AMERICAN EDUCATION
Foundations and Policy

AMERICAN EDUCATION
Foundations and Policy

John H. Walker

Ernest J. Kozma

Robert P. Green Jr.

Clemson University

WEST PUBLISHING COMPANY

St. Paul   New York   Los Angeles   San Francisco

Photo Credits

Part I © 1985 Barbara Rios/Photo Researchers, Inc.

Chapter 1 1.1 © Rohn Engh/Photo Researchers, Inc. 1.2 © 1979, Jan Lukas/Photo Researchers, Inc. 1.3 © 1984, Barbara Rios/Photo Researchers, Inc. 1.4 © David M. Grossman/Photo Researchers, Inc.

Chapter 2 2.1 © 1987, Roberta Hershenson/Photo Researchers, Inc. 2.2 © 1988, Barbara Rios/Photo Researchers, Inc. 2.3 © 1985, Miriam Reinhart/Photo Researchers, Inc. 2.4 © Hella Hammid/Photo Researchers, Inc.

Part II © 1987, Robert Houser/Comstock.

Chapter 3 3.1 © Print Collection of Miriam & Ira D. Wallach, Division of Art, Prints and Photographs, The New York Public Library, Astor, Lenox and Tilden Foundations. 3.2 Historical Pictures Service, Chicago. 3.3 Library of Congress. 3.4 © 1987, Roy Attaway/Photo Researchers, Inc. 3.5 Historical Pictures Service, Chicago.

Chapter 4 4.1 Library of Congress. 4.2 © 1984, Olof Källström/Jeroboam, Inc. 4.3 Historical Pictures Service, Chicago.

Chapter 5 5.1 Library of Congress. 5.2 Library of Congress. 5.3 © 1966, D. Berretty-Rapho/Photo Researchers, Inc. 5.4 Library of Congress

Chapter 6 6.1 © 1987, Vivienne della Grotta/Photo Researchers, Inc. 6.2 © 1984, Barbara Rios/Photo Researchers, Inc. 6.3 © Laimute Druskis/Jeroboam, Inc. 6.4 © 1981, Steve Malone/Jeroboam, Inc.

Chapter 7 7.1 © Bob Clay/Jeroboam, Inc. 7.2 © Four By Five. 7.3 © 1980, Frank Siteman/Jeroboam, Inc.

Photo Credits continue following index.

COPYRIGHT © 1989 By WEST PUBLISHING COMPANY
50 W. Kellogg Boulevard
P.O. Box 64526
St. Paul, MN 55164-1003

All rights reserved

Printed in the United States of America

96 95 94 93 92 91 90 89   8 7 6 5 4 3 2 1 0

Library of Congress Cataloging-in-Publication Data

Walker, John H. (John Henry), 1944–
    American education : foundations and policy / John H. Walker, Ernest J. Kozma, Robert P. Green.
        p. cm.
    Includes bibliographies and index.
    ISBN 0-314-46553-7
    1. Education and state—United States. 2. Education—United States—Aims and objectives. I. Kozma, Ernest J. II. Green, Robert P. III. Title.
LC89.W29 1989
379.73—dc19

Index: **Virginia Hobbs**
Copyeditor: **Deborah Cady**
Design: **John Osborne**
Cover Image: **Four By Five**
Composition: **Carlisle Communications**

88-28643
CIP

Contents

v

Preface

Many different approaches have been used by colleges and departments of education to introduce students to the area of study called "foundations of education." Courses in philosophy of education, history of education, politics of education, and sociology of education have all been offered as a part of this effort. Recent introductory textbooks in foundations have incorporated combinations of the above areas, and many of them have also covered such areas as school law, school administration, and the professional aspects of teaching. *American Education: Foundations and Policy* reflects these developments but has a focus on educational policy.

The authors of this text believe that study in the foundations of education will help students develop a firm basis for participation in the ongoing debate over educational policy. Analysis of the links that inevitably exist between educational policy and school history, of the theoretical perspectives that influence lay and professional views on schooling policy, and of the impact that social and political change have on schooling will bring students to understand both the participants and the processes that are involved in the development and administration of educational policy. It is hoped that such understanding will foster a more critical perspective while it contributes to greater participation in the policy-making process.

American Education: Foundations and Policy connects the traditional focus on the historical, philosophical, and social foundations of education to educational policy in the United States. The authors argue that educational policy is developed out of perceptions of and reactions to public problems that citizens want the schools to solve. Social change brings about different perceptions of what the "real" problems are that should be addressed through public schooling. The foundations section of the book provides (1) historical overview of the problems that educational institutions have addressed in the past; (2) a review of the philosophical and ideological perspectives that affect the way people perceive public educational problems and solutions; (3) a review of the social and cultural issues—socialization, poverty, unemployment, social mobility—that schools have been asked to deal with; and (4) a treatment of curriculum as an expression of educational policy.

The policy section of the text reviews the kinds of educational policy that result from the relationships and interactions between the formal and informal political systems in the United States. Policy models are used to simulate these interactions and relationships, to describe the kinds of policy solutions adopted, and to analyze the effects these solutions may have. Separate chapters are devoted to educational policies relating to teachers, to students, to equality, to school finance, and to church/state relations. The final chapter focuses on the impact that social change might have on the development of educational policy in the future. An instructor's manual with test questions and pedagogical aids is available.

Acknowledgments

Many students, colleagues, and former teachers have contributed to the authors' views on studies in foundations of education. We express our sincere gratitude for the ideas and insights we have gained from them through the years. We also appreciate the helpful suggestions given to us by the following reviewers in different stages of the book's development:

Edward Petkus, William Paterson College, NJ
William Persons, Mississippi State University
John Jensen, Boise State University
Richard Roames, Purdue University–Calumet, IN
Vincent P. Mikkelson, Indiana University of Pennsylvania
David Adams, Cleveland State University, OH
Wayne Urban, Georgia State University
Paul Farber, Western Michigan University
Hans Jellen, Southern Illinois University–Carbondale
Val D. Rust, University of California–Los Angeles
W. Thomas Jamison, Appalachian State University, NC
Samuel Carver, Virginia Commonwealth University
Joseph Newman, University of South Alabama
Mary Yeazell, West Virginia University
Thomas Gwaltney, Eastern Michigan University
Charles Clark, Harrisburg Area Community College, PA
Mary Nell Legg, Valencia Community College, FL
Kenneth Bailey, University of California–Irvine
Robert Bartos, Georgia College
Svi Shapiro, University of North Carolina–Greensboro
James Carper, Mississippi State University

The authors also express their sincere appreciation to three people at West Publishing Company for their help in developing the manuscript. Peter Marshall, Executive Editor, provided valuable insights in the initial stages of the book. Christine Hurney, Production Assistant, and Maralene Bates, Developmental Editor, provided much-needed professional and technical assistance in the final phases of the book's development and publication.

John Walker

Ernest Kozma

Robert Green

AMERICAN EDUCATION
Foundations and Policy

I INTRODUCTION TO EDUCATION TODAY

The first two chapters of *American Education: Foundations and Policy* introduce the reader to American education today. Chapter 1 emphasizes the importance of, as well as the dissatisfaction with, our schools. The chapter discusses the magnitude and diversity of the educational enterprise and introduces the complicated educational policymaking process. In addition, Chapter 1 outlines the organization of the book. Chapter 2 introduces the reader to the educational professional, specifically the role of the teacher, and provides a rationale for foundational studies, the topic of Part II.

The Challenge of Teaching Today

"If critics are tempted to condemn educational leaders for isolating the schools from the actualities of American life, for unrealistic assumptions and procedures, they must remember that American leaders in other fields have seldom tried to think out the relationship between their own problems and the problems and institutions of the country as a whole. General planlessness, a love of freedom, of individual enterprise, and of open goals have been characteristic of American life."

Merle Curti, *The Social Ideas of American Educators* (1935)

"All social movements involve conflicts which are reflected intellectually in controversies. It would not be a sign of health if such an important social interest as education were not also an area of struggles, practical and theoretical."

John Dewey, *Experience and Education* (1939)

". . . Continued failure by the schools to perform their traditional role adequately, together with a failure to respond to the emerging needs of the 1980's, may have disastrous consequences for this nation."

President's Commission for a National Agenda for the Eighties, *A National Agenda for the Eighties* (1980)

Social, political, economic, and technological developments in recent years have focused our attention on the weaknesses and failures of some American

Photo 1.1
Public schools serve rural children.

institutions. People have been made aware of America's competitive weakness in the commercial markets of the world. Media attention has been focused on the loss of jobs and industries to foreign countries. The reliability of American products has been questioned, and more people are purchasing foreign-made manufactured goods. Our political power has been questioned as the nation has faced such difficult problems as the taking of American hostages in the Middle East and the continuing turmoil in a number of Central and South American nations. On the domestic front, drug problems, teenage pregnancy, sex-related diseases, and a perceived changing morality have received considerable attention. Inevitably, problems such as these will focus our attention on our institutions of education. The schools were criticized when information was publicized that indicated that American pupils had lower average Scholastic Achievement Test (SAT) scores in recent years. Studies revealed that many of our public school

Photo 1.2
Public schools serve urban children.

students lacked proficiency in basic skills and were not as competent in math and science as comparable pupils in other nations. Soon critics began to issue reports asking for changes in American education. The media attention given to the criticism of education has made the educational enterprise one of the focal points in the debate concerning the future direction of our nation.

The Schools' Magnitude and Diversity

The United States has fifty-one systems of public education, fifty state systems and one in the District of Columbia. Each system operates under a constitution and statutes peculiar to that state or district. Within the state systems are approximately 15,750 local school districts. Hawaii has one school district that covers the entire state, while Texas has 1,000 local districts. Each local district has a board of education that acts as a policymaking body.

Public school districts that have fewer than 1,000 pupils enroll fifty percent of the elementary and secondary pupils, while four percent attend schools in districts that enroll 10,000 or more pupils.[1] Minorities constitute approximately twenty-seven percent of the elementary and secondary school enrollment.

The elementary and secondary schools of our nation serve over forty-six million pupils, approximately eleven percent of whom attend private schools. Each of the states has an assortment of these schools; some are independent, but most are affiliated with a religious denomination (approximately eighty-five percent of the private school population attends religious-affiliated schools).

The percentage of school-age children in private schools has remained relatively stable at eleven percent. It is interesting to note, however, that the types of private schools have undergone considerable change. A significant drop in enrollment has occurred in Roman Catholic parochial schools, while fundamentalist Christian schools and home schooling have had remarkable increases.[2] The state of Delaware has the highest percentage of children in private schools—nineteen percent. This figure is in contrast to a low of 1.6 percent enrollment in Utah.

The National Education Association (NEA) reports that over 116 billion dollars was received as revenue by the nation's public schools in 1983.[3] These revenues, however, were not distributed equally among the states. Great differences exist in the amount of taxable wealth among the states, and even greater differences exist among the school districts within a state.

The public schools in America employ more than 2.1 million teachers; roughly eleven percent of these teachers represent minorities. Two major teacher organizations compete for the loyalties of the teachers. The NEA is the largest and represents 1.8 million members. The American Federation of Teachers (AFT), largely centered in large urban areas and affiliated with the American Federation of Labor (AFL), represents approximately 625,000 members.

The diversity of the educational endeavor in America makes it difficult to assess and understand the role played by the public schools in the continuing development of the nation. To successfully meet the challenge of teaching today, an understanding of the operation of America's public education system and the societal issues that have focused attention on the schools is indispensable.

Photo 1.3
The public schools serve the young in kindergarten classrooms.

The Issues

The American public is being bombarded with news about the "crisis" in education in the United States. A significant number of reports have been released and disseminated that purport to have solutions to the education crisis. Many of these reports are dealt with in detail throughout this text. The following representative list of recommendations taken from *The Reports: Challenge and Opportunity*, published by Phi Delta Kappa, an honor society in education, illustrates the variety of proposals. (The publication summarizes and compares only three of the many reports.)

Photo 1.4
The public schools serve those who desire college preparation.

1. The schools should stress literacy in English language.
2. The schools should increase graduation requirements.
3. The schools should stress proficiency in a second language.
4. The schools should stress productive employment.
5. There should be a longer school day and a longer school year.
6. Textbooks should be upgraded.
7. More homework should be required.
8. Standardized tests should be administered.
9. Emphasis should be on quality teaching and quality teachers.
10. Teacher salaries should be increased.
11. More money should be provided for education.[4]

Recently, several widely read books have joined the cries for educational reform, claiming that youngsters in America are culturally illiterate. The authors of these books believe that there is some information and knowledge that is so important that all members of our society must grasp and understand it. Without such understanding, a person is culturally illiterate, and if enough people are ignorant of this material, our society will be threatened (see Box 1.1).

Box 1.1
Are Americans Cultural Illiterates?

Can you answer these questions?

During which of the following periods did the Civil War take place. When was the Civil War?	**A.** Before 1750 **B.** 1750–1800 **C.** 1800–1850 **D.** 1850–1900 **E.** 1900–1950 **F.** After 1950
Social critics such as Lincoln Steffens, Ida Tarbell, and Upton Sinclair were known as	**A.** Carpetbaggers **B.** Muckrakers **C.** Abolitionists **D.** Trustbusters
Who was the Spanish knight who attacked windmills, thinking they were giants?	**A.** Sancho Panza **B.** Don Quixote **C.** El Cid **D.** Zorro
Name the two largest states in area.	**A.** **B.**
Name the Great Lakes.	**A.** **B.** **C.** **D.** **E.**

List the four oceans in order of size.	1. 2. 3. 4.	
Can you identify these words, terms names, or dates?	G.I. Bill galaxy gay rights Greshams's Law	gung-ho Genghis Khan gerrymander
What is the major cause of air pollution in most large American cities:	**A.** Factories **B.** Fog **C.** Cars **D.** Open trash burners	

These questions are adapted from such current discussions of cultural literacy as Allan Bloom's *The Closing of the American Mind* (New York: Simon & Schuster, 1987), E. D. Hirsch, Jr.'s *Cultural Literacy: What Every American Needs to Know* (Boston: Houghton Mifflin, 1987), and Diane Ravitch & C. E. Finn, Jr.'s *What Do Our 17 Year Olds Know?* (New York: Harper & Row, 1987). Do these kinds of questions truly reflect America's rich and diverse cultural heritage? Are these questions adequate measures of cultural literacy?

Many of our popular publications have carried accounts of the shortcomings of our public schools, adding to the debate concerning the proper direction for educational policymakers. A feature article in *U.S. News & World Report,* September 18, 1987, on "what Americans should know" cited a number of reasons for school failure:

1. Poor textbooks.
2. Using books such as *Dick and Jane* to teach reading.
3. The combining of disciplines into "Social Studies" and "Language Arts."
4. Cultural relativism of the 1960s.
5. Concern with process rather than content.
6. Television.
7. Use of standardized tests.
8. The short academic year in America.

Do these reasons explain to your satisfaction the weaknesses *you* perceive in America's public schools?

It should not be surprising that there are so many controversies over educational policy, considering the fact that we live in a very heterogeneous, highly complex society experiencing rapid change in its economic, political, and social institutions. Diverse groups, each with its own agenda concerning the objectives and programs for schooling, present divergent demands to lo-

Figure 1.1   Economic Issues Addressed Through Schooling

Issues Addressed   Programs/Activities in School

Training of work force   Develop basic competency skills

                                                    Develop specific job skills

                                                    Socialize students in career
                                                    and work ethic

Consumer education   Promote consumer education curricula

                                                    Require students to study principles
                                                    of economic system

Appreciation for
free enterprise capitalism   Sort students on basis of merit

                                                    Base credentialing process on merit

                                                    Administer special job training/
                                                    retraining programs

Inequality in the work force   Provide sex education

                                                    Provide drug and alcohol
                                                    abuse education

Poverty and unemployment   Prevent juvenile delinquency and crime

cal, state, and federal government officials regarding school policy. Government officials respond to these conflicting demands by issuing court decisions, administrative regulations, and statutes that placate some groups and create dissatisfaction among others. Figure 1.1, 1.2, and 1.3 illustrate the kinds of economic, political, and social issues thrust on the schools and the responses that school officials make to the demands that schools deal with such issues.

Prospective teachers as well as citizens can be overwhelmed by the number of issues being debated and the voluminous amount of information that is generated in the debate over educational policy. So many economic, political, and social issues are linked to schooling policy that dealing with all of them in a reasonable and objective manner seems to be an insurmountable task. Citizens and professional educators need some systematic framework for conceptualizing educational policy issues, evaluating existing

Figure 1.2   Political Issues Addressed Through Schooling

Issues Addressed   Programs/Activities in School

Citizenship training   Require study of constitutional
                                                    documents/government process
Development of political
leadership   Develop programs that identify talent

Fostering of political
consensus necessary
for political stability   Require study of cultural
                                                    and political heritage
Promotion of national security
and national defense   Foster technical, scientific development

Stimulation of patriotism   Engage students in patriotic observances

Figure 1.3   Social Issues Addressed Through Schooling

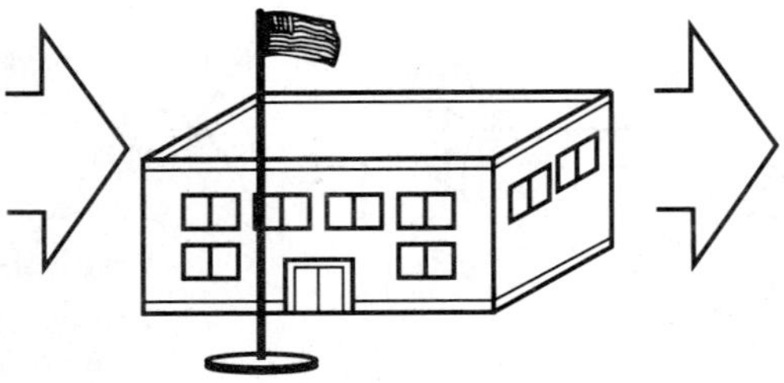

Issues Addressed

Programs/Activities in School

Promotion of social mobility based on meritocracy

Socialization of children and youth

Promotion of equality

Elimination of injustice

Changing demographic structure

Changes in institutions such as the family

Develop competence skills

Promote meritocratic ideal

Deal with social class biases in school programs

Promote acculturation/enculturation

Foster understanding of and adaptation to changing social roles

Desegregate schools

Provide compensatory/remedial education

Prevent school dropout

Promote cultural pluralism

Accommodate ethnic, racial, sexual, religious differences

Provide sex education

Provide drug and alcohol abuse education

Prevent juvenile delinquency and crime

policy, and analyzing the policies being promoted by interest groups seeking to use the schools to achieve their goals.

The authors are not optimistic that the persistent policy issues in education will be "solved." Informed people with strong convictions will continue to defend different policy positions. More research and investigation, resulting in findings that clog university library shelves, will not settle the debate. Future teachers and citizens need to learn how to conceptualize the issues, examine historical perspectives, analyze the philosophical bases for differences of opinion, and encourage calmer and more reasoned thinking among policymakers as they work to develop policy solutions.

Understanding educational policy in the United States begins with the realization that policy for schools evolves from perceptions of and reactions to public issues that citizens want schools to "solve." Cultural change brings about different perceptions of what the "real" issues are and creates demands for different solutions to cope with the changes that are taking place. Most public policy offers only tentative solutions. Policies will change as new issues arise. Citizens are having a free-for-all discussion about a host of issues such as the quality and quantity of teachers needed, what constitutes appropriate academic standards and regulations, how we should fund our schools, and the role of schools in providing sex education and moral education. This textbook is organized in a way that leads the reader to questions concerning some serious educational policy alternatives. In confronting the possible solutions, the reader will be offered a method of analysis of the proposed policy and the effects of implementing the policy.

This book is organized so that it will aid the reader in understanding the challenge of teaching today. Chapter 2 is devoted to the study of teaching as a profession. Part II, entitled Educational Foundations, begins with Chapters 3 and 4, which provide an historical overview of schooling and the various issues that educational institutions have been asked to solve in the past. New institutions, programs, and standards evolved as schools responded to different economic, political, and social issues. Chapter 5 reviews the major belief systems and political perspectives held by different groups interested in education in the United States. These belief systems affect the way people perceive public education issues and the proposed solutions to them. Chapter 6 is devoted to the social and cultural considerations that are important in understanding our educational system, and Chapter 7 focuses on what and whom we teach.

Part III, Educational Policy, relates the study of the educational foundations to educational policymaking. Chapters 8 and 9 describe the formal and informal political systems involved in educational policy development in the United States. Several chapters in the text are devoted to the products of educational policy resulting from the interactions and relationships between the formal and informal political systems. Chapter 10 concentrates on the teachers, Chapter 11 on the student. Equality concepts are studied in Chapter 12; church and state issues are the topics of Chapter 13; financial policies are studied in Chapter 14; and Chapter 15 lists the topics and issues that educational policy will have to address in the future.

Summary

Attention in recent years has been focused on the weaknesses and failures of American institutions. Eventually, criticism of our education system moved to center stage. If the nation were to solve its problems, the schools were going to have to improve. Soon reports began to appear asking for changes in our education system. To be successful, any changes would have to take into account the magnitude and diversity of our educational enterprise.

The public system comprises fifty state school systems with thousands of local school districts serving a heterogeneous population. In addition, numerous private schools exist, most of which are affiliated with various religious denominations. These schools are staffed by over two million teachers. This diversity makes it difficult to assess and understand the role played by our education system in meeting the needs of our nation.

Diverse groups, each with its own agenda concerning the objectives and programs for schooling, present divergent positions and demands on our schools. Citizens can be overwhelmed by the number of issues and information being generated. Citizens and professional educators need some systematic framework for conceptualizing educational policy issues, evaluating existing policy, and analyzing the solutions being promoted by interest groups seeking to use the schools to achieve their goals.

This text starts with a description of the challenge of teaching today followed by a unit on the Foundations of Education. A unit on Educational Policymaking follows. Topics such as the formal and informal legal structure, the teacher, the student, equality, finance, and church and state issues are included. The organization of this textbook will aid the reader in understanding the enormity and the importance of the challenge of teaching today.

Key Words

Scholastic Achievement Test (SAT)

State systems

Local district

Public schools

Private schools

National Education Association (NEA)

American Federation of Teachers (AFT)

Phi Delta Kappa

Heterogeneous

Foundations of education

Discussion Questions

1. When critics emphasize economic, social, or technological shortcomings of America, why do the criticisms eventually focus on the schools?

2. What factors make it difficult for schools in the United States to respond quickly to demands for change? Is your response a strength or weakness?

3. The chapter indicates that the heterogeneous makeup of our population must be considered in our debates about educational policy. What problems and considerations reflect the population's diversity?

For Further Reading

A Nation Responds. Washington, D.C., U.S. Department of Education, 1984.

Frankel, M. M., and Gerald, D. E. *Projections of Education Statistics to 1990–91 Volume I: Analytical Report.* National Center for Educational Statistics.

Goodlad, J. I. "A Study of Schooling: Some Findings and Hypotheses," *Phi Delta Kappan,* January 1983, 465–70.

Lines, Patricia M. "The New Private Schools and Their Historic Purpose," *Phi Delta Kappan,* January 1986, 373–79.

National Commission on Excellence in Education. *A Nation at Risk: The Imperative for Educational Reform.* Washington, D.C., U.S. Department of Education, 1983.

Phi Delta Kappan, The 19th Annual Gallup Poll of the Public's Attitudes Toward the Public Schools, September 1987, 17–30.

Today's Education (1986–87 Annual Edition). Washington, D.C.: Journal of the National Education Association.

Notes

1. M. M. Frankel, and D. E. Gerald, *Projections of Education Statistics to 1990–91, Volume I: Analytical Report,* National Center for Educational Statistics, pp. 71–91.

2. Patricia M. Lines, "The New Private Schools and Their Historic Purpose," *Phi Delta Kappan,* January 1986, pp. 373–79.

3. *Estimates of School Statistics 1982–83,* published by National Education Association, Washington, D.C., 1983, p. 37.

4. *The Reports: Challenge and Opportunity,* published by Phi Delta Kappa, Bloomington, Indiana.

2 Educational Professionals

"It is not the quality of the textbooks, the quality of the pupils or their environment, or the quality of the community, the administration, or the professional staff that makes the difference between learning and not learning for students—rather it is the capability of the teacher as a developing person to facilitate the learner's interaction with important, ever-changing factors which he or she encounters."

Shirley F. Heck and C. Ray Williams, *The Complex Roles of the Teacher* (1984)

"Education is a moral undertaking. What kind of life should a child lead in school? The answer to this question is not a matter of science. It is not a matter of technique. It is not a matter of controlled experiment. It is not a matter of rational reform. The dilemma of science is that there are no scientific answers to fundamental educational questions. Education is a moral activity and if we ever improve it we will have to engage in moral struggle."

Millard Clements, "Dilemmas of the Holmes Report" (1987)

The various state school systems are staffed by educational professionals: teachers, guidance counselors, building and central office administrators, supervisors, paraprofessionals, and others. The backbone of the profession, however, is the teacher. As such, the teacher has received much attention in the educational reform literature of the 1980s. This chapter looks at a profile of today's teacher, the motives of those expressing a desire to teach, the roles teachers play in the schools, and the characteristics of those who are attracted to playing those roles. A number of these characteristics raise

15

issues that educational policymakers must face. The chapter also considers the variety of other professional positions found in the schools. Finally, given the issues discussed in Chapter 1 and here, this chapter considers the importance of foundational studies in addressing educational issues.

Today's Teachers

The stereotypical view of the teacher as a middle-aged schoolmarm is not far from wrong. The great majority of teachers today are women. At the elementary level during the 1984–85 school year, female teachers outnumbered males by a ratio of five to one (988,508 to 195,829). At the high-school level, the teaching force was split roughly 50–50 between females and males, 481,249 (50.1 percent) to 479,956 (49.9 percent), respectively. Most of today's teachers are just entering middle age, averaging five years older than the typical American worker. Only one percent are under twenty-five. This represents a dramatic change from 1970, when some seventeen percent of the teacher force was under twenty-five. Unlike the schoolmarm, however, the teacher today is likely to be married. Some seventy-four percent of the American teaching force is married, compared with sixty-four percent of the working public. Nearly nine of every ten teachers are white. Blacks constitute some 8.6 percent of the teaching force, while Hispanics represent 1.8 percent, and Asian-American and native Americans compose less than one percent.[1] (See Figure 2.1.) These characteristics lead Emily Feistritzer to portray the "typical" American teacher in the following manner:

> A "typical" American teacher today would be a woman in her early forties who had taught for fifteen years, most in her present district. Over those years, she would have returned to her local college or university often enough to acquire enough credits for a master's degree. She would be married and the mother of two children. She would be white and not politically active. Her formal political affiliation, if she had one, would be with the Democratic Party. She would teach in a suburban elementary school staffed largely by women, although, in all likelihood, the school principal would be male. She would have about twenty-three pupils in her class. Counting her after-hours responsibilities, she would put in a work week slightly longer than that of the average worker.[2]

During that work week, the teacher plays a variety of roles.

The Roles of the Teacher

Teaching is a demanding, trying, exhausting, yet rewarding, job. Few positions provide a comparable setting for the wide range of human interactions that take place in the classroom. In The *Complex Roles of the Teacher: An Ecological Perspective,* Shirley F. Heck and C. Ray Williams describe a number of the roles that the teacher plays.[3]

Teacher As Person: A Caring Role   Heck and Williams point out that one does not suddenly become a teacher; rather, becoming a teacher is a process of growing and developing. Teachers must first understand themselves before they can care for others. "The focus on the teacher as a

Figure 2.1
Characteristics of the
Teacher Force

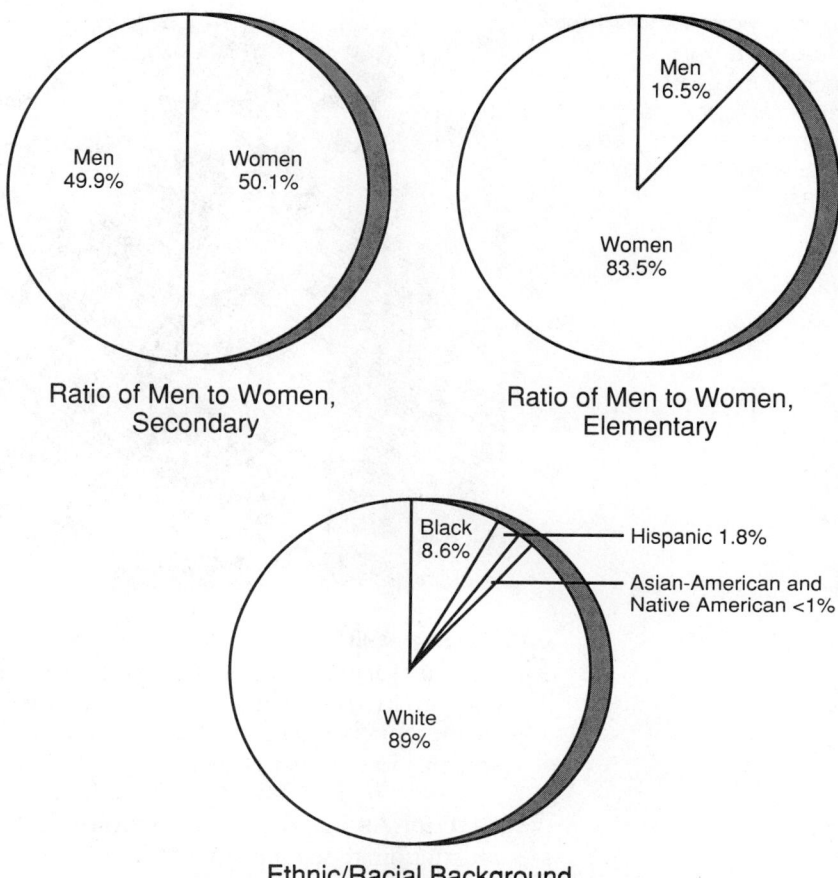

Ratio of Men to Women,
Secondary

Ratio of Men to Women,
Elementary

Ethnic/Racial Background

Source: From C. Emily Feistritzer, *The Condition of Teaching:. A State by State Analysis* (Princeton: The Carnegie Foundation for the Advancement of Teaching, 1985).

developing person is extremely critical, for it is the teacher who ultimately 'becomes the curriculum.' "[4] Teachers must model a positive self-concept, have enthusiasm for their teaching, and internalize and integrate learning theory if student learning is to take place. "Unless teachers understand their own unique learning processes, they will not be able to understand their students' learning processes."[5]

Teacher As Colleague: A Supporting Role   According to Heck and Williams, "Teachers can serve as powerful resources in helping each other grow as professional educators."[6] Each teacher is responsible for helping to create a supportive environment for all teachers—sharing ideas, listening, and helping.

Teacher and Parents As Partners: A Complimentary Role   It is the teacher's job to foster interactive, supporting relationships between the school and the home. Teachers must be aware of the home context in which students live, be aware of the students' backgrounds, and be willing to listen to parents. Communication is a key.

Photo 2.1
According to Emily Feistritzer, a "typical" teacher today would be a white woman in her early forties.

Teacher As Understander of the Learner: A Nurturing Role   Teachers must demonstrate awareness of the various contexts—home, school, community, social groups—in which their students live. They must be aware of individual differences in their students and be willing to observe students in nonclassroom settings.

Teacher As Facilitator of Learning: An Interacting Role   Teachers must facilitate natural student interest in learning through the creation of conditions that foster problem solving and creativity. "Teachers must create a climate that permits freedom for thinking beyond the classroom—a supportive environment in which students feel free to take risks, make mistakes, question, explore, and disagree."[7]

Teacher As Researcher: An Experimenting Role   As teachers interact with students, they make observations, derive generalizations or hypotheses, and test these generalizations—the classical model of experimental inquiry. Based on such experimentation, teachers evaluate the curriculum and instructional strategies and adopt changes.

Teacher As Program Developer: A Creating Role   Teachers must be involved in general curriculum development. As program developers, they must apply philosophies of education in helping to shape the goals of their schools. They must decide if those goals should not only focus on academic matters but also include student personal and social development.

Teacher As Administrator: A Planning Role   Teachers are responsible for both long-range and short-range classroom planning. Such responsibilities range from decisions concerning the physical arrangement of the classroom to the scheduling of field trips. Administrative duties include counting, grading, recording, and reporting.

Photo 2.2
Teachers are responsible for both long- and short-range planning for their classes.

Teacher As Decision Maker: A Problem-Solving Role   Teachers are constantly making decisions, from the trivial to the momentous. Some of these decisions might include the following:

> *...which discipline approach to use in a specific situation; how to evaluate the students; how to individualize instruction; when to be flexible; how to evaluate curriculum; how to organize time; how to deal with trauma and stress in students; how to choose correct student placement and appropriate learning activities; how to select the teaching method for use at a specific moment; how to communicate with parents, peers, and students on specific issues; how to distribute classroom responsibilities; how to design the physical arrangement of the class; when to give homework; how to deal with one's own personal evaluations; and how to separate personal values from professional life.[8]*

Teacher As Professional Leader: A Challenging Role   "A leader is one who 'dreams dreams' and is successful in translating these dreams into reality." A teacher serves as leader by reflecting the personal qualities associated with leadership: "concern; belief and trust in human potential; enthusiasm; confidence; high ethical standards; willingness to admit errors; a sense of spontaneity and emotional involvement; and an innate drive to achieve."[9]

The teacher, then, plays a number of roles in the school. He or she is the leading actor. In fact, Stuart Palonsky called his two-year experience as a classroom teacher in the early 1980s "900 Shows a Year."[10] Permeating all these roles must be a spirit of enthusiasm—enthusiasm for teaching and continuous learning. That spirit, while humorously put, is reflected in Box 2.1.

Other Educational Professionals

Teaching can also be the starting point for a number of other careers in education. Traditionally, teachers who have wanted to advance professionally have had to change the direction of their careers to enter administration, supervision, or support fields. The typical means for this transition has been to pursue masters and doctoral degrees or certificates in administration, supervision, or support fields. Most superintendents and principals were

Photo 2.3
Most administrative and supervisory personnel were once teachers themselves.

once teachers, as were most guidance counselors and central office personnel. The latter group is often divided into administrative and supervisory categories. Administrative personnel might include assistant superintendents and other officers responsible for building maintenance, transportation, personnel, federal programs, and the like. Supervisory personnel might include supervisors and coordinators of curricular and instructional areas as well as specialists in such areas as reading, special education, and psychological testing. Experience in teaching, then, has provided the background for a wide variety of professional educational positions. But why do individuals decide to teach, and what are some of the characteristics of those who decide to play that multifaceted role? These questions are addressed in the following sections.

Why Does One Choose Teaching?

Students training to become teachers are an idealistic lot, and that is good. This idealism is reflected in their responses to queries about their motives for choosing teaching as a career. When education students in their first year of professional preparation (juniors) at a southeastern university were recently asked to describe their motives for going into teaching, typical responses ranged from a desire to work with children to a desire to improve society. "I enjoy working with and being around kids," wrote one student. "I like to watch them grow, and I would like to be a part of their growth." "To watch a child understand something you have just taught him or her is the most satisfying feeling in the world," wrote another. And another: "Children are very special people, and they are our future." While most students pointed out a desire to work with children, others also emphasized the idea that they would be sharing knowledge. "I want to teach because I have a strong interest in French," wrote one secondary trainee. "Passing on one's knowledge to others gives one a feeling of accomplishment," wrote another.

Box 2.1
My First Twelve
Years

During my first twelve years of teaching I was desperate for new ideas, constantly foraging for schemes with which to engage the children. My frenetic activity was due, in part, to the fact that I was given a different teaching assignment every two years. I figured, "Different children require different methods, different materials." So I would race off to the library or to the arts-and-crafts store. I'd buy another filing cabinet and join another book club for teachers.

But even when I settled in with the same assignment for a six-year stretch, my frenzy did not abate. My classroom became a veritable curriculum warehouse, stuffed with every innovative whiz-bang gizmo I could buy, borrow, or invent. I spent hundreds of hours reading, constructing, laminating. My husband gave up reminding me that I had promised to put the cut-and-paste factory in our living room out of business, once I figured out what to teach. When I wasn't inventing projects, I was taking courses: cardboard carpentry, architectural awareness, science process, Cuisenaire rods, Chinese art, test construction and evaluation, curriculum development, and so on. I even took two courses in the computer language, BASIC. (I thought maybe I'd missed the point in the first course, so I took another—just to be sure.)

Source: Susan Ohanian, "On Stir-and-Serve Recipes for Teaching" *Phil Delta Kappan*, Vol. 66, No. 10, June 1985.

Awareness of educational reform was reflected in student responses. One student wrote, "I want to be a teacher because I want to be a part of improving general education." Others tied education to the welfare of society. "I believe that education is very important to the future of our country. We need good, devoted, and caring teachers, and I think I'm qualified." One student summed up the feelings of many when she wrote: "I want to be able to have an effect on my nation and feel that I have contributed to the welfare of its people. Through teaching, I will have a small but important effect on the future." Finally, while a number of students pointed out that they did not expect to get rich through teaching, perceptions of lower pay seemed to be offset by an annual schedule allowing more free time. "I like the advantage of summers off and getting out of school with the children so that I can balance a career and a family."[11]

Many of the same feelings were reflected in a recent survey of students completing their professional preparation for teaching. In 1985, *Instructor* magazine surveyed some 1,300 teacher trainees in their final year of preparation and followed the survey with twenty-five telephone interviews.[12] The results showed that in the two to three years of teacher training, student explanations of their motives change very little. "More than 90 percent of new teachers say they chose their profession because they love children and believe that teaching is important and honorable work," wrote Mary Harbaugh. "In telephone interviews, new teachers cited two additional reasons—the intellectual rewards of good teaching and a personal commitment to improving instruction."[13] The survey also revealed that students had begun to shape opinions concerning foundational and policy issues—issues that are treated throughout this book. As you read the following survey results, consider your own ideas at this stage in your professional preparation.

Students indicated a strong interest in a number of the reform proposals of the mid-1980s. A majority felt schooling would be improved by career ladders (that is, professional ladders of three to five steps with increasing levels of compensation, selection criteria, and work responsibility). Two-thirds approved of merit pay (extra pay based upon demonstrated productivity). Forty percent endorsed educational vouchers and tuition tax credit plans (vehicles that would allow parents more options in choosing schools for their children, including private schools, either through entitlements to a certain number of years of education or through tax breaks). Over half felt that all teachers should be tested periodically. Close to three-fourths supported raising minimum grade-level requirements for students, and over half opposed social promotion. Interviews suggested strong support for reform in teacher education.

Students were very much aware of what some groups called "social issues" in the mid-1980s. Forty-one percent supported school prayer. Over eighty percent advocated values or character education in the schools. "What we need is more values education. I think that's what most people who support prayer really want," argued one interviewee. Eighty-six percent supported sex education. "I think that kids should have morality taught along with sex education," responded one. "I think responsibility is important. I think sometimes the morality is lacking." Another claimed, "Sex education has become very necessary in a world where parents aren't around."

Responses to curricular issues were mixed. The students split evenly over a question asking whether or not the elementary curriculum should address the threat of nuclear war. Only fifty-three percent expected to use computer software at least occasionally. Seventy-two percent, however, expected to use videos and video equipment frequently or occasionally.

When asked to state their greatest concerns as they enter classrooms, students mentioned class size, lack of parental and administrative support, student behavior problems, lack of good texts and other materials, and too much paperwork. Many students also felt unprepared to teach children with special needs, including mentally handicapped children and those with limited proficiency in English.

As you will see, these responses reflect positions on a number of current policy issues in education. (For an interesting contrast, see Table 2.1.) These positions, however, must be based on an individual's understanding of the history of public schooling in the United States, the individual's educational philosophy, an understanding of the social role of the school, and an awareness of the process of educational policy formation. Teachers' opinions must be well informed. This text is designed to provide the basis for well-informed opinions. We begin with a look at who goes into teaching.

Table 2.1
Teacher Support for
Reform

	FAVOR CAREER LADDER	FAVOR MERIT PAY
BASE (TEACHERS FAMILIAR WITH REFORM)	617	1149
	%	%
TOTAL TEACHERS	49	26
RECEIVE PERFORMANCE-BASED PAY	50	27
DO NOT RECEIVE PERFORMANCE-BASED PAY	49	26
TYPE OF SCHOOL		
Elementary	47	23
Junior High	45	28
High School	52	30
REGION		
East	64	27
Midwest	57	31
South	40	23
West	53	21
SIZE OF PLACE		
Inner City	52	31
Other Urban	53	26
Suburban	53	29
Small Town	45	25
Rural	48	22
SEX OF TEACHER		
Male	52	30
Female	48	24
EXPERIENCE OF TEACHER		
< 5 Years	65	45
5–9 Years	50	28
10–19 Years	46	25
> 20 Years	50	23
TRAINING OF TEACHER		
Through 4 Years College	36	28
Some Graduate Credits	50	24
Masters	57	27
Masters +	45	26
UNION MEMBER	46	24
NONUNION	59	38

Source: Adapted from the Metropolitan Life Survey of the American Teacher, 1986.

Who Teaches?

Richard E. Kemper and John N. Mangieri surveyed 589 high-school seniors who ranked in the top fifty percent among their college-bound classmates to determine some of the characteristics of those who might become teachers.[14] Of those students surveyed, only eight percent indicated that they were "very interested" in becoming teachers. A further twenty-five percent indicated that they were "somewhat interested." Those who indicated a lack of interest in teaching noted that better salaries or better chances for professional advancement might attract them to the profession.

Among the two groups reflecting interest in teaching, four percent of the males and sixteen percent of the females indicated that they would like to teach in kindergarten; four percent of the males and twenty-six percent

---

Table 2.2	Earnings of Teachers and Workers in Other Selected Occupations, by Sex: 1982–85 (In Constant 1985 Dollars)							
OCCUPATION HELD LONGEST DURING THE YEAR	MEN				WOMEN			
	1982	1983	1984	1985	1982	1983	1984	1985
TEACHERS	$23,593	$24,181	$25,758	$25,575	$19,069	$19,754	$20,869	$20,810
ALL FULL-TIME WORKERS	23,364	23,393	23,892	24,195	14,426	14,876	15,209	15,624
PROFESSIONAL SPECIALTY	30,972	31,588	32,336	32,688	20,422	20,529	21,506	21,781
Engineers	36,155	35,346	36,335	36,615	27,132	29,132	28,666	31,361
Natural Scientists & Mathematicians	33,609	33,517	32,304	34,632	26,870	27,491	25,375	28,530
Health Workers (Except Diagnosing)	24,805	26,335	27,155	29,017	21,580	21,845	22,590	23,075
EXECUTIVE, ADMINISTRATIVE, & MANAGERIAL	31,947	32,540	33,091	32,872	19,206	19,540	19,408	20,565
Accountants & Auditors	29,647	30,417	31,208	30,098	19,115	19,679	19,833	20,364
TECHNICAL AND SALES	23,722	24,051	24,581	24,957	13,938	14,456	14,698	15,117
ADMINISTRATIVE SUPPORT, CLERICAL	22,733	22,272	22,783	22,997	14,070	14,404	14,836	15,157
PRECISION PRODUCTION, CRAFT & REPAIR	23,182	23,007	23,236	23,269	15,066	14,160	14,177	15,093
OPERATORS	19,092	19,050	19,173	19,648	12,226	12,103	12,196	12,309

Source: U.S. Department of Commerce, Bureau of the Census, *Current Population Reports*, "Money Income of Households, Families, and Persons in the United States: 1982 through 1985," Series P-60.

---

of the females said that they would prefer to teach in grades 1–3; twenty-one percent of the males and twenty percent of the females said that they would prefer to teach in grades 4–6; and seventy-two percent of the males and thirty-nine percent of the females said they would prefer to teach in grades 7–12. Of those reflecting a preference for grades 7–12, five percent of the males and thirty-eight percent of the females indicated a primary interest in teaching English; seventeen percent of the males and seven percent of the females indicated interest in teaching history, geography, or civics; and twenty-four percent of the males and thirteen percent of the females indicated interest in teaching math.

While the results of this research tell us a number of things about the teacher force of the mid- to late 1980s, they also reveal some general characteristics of teaching today. First, the study revealed that relatively few of the top high-school students of the mid-1980s—eight percent—showed a great deal of interest in becoming teachers. Other research suggests that teaching fails to attract the best students, and those it does attract leave the profession earlier than others who are less capable academically.[15] Second, the general perception exists that teaching as a career fails to provide either high enough pay or enough opportunity for professional advancement (see Tables 2.2 and 2.3). Third (as suggested in our profile of the "typical" teacher today), gender appears to play a significant role in the distribution of teachers: Women tend to predominate in earlier grades, men in later; and certain high-school subjects are taught by women (e.g., English) and others by men (e.g., mathematics). Finally, although Kemper and Mangieri found that twenty-two percent of the students surveyed were minorities, they did not report any findings in terms of race.

Figure 2.2
Percentage of Minority
Students in Public Schools
with Projection for 2000

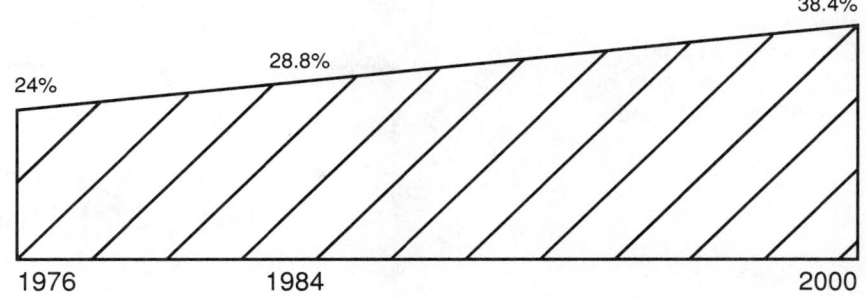

Source: U.S. Department of Education, Center for Education Statistics.

Other researchers suggest that blacks and other minorities are not being attracted into teaching. Patricia A. Graham of Harvard, for example, points out that although twelve percent of the nation's population is black, blacks today make up a much smaller percentage of the teaching force. This comes at a time when experts are predicting that by the end of the century, from one third to two fifths of the student population in America will be composed of minorities.[16] (See Figures 2.2 and 2.3 and Table 2.4.) Underlying all these numbers are two major areas of concern among educational analysts: the quality and the quantity of future teachers.

Quality   The Kemper and Mangieri study revealed that relatively few of the top high-school students—eight percent—showed a great deal of interest in becoming teachers. Critics of the schools frequently cite SAT

Table 2.3

Ratio of Earnings of Other Workers in Selected Occupations to Teacher Earnings, by Sex: 1982–85

OCCUPATION HELD LONGEST DURING THE YEAR	MEN				WOMEN			
	1982	1983	1984	1985	1982	1983	1984	1985
TEACHERS	1.00	1.00	1.00	1.00	1.00	1.00	1.00	1.00
ALL FULL-TIME WORKERS	.99	.97	.93	.95	.76	.75	.73	.75
PROFESSIONAL SPECIALTY	1.31	1.31	1.26	1.28	1.07	1.04	1.03	1.05
Engineers	1.53	1.46	1.41	1.43	1.42	1.47	1.37	1.51
Natural Scientists & Mathematicians	1.42	1.39	1.25	1.35	1.41	1.39	1.22	1.37
Health Workers (Except Diagnosing)	1.05	1.09	1.05	1.13	1.13	1.11	1.08	1.11
EXECUTIVE, ADMINISTRATIVE & MANAGERIAL	1.35	1.35	1.28	1.29	1.01	.99	.93	.99
Accountants & Auditors	1.26	1.26	1.21	1.18	1.00	1.00	.95	.98
TECHNICAL AND SALES	1.01	.99	.95	.98	.73	.73	.70	.73
ADMINISTRATIVE SUPPORT, CLERICAL	.96	.92	.88	.90	.74	.73	.71	.73
PRECISION PRODUCTION, CRAFT & REPAIR	.98	.95	.90	.91	.79	.72	.68	.73
OPERATORS	.81	.79	.74	.77	.64	.61	.58	.59

Source: U.S. Department of Commerce, Bureau of the Census, *Current Population Reports,* "Money Income of Households, Families, and Persons in the United States: 1982 through 1985," Series P-60.

Figure 2.3
Demographics of
Education Students by
Race/Ethnicity/Gender

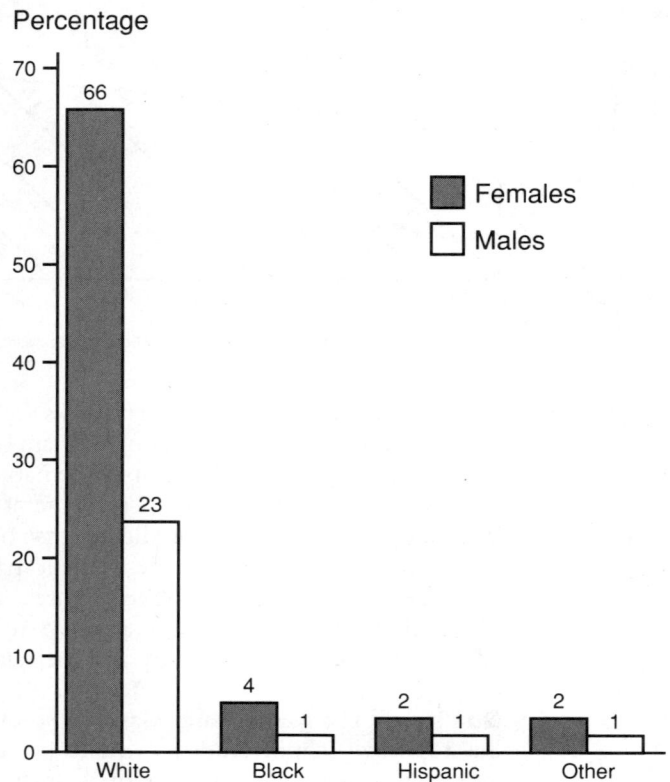

Source: *Teaching Teachers: Facts and Figures, 1987*. American Association of Colleges for Teacher Education, Washington, D.C., 1987.

scores in support of their attack on the academic quality of teacher-trainees. For example, in 1973, the average SAT score of high-school seniors indicating an intention to become teachers was 878—lower than the average for all majors (937) by 59 points. During the next decade, as average SAT scores dropped, the scores of those intending to become teachers dropped faster. In 1982, the national average SAT score had dropped to 893, while the average score among students intending to major in education had dropped to 813. By the mid-1980s, however, SAT score averages had increased, with the scores of those intending to become teachers improving at a rate faster than those of other majors.[17]

While the SAT score is only one measure of academic ability, and one that neither predicts nor claims to predict how well future teachers will actually do in the classroom—competence in which requires a number of factors other than pure academic ability—low scores as well as other criticisms fostered a wave of measures attempting to encourage higher quality. South Carolina, for example, implemented a series of evaluations intended to weed out weaker students from the ranks of potential teachers. Students majoring in education were required to pass a minimal competency test prior to admission to the final two years of teacher training (at the same time achieving a certain grade point average in their classwork), a content area test in the subject in which they majored prior to probationary

Table 2.4
Education Professoriate
by Rank and
Race/Ethnicity

RACE/ETHNICITY	PROFESSOR	ASSOCIATE PROFESSOR	ASSISTANT PROFESSOR
White	96.0	92.0	89.5
Black	1.6	3.9	3.6
Hispanic	1.3	2.8	5.5
Asian/Pacific	0.8	0.8	1.4
American Indian/ Alaskan Native	0.2	0.2	
Other	0.2	0.2	

Source: *Teaching Teachers: Facts and Figures, 1987.* American Association of Colleges for Teacher Education, Washington, D.C., 1987.

certification, and an evaluation of minimal classroom skills during their first, probationary year as teachers. Other states adopted similar measures.

Recognizing that relatively low teacher salaries and limited opportunities for professional advancement kept a number of bright students from choosing teaching as a career, some states during the mid-1980s raised teacher salaries and/or developed new programs for professional advancement. Typical of the latter were merit pay, career ladders, and teacher recognition programs.[18] Thus, between the 1982–83 and 1984–85 school years, average teacher salaries increased some twenty-two percent, a rate of increase that outstripped inflation.[19]

In an attempt to maintain developments fostering higher quality on the state level, national groups during the mid-1980s called for higher teacher salaries and the improvement of both undergraduate teacher education and the teacher certification process. The Carnegie Forum on Education and the Economy's Task Force on Teaching as a Profession, for example, called for the abolition of the undergraduate teacher education curriculum and the establishment of teacher-training programs requiring a bachelor's degree in the arts and sciences at the undergraduate level and professional education training on the graduate level.[20] The Holmes Group, an organization composed of the deans of the colleges of education of major research universities, proposed a similar program in a publication entitled *Tomorrow's Teachers*.[21] An important part of the Holmes proposal was the emphasis on a growing knowledge base, derived from research, for teacher education. To promote more rigorous certification standards, The Carnegie Task Force also called for a National Board for Professional Teaching Standards, the primary function of which would be "to establish standards for high professional teaching competence and issue certificates to people who meet those standards."[22]

Quantity   Although the major focus during the mid-1980s has been on teacher quality, some analysts have grown concerned over the possibility of a teacher shortage by the end of the decade and early 1990s (see Table 2.5). Shortages in some teaching fields—notably science and math—in some regions of the country have already been reported (see Table 2.6). The aging of the teaching force, the currently large numbers of retirees from teaching, and the growth of the school-age population because of the "baby boomlet" of the 1970s all suggest that more teachers will be needed in the near future.

Table 2.5   Trends in Estimated Demand for Classroom Teachers in Elementary/Secondary Schools and Estimated Supply of New Teacher Graduates: Fall 1985 to Fall 1993 (Numbers in Thousands)

FALL OF YEAR	TOTAL EST. TEACHER DEMAND	ESTIMATED DEMAND FOR ADDITIONAL TEACHERS					EST. SUPPLY OF NEW TEACHER GRADS	SUPPLY AS % OF DEMAND
		TOTAL	PUBLIC	PRIVATE	ELEMENTARY	SECONDARY		
1985	2413	158	134	24	96	62	146	92.4
1986	2438	165	139	26	109	56	144	87.3
1987	2452	171	144	27	125	46	142	83.0
1988	2468	162	140	22	124	38	139	85.8
1989	2493	177	146	31	130	47	139	78.5
1990	2527	188	160	28	136	52	139	73.9
1991	2569	204	176	28	138	66	138	67.6
1992	2624	215	181	34	135	80	137	63.7
1993	2737	211	175	36	125	86	133	63.0

Source: U.S. Department of Education, National Center for Education Statistics.

The National Center for Education Statistics (NCES) projects that the nation will need to hire 1.65 million new public and private school teachers between the fall of 1985 and the fall of 1993, or more than two-thirds of the current teaching force. But, based on studies indicating declining enrollment in teacher training programs in the early 1980s, the NCES also projects that the supply of new teacher graduates by 1993 will be less than two-thirds of that demand. The resulting shortage could have a tremendous impact on schooling in the early 1990s. The U.S. Bureau of Labor Statistics and some other groups, however, argue that the data used by the NCES is flawed and that there will not be a teacher shortage. They point out that the pool of potential teachers is composed of many people besides education majors, including those who have been certified and have left teaching and those who have graduated in majors other than education. Many states, for example, will give temporary certificates to degree holders in an academic discipline if they agree to take the courses required for certification.[23]

This overview of some of the problems that policymakers must deal with in relation to teachers suggests a frustrating but all too common aspect of policy development. Policies designed to address one problem often worsen or cause another. Thus, policymaking is almost always controversial. One purpose of this book is to provide students of education with an analytical framework through which policymaking can be studied. Part III introduces the reader to models for the analysis of policy development.

Foundations and Policy

The authors of this text contend that teachers must play a role in educational decision making and that role must be based upon an understanding of the historical, philosophical, and social foundations of American education. The issues raised in these first two chapters illustrate the need for thought before action. The reform reports of the 1980s call for emphasis on

Table 2.6

Relative Demand by Teaching Area and Year in the Continental United States (Based Upon a Survey of Teacher Placement Officers)

	1988*	1987	1986*	1985	1984	1982	1976*
TEACHING FIELDS WITH CONSIDERABLE TEACHER SHORTAGES . . . .(5.00–4.25)							
Bilingual Education	4.35	4.42	4.27	4.12	4.04	4.13	—
Special Education—ED/PSA	4.33	4.30	4.20	4.02	3.84	3.98	3.42
Special Education—LD	4.26	4.46	4.23	3.95	3.98	4.20	4.00
Special Education—Multi. Handi.	4.26	3.85	4.25	3.94	3.77	3.93	—
TEACHING FIELDS WITH SOME TEACHER SHORTAGE . . . .(4.24–3.45)							
Special Education—MR	4.15	3.97	4.25	3.76	3.55	3.84	2.87
Science—Physics	4.01	4.26	4.44	4.57	4.45	4.41	4.04
Mathematics	4.00	4.35	4.55	4.71	4.78	4.81	3.86
Speech Pathology/Audio.	4.00	4.21	4.09	4.01	3.83	3.95	3.68
Science—Chemistry	3.96	4.21	4.40	4.42	4.25	4.13	3.72
Special Education—Deaf	3.91	3.81	3.72	—	—	—	—
Computer Science	3.79	3.98	4.22	4.37	4.34	—	—
Special Education—Gifted	3.74	3.88	3.91	3.85	3.74	3.81	3.85
Data Processing	3.59	3.81	3.97	4.30	4.18	3.86	—
Language, Mod.—Spanish	3.59	3.57	3.64	3.43	3.18	2.68	2.47
Psychologist (School)	3.57	3.46	3.43	3.65	2.98	3.56	3.09
Library Science	3.56	3.33	3.39	3.49	3.30	3.12	—
Science—Earth	3.52	3.43	3.86	3.79	3.70	3.89	3.44
TEACHING FIELD WITH BALANCED SUPPLY AND DEMAND . . . .(3.44–2.65)							
Special—Reading	3.43	3.45	3.46	3.39	3.48	3.73	3.96
Language, Mod.—French	3.43	3.24	3.34	3.31	3.00	2.49	2.15
Science—General	3.42	3.32	3.82	3.65	3.65	—	—
Science—Biology	3.37	3.33	3.65	3.58	3.40	3.66	2.97
Language, Mod.—German	3.34	3.15	3.26	3.11	3.08	2.48	2.03
Counselor—Elementary	3.12	3.31	3.04	3.05	2.80	2.72	3.15
English	3.11	3.02	3.25	3.14	3.13	3.21	2.05
Industrial Arts	3.07	3.24	3.30	3.65	3.50	4.36	4.22
Counselor—Secondary	3.03	3.24	3.05	3.08	2.67	2.79	2.69
Social Worker (School)	3.01	2.82	2.77	2.81	2.33	2.34	—
Music—Instrumental	3.00	3.29	3.14	3.29	3.25	3.28	3.03
Journalism	2.91	3.00	2.93	2.74	2.60	2.61	2.86
Speech	2.91	2.86	2.72	2.91	2.70	2.76	2.46
Business	2.90	2.94	3.11	3.32	3.11	3.47	3.10
Music—Vocal	2.89	3.11	2.95	3.19	3.00	2.95	3.00
Agriculture	2.88	2.81	3.23	3.11	3.44	4.36	4.06
Elementary—Intermediate	2.72	2.61	2.78	2.53	2.20	2.26	1.90
Elementary—Primary	2.71	2.58	2.70	2.57	2.13	2.02	1.78
Driver Education	2.70	2.67	2.46	2.65	2.61	2.77	2.44
TEACHING FIELDS WITH SOME SURPLUS OF TEACHERS . . . .(2.64–1.85)							
Art	2.35	1.89	2.20	2.04	1.89	1.84	2.14
Home Economics	2.26	2.16	2.51	2.79	2.43	2.43	2.62
Health Education	2.02	1.95	1.92	2.08	1.90	1.90	2.27
Social Science	2.00	2.05	2.11	2.17	1.91	2.11	1.51
TEACHING FIELD WITH CONSIDERABLE SURPLUS OF TEACHERS . . . .(1.84–1.00)							
Physical Education	1.67	1.53	1.60	1.75	1.61	1.72	1.74

5 = Greatest demand, 1 = Least demand

*Mailings for the 1976, 1986, and 1988 reports included all teacher placement offices that were members of ASCUS.

Source: Report Prepared by James N. Akin, Kansas State University, for the Association for School, College, and University Staffing. January 1988.

academics and testing, higher standards for student advancement and teacher recruitment, and changes in teacher training. Implicit in these reports are certain assumptions about the nature of schooling in the United States. These assumptions, the recommendations of the various groups, and the educational policies derived from these recommendations must be critically analyzed. One may agree or disagree with them, but everyone should ask the fundamental questions, Whom do we teach?, What do we teach them?, and Why? The answers to these questions should be informed by an understanding of the historical and social roles of the schools and, growing out of that understanding, a basic philosophical position concerning the nature of education.

In 1983, the National Commission on Excellence in Education published *A Nation At Risk*. The nation was at risk, argued the report, because Americans were becoming less and less competitive in international corporate markets. Schools were seen as both part of the problem and a part of the solution. Schools were blamed for inadequately preparing the work force, but reform of the schools—with renewed emphasis upon academics, especially science and mathematics—was seen as a solution to the nation's precarious position. As the reader will learn, the call for the schools to do something about this national crisis was nothing new. In the late 1950s and early 1960s, the schools were called upon to address the perceived failure of the United States to keep up with the Soviet Union in the race for space; in the 1960s, schools were used to address the problems of racial segregation and poverty; and in the 1970s, schools concentrated on the problem of youth unemployment. In fact, the call for schooling to address the perceived needs of the larger society is, in this country, as old as public schooling itself. But can the schools continue to serve this function, and should they?

In *A Nation At Risk,* schools received a large part of the blame for failings in American competitiveness. Educational analyst Joel Spring, however, challenges this blame. "After all," he writes, "the decision of business not to invest in new plants and equipment in the 1970s and instead to reap short-term profits is partly responsible for the present technological crisis." Furthermore, he asks if the schools even *should* be geared to meet the continually changing needs of American business. "Meeting the short-term needs of U.S. business and industry does not necessarily result in economic benefits either to the economy or to the individual . . . . In fact, if the schools continue to be geared to meet the changing needs of U.S. business, we can expect still another change in educational policy in the next decade to meet those changing desires. Thus the public school system becomes a captive of the profit motive of U.S. industry."[24] Whether one agrees with Spring or not, the issues that Spring raises reflect the kind of critical perspective that educators need.

Should schools conserve or foster change in society? Social studies educator Catherine Cornbleth is concerned, for example, over *A Nation At Risk*'s argument that the teaching of social studies in high school should be, among other things, designed to "enable students to fix their places and possibilities within the larger social and cultural structure." Cornbleth argues: "At best this advice is vague. What does it mean for 'students to fix their places and possibilities within the larger social and cultural structure?' . . . At worst, it is extremely conservative, if not reactionary." Cornbleth

Photo 2.4
Ethnic and racial diversity is a characteristic of today's public school students.

goes on to argue, ". . . no mention is made of contributing to the resolution of persistent social problems, developing democratic values (for example, human dignity, social justice) or the skills necessary to active citizen participation, or fostering constructive social change. *A Nation At Risk* offers us an agenda for conservative reaction, not reform." Cornbleth also raises questions about the Carnegie and Holmes reports on the reform of teaching. She is particularly disappointed with their failure to see teaching as a reflective, interpretive, critical activity.

> *If tomorrow's teachers are to be reflective practitioners, we ought not to rely on "imparting" research findings with the expectation that they be instrumentally applied. The technocratic rationality implicit in the Holmes and Carnegie reports, like that of the earlier school reform reports, is inadequate to the task of reform; it tends to perpetuate what it purports to change. It also fosters expert control and demeans teachers. School teaching and learning are social activities, not technical ones; even if they could be made technical, we do not know enough to prepare teachers as competent technicians.*
>
> *While technocratic rationality may indeed be productive in other arenas (for example, engineering), it is inappropriate to social activities. The irony of technocratic rationality in social affairs is that, by deflecting attention from questions of purpose and substance and their social and political implications, it precludes the institutional reform that it claims to further.*[25]

Others have attacked the Holmes Report for its failure to adequately address the issue of minorities in education. Carl A. Grant and Maureen

Gillette, for example, point out that a mere one paragraph of twenty-two lines (in a report of sixty-eight pages) is devoted to minority teachers. Reminiscent of social and educational critics of the 1960s, and viewing all of American education from a critical perspective, Grant and Gillette argue, *"Tomorrow's Teachers* offers an excellent case study of how the dominant society reproduces its power and political relations while maintaining its dominance over minority groups. Control of teacher education is in large measure control of the school. The Holmes Group is continuing to insure that our schools remain racist and classist and that minority students remain cut off from mainstream society and servants to the dominant culture."[26] Again, while one might not agree with Grant and Gillette—their viewpoints are based on a particular interpretation of the relationship between school and society—their critical perspective is one that should be fostered among all educators. It is their study of the historical and social roots of American education that informs this perspective.

In short, critics of the reports of the 1980s argue that schools should focus on goals other than those described in the reports. These critics reflect basic philosophical differences with the authors of the reports. Some are simply not sure that the emphasis on academic subjects is meaningful or valuable for all students. At least, many argue, the schools should also foster such things as compassion for others, interpersonal skills, and socially responsible behavior. Thus, the goals of schooling should include not only the intellectual but also the social and personal needs of children. Others, like Joel Spring, are critical of the reports from a libertarian perspective. Still others, like Grant and Gillette, seem to reflect the other end of the ideological spectrum, what one might call a neo-Marxist perspective. (The ideological perspectives of libertarian and neo-Marxist are treated in some detail in Chapter 5, along with some basic educational philosophies.) The point in each case, however, is that these individuals do not blindly endorse every shift in educational policy. They critically approach recommendations and developments in educational policy from their own individual philosophical perspectives, perspectives grounded in an understanding of the historical and social foundations of American education. It is the hope of the authors that the rest of this book will help to foster a critical perspective in its readers.

Summary

The typical teacher today has many of the characteristics of the stereotypical schoolmarm of the past. The teacher today, however, plays a variety of roles. It takes a special person to play those roles, and those who express a desire to become teachers most frequently cite a love for children as the primary motive for choosing teaching as a career. Teaching can also provide a springboard into other professional educational positions.

Studies of the teacher force of the 1980s reflected renewed concern with both the quality and quantity of teacher-trainees. Motivated by a series of reform reports during the mid-1980s, a number of states attempted to address the issues of teacher-trainer quality and quantity. While many of the recommendations of the reform reports were incorporated into educational policy during the 1980s, some observers—reflecting philosophical positions that differed from those implicit in the reports—criticized the assumptions and directions of the reports. It is important for all educators to develop their own philosophical positions, positions that foster a critical frame of mind. Such a frame of mind requires an understanding of the historical, philosophical, and social foundations of American education.

Key Words

Merit pay

Career ladders

Educational voucher

Tuition tax credits

Technocratic/rational teaching

Reflective/interpretive teaching

Holmes Report

National Commission on Excellence in Education

Discussion Questions

1. Review the discussion of Heck and Williams' treatment of teacher roles. Do you think their treatment suggests that teachers' roles are, in Cornbleth's terms, technocratic and rational or reflective and interpretive? Why?

2. Why did you choose to train in teaching? Are your reasons similar to those discussed in the chapter? What are your opinions concerning the issues raised in the survey conducted by *Instructor* magazine?

3. Review Table 2.1. How might you explain the difference of opinion between teacher-trainees and experienced teachers over merit pay?

4. What problems arise for educational policymakers in the attempt to foster both the quality and quantity of the teacher pool?

5. Why is a sound understanding of the philosophical, historical, and social foundations of American education important for today's teachers?

For Further Reading

Heck, Shirley F., and Williams, C. Ray. *The Complex Roles of the Teacher: An Ecological Perspective.* New York: Teachers College Press, 1984.

Holmes Group, J. E. Lanier, Chair. *Tomorrow's Teachers.* East Lansing, Michigan: The Holmes Group, 1986.

Palonsky, Stuart B. *900 Shows A Year: A Look at Teaching from the Teacher's Side of the Desk.* New York: Random House, 1986.

Popkewitz, Thomas S., ed. "Educating Teachers to Educate Students" Special Section, *Social Education,* Vol. 51, No. 7, November/December 1987.

Task Force on Teaching as a Profession. *A Nation Prepared: Teachers for the 21st Century.* New York: Carnegie Forum on Education and the Economy, 1986.

Notes

1. C. Emily Feistritzer, *The Condition of Teaching: A State by State Analysis* (Princeton: The Carnegie Foundation for the Advancement of Teaching, 1985), xix–xxi.

2. Ibid., xix.

3. Reprinted by permission of the publisher from Heck, Shirley F., & Williams, C. Ray, *The Complex Roles of the Teacher: An Ecological Perspective.* (New York: Teachers College Press, © 1984 by Teachers College, Columbia University. All rights reserved.)

4. Ibid., p. 2.

5. Ibid., p. 3.

6. Ibid., p. 14.

7. Ibid., p. 74.

8. Ibid., p. 169.

9. Ibid., p. 189.

10. Stuart B. Palonsky, *900 Shows A Year: A Look at Teaching from the Teacher's Side of the Desk* (New York: Random House, 1986).

11. Unpublished Survey, Clemson University College of Education, November 1987.

12. Mary Harbaugh, "Who Will Teach the Class of 2000?" *Instructor,* September 1985, 31–37.

13. Ibid., p. 31.

14. Richard E. Kemper and John N. Mangieri, "America's Future Teaching Force: Predictions and Recommendations," *Phi Delta Kappan,* Vol. 68, No. 5, January 1987, 393–395.

15. Victor S. Vance and Phillip C. Schlechty, "The Distribution of Academic Ability in the Teaching Force," *Phi Delta Kappan,* Vol. 64, No. 1, September 1982, 22–27.

16. Patricia A. Graham, "Black Teachers: A Drastically Scarce Resource," *Phi Delta Kappan,* Vol. 68, No. 8, April 1987, 598–605.

17. Feistritzer, 72.

18. *Time for Results: The Governors' 1991 Report on Education* (Washington, D.C.: National Governors' Association, 1986).

19. Feistritzer, 35.

20. Task Force on Teaching as a Profession, *A Nation Prepared: Teachers for the 21st Century* (New York: Carnegie Forum on Education and the Economy, 1986), 73–77.

21. The Holmes Group, J. E. Lanier, Chair, *Tomorrow's Teachers* (East Lansing, Mich: The Holmes Group, 1986).

22. Task Force on Teaching as a Profession, 66.

23. Lynn Olson & Blake Rodman, "Is There a Teacher Shortage?" *Education Week,* Vol. VI, No. 39, June 24, 1987, 1, 14–16.

24. Joel Spring, "Education and the Sony War," *Phi Delta Kappan,* April 1984, 534–537.

25. Catherine Cornbleth, "Knowledge in Curriculum and Teacher Education" *Social Education,* Vol. 51, No. 7, November/December 1987, 513–516.

26. Carl A. Grant and Maureen Gillette, "The Holmes Report and Minorities in Education," *Social Education,* Vol. 51, No. 7, November/December 1987, 517–521.

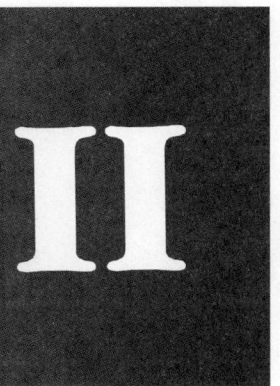

II FOUNDATIONS

Policy attempts to solve problems. Public policy is the attempt to solve the basic problem of who gets what, when, where, how, and why. In this textbook, public education is seen as one aspect of public policy. Thus, public educational policy addresses these same questions. In our pluralistic society, however, that which one perceives as a satisfactory answer or answers to these questions might be quite different from that which another perceives. Thus debate ensues. Informed debate, however, requires a firm understanding of the historical, philosophical, and social foundations of American education. Thus, one must understand how public education in America has developed, the idea systems that animate current debates over the nature of schooling, and the social implications of American schooling. This part is designed to introduce the reader to these areas of study. Chapters 3 and 4 survey the historical antecedents to American schooling today; Chapter 5 deals with various idea systems, both philosophical and ideological; and Chapter 6 treats the social roles of schools and social implications of schooling. Chapter 7 begins to form the bridge between foundational studies and policy by synthesizing elements of foundational studies around the topic of curriculum and instruction.

3 The Roots of American Public Education

"That education should be regulated by law and should be an affair of state is not to be denied, but what should be the character of this public education, and how young persons should be educated, are questions which remain to be considered."

Aristotle, *Politics* (4th century B.C.)

"In regard to the . . . extent of the education to be provided for all, at the public expense, some differences of opinion may fairly exist, under different political organizations; but under a republican government, it seems clear that the minimum of this education can never be less than such as is sufficient to qualify each citizen for the civil and social duties he will be called to discharge; such an education as teaches the individual the great laws of bodily health; as qualifies for the fulfilment of parental duties; as is indispensable for the civil functions of a witness or a juror; as is necessary for the voter in municipal affairs; and finally, for the faithful and conscientious discharge of all those duties which devolve upon the inheritor of a portion of the sovereignty of this great republic."

Horace Mann, "Tenth Annual Report to the Massachusetts Board of Education" (1847)

The question of the nature of education most appropriate for their children has been with mankind for centuries. The answer to that question, as the quotation from Aristotle suggests, has been debated for just as long. Horace Mann, the best-known reformer in nineteenth-century American public education, had a rather comprehensive answer. Others, however, disagree with Mann's conception. A growing number today even question Aristotle's opening assertion, that it should be an affair of state. The purpose of this chapter is to survey the antecedents to American elementary and secondary education and trace the development of some major themes in what has indeed become, in the United States, a largely public enterprise.

Before beginning such a survey, however, it is important to distinguish between *education* and *schooling*. If education is defined, in the words of educational historian Lawrence A. Cremin, as "the deliberate, systematic, and sustained effort to transmit or evoke knowledge, attitudes, values, skills, and sensibilities,"[1] then education includes far more than schooling. When we speak of schooling, we mean the formalized, institutional aspect of education. The development of schooling—and especially public schooling—is central to the American experience. It is that development upon which we focus.

Of course, American schools did not develop without precedent. Throughout history, societies that have reached a certain stage of maturity have reflected an interest in schooling or formal education. The experiences of those societies as well as the records of those experiences have been influential in the formation of the American educational system. It is therefore useful to review briefly some of the classical and Western European antecedents to the American educational experience.

Classical Antecedents

Western civilization owes much to its Greek and Roman heritage. Classical Greek achievements in art and literature still provide models for study today; Greek philosophers raised most of the questions about the nature of life and the universe with which thinking people still grapple; the Greek spirit of inquiry underlies modern scientific thought; and Greek social and political ideas influenced the development of Western democracy. While the contributions of the Greeks were largely in the artistic and philosophical world, those of the Romans came in practical applications to the everyday world: administration, organization, and engineering. Roman civil law, for example, laid the foundation for much of Western legal thought. Roman organizational and administrative skill maintained a world empire and, more permanently, transformed a small sect into a worldwide church. Both societies contributed much to both educational thought and practice.

In his *Politics,* Aristotle made the following assertion:

> *The legislator should direct his attention above all to the education of youth; for the neglect of education does harm to the constitution [of the state]. The citizen should be moulded to suit the form of government under which he lives. For each government has a peculiar character which originally formed and which continues to preserve it. The character of democracy creates democracy, and the character of oligarchy creates oligarchy; and always the better the character, the better the government.*[2]

One might infer from this passage that the nature of schooling is closely related to the nature of the society that produces the schools. This was true in classical Greece and Rome, and it is true today in the United States. But a study of classical schooling—and of thoughts about schooling—does more than demonstrate this characteristic of schools. It also provides insight into some of the intellectual foundations of American schooling. While Greek and Roman schools provided models for later development, some of the ideas most influential in shaping Western European and early American educational thought were provided by individual Greek and Roman visionaries responding to what they saw as challenges in or to their societies. Who should be educated? Who is responsible for providing education? What kind of education is of most worth? These were questions raised by Greek thinkers. Thus, as it is with so much of the Western intellectual tradition, one must turn to ancient Greece and Rome for insights into the development of Western European and American schools.

Greek Schooling

The Greece of antiquity was a land of city-states. Most great classical Greek thinkers believed that the noblest goal of the citizen was rational and virtuous service to the state. But Greek states differed dramatically. Each city-state had its own distinguishing characteristics, characteristics that were reflected in the various systems of schooling that developed. The hard, militaristic life of the Spartans, for example, can be contrasted to the Athenian emphasis upon individual development in aesthetics and culture.

Sparta   Sparta was founded by a branch of Greeks who conquered the tribes that lived in the Peloponnesus. The subjugated peoples comprised two classes: slaves and those who occupied lands adjacent to the city. Neither group was fond of its conquerors, and the Spartans constantly felt threatened. Consequently, Sparta became a military state that valued physical perfection and complete obedience. Thus, the aims of education were courage, obedience, and physical strength. Children belonged to the state, and the state provided an educational system. The system actually began before birth, and only fit individuals were allowed to marry and have children. At birth, children were presented to government administrators who determined the children's fitness for potential citizenship. Those judged unfit were left to die. The fit went on through the educational system.

Young children received their earliest training at home, where mothers taught them to be resourceful, endure pain, and enjoy strenuous exercise. At the age of seven, boys went on to state boarding schools that toughened them further. There, physical training continued, along with instruction in moral and civic issues and the affairs of state. Young girls were organized into "packs" where group spirit was emphasized and physical training continued. Such training was designed to enable them to bear strong children and endure hardships. At eighteen, strenuous military training began for the young men. At the age of thirty, young men who had proven themselves worthy became full citizens.

Athens   In the early Athens of the sixth and seventh centuries B.C., emphasis was placed on individual development in aesthetics and culture. The ideal was the well-rounded individual who, through civic virtue, would provide excellent public service. The man of wisdom was valued in contrast to the Spartan man of action. Again, young children were educated in the home: girls under the care of a slave nurse (some 80 percent of those who lived in Athens were slaves) and boys under the care of a pedagogue, usually an old and trusted male slave. At seven or eight, boys began to attend a variety of public schools, some emphasizing reading, writing, and arithmetic; others sports and games; and yet others music, which was not limited to our modern understanding of the word but came to include history, drama, poetry, speaking, and science. Girls continued to be trained for their duties at home. In their late teens, boys received military and citizenship training.

By the fifth century B.C., Athens had begun to change. The nature of the change and the response of the leading thinkers of Athens to that change are particularly informative to students of American educational history. A leader in the successful repulsion of the Persians, Athens became the center of Greek life, more cosmopolitan and diversified. The expansion of trade led to great wealth among some individuals. Consequently, the old ideal of civic virtue became replaced by a concern for personal advancement. It was in this atmosphere that the Sophists became popular. Sophists were teachers of "practical wisdom" designed to prepare students for success in the public forums of Athens. When asked, "What knowledge is of most worth?" they replied, "Knowledge of the art of presenting viewpoints in public." While the Sophists guaranteed the effectiveness of their teaching of rhetoric—the preparation and presentation of an oration—they cared little for the substance of the argument—thus the modern term, *sophistry*. The success of an oration was in itself an indication of the value of the effort.

Reaction to both the changes in Athenian values and the arguments of the Sophists produced three of Greece's greatest philosophers: Socrates, Plato, and Aristotle. While these men recognized the importance of individual growth and development, they sought to place that development within a context that would maintain social stability. Virtuous living supplied that context. Socrates (c. 470–399 B.C.), for example, rejected the Sophist maxim that "man [i.e. the individual] was the measure of all things" and argued instead that there were certain universal concepts (e.g., piety, temperance, justice) that man could identify through the use of reason and apply in his life. Sophistry, he felt, fostered unrestrained individualism. Rather, education should foster the critical analysis of one's motives and the development of virtue. "The unexamined life," Socrates argued, "is not worth living."

Socrates' student, Plato (c. 429–347 B.C.), continued to address the question of the individual's relationship to society. In so doing, Plato advocated a much greater role for the state. Ideally, the state would foster an individual's development to his or her potential, enriching individual life while promoting devotion to the general welfare. Education provided by the state would play a key role. Plato believed that not all individuals were capable of achieving true knowledge of the universal, abstract ideas that Socrates discussed, true wisdom. Therefore, in his *Republic*, Plato posited an ideal society composed of three classes of people—artisans, guardians, and philosophers—each fulfilling social roles associated with his or her level of development. But these classes would not be hereditary. Rather, each generation of children would receive a basic education, and those of merit would be promoted to their appropriate station in life. Plato's utopian

Photo 3.1

"The unexamined life," argued Socrates, "is not worth living."

society would be ruled by the most capable and intelligent—philosopher-kings. While the educational system fostered a meritocracy—a society where one advances through merit—it also trained individuals in the virtues of their stations in life: temperance and moderation for the artisans, courage for the guardians, and wisdom for the philosopher-kings. Aspects of Plato's conception of schooling are readily discernible in the schools of today.

Just as influential as Plato was his pupil, Aristotle (384–322 B.C.). As reflected in the introductory quotation, Aristotle believed that the state should educate all its citizens. Education was too important to leave to individual families where social and economic factors would determine its quality. The state, argued Aristotle, should see to it that all children of citizens received that common body of knowledge necessary to good citizenship: reading, writing, music, and—to provide "a healthy body for a healthy mind"—gymnastics. Although Aristotle did not specifically address what we would call secondary education in any of his surviving works, scholars have inferred that he would have had youths study such topics as mathematics, instrumental music, poetry, grammar, rhetoric, literature, and geography.[3]

Aristotle's thoughts on schooling had a tremendous impact on Western European and Arabic practices. For Aristotle, the purpose of education was to produce rational living; the virtuous life was the life of reasoned thought and conduct. Since such a life required contemplation, Aristotle distinguished between liberal studies—those that expanded the mind—and vocational training, which he disparaged. The distinction between the two—and the debate over their relative merits—remains with us to this day. From the fall of Rome until the end of the Renaissance, Aristotle's works were the most influential in Western society. Aristotle's categorization of learning into logic and reality was translated by scholars of the Middle Ages into the "seven liberal arts" (the *trivium,* grammar, logic, and rhetoric; and the *quadrivium,* music, arithmetic, geometry, and astronomy).

Socrates, Plato, and Aristotle were visionaries whose ideas had greater impact on the future than on their own times. Their lifetimes saw the decline of the Athenian empire. The Golden Age of Greece had passed. However, one result of their style of teaching and that of other philosophers—informal gatherings where students listened to the great teachers—was the rise of centers of learning in Greek cities. Over time, these centers evolved into what might be called the first universities. Yet in these centers of learning, education withdrew from practical affairs, and the life of contemplation replaced that of service to the society.

Roman Schooling

During the second century B.C., Greece was conquered by expanding Rome. The Romans were characterized by their utilitarianism. Over time, however, Greek culture shaped the culture of the younger civilization. During the early years of Roman development and expansion, education of Roman youth was military in character. Informal, with the family as key agent, it trained men to be active and efficient, and it taught women the domestic arts and moral virtues. Reading and study were held in low esteem. Under the influence of Greek culture, however, the Romans developed a more extensive system. By the middle of the first century B.C., they had appropriated and organized the Greek system of education. On the elementary level, a Roman child might attend the school of a *litterator* (teacher of letters), learning reading, writing, and arithmetic, then—if male—progress to the secondary level, the school of the *grammaticus* (teacher of either Greek or Latin), and later, the school of the *rhetor* (teacher of rhetoric). As with their Greek predecessors, the great Roman teachers (Cicero, Quintilian, Tacitus, et al.) sought to prepare students for a life of public service, emphasizing moral character and wide culture along with rhetoric. Later, as the empire began to decay, Roman education devolved to sophistry.

As the Roman Empire expanded, so did the influence of Greek thought and culture. Latin became the universal language of the western world and, with the coming of Christianity, the official language of the Church. After the fall of Rome, Greek ideas in Latin translation were preserved in the vaults of medieval Roman Catholic churches.

The Middle Ages

With the fall of Rome and the onset of the Dark Ages, state-supported systems of education disappeared. Education for one's hereditary position in the feudal hierarchy took place largely through the home. Feudal nobles were trained in government, estate management, and war. Peasants were trained in their menial duties by their parents. Illiteracy was widespread.

Interest in academic learning was confined largely to the Church. In that context, the purpose of schooling was to foster the Christian experience. The typical school of the early Middle Ages was the monastery school. There, of course, the emphasis was upon religious studies—the nature of

God and the Bible. The major teaching technique was the catechism—rote recitation of a series of questions and answers. Later, students did study secular subjects in the form of the Greek rhetoric, dialectics (discussion and reasoning through dialogue), and elements of the quadrivium (especially arithmetic and geometry). Young scholars also studied the Bible as history and the geography of the Holy Land.

Thus, over time, a synthesis took place between Christian theology and Greek learning. In the early Middle Ages, the church father Origen, for example, called for studies in Greek science, literature, and philosophy as stepping stones to Christian faith. In the later Middle Ages, the Crusades brought contact with Byzantine Greek and Arabic culture, further fostering that synthesis. In fact, as exposure to new ideas brought skepticism, church fathers sought to support doctrine through reasoned analysis. This attempt to rationalize Church doctrine is known as Scholasticism. In the teachings of figures such as Abelard, Anselm, and especially Thomas Aquinas, Aristotelian emphasis on knowledge derived from the senses was synthesized with knowledge through faith.

As the fame of certain Scholastics spread, more mature students traveled to hear them, and from these gatherings the medieval universities grew. The early universities were associations of teachers chartered by a pope or secular leader and granted certain privileges and immunities. Students came to study under masters who, by the end of the Middle Ages, were typically organized into four faculties: arts, medicine, law, and theology. Once a student was able to demonstrate proficiency in the reading, writing, and speaking of Latin, he was declared a "bachelor." Those who continued their studies for several more years and who successfully wrote and defended a thesis were admitted to the ranks of the teaching masters.

Through much of the Middle Ages, schooling was confined to religious institutions. Where larger towns began to develop, however, changes took place. There, wealthier townspeople established schools where Latin and theology gave way to such practical subjects as letter writing and bookkeeping. Training for work in the crafts took place through the guild system, where young men rose from apprentice through journeyman to master craftsman.

Renaissance and Reformation

Europe from the fourteenth through mid-sixteenth centuries underwent a period of dramatic transformation. Major political, social, and economic changes took place as the feudal system gave way to developing nation-states. Renewed interest in the works of classical antiquity led to the Renaissance and the growth of humanism—a concern for the individual's role in this world as well as his preparation for the next. Since Italy was, for Western Europeans, the gateway to the East, the effects of this new intellectual ferment first appeared there. Humanism appeared in Italian literature in the works of such figures as Dante, Petrarch, and Boccaccio and in the painting, sculpture, and architecture of men such as Raphael, Michelangelo, and da Vinci. Humanism influenced schoolmasters such as Vittorino (1378–1446), who continued the synthesis of Christian and classical values. By his time, Latin had become the universal language of the Christian West, and Vittorino had his students learn Latin and Greek in order to read the classics. Study of the classics, besides providing lessons in the decline and downfall of Roman and Greek civilizations, was meant to provide moral lessons, breeding character and civic responsibility.

While humanism in southern Europe was expressed through aesthetic experimentation, the humanism of northern Europe was preoccupied with weightier questions concerning the relationship of the individual to God and the moral vitality of the Christian Church. Familiarity with the classics bred an atmosphere of critical thinking that was applied to all aspects of life, including the practices of the Church. The preeminent figure of the northern Renaissance was Erasmus of Rotterdam (1466–1536). In his most famous work, *In Praise of Folly,* Erasmus satirically attacked the foibles of humanity, especially those of theologians, philosophers, and grammarians. He was particularly critical of the abuses of the Church and the ignorance and corruption of its clergy. Anything but a revolutionary, Erasmus put his faith in gradual moral improvement based upon education. Consequently, he wrote a number of treatises on education reflecting his combination of Christian and classical virtue:

> *The first and most important function of education is to ensure that the youthful spirit may be given the seeds of piety; the next, that it may live and learn the liberal studies; the third, that it may be prepared for the duties of life; and fourth, that it may from earliest childhood, become habituated in good manners.*[4]

While Erasmus placed the primary responsibility for education on the family, he came to recognize that only a well-funded and staffed state establishment could provide the kind of training he advocated.

Erasmus never questioned the legitimacy of the Roman Catholic Church, although he did advocate reading the New Testament in the vernacular, and his work contributed to the growing dissatisfaction with Rome. The resultant Protestant Reformation was yet another watershed in European life.

The most influential figure of the Reformation was Martin Luther. In 1517, Luther, a Roman cleric, posted his ninety-five theses on the gates of the monastery in Wittenberg, attacking the Church's sale of indulgences and beginning the Protestant Reformation. Central to Luther's thinking were the concept of the priesthood of all believers and a belief in the ultimate authority of the Bible. Individuals, Luther thought, should read the Bible and interpret it for themselves. The implications for education were obvious. The ability to read became paramount.

Thus, in the German principalities that broke with the Church, Luther called for the establishment of school systems. In his *Address to the Christian Nobility,* for example, he urged rulers to create elementary schools where all children would be taught such subjects as religion, languages, history, mathematics, singing, and instrumental music. Towns were encouraged to establish and support Latin grammar schools where more talented students could study Latin, Greek, Hebrew, the scriptures and Church Fathers, history, and music.

Interestingly enough, Luther's ideas fueled a growing social revolt in Germany. Spurred in their efforts to effect greater freedom and civil rights by the basically democratic aspects of Luther's thought, peasants and extreme reformers in some regions revolted against constituted authorities. While Luther rejected the use of force to effect reform, he was sympathetic to the plight of the peasants. In fact, he was appalled by the conditions he found: ignorance, immorality, impiety. But what could serve to address these problems? Schooling. In the absence of the overarching authority of the Church, schools were necessary to educate the people in their new responsibilities. In his sermon, *On the Duty of Sending Children to School,* for example, Luther emphasized the importance of education to all aspects of life.

As the Protestant Reformation spread, so did the argument for the importance of schooling. The Calvinist John Knox of Scotland, for example, proposed a system of education comprising elementary schools in every church, secondary schools in every town, and a university in every city. In the Protestant Dutch Republic, a three-level system existed. Common schools prepared children in the basic skills needed for effective citizenship in growing commercial centers, including basic principles of democracy as well as moral and religious training. Latin grammar schools, teaching Latin, Greek, and—in some cases—French, mathematics, and philosophy, served to prepare boys for the professions. The system was capped by the university. In Tudor and early Stuart England, a system of universal compulsory education developed that was centered in the Anglican parishes. The curriculum focused on the Bible and the Book of Common Prayer.

Perhaps the best-known educationist of the Reformation era, however, was the Czech John Amos Comenius (1592–1670), whose *Great Didactic* suggested a comprehensive school system that looked very similar to school systems today. Comenius firmly believed that education could reform humankind and that it should be afforded to all. "As far as is possible," he wrote, "all should be educated together, that they may stimulate and urge on one another."[5] Education for younger children would take place in the home, but at age seven, children would attend the vernacular school where instruction in the native tongue would take place in reading, writing, arithmetic, history, geography, and religion. At thirteen, children would attend the Latin school for instruction in classical languages, sciences, math, ethics, dialectic, music, theology, and—integrating them all—history. After six years of schooling at this level, the very best students would then attend the university, where Comenius recommended a curriculum that was encyclopedic in scope.

Seventeenth Century England

English education is of particular interest to us, of course, because it was the English village experience that was transplanted to America. By the seventeenth century, the "system" of education in England was composed of the household, the church, and the school. The family was the most important element—responsible for the primary socialization of the children and introduction to the world of work. Through the church, families submitted to systematic teaching and discipline by the clergy. The school was the least significant of the educational institutions, because most English children did not attend at all. Those who did, attended dame schools, where they were exposed to basic reading and writing. A small proportion of boys might go on to a local grammar school, where they learned Latin, Greek, and Hebrew. An even smaller percentage might go on to the university.

The grammar school, however, played an important role in another way. Although few boys attended the schools, those who did were the youth of the growing middle class. It should be remembered that the great classical authors, attempting to identify the virtuous life, emphasized civic virtue—service to society. Grammar school education came to be seen as education for civic leadership, conferring social status. Thus, for the first time in history, schooling was associated with upward social mobility. This was a theme that would become an important element in the thought of Americans.

This brief survey of classical and Western European antecedents provides a number of themes that will reappear in the discussion of American education. Classical and Western European societies created schools that reflected the characteristics, values, and aspirations of those societies. Major proponents of schooling argued for education in civic virtue and social responsibility. Schooling generally emphasized the liberal studies—contemplative and rational study of the great writers of antiquity—although practical studies appeared with the municipal schools of the Middle Ages. The concept of schooling as a function of the state was introduced, and the association of schooling with both social mobility and meritocracy had been made. It is time now to turn to the American experience.

Colonial Beginnings

America's system of public education did not develop in a vacuum. Precedent abounded in the European experience. However, just as in Europe, schooling in America was shaped by the particular needs and experiences of the larger society. During most of America's history, that society was characterized by tremendous dynamism. From its inception, America was a nation in motion. Dynamism, however, produced tensions, problems, and social friction as traditional institutions were challenged or modified. American public education developed as one response to these tensions or problems.

The reader should note at this point that the following treatment of the development of American schooling is not intended to be a comprehensive survey. Rather, certain issues, themes, and expectations related to public education are raised to provide historical background for today's policy issues in education. If the reader wishes to pursue a comprehensive treatment of the history of American education or study in depth a particular issue, the list of readings at the end of the chapter might be of interest.

Traditional Institutions

As it was in traditional English society, education in colonial society was centered in the family, the community, and the church. The traditional extended family was the key. As the principal agent of socialization, it also provided—through apprenticeship—vocational training. Since the typical extended family included a wide range of children as well as nieces, nephews, cousins, and servants, it was hard to tell where the family ended and the larger community began. The larger community was, in effect, a further extension of the family and its instruction in the world of work and conduct of life. The church provided further socialization and some formal education. As the child grew, older brothers and sisters and, especially, parents modeled the behaviors required for survival in a traditional, stable, and ordered society.

It was this pattern of education that had been transplanted from England. Although there were variations from region to region in the colonies, the basic pattern held. Schools did not play a major role. By the end of the colonial period, however, the pattern had begun to change, and schools began to play a more significant role.

Life in colonial America significantly altered traditional patterns of family life. Settling a wilderness required new skills, and traditional modes of behavior were often ineffective. In short order, the prescriptive role of adults was undercut. In fact, those who most easily adapted to the new environment were the young. The availability of new land and the independence it provided further undermined parental authority.

A Problem and a Solution

Within a short period of time following settlement, colonial leaders recognized the changes taking place. In the 1640s, laws were passed in Virginia and Massachusetts, and in 1665 in New York, aimed at shoring up the family and its educative functions. The laws of colonial Massachusetts are of particular interest.

To the leaders of Massachusetts society, loss of parental authority portended chaos. Any breakdown in the hierarchical order of the family threatened the very orderliness and stability of society. Consequently, action was taken to reinforce both traditional patterns and functions of family life. To reinforce traditional patterns, Massachusetts began passing laws requiring obedience from children and prescribing penalties for contempt and abuse. To reinforce traditional functions, laws like the Massachusetts statute of 1642, condemning "the great neglect of many parents and masters in training up their children in learning and labor," required families to provide their children with the "ability to read and understand the principles of religion and the capital laws of this country."[6]

Such measures evidently proved inadequate in stemming the failure of families to provide traditional functions. Thus, in 1647, an even more far-reaching statute was enacted. The "old deluder, Satan" act required townships of 50 households to establish primary schools and those of 100 or more to establish grammar schools. In short, by 1647 Massachusetts had begun to look to the schools to provide one of the family's traditional roles.

This transfer of roles from the family to a formal educational institution is also evident in the area of vocational training. As previously noted, the family was the traditional source of education in a vocation. The most common means for this education was apprenticeship—a contractual arrangement whereby vocational training was provided by a master in return for absolute personal service over a specified number of years on the part of the apprentice. The contractual obligation on the part of the master, however, went beyond mere training in the skills of his craft. Masters were required by law to bring their apprentices up morally, to provide for their "Christian cultivation . . . and . . . proper deportment."[7] Frequently, the terms of indenture also required the master to provide instruction in reading, writing, and ciphering. The master, in effect, took over the role of parent to his apprentice.

Over time, however, the persistent shortage of labor in the colonies transformed the nature of apprenticeship. Masters began to view apprenticeship as merely a source of labor. In that context, skills instruction continued, but instruction in other areas began to disappear. Instead, masters hired teachers to instruct apprentices in nonvocational matters. Soon this change was institutionalized in the "evening school." In the words of historian Bernard Bailyn, "there took place a reduction in the personal, non-vocational obligations that bound master and servant and a transfer of general educational functions to external agencies."[8] The inability or unwillingness of families to continue traditional functions led to reliance on another institutional device, the school.

Implications

The establishment of the first public schools in the context of social change and the attempt to address that change are significant to our understanding of American public schooling for a number of reasons (see Box 3.1 for an early interpretation). First and foremost, this earliest version of the public school was created in response to the perceived failure of another institution. The acquisition of functions of other institutions has become a common characteristic of American public schools.

Second, these first public schools closely reflected the cultural milieu in which they were established. Colonial Massachusetts was Puritan Massachusetts. Attribution of social ills to "that old deluder, Satan" symbolizes for us the deeply religious perspective of the people, the belief that social order could be maintained through proper religious instruction. Religious indoctrination was, indeed, a primary function of the schools throughout the colonial period. The early schools also reflected colonial assumptions concerning the hierarchical nature of society. The lower level schools, designed for the bulk of the population, were to produce good workers and law-abiding citizens. Only the social and intellectual elite attended the Latin grammar schools, designed to provide preparation for college.

Finally, the schools relied for their existence on support from community resources. Schools were not autonomous agencies. Rather, they were controlled by their benefactors. Over the years, this precedent has become firmly established. Consequently, schools have continued to be sensitive to the concerns of the communities that they serve. In sum, public schooling has developed as an institution controlled by the people that can be used to address problems perceived by the people; that is, the school has been perceived as an instrument for the implementation of public policy.

The Colonial and Early National Cultural Milieu

An important characteristic of American public schools is that they reflect the cultural concerns and social developments of the broader society. A major feature of early American public schools was the preeminence of religious instruction. Religious instruction was believed to foster virtue, a characteristic many of the founding fathers emphasized as necessary to the citizenry of a republic. By the early nineteenth century, however, a new function for public schools appeared: Schooling became a means for social and economic advancement.

Box 3.1
An Early
Interpretation of
Massachusetts
School Laws

In 1894, George H. Martin published *The Evolution of the Massachusetts Public School System,* which he argued that when taken together, the Massachusetts school laws of the 1640s and tax laws of the 1630s—which provided equalized and compulsory taxation of all for all town charges—established the following underlying principles of public education. Do these principles appear to hold today?

1. The universal education of youth is essential to the well-being of the state.

2. The obligation to furnish this education rests primarily upon the parent.

3. The state has a right to enforce this obligation. . . .

4. The state may fix a standard which shall determine the kind of education, and the minimum amount. . . .

5. Public money, raised by a general tax, may be used to provide such education as the state requires. The tax may be general, though the school attendance is not.

6. Education higher than the rudiments may be supplied by the state. Opportunity must be provided at public expense for youths who wish it to be fitted for the university.

Source: George H. Martin, *The Evolution of the Massachusetts Public School System* (New York: D. Appleton, 1894), pp. 14–15.

Religion and the Schools

The earliest public schools were seen as instruments for the preservation of religious faith. Religious indoctrination was practiced throughout the colonial period. Cotton Mather's eulogy of schoolmaster Ezekiel Cheever lauded Mr. Cheever's pursuit of this end:

> *He so constantly* Pray'd *with us every* Day, *and Catechis'd us every* Week, *and let fall such Holy* Counsels *upon us; He took so many Occasions, to make* Speeches *unto us, that should make us Afraid of Sin, and of incurring the fearful Judgments of God by Sin; That I do propose him for* Imitation."[9]

In fact, a 1654 Massachusetts law required selectmen (town officers) "not to admit or suffer any such to be continued in the office or place of teaching, educating or instructing of youth or children in the college or schools, that have manifested themselves unsound in the faith, or scandalous in their lives, and not giving due satisfaction according to the rules of Christ."[10]

Despite the secularization of society throughout the eighteenth and into the nineteenth century, religious indoctrination remained in the schools. Religious themes found in the early *New England Primer* ("In Adam's fall, we sinned all.") were still reflected in texts like Jonathan Fisher's *The Youth's Primer* (1817), which illustrated the letter Y with:

Take ye my Yoke
So Jesus spoke
Born with delight
'Tis easy quite.[11]

Even as late as 1848, Webster's *Elementary Speller* taught students that the Scriptures were to be examined "daily and carefully."

A number of historians have suggested that during periods of rapid social change, emphasis upon traditional religious values and precepts reflects a desire to maintain some sense of stability. There seems little doubt that this argument can be applied to the religious indoctrination of the schools during the seventeenth and eighteenth centuries. Yet another reason for religious instruction in the schools was the belief that such instruction fostered virtue.

A Virtuous Citizenry

Many of the founding fathers felt that a virtuous and educated citizenry was necessary for the survival of the infant republic. These views were reflected by Noah Webster:

(S)ociety requires that the education of youth should be watched with the most scrupulous attention. Education, in a great measure, forms the moral characters of men, and morals are the basis of government. Education should therefore be the first care of a legislature; not merely the institution of schools, but the furnishing of them with the best men for teachers. A good system of education should be the first article in the code of political regulations; for it is

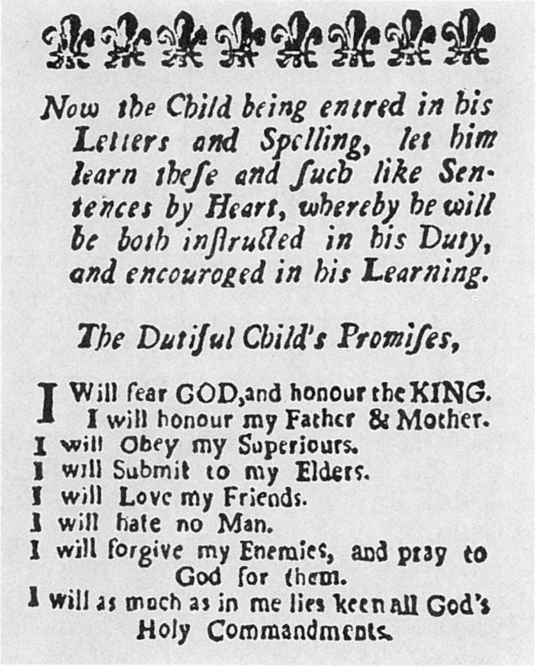

Photo 3.2
The religious character of schooling was reflected in textbooks such as the popular *New England Primer*.

Now the Child being entred in his Letters and Spelling, let him learn these and such like Sentences by Heart, whereby he will be both instructed in his Duty, and encouraged in his Learning.

The Dutiful Child's Promises,

I Will fear GOD, and honour the KING.
  I will honour my Father & Mother.
I will Obey my Superiours.
I will Submit to my Elders.
I will Love my Friends.
I will hate no Man.
I will forgive my Enemies, and pray to
      God for them.
I will as much as in me lies keep all God's
      Holy Commandments.

much easier to introduce and establish an effectual system for preserving morals, than to correct, by penal statutes, the ill effects of a bad system. . . .

Two regulations are essential to the continuance of republican governments: 1. Such a distribution of lands and such principles of descent and alienation, as shall give every citizen a power of acquiring what his industry merits. 2. Such a system of education as gives every citizen an opportunity of acquiring knowledge and fitting himself for places of trust. . . .

In our American republics, where government is in the hands of the people, knowledge should be universally diffused by means of public schools. Of such consequence is it to society, that the people who make laws should be well informed, that I conceive no legislature can be justified in neglecting proper establishments for this purpose.[12]

Soon after the Revolution, some Americans looked to public schooling as a means to foster citizenship. By the same time, discussions of schooling were reflecting yet another theme: schooling for social and economic advancement.

Schooling and Social Mobility

Although social dynamism might threaten traditional institutions, it can also provide opportunity. Such was the case in colonial and early national America. By the end of the colonial period, education had begun to be seen as means to social betterment. Two famous Americans, Benjamin Franklin and Thomas Jefferson, contributed to a theme that has become a central aspect of America's faith in schooling.

Benjamin Franklin   Benjamin Franklin represents a link between the old idea of education for religion and maintenance of social order and the new idea of education for self-improvement. In his *Autobiography,* Franklin tells us that a most influential book on his life was Cotton Mather's *Essays to Do Good,* a basic theme of which—greatly simplified—was that a virtuous life signaled salvation. Franklin translated "virtuous life" into the idea of doing good for others. One way he "did good" was in his role as educator. The instruction he provided through his *Autobiography* and *Poor Richard's Almanack* was that virtue led to wealth:

The way to wealth is as plain as the way to market. It depends chiefly on two words, industry and frugality; that is, waste neither time nor money, but make the best of both. Without industry and frugality nothing will do, and with them everything.[13]

Initially, Franklin promoted institutions that would facilitate self-education: the Junto (a study group for mutual improvement), the subscription library, and the American Philosophical Society. His most famous educational effort, however, was his Academy of Philadelphia. In the mid eighteenth century, secondary educational institutions functioned primarily to supply ministers. The colleges trained ministers, and the Latin grammar schools prepared students for college. Other than special schools run by individuals, no institutions existed to train young people for other professions or businesses. Thus, with his publication in 1749 of "Proposals Related to the Education of Youth in Pennsylvania," Franklin advocated an education that was secular and practical rather than religious and classical.

> *As to their STUDIES, it would be well if they could be taught* every Thing *that is useful, and* every Thing *that is ornamental: But Art is long, and their Time is short. It is therefore proposed that they learn those things that are likely to be* most useful *and* most ornamental, *Regard being had to the several Professions for which they are intended.*[14]

For Franklin, the most useful studies were those that gave the student mastery over his own language: the ability to read with understanding, write clearly, and speak effectively. Art would be studied as an aid to creative expression. Practical aspects of mathematics, especially accounting, would be emphasized as well as natural history. A large part of the curriculum would be devoted to what we now call social studies: history, geography, political science. Finally, languages would be offered: Latin and Greek for those who wished to prepare for the ministry and modern foreign languages for others.

According to educational historian Henry J. Perkinson, Benjamin Franklin was in many ways the prototypical American educator. His emphasis on pragmatism—practical outcomes—grew to thoroughly permeate American educational thought. His faith in the power of education to improve the individual's lot in life anticipated an American belief that borders on dogma. His proposal for an academy, however, was somewhat ahead of his time, and it was not until the nineteenth century that the educational institution he advocated became commonplace in America. In fact, the private academy—although sometimes receiving different kinds of public support—became the predominant form of secondary education in the United States well into the second half of the nineteenth century.

Thomas Jefferson   Closely related to the belief in the school as a means for social mobility is the idea that the school rewards those with talent and ability—regardless of their social background. Perhaps the first American to explain the role of the school as that of fostering the development of a meritocracy was Thomas Jefferson. Jefferson's view of the school as a means for promoting meritorious individuals grew out of his fundamental concern for protecting the freedom of the people. Jefferson believed that an educated populace was necessary to democratic society, that people could not remain uneducated and free:

> *Even under the best forms [of government], those entrusted with power have, in time, and by slow operations, perverted it into tyranny; and it is believed that the most effectual means of preventing this would be to illuminate, as far as practicable, the mind of the people at large . . . whence it becomes expedient for promoting the publick happiness that those persons, whom nature hath endowed with genius and virtue, should be rendered by liberal education worthy to receive, and able to guard the sacred deposit of the rights and liberties of their fellow citizens, and that they should be called to that charge without regard to wealth, birth or other accidental condition or circumstance.*[15]

A meritocracy is a social system that allows individuals an equal chance to rise in the social hierarchy. People rise— or fall—according to their abilities, their merit. A public educational system can play a key role in identifying and promoting meritorious individuals. That is precisely what Jefferson proposed when, in 1779, he introduced a "Bill for the More General Diffusion of Knowledge" to the Virginia legislature.

According to Jefferson's proposal, the state would provide three years of elementary education, free to all children—male and female. During these three years, the children would be taught reading, writing, and "common arithmetic." After elementary education, students could move on to one of twenty grammar schools throughout the state. These schools would charge tuition; however, the state would provide scholarships to a number of the talented poor. Each year, each elementary school would be able to send one male scholarship student on to this level. In these schools, Latin and Greek, English grammar, geography, and "higher arithmetic" would be taught. After two more years of free education, each grammar school would then select one scholarship student for four more years of schooling at state expense. "In this manner," argued Jefferson, "twenty of the best geniuses will be raked from the rubbish annually, and be instructed, at the public expense, so far as grammar schools go."[16]

At the top of this educational pyramid would be the state university. Every year, each grammar school would select ten of its best students to receive three-year scholarships to William and Mary. (At the time, William and Mary was an Anglican school, but Jefferson proposed its conversion to state control. He eventually oversaw the establishment of the University of Virginia.)

Under Jefferson's proposal, a "natural aristocracy" of talent and ability would be promoted through the school system. Jefferson, however, was ahead of his time. The bill did not pass. Critics argued that the state should not be involved in educating the populace and that, in any case, public funds were too limited. Yet Jefferson's thinking was influential in promoting an idea that has since become widely accepted.

Box 3.2
European Influences
Continue

Despite American independence, European educational ideas remained influential in the new nation, especially those ideas that could be implemented without cost to the state. In the early years of the republic, for example, before the common school movement, the ideas of Englishmen Joseph Lancaster and Robert Raikes were adopted in some areas. Lancaster's monitorial system provided an inexpensive means by which one teacher could supervise the instruction of hundreds of students. Under this system, the teacher would instruct a few more capable students who would each, in turn, be responsible for the instruction of a small group of other children. In this manner, schooling was indeed inexpensive and, advocates felt, more palatable to cost-conscious supporters. Raikes' Sunday school, originally conceived to educate English children who worked in the mills on their one day off—Sunday—was adopted in a number of American cities. Sunday school societies were designed primarily for the poor.

Photo 3.3

Thomas Jefferson believed that a public educational system would help foster a natural aristocracy.

Jefferson and Franklin, then, were significant figures. Writing in an era when schooling was religious and conservative, they reflected a new theme. A dynamic American society—a society where social mobility was a reality—fostered new educational ideas. Significant developments in American public education would not come, however, until the public school was seen as a means to address yet another social change.

The Common School Movement

Despite the efforts of such thinkers as Noah Webster and Thomas Jefferson, the idea of public schools did not catch on. During the early part of the nineteenth century, private education remained the norm. Even the public schools in Massachusetts fell into disarray. Changes were occurring in American society, however, that would see new advocates call for and establish public school systems in many of the states.

America on the Move

The United States during the first half of the nineteenth century was a nation on the move, a nation of change. Movement and change came not only in geographic terms but also in economic and social terms.

By the close of the 1840s, the United States stretched from the Atlantic Ocean in the East to the Pacific Ocean in the Far West and the Rio Grande in the Southwest. As the boundaries of the country moved westward, so did the people. By 1840, over six million Americans—more than one third of the total population—lived west of the Appalachian Mountain Range.

While the vast majority of Americans remained independent farmers, Thomas Jefferson's ideal, the industrial and transportation revolutions fostered a society of much greater diversity than that known by earlier Americans. One aspect of that diversity was the growing importance of cities and those who lived in them. As transportation and industrial centers, cities became more and more significant in the life of the nation.

The revolution in industry brought a factory system to the cities, new machinery to the factories, and new workers to run the machines. Some of these workers came from American farms, as did the young women who worked in the Lowell Mills of Massachusetts. Others, however, were immigrants from Europe.

During the second quarter of the century, hundreds of thousands of immigrants came to the United States. Trying to escape a variety of problems at home, from political oppression to economic hard times, they came from all over Western Europe. During the 1840s, hundreds of thousands of Irish farmers and their families came to America seeking to flee the tragedy of famine in their homeland. Most of the Irish were poor. Because they could not afford to travel the United States looking for jobs, they remained for the most part in the major cities along the East Coast. There they lived in the poorest parts of town under conditions so unhealthy as to be almost unimaginable today. Furthermore, they brought with them a religion, Roman Catholicism, and customs with which many Americans of English and Protestant background were unfamiliar. Tension between immigrants and "native Americans"—those who could trace their roots back to Colonial times—often ran high. All too frequently, violence resulted.

The factory system also had a tremendous impact on the nature of work. Since machines simplified work, unskilled immigrants, women (like those at Lowell), and children were added to the labor force. One observer estimated that fifty-eight percent of the employees in the cotton-textile industry in New England were women and seven percent were children. Wages were low and hours were long. Furthermore, the factory system reduced the need for skilled craftsmen. As a result, lower wages were paid to, and longer hours demanded of, factory workers.

Movement and change are key words in describing America during the first half of the century. People moved from east to west, from farm to city. Changes came in the nature of work and in those who became members of the work force. This was an era of expanding opportunities, when people felt that if given the chance, they could make a better life for themselves and their families. For others, however, rapid change was disturbing. The story of American public education during this period encompasses both perspectives. In fact, both were reflected in the thought of the leading educational figure of the era, Horace Mann.

Horace Mann

In 1837, the Massachusetts legislature passed a bill establishing a state board of education. The bill had been introduced by James Carter, an advocate of public schooling. Carter had been dismayed over the deterioration of Massachusetts public schools and the consequent development of what he saw as a dual system of education, public schools for the poor and private schools for the wealthy. He had hoped that a state board, functioning in an advisory capacity, would foster renewed interest in public schooling. Under the direction of its first executive secretary, Horace Mann, the board did just that.

Horace Mann, at the time president of the Massachusetts senate, gave up a promising career in law and politics to take on the position of executive secretary of the state school board. A typical Whig of that era, Mann believed that government action could be pursued to address problems facing the nation—that active government could foster economic growth and equality of opportunity. State and local governmental support of public schools was one manifestation of Mann's belief.

For twelve years, Mann toured the state promoting popular education. He used his position, especially his annual reports to the legislature and his editorship of the *Common School Journal,* as a pulpit to call for educational reform. He advocated innovation in instruction and curriculum, helped establish some of the first normal schools (teacher training institutions) in the country, and fostered the growth of high schools (an 1827 Massachusetts law, promoted by George Carter, had established public secondary schools).

Horace Mann is one of the most famous names in public education. Of particular interest are his ideas concerning the purpose of the schools. It is here that we find reflected the theme of educational reform in response to social change.

As with many Americans, Mann was alarmed by a number of the changes taking place in American society. The rise of the common man, represented by the presidency of the wild and intemperate—to a Whig—Andrew Jackson, was disturbing. So was the appearance of the new and culturally different immigrants. These new forces in American life were associated with political and social upheaval and even moral decay. Yet how, in a republic, could these problems be addressed? For Mann the answer was found in a common education. "The mobs, the riots, the burnings, the lynchings, perpetrated by the men of the present day," he wrote, "are perpetrated, because of their vicious or defective education when children."[17] Evident in his writing, then, was the theme of education for social control:

> *Let the intelligent visit the ignorant, day by day, as the oculist visits the blind mind, and detaches the scales from his eyes, until the living sense leaps to light. . . . Let the love of beautiful reason, the admonition of conscience, the sense of religious responsibility, be plied, in mingled tenderness and earnestness, until the obdurate and dark mass of avarice and ignorance and prejudice shall be dissipated by their blended light and heat.[18]*

The very future of the republic depended upon education:

> *If we do not prepare children to become good citizens—if we do not develop their capacities, if we do not enrich their minds with knowledge, imbue their hearts with the love of truth and duty, and a reverence for all things sacred and holy, then our republic must go down to destruction, as others have gone before it; and mankind must sweep through another vast cycle of sin and suffering, before the dawn of a better era can arise upon the world.[19]*

Yet there is an interesting tension in Mann's thought. While the theme of social control is obvious, so too is his argument that the schools provide a means for social mobility. In this sense, Mann is a truly transitional figure. The traditional concern for social stability is evident—a concern remaining from colonial times—but so, too, is an explicit statement of the school's role

Photo 3.4
By the latter half of the nineteenth century, the schoolhouse had become a common feature of the American landscape.

in providing economic and social opportunity. Mann's recognition of poverty and ignorance led him not to the argument that poorer people should be kept in their place but rather to the argument that the school could provide them with the means for upward mobility:

> . . . *If education be equably diffused, it will draw property after it, by the strongest of all attractions; for such a thing never did happen, and never can happen, as that an intelligent and practical body of men should be permanently poor. . . .*
>
> *Education, then, beyond all other devices of human origin, is the great equalizer of the conditions of men—the balance wheel of the social machinery. . . . It does better than to disarm the poor of their hostility towards the rich; it prevents being poor.*[20]

Horace Mann is considered by many as America's greatest educational reformer. His argument that a common education can address social problems and facilitate social mobility has itself become as institutionalized as the schools he fostered.

The Common School Spreads

Influential figures in other states shared Mann's vision during this period, and in some cases, with the support of workingmen's associations that also recognized the benefits accruing to education, a veritable movement for the establishment of common schools occurred. Henry Barnard promoted programs similar to Mann's in Connecticut and Rhode Island. With the support of Thaddeus Stevens, Pennsylvania transformed its state-supported system from pauper schools (parents had to admit indigence to receive state aid) to public schools for everyone. New Jersey and New York followed suit. By the time of the Civil War, common school systems were widespread in the northern and western states, and the South had made progress toward abolishing pauper schools and establishing free public school systems.

The Opposition

The typical state legislation promoting public schools allowed localities to tax their citizens to support the schools. Resistance to this legislation was, of course, not uncommon. Those who had no children and those who chose to send their children to private schools argued that taxation to pay for "other people's children" was unjust. Others argued that public schools would sap individual initiative and independence. Immigrant groups often sent their children to parochial schools and opposed taxation for Protestant-dominated public schools. Irish Roman Catholics, in particular, were sensitive to the cultural implications of Protestant public schooling and developed their own system of schools.

By the end of the antebellum era, however, public schools supported by local—frequently property—taxes and state aid were becoming an important part of American education. State centralization was also beginning, with the creation of state school boards, normal schools, and statewide educational publications. Other institutions, however, continued to play major roles. Public high schools were uncommon, and most secondary education took place in private academies. Informal education—the education of "living and learning" through the family, the job, the church, newspapers, and voluntary associations—remained significant.

Women and Minorities

While progress in common schooling was uneven throughout the country, it was even more so with relationship to sex and race. Nineteenth-century attitudes toward women, blacks, and native Americans greatly influenced these groups' opportunities— or lack thereof—for schooling.

Women   The role of the female in Western European and American society had traditionally been that of homemaker and helpmate. With few exceptions, the argument ran well into the nineteenth century (and beyond) that women were intellectually and physically inferior to men, that deep thought was too taxing for them and schooling might harden and deform them, making them unsuited for marriage. If schooled at all, it was to have been in "Morality, Humility, and the love of Virtue." As a result, schooling for women beyond the rudiments of literacy was limited. Nevertheless, change did occur during the first half of the century. Slowly, girls were incorporated into the schools and by midcentury were not uncommon in some schools, although usually the emphasis for them tended to be in areas such as poetry, music, and dancing. Education beyond the primary level could be obtained in the academies, some of which admitted both sexes. From there, girls might return to the towns and teach in the district schools, where they were paid half of what a male received for the same job.

In fact, it was in teacher training that one found the pioneers of female education in the early nineteenth century. Catherine Beecher, whose *Essay on the Education of the Female Teacher* was considered a classic, worked for the preparation of missionary teachers, emphasizing physical education and domestic science. Unlike Beecher, Emma Willard, author of *Plan for Improving Female Education* (1819), felt young women should address the serious subjects, and the course of study at her Troy Female Seminary included mathematics, history, geography, and physics. Perhaps the best-known of the early advocates of women's education was Mary Lyon, founder of Mount Holyoke College (1837). At Mount Holyoke, entry requirements—with the exception of foreign languages—and instruction were on the same level as men's colleges.

Blacks   Education for blacks was extremely limited. In the South, some support for the education of slaves could be found in the early part of the century—under the assumption that religion would help pacify them—but after Nat Turner's Rebellion in 1831, the education of slaves was generally forbidden. In the North, if public schooling was provided, it was usually separate and inferior. Such a situation in 1846 prompted Benjamin Roberts to file suit over the requirement that his daughter attend a segregated school for blacks in Boston. In the ensuing precedent-setting case, *Roberts* vs. *City of Boston,* the Massachusetts Supreme Court held that the local school committee had the right to operate separate schools for blacks and whites. Even in cases where blacks and whites attended the same schools, blacks frequently had to sit in special seats and were subjected to other mistreatment. As a result, Northern blacks began to operate their own schools. Usually the schools were run by black churches or charities. Funds were often obtained from antislavery groups.

Native Americans   As whites moved west and native Americans were subdued, the attempt to "civilize" the Indians was pursued. One aspect of this program was federal support for schools established for the Indians by various missionary groups. In March 1819, an "Act making provision for the civilization of the Indian tribes adjoining the frontier settlements" became law, appropriating funds to employ "capable persons of good moral character, to instruct them in the mode of agriculture suited to their situation; and for teaching their children in reading, writing, and arithmetic."[21] These funds were offered to private benevolent societies for the education of the Indians. Although a number of schools received support as a result of this effort and some Indians learned to read and write, basic cultural differences between the Indians and their teachers prevented any real success with formal education.

Thus, at the time when the concept of the common school was spreading throughout the country, traditional attitudes toward sex and race shaped developments in schooling for women, blacks, and native Americans. These developments held implications for the future. Teaching became the only "profession" practically available for women, and the nation had still to deal with the questions of slavery and policy toward native Americans.

The Late Nineteenth Century

The period after the Civil War saw a dramatic continuation of the urbanization and industrialization begun in the antebellum years. In effect, a new, urban America emerged. In 1860, less than twenty-one percent of the population lived in urban areas. By 1900, almost forty percent did—and they congregated in the larger cities. During this period, New York more than tripled its 1860 population of over a million. Chicago grew from 440,000 to 1.7 million, and both Boston and Baltimore grew from around 200,000 to over 500,000. While the greatest growth occurred in the Northeast, cities across the nation experienced the same phenomenon. Even the South became more urban, although beginning at a lower level of urbanization and moving at a slower pace. The South, however, had a number of problems that slowed its return to the mainstream of national life. Those problems require special treatment here.

Box 3.3
Experimental Schools

As it is today, nineteenth-century Americans interested in education avidly read the latest ideas in teaching and attempted to apply them in practice. Particularly influential during the antebellum period were the ideas of Jean Jacques Rousseau as implemented by the Swiss educator, Johann Heinrich Pestalozzi (1746–1827). In the novel *Émile,* Rousseau had proposed a child-centered curriculum, where the teacher provided a variety of experiences but allowed the child to pursue his "natural" interests, inclinations, and development. Rousseau's ideas influenced Pestalozzi, who wrote, "According to my experience, success [in teaching] depends upon whether what is taught to children commends itself to them as true through being closely connected with their own personal observation and experience."* Thus, in his writing and at his experimental school in Yverdon, Pestalozzi promoted the idea of matching instruction to the developmental characteristics of the child.

Perhaps the most famous practitioner of Pestalozzian ideas in America was Bronson Alcott. In his Temple School in Boston, Alcott individualized instruction, allowing each student to progress at his own rate. Each child had his own blackboard, desk, and chair. The curriculum was designed to develop the "spiritual," "imaginative," and "rational" faculties of the children. To enhance "The Spiritual Faculty," students were exposed to such topics as "Listening to Sacred Readings," "Conversations on the Gospels," "Writing Journals," "Self-Analysis and Self-Discipline," and "Listening to Readings from Works of Genius"; to enhance "The Imaginative Faculty," such topics as "Spelling and Reading," "Writing and Sketching from Nature," "Picturesque Geography," and "Illustrating Words", and for "The Rational Faculty," such topics as "Defining Words," "Analyzing Speech," "Self-Analysis," "Arithmetic," "Study of the Human Body," and "Reasonings on Conduct." Alcott rejected corporal punishment, advocating the maintenance of order through interesting activities. Disciplinary matters were resolved by the whole school.

*Quoted in E. H. Gwynne—Thomas, *A Concise History of Education to 1900 A.D.* (New York: University Press of America, 1981), p. 240.

The Postwar South

Unlike the North, the South was devastated by the Civil War. Added to the tremendous loss of life was the fact that the war had been fought on Southern territory. Fields, homes, factories, and even cities had been destroyed. The South had been dislocated economically, politically, and—with emancipation—socially. It faced the long, hard task of reconstruction. Central to the issue of reconstruction was the question of the role of the freedmen.

Many Northerners, along with the freedmen themselves, felt that free blacks could play an important role in Southern society if only they were educated. Thus, Northern educators under the auspices of various philanthropic agencies and the Freedmen's Bureau flocked to the South. They were received with open arms by the freedmen. Later, Booker T. Washington would write:

I can recall vividly the picture not only of children, but of men and women, some of whom had reached the age of sixty or seventy, tramping along the country roads with a spelling-book or a Bible in their hands. It did not seem to occur to any one that age was any obstacle to learning in books. With weak and unaccustomed eyes, old men and old women would struggle along month after month in their effort to master the primer in order to get, if possible, a little knowledge of the Bible. Some of them succeeded; many of them failed. To these latter the thought of passing from earth without being able to read the Bible was a source of deep sorrow.

The places for holding school were anywhere and everywhere; the freedmen could not wait for schoolhouses to be built or for teachers to be provided. They got up before day and studied in their cabins by the light of pine knots. They sat up until late at night, drooping over their books, trying to master the secrets they contained. More than once, I have seen a fire in the woods at night with a dozen or more people of both sexes and of all ages sitting about with book in hands studying their lessons. Sometimes they would fasten their primers between the ploughshares, so that they could read as they ploughed.[22]

Reaction by the whites, however, was altogether different. They resented "outside interference" with "their problem." While many Southern states initiated systems of free public education during the period of Confederate Reconstruction—the first two years after the war and before congressional Radical Reconstruction began—such systems were almost exclusively systems devised for whites. One South Carolinian argued, for example, "The sole aim should be to educate every white child in the Commonwealth."[23] As historian John Hope Franklin put it:

The hostility to the education of Negroes was a part of the scheme to keep the whites superior. Within the first two years after the war Southerners themselves not only did little to educate the Negro but they also resisted the efforts of others . . . (O)rganizations and individuals interested in educating the Negro were vigorously opposed. White teachers from the North were ostracized and occasionally run out of the community. Negro schools were often burned or razed. In dozens of other ways Negroes were discouraged from seeking education. While many whites insisted that they were not opposed to the education of the freedmen, they did little or nothing to make it possible.[24]

Stories of violence reached the North and, along with knowledge of Southern adoption of Black Codes—restrictions on the rights of freedmen—went a long way toward fostering the attitude in the North that more stringent measures were needed to "reconstruct" the South. Radical Reconstruction followed.

Under Radical Reconstruction, the franchise and other civil rights of the freedmen were protected, and the freedmen played an important role in the governments of the ex-Confederate states. Along with franchisement of the blacks, however, many ex-Confederates were disfranchised, and white

bitterness remained high. The fact that the radical regimes were characterized by corruption and misadministration only heightened white resentment. Most Southern states under radical regimes established or otherwise fostered free public schools for all children, but whites resisted integration.

As Radical Reconstruction ended in the 1870s and white Southerners regained control of their governments, a dual system of education remained. In the retrenchment that followed, monies for public education were reduced, and methods were developed to funnel the bulk of the remainder into white schools. The results were doubly unfortunate. Reduced funding for public education hamstrung the development of public schools in the South, and the dual system ensured even less educational opportunity for blacks. In 1896, the Supreme Court decision *Plessy* vs. *Ferguson* promulgated the "separate but equal" doctrine, which allowed the dual system to continue. Despite these developments, black faith in education, although dimmed for a while, remained high. Major developments in both black and white education, however, would await a later period.

Although the development of formal education in the South lagged behind that in the North, the South did make strides toward modernity. The South, the "New South," became more urban and began to achieve a more diversified economy. Major tensions surrounding urbanization, however, were a northern phenomenon.

Urban America

A key aspect of American society during the late nineteenth century was the country's growing urbanization. The people who inhabited the cities came from both rural America and Europe. Young, rural Americans, displaced from the farm by technological developments, flocked to the cities in search of opportunity. Immigrants sought the same.

Between 1880 and 1920, some 25.5 million immigrants came to the United States. Unlike the immigrants of an earlier era, however, these were not Northern and Western Europeans. Most of these "new" immigrants came from Southern and Eastern Europe. Italians and Slavs fled economic disaster in their homelands, while Eastern European Jews fled persecution. While the old immigrants tended to be white, Anglo-Saxon, and—with the notable exception of the Irish—Protestant, the new were Catholic, Jewish, and Eastern Orthodox. They had different languages and customs and even "looked different."

In many respects, the new immigrants' experiences repeated those of the Irish in antebellum America. With no money and few skills, the new immigrants found only menial employment. Poor pay restricted their mobility to areas of the city near their jobs. In these areas, population was dense and living standards low. Ghettoes—ethnic neighborhoods—became slums.

Different languages and customs, substandard living conditions, and the willingness to accept extremely low pay—thus undercutting native-born workers—led many "native" Americans to react negatively to the new immigrants. While the move to restrict immigration grew, many felt that something had to be done to "Americanize" the immigrants already here. The answer seemed to be in the schools.

Educational Developments

Just as Horace Mann turned to the schools to address the social changes of his era, many Americans sought the same solution in the late nineteenth century. Urbanization and modernization created concern over immigration, child labor, political and social radicalism, and even the very nature of American social mobility. A number of the developments in American schooling during this period must be considered in the context of these larger social concerns. As these developments are discussed, it is important to keep in mind that changes had continued to take place in the family.

By the late nineteenth century, the nuclear family had become the norm in much of urban society. No longer was it difficult to draw a line at the point where family ended and community began. No longer did the family provide a series of models—older siblings, adult relatives—which, by example, prepared children for adulthood. Success in the modern world required the postponement of children and a reduction in the size of the family. The family in urban America—particularly the middle-class family—was clearly distinguished from the larger community. Indeed, the family and its life came to be seen as a haven from the stresses of modern, industrial society.

Even where people tried to retain the traditional, extended structure—in the immigrant communities—urban society undercut traditional roles. Just as children during the early stages of colonization more readily adapted to a wilderness society, so too did the children of immigrants more readily adapt to urban society. Again, the prescriptive role of adults was undermined. What we see during this period, then, is a further erosion of the educative function of the family. This change serves as background for many of the developments in schooling.

Compulsory Education   The "battle for the slums," argued journalist Jacob Riis, "would be fought out, in, and around the public school."[25] That laconic statement reflected the growing belief that the schools could address social problems. In the schools, immigrants would be "Americanized." In the schools, wrote Andrew Carnegie, "the children of Irishmen, Germans, Italians, Spaniards, and Swedes, side by side with the native Americans . . . are transmuted into republican Americans and are made one in love for a country which provides equal rights and privileges for all her children."[26] The schools would even fight radicalism. Argued J. E. Seaman before the NEA in 1885: "The high school education detects and exposes the falacies of socialism; the poor learn that they have an interest in respecting the property of the rich, and that their powers and their labors are also real property, which require to be respected in turn."[27]

Yet how could one be sure that all children were exposed to the beneficial aspects of schooling? Require them to attend. By 1900, thirty-one states had passed compulsory education laws. In 1870, some 6.5 million children between the ages of five and eighteen (fifty-seven percent of the age group) were enrolled in schools. By 1880, the numbers had increased to 15.5 million and seventy-two percent. In 1916, roughly twenty million American children were enrolled in public schools.

Organization and Specialization   The tremendous increase in the number of enrollees fostered the application of principles of organization and specialization to schooling. These were skills, however, that had been well learned during the Civil War, as both North and South had had to become efficient in dealing with large-scale numbers. Urban centers saw the development of centralized school boards and the hiring of education experts—the superintendent and his staff. A number of cities even established their own normal schools. Specialization came to the schools with the adoption of the graded-school plan, whereby classes were composed of students at the same level or age, and with departmentalization in the high schools.

A concern for standardization was reflected in the formation of the forerunners of modern accrediting associations. Although the New England Association of Colleges and Secondary Schools was founded in 1789, the 1890s saw the establishment of the Middle Atlantic States Association (1892), the North Central Association (1894), and the Association of Colleges and Preparatory Schools of the Southern States (1895). The Northwest Association of Secondary and Higher Schools was formed in 1918. The power of a united voice was recognized when, in 1870, the National Education Association (NEA) was formed from the National Teacher's Association, the National Association of School Superintendents, and the American Normal School Association. At its annual conventions and in published reports, the NEA considered the variety of issues impinging upon education. Throughout the period, education was taking on the trappings of a profession.

The High School   While the bulk of the increase in enrollment came at the elementary level, the latter part of the nineteenth century saw the rapid growth of the high school. Although originally conceived as a more democratic form of secondary education than the private academies, public high schools enrolled fewer than 25,000 students in 1875. During the 1880s, however, enrollment surpassed that of the academies, and by 1900 there were over 6,000 high schools in the United States enrolling over 500,000 students. The development of high schools was fostered in part by the famous Kalamazoo Case in Michigan. In 1872, the Supreme Court of Michigan recognized the Kalamazoo school district's right to levy taxes in support of a public high school. An important precedent was thus established, making the high school a part of the common school system.

The story of the high school illustrates what has become one source of tension over the goals of public schooling in the United States. That is, should schooling be academic or practical in nature? The high school had originally been designed to meet the needs of boys who did not intend to attend college. Despite the fact that many high schools offered options in English, classical, and practical curricula, emphasis was usually placed on preparation for college. Yet, even by 1900, only one in ten students in high school expected to attend college. What should be done for the larger group of high-school students, or the even larger group of working-class children who did not even attend high school? The answer seemed to lie in commercial and vocational options.

In the late 1870s, Calvin Woodward established the first manual training school in St. Louis to train students "for the actual duties of life in a more direct and practical manner than is done in the ordinary American School."[28] Throughout the 1880s and 1890s, Woodward's model was followed in many cities. In 1903, A. H. Chamberlain told members of the NEA, "Manual training schools have come to stay because there is a demand for that form of education which shall connect itself with productive industries and with the employments which the youths of our land are by force of circumstances bound to follow."[29] In the fall of 1906, the National Society for the Promotion of Industrial Education was formed.

The vocational education movement was so successful that in 1917, the United States Congress passed the Smith-Hughes Act providing federal funds for the establishment of high-school vocational programs in agriculture, home economics, and trade and industrial subjects. While vocational training programs developed, so did commercial programs and commercial high schools. Through these programs, bookkeepers, stenographers, typists, and the like were trained. In 1896, the department of business education was created in the NEA.

Despite these developments, the emphasis on college preparatory programs remained. The real key to success in America, it seemed, was a college education. Yet representatives of the colleges, pointing to the diversity of programs in high schools, argued that the high schools were inadequately preparing pupils for higher education. In 1892, the NEA addressed this issue by appointing a Committee of Ten to examine the high-school curriculum and make recommendations concerning methods, standards, and programs. One of the most influential members of the Committee of Ten was Charles W. Eliot, president of Harvard and critic of diversity in high-school programs.

Eliot was known as an educational reformer. As president of Harvard, he had introduced the elective system, a major break from the traditional classical curriculum in American higher education. Eliot believed that the most important function of the schools was to develop the student's reasoning power. Practically any academic subject that could be studied in depth would serve to achieve that function, not just—as had been argued by many college professors— Greek, Latin, and mathematics. When he turned his attention to secondary education, Eliot rejected the argument that academic subjects were appropriate only for those students planning to attend college. Arguing that "the proportion of grammar school children incapable of pursuing geometry, algebra and foreign language would turn out to be much smaller than we now imagine," Eliot called for academic preparation for all children.[30]

Eliot's hand could clearly be seen in the report of the committee, published in 1893. That report argued that any of nine subjects was equally valuable in training the mind of the young scholar: Latin, Greek, English, modern languages, mathematics, physical sciences, natural history (biology), history, and geography. It argued that all students should be taught by the same methods. It largely ignored vocational and commercial courses.

The Report of the Committee of Ten was tremendously influential. It was followed—and reinforced—in 1895 by the Report of the Committee of Fifteen on elementary education. The leading force on that committee was William T. Harris, U.S. Commissioner of Education and advocate of traditional, academic schooling. While recognizing the changes taking place in American society, Harris maintained that the best elementary curriculum would be one organized around what he called the "five windows of the soul," grammar, literature and art, mathematics, geography, and history. That curriculum would achieve the primary goal of the school: to pass along the Western cultural heritage. These ideas as well as Harris' opposition to specialized vocational training were reflected in the report. Relatively minimal amounts of time were allocated by the report to manual training.

Thus, curricula maintaining the traditional subject matter and its orientation toward college study seemed preeminent at the end of the century. In 1895, the NEA established a Committee on College Entrance Requirements that endorsed the basic findings of the Committee of Ten, with the recommendation of a set of core academic subjects to be taken by all high-school students. Subsequently, the Carnegie Foundation for the Advancement of Teaching's adoption of the same courses—which came to be known as Carnegie Units—went a long way toward establishing a standard high-school program across the nation.

By the turn of the century, then, the United States truly had a "system" (although composed of many state systems) of education. Yet in trying to provide something for everyone, the system was based upon contradictory aims that would continue to breed conflict and debate. Should everyone receive the same education—preparation for college? If so, what about those who were really unsuited for higher education? If, in the school's attempt to be practical, those unsuited for higher education were tracked into commercial or vocational programs, would the schools be fulfilling their perceived function as a means of social mobility? This debate over the function of schools in a democracy underlay the developments in education into the twentieth century.

Summary

By the end of the nineteenth century, the United States had a "system" of public education. The system developed in response to changes in the larger society. Throughout much of its history, American society was extremely dynamic. Dynamism was fostered by factors such as the presence of a frontier, industrialization, and urbanization. The roles various institutions played in society changed as a result of this dynamism. In particular, the traditional educative functions of the family were affected.

Beginning with the assumption that education was important to an individual's life in this world, Americans gradually asked schools—and especially public schools—to do more and more to help address life's problems: to provide virtuous citizens, to enhance social and economic advancement through merit, to address social problems associated with urbanization. By the end of the century, however, Americans were still grappling over the question of appropriate goals for public schools in a democracy.

Key Figures

Socrates	Noah Webster
Plato	Benjamin Franklin
Aristotle	Thomas Jefferson
Quintilian	Horace Mann
Origen	Emma Willard
Aquinas	Calvin Woodward
Erasmus	Charles W. Eliot
Luther	William T. Harris
Comenius	

Discussion Questions

1. What evidence is there that early proponents of education in the United States were influenced by the works of classical thinkers like Socrates, Plato, and Aristotle?

2. What precedents or arguments can you find in the European experience for education as a concern of the state?

3. What elements of the thinking of Franklin and Jefferson are still reflected in American views of education today?

4. Educational historian Carl Kaestle argues in his *Pillars of the Republic: Common Schools and American Society, 1780–1860* that the common school movement was designed primarily to protect the ideology of an American Protestant culture. What evidence do you find in this chapter to support that viewpoint?

5. What similarities do you find, if any, between the responses to urbanization and immigration in the antebellum period and late nineteenth centuries?

6. Consider your own high-school experience. What evidence, if any, can you find of the debate over liberal versus vocational education in your school? Do there appear to be social and economic implications in this debate?

For Further Reading

Bailyn, Bernard. *Education in the Forming of American Society.* Chapel Hill: University of North Carolina Press, 1960.

Cremin, Lawrence A. *American Education: The Colonial Experience, 1607–1783.* New York: Harper & Row, 1970.

———. *American Education: The National Experience, 1783–1876.* New York: Harper & Row, 1980.

Frost, S. E., Jr. *Historical and Philosophical Foundations of Western Education.* Columbus: Charles E. Merrill, 1966.

Gwynne-Thomas, E. H. *A Concise History of Education to 1900 A.D.* New York: University Press of America, 1981.

Kaestle, Carl. *Pillars of the Republic: Common Schools and American Society, 1780–1860.* New York: Hill & Wang, 1983.

Perkinson, Henry J. *The Imperfect Panacea: American Faith in Education, 1865–1965.* New York: Random House, 1968.

———. *Two Hundred Years of American Educational Thought.* New York: David McKay Co., 1976.

Spring, Joel. *The American School: 1642–1985.* New York: Longman, 1986.

Ulrich, Robert. *Education in Western Culture.* New York: Harcourt, Brace & World, 1965.

Wilds, E. H. and Lottich, K. V. *The Foundations of Modern Education.* New York: Holt, Rhinehart & Winston, 1961.

Notes

1.   Lawrence A. Cremin, *American Education: The Colonial Experience. 1607–1783* (New York: Harper & Row, 1970).

2.   Mortimer J. Adler and Charles Van Doren, *Great Treasury of Western Thought* (New York: R. R. Bowker & Co., 1977), p. 515.

3.   S. E. Frost, Jr., *Historical and Philosophical Foundations of Western Education* (Columbus: Charles E. Merrill, 1966), p. 71.

4.   Quoted in E. H. Gwynne-Thomas, *A Concise History of Education to 1900 A.D.* (New York: University Press of America, 1981), p. 82.

5.   Quoted in E. H. Wilds and K. V. Lottich, *The Foundations of Modern Education* (Holt, Rhinehart & Winston, 1961), p. 215.

6.   Bernard Bailyn, *Education in the Forming of American Society* (Chapel Hill: University of North Carolina Press, 1960), pp. 23–26.

7.   *Ibid.,* p. 17.

8.   *Ibid.,* p. 32.

9.   Quoted in Merle Curti, *The Social Ideas of American Educators* (Towata, New Jersey: Littlefield, Adams & Co., 1974), p. 12.

10. *Ibid.,* pp. 11–12.

11. *Ibid.,* p. 17.

12. Noah Webster, "On the Education of Youth in America," in James W. Noll and Sam P. Kelly, *Foundations of American Education: An Anthology of Major Thoughts and Significant Actions* (New York: Harper & Row, 1970), pp. 155–156.

13. Quoted in Henry J. Perkinson, *Two Hundred Years of American Educational Thought* (New York: David McKay Co., 1976), p. 4.

14. Benjamin Franklin, "Proposals Relating to the Education of Youth in Pennsylvania," in *Ibid.*, p. 23.

15. Quoted in Alice Felt Tyler, *Freedom's Ferment* (New York: Harper & Row, 1962), p. 230.

16. Quoted in Perkinson, p. 45.

17. *Ibid.*, p. 63.

18. Quoted in John L. Thomas, "Romantic Reform in America," in David B. Davis, *Ante-Bellum Reform* (New York: Harper & Row, 1967), p. 165.

19. Quoted in Tyler, p. 239.

20. Horace Mann, "Twelfth Annual Report" in Walter Hugins (ed.), *The Reform Impulse: 1825–1850* (New York: Harper & Row, 1972), p. 142.

21. Francis Paul Prucha, *American Indian Policy in the Formative Years* (Lincoln, University of Nebraska Press, 1971), p. 222.

22. Quoted in Lawrence A. Cremin, *American Education: The National Experience, 1783–1876* (New York: Harper & Row, 1980), p. 518.

23. John Hope Franklin, *Reconstruction After the Civil War* (Chicago: University of Chicago Press, 1965), p. 46.

24. *Ibid.*, p. 52.

25. Quoted in Henry J. Perkinson, *The Imperfect Panacea: American Faith in Education,* 1865–1965 (New York: Random House, 1968), p. 68.

26. *Ibid.*, p. 122.

27. Curti, pp. 220–221.

28. Perkinson, *The Imperfect Panacea*, p. 140.

29. *Ibid.*, p. 141.

30. See C. W. Eliot, "Shortening and Enriching the grammar school course," *Journal of Proceedings and Addresses of the National Education Association, Session of the Year 1892*, pp. 617–625.

4 American Education in the Twentieth Century

"The ideal education is not an *ad hoc* education, not an education directed to immediate needs; it is not a specialized education, or a preprofessional education; it is not a utilitarian education. It is an education calculated to develop the mind.

I have old-fashioned prejudices in favor of the three R's and the liberal arts, in favor of trying to understand the greatest works that the human race has produced. I believe that these are the permanent necessities, the intellectual tools that are needed to understand the ideas and the ideals of our world."

Robert Hutchins, *On Education* (1963)

"Love is the ability to communicate by demonstrative acts to others our profound involvement in their welfare. We communicate our deep interest in them because we are aware that to be born human is to be born in danger, and therefore we will never commit the supreme treason against others of not helping them when they are most in need of us. We will minister to their needs and give them all the supports, all the stimulation, all the succor that they need or want.

That's love, and that's what we should be teaching in the schools, and everything else should be secondary to that. Reading, writing, and arithmetic, yes—but not of primary importance, of secondary importance in the development of a warm, loving human being."

Ashley Montagu, "My Idea of Education" (1980)

The above comments reflect real differences in opinion concerning the primary goals of schooling in the United States. Some Americans believe that the school should focus on academic learning. Others argue that schools should foster individual growth across a wide spectrum of developmental characteristics. Still others feel that schools should prepare individuals for their adult roles. During the course of the twentieth century, the question, What education is most appropriate in a democracy? has been a central one, shaping the evolution of the modern school. The answer to this question is the subject of this chapter.

By the turn of the century, public schools had become a central element in the American conception of education. As social institutions, schools had reflected and responded to the changes in American life. In particular, they had come to be seen as a means to address the variety of problems besetting a dynamic, democratic society. Born in an attempt to address perceived shortcomings in the family's ability to perform traditional functions, public schools by the end of the nineteenth century were expected to help overcome a variety of problems associated with urbanization and industrialization. Yet attempts to address diverse and complex problems raised questions about the nature of public education in a democratic society. Should all students receive the same education, or should education be differentiated according to the abilities and interests of the students? Which was the more "democratic"? Who should decide? Around these and similar questions revolved an educational debate that continues through this day.

Education for Democracy

The years between the turn of the century and World War I were years of widespread political, economic, and social reform in America. These were years during which democratic political reforms such as the initiative, referendum, recall, secret ballot, and direct election of U.S. senators were adopted. Economic reform ranged from attempts to control abusive business practices to the establishment of a sound, national banking system. Social reformers focused on the problems of urban slums, child labor, and women's rights. Beginning in the growing urban centers, the spirit of reform spread to all levels of government and, on the national level, produced reform-minded presidents like Theodore Roosevelt and Woodrow Wilson. This period of reform is known as the Progressive Era. Students of American educational history know that the period also had a tremendous impact on American educational thought and practice.

The Progressive Mind

Most historians argue that progressivism was an urban, middle-class movement. Middle-class Americans, disturbed by the growing gulf between wealth and poverty in America, outraged by local political corruption, and inflamed by the revelation of dishonest and, in some cases, dangerous business practices, called for a wide range of reforms. Of special concern were the monopolistic practices of the great corporations and the tremendous power and evident social irresponsibility of the wealthy industrialists, the plutocrats. A number of historians argue that underlying these concerns, progressives feared the possibility of social revolution. Basically conservative in their outlook and advocates of capitalism, progressives nevertheless recognized the problems inherent in an extremely uneven distribution of wealth and power. In an attempt to preserve a basically middle-class society, they advocated measures that would both control the plutocrats and help the working poor. It was hoped that these measures would counteract the social disorganization that many felt was the result of rampant individualism.

Yet in a typically American fashion, many also looked to the schools for help in addressing the concerns of the era. John Dewey reflected this faith in schooling:

> *It is fatal for a democracy to permit the formation of fixed classes. Differences of wealth, the existence of large masses of unskilled laborers, contempt for work with the hands, inability to secure the training which enables one to forge ahead in life, all operate to produce classes, and to widen the gulf between them. Statesmen and legislation can do something to combat these evil forces. Wise philanthropy can do something. But the only fundamental agency for good is the public school system.*[1]

John Dewey

In 1894, John Dewey (1859–1952) was appointed chair of the Department of Philosophy, Psychology, and Pedagogy at the University of Chicago. As with so many other Americans at the turn of the century, Dewey was disturbed by the social disorganization that he felt was taking place in American society. In earlier times, he argued, the family and the community had given children "training in habits of order and of industry, and in the idea of responsibility, of obligation to do something, to produce something, in the world."[2] Modern industrial society, however, had destroyed the traditional relationships between individual, household, and community. No longer did children experience the total productive process of the community. No longer did children, by sharing in the work of the community, learn how people solved the shared problems of daily living. In the absence of a shared sense of community, a "disintegrative individualism" characterized modern society.

Worse yet, the educational practices of the schools fostered this disintegrative individualism. When all children, regardless of background and ability, were forced to do the same work in competition for a grade, individualistic competition was reinforced. The consequences were unfortunate: "The weaker gradually lose their sense of capacity, and accept a position of continuous and persistent inferiority. . . . The stronger grow in glory, not in their strength, but in the fact that they are stronger."[3]

To address these problems, Dewey recommended the reconstruction of the schools. Schools and their practices needed to be redesigned to foster the social character and social understanding of children. That meant that the schools had to become little communities themselves, where children engaged in "common and productive activity." "The school, as an institution," wrote Dewey, "should simplify existing social life; should reduce it, as it were, to an embryonic form."[4] Learning situations should revolve around "the child's own social activities."

Photo 4.1

John Dewey is one of the most respected—and most maligned—names in educational history. Many critics mistakenly attribute to him the ideas of others.

This gives the standard for the place of cooking, sewing, manual training, etc., in the school.

They are not special studies which are to be introduced over and above a lot of others in the way of relaxation or relief, or as additional accomplishments. I believe rather that they represent, as types, fundamental forms of social activity; and that it is possible and desirable that the child's introduction into the more formal subjects of the curriculum be through the medium of these constructive activities.[5]

Dewey implemented these ideas in his Laboratory School at the University of Chicago. There, children studied how people at different times and in different places secured the basic needs of life. In that fashion, they also learned traditional information in such subjects as history, geography, math, and science. But they learned this information in "socially meaningful" contexts. Thus, the school trained "each child of society into membership within such a little community, saturating him with the spirit of service, and providing him with the instruments of effective self direction."[6] These constructive activities would produce children with initiative, independence, and resourcefulness—the type of individual needed in a democracy. The retention of traditional educational practices produced individuals more suited for autocratic society, training such individuals "to docility and obedience, to the careful performance of imposed tasks because they are imposed, regardless of where they may lead."[7]

Other Educational Reformers

Dewey was a significant figure in American life, a major contributor in both philosophy (see Chapter 5) and education. Perhaps as a result of his great fame, Dewey's name has been associated generally with the educational reforms of the Progressive Era, reforms that have been combined loosely under the concept progressive education. Many of the educational reforms of the first half of the twentieth century, however, were only indirectly related to Dewey's ideas, and some were completely foreign to his views. Dewey was concerned that the nation's schools were inadequately addressing the needs of its students and the needs of a modern, industrial society. Other individuals and groups whose proposals influenced "progressive" educational reform—and continue to influence education today—shared the same concerns, but they addressed those concerns in different ways. Two of these groups have been labeled by historians as child-centered reformers and social efficiency reformers.

Child-Centered Reformers   Although Dewey was certainly child centered, his fundamental idea was to foster child participation in naturally interesting social situations as a springboard into the study of the knowledge of the culture as reflected in the traditional academic areas. Dewey wanted to prepare individuals who could critically analyze and effectively deal with situations in the modern world.

Others were more interested in the child as child. The famous psychologist G. Stanley Hall (1844–1924), for example, noted for his developmental studies of childhood and adolescence, argued that schools should defend the happiness and rights of children and not impose civilization on them. Hall believed that children, in their development, recapitulated the stages of development of the human race. Schools should take advantage of this natural process, he reasoned, by shaping the curriculum around the cultural content of the various epochs of human history.

Hall argued that the typical curriculum of the schools squelched children's natural spontaneity, ignored their need for activity, and failed to comprehend the wide diversity in student ability. Critical of the Committee of Ten's recommendation of a common academic experience, Hall called for individualization, the adjustment of schooling according to the natural abilities of the students. This concern for differences in ability and, by extension, the variety of future occupations children would find, was a major concern of a second group of educational reformers, the social efficiency reformers.

Social Efficiency Reformers   Dewey was concerned with what he perceived as social disorganization, but his solution to that phenomenon included a vision of a better and stronger democratic society. Others, also alarmed by developments in modern society, called upon the schools to help maintain social stability by training youth for their probable positions in life. Concerned over the number of dropouts from the traditional academic curriculum and the potential threat to society of these dislocated youth, the social efficiency reformers concluded that the academic curriculum was irrelevant to those students' needs and interests. Thus, these critics of traditional education urged the schools to prepare students for the roles they would fulfill as adults. In such a fashion, schooling would be meaningful for all students and more useful to society. According to these critics, the major function of the school should be to prepare students to earn a livelihood.

This perspective grew out of a major thrust of the Progressive Era, a concern for efficiency. Influenced by the work of Frederick Winslow Taylor in "scientific management," many Americans felt that modern industrial society demanded efficiency through specialization. For educators this meant the education of individuals according to their abilities. The leading spokesperson for this perspective was Franklin Bobbitt (1876–1956):

> *Work up the raw material into that finished product for which it is best adapted. Applied to education this means: Educate the individual according to his capabilities. This requires that the materials of the curriculum be sufficiently various to meet the needs of every class of individuals in the community; and that the course of training and study be sufficiently flexible that the individual can be given just the things that he needs.*[8]

Unfortunately, implicit in this perspective was a potentially undemocratic element. The ultimate form of efficient organization based on specialization would have human beings assigned tasks based on their talents or abilities. As a result of experiments and developments during World War I in intelligence testing, it appeared that society had a tool that predicted those capabilities. Educators began to use intelligence tests to place students in curricula according to their test scores. From this perspective, the function of the schools would be to adjust individuals to the roles for which they were most suited. Such determinism—"experts" deciding what direction a person's life should take—became and still is a part of educational practice, but it was a long way indeed from John Dewey's thinking:

> *There must not be one system for the children of parents who have more leisure and another for the children of those who are wage-earners. The physical separation forced by such a scheme, while unfavorable to the development of a proper mutual sympathy, is the least of its evils. Worse is the fact that the overbookish education for some and the over-"practical" education for others brings about a division of mental and moral habits, ideals, and outlook.*
>
> *The academic education turns out future citizens with no sympathy for work done with the hands, and with absolutely no training for understanding the most serious of present-day social and political difficulties. The trade training will turn out future workers who may have greater immediate skill than they would have had without their training, but who have no enlargement of mind, no insight into the scientific and social significance of the work they do, no education which assists them in finding their way on or in making their own adjustments. A division of the public school system into one part which pursues traditional methods, with incidental improvements, and another which deals with those who are to go into manual labor means a plan of social predestination totally foreign to the spirit of a democracy.*[9]

Box 4.1
Dewey on Subject
Matter

One consideration stands out clearly when education is conceived in terms of experience. Anything which can be called a study, whether arithmetic, history, geography, or one of the natural sciences, must be derived from materials which at the outset fall within the scope of ordinary life-experience. In this respect, the newer education contrasts sharply with procedures which start with facts and truths that are outside the range of the experience of those taught, and which, therefore, have the problem of discovering ways and means of bringing them within experience. Undoubtedly one chief cause for the great success of newer methods in early elementary education has been its observance of the contrary principle.

But finding the material for learning within experience is only the first step. The next step is the progressive development of what is already experienced into a fuller and richer and also more organized form, a form that gradually approximates that in which subject-matter is presented to the skilled, mature person. That this change is possible without departing from the original connection of education with experience is shown by the fact that this change takes place outside of the school and apart from formal education. The infant, for example, begins with an environment of objects that is very restricted in space and time. That environment steadily expands by the momentum inherent in experience itself without aid from scholastic instruction. As the infant learns to reach, creep, walk, and talk, the intrinsic subject matter of his experience widens and deepens. It comes into connection with new objects and events which call out new powers, while the exercise of these powers refines and enlarges the content of its experience. Life-space and life-durations are expanded. The environment, the world of experience, constantly grows larger and, so to speak, thicker. The educator who receives the child at the end of this period has to find ways for doing consciously and deliberately what "nature" accomplishes in the earlier years. . . .

It is a mistake to suppose that the principle of the leading on of experience to something different is adequately satisfied simply by giving pupils some new experiences any more than it is by seeing to it that they have greater skill and ease in dealing with things with which they are already familiar. It is also essential that the new objects and events be related intellectually to those of earlier experiences, and this means that there be some advance made in conscious articulation of facts and ideas. It thus becomes the office of the educator to select those things within the range of existing experience that have the promise and potentiality of presenting new problems which by stimulating new ways of observation and judgment will expand the area of further experience.

Source: John Dewey, *Experience and Education* (New York: The Macmillan Co., 1938.) Printed by permission of Kappa Delta Pi, an Honor Society in Education.

Seven Cardinal Principles

Each group of educational reformers expressed dissatisfaction with the recommendations of the Committee of Ten and traditional academic education, and this dissatisfaction soon led to a call for a new statement concerning the goals of education. In 1918, the NEA's Commission on the Reorganization of Secondary Schools made its report. While reflecting primarily the influence of the social efficiency reformers, the report can be seen as a compromise between the various reform perspectives. Unlike the report of the Committee of Ten, the NEA's Commission's report advocated a wide range of curricula designed to meet diverse student interests and needs. "Secondary education should be determined by the needs of society to be served, the character of the individuals to be educated, and the knowledge of educational theory and practice available," wrote the Commission.[10]

> *The purpose of democracy is so to organize society that each member may develop his personality primarily through activities designed for the well-being of his fellow members and of society as a whole. . . .*
>
> *Education in a democracy . . . should develop in each individual the knowledge, interests, ideals, habits, and powers whereby he will find his place and use that place to shape both himself and society toward ever nobler ends.*[11]

To achieve that broad purpose of education, the Commission described seven objectives, or cardinal principles, of secondary education: health, command of fundamental processes (reading, writing, arithmetic, and oral and written expression), worthy home membership, vocation, citizenship, worthy use of leisure, and ethical character. These objectives were to be achieved for all students in the comprehensive high school.

The Commission recognized that a wide variety of curricula based on individual needs would foster specialization. The problematic nature of this phenomenon, however, was also addressed. "With increasing specialization in any society comes a corresponding necessity for unification. So in the secondary school, increased attention to specialization calls for more purposeful plans for unification."[12] Unification would be achieved through required courses of all students, revolving around the objectives of health, command of fundamental processes, worthy home membership, citizenship, and ethical character. It would also result from student participation in school government and athletics and other social activities.

The Commission took a number of stands that reflected current thought on adolescent growth and development. Arguing that individual development was a continuous process, the Commission endorsed the division of secondary education into junior and senior high-school components. The purpose of the junior high school would be to expose students to a wide variety of vocations. Students could thus explore their individual interests and abilities before the specialization pursued in the high school. The Commission also recommended against retaining overage pupils in elementary schools. "Experience has shown that the secondary school can provide special instruction for overage pupils more successfully than the elementary school can."[13] Given a secondary school with such a wide variety of students, the Commission advocated differentiated teaching methods based on student abilities and interests.

The report of the Commission on the Reorganization of Secondary Schools is seen by many as the quintessential statement of progressive education. The differences between it and the report of the Committee of Ten should be obvious. In fact, these differences form the basis for much of the educational debate in the twentieth century. The Committee of Ten, dominated by college people, advocated an academic core for all students. The Committee argued against differentiation in curriculum and instruction as undemocratic. It was undemocratic, the Committee felt, because distinguishing between those going to college and those not fostered an educational caste system. Committee speaker Francis Parker stated, "There is no reason why one child should study Latin and another be limited to the 3R's."[14] The Commission for the Reorganization of Secondary Schools felt, however, that academic subjects imposed on the students without reference to their individual needs—and here progressives disagreed over interpretation, some calling for concern with developmental needs, others for growth in a social context, and still others for preparation for adult social role—were of little value. To them, ignoring individual needs and capacities in favor of a traditional curriculum associated with a life of leisure was undemocratic.

The progressives recognized that many students lacked either the interest or ability to study college preparatory material. These students frequently came from lower socioeconomic levels. Given the wide range of student interests and needs, high schools had to offer a differentiated curriculum. The progressives saw the comprehensive high school as responsible for meeting the needs of all children in a common environment. Progressives argued that those features of the comprehensive high school that fostered "unification" would offset the ill effects of differentiation.

Expressions of Progressivism

Progressive education, or the "new education," was adopted in one form or another in a number of schools across the nation. Yet even where the new education did not provide the basic program, the impact of progressivism could be seen. This was particularly true in terms of the social functions adopted by the schools and the further development of educational professionalism.

Social Functions

As noted earlier, a major concern of the period was the impact of urbanization and industrialization on the family—especially the immigrant family—and community. The school, of course, was seen as a device to offset the shortcomings of the urban family and rekindle a sense of community in the urban environment. Schools could serve this function by becoming social and community centers. In practice, the schools adopted a number of social functions during the late nineteenth and early twentieth centuries. Among them were the establishment of playgrounds at schools for more wholesome urban recreation and the provision of school nurses, school lunches, and shower facilities. Even the adoption of the public kindergarten was perceived as a means of addressing urban social problems.

As originally conceived by the German Friedrich Froebel (1782–1852), the kindergarten was a child-centered educational environment in which children were nurtured from egocentrism to a social orientation. By the late nineteenth century, however, many American

Photo 4.2
In the early nineteenth century, the kindergarten was perceived as a means to address urban social problems.

educators saw the kindergarten as a means for addressing urban poverty. In the kindergarten, slum children would be taught the virtues and manners necessary to community living that the family no longer provided. Children would also, at an early age, be removed for at least a part of the day from an unsound environment. Laura Fisher, the first director of Boston's kindergartens wrote:

> The mere fact that the children of the slums were kept off the streets, and that they were made clean and happy by kind and motherly young women; that the child thus being cared for enabled the mother to go about her work in or outside the home—all this appealed to the heart of America, and America gave freely to make these kindergartens possible.[15]

It was even hoped that teaching the children positive habits and behaviors would have an impact on the home life, especially influencing the mother. Joel Spring summed up the kindergarten movement:

> The concept of parental education introduced by the kindergarten movement extended the role of the school in a new direction that gave the kindergarten a social role far beyond anything originally intended by Froebel. As a new educational institution, the kindergarten was to compensate for the supposed loss of socialization within the slum family, to protect the young child from the influences of the street, to provide preparation for entrance into regular elementary school classes, and to educate the parents, particularly the mother.[16]

Professionalization

Yet another area in which progressivism had an impact on American education was the further professionalization of educators. A major characteristic of American society at this time was a concern with efficacy, with that which "worked." Yet in an increasingly complex society, it was difficult to predict what would work. That task, then, fell to experts. As noted earlier, one major direction that progressivism took was the application by experts of scientific management and organizational principles to various problems. "The heart of progressivism," wrote historian Robert Wiebe, "was the ambition of the new middle class to fulfill its destiny through bureaucratic means."[17]

The implications of this aspect of progressivism for public schooling were manifold. First, the early twentieth century saw a clear distinction drawn among educational leaders between the role of the school board and that of the administration. School boards, which originally had been involved in many aspects of education, were relegated the task of devising policy. Administrators—experts in education—were to administer that policy without interference from the board. Second, school administrators adopted the arguments for scientific organization and management within their school systems. The result of what educational historian Raymond E. Callahan has called the cult of efficiency[18] was a hierarchical ordering of authority from the central office, through the school principals, and down to the teachers. Standardization—in forms, records, procedures—and cost efficiency became major concerns of school superintendents. Finally, and especially, educational professionals advocated special training for the variety of educational roles.

All of these aspects of "organizational progressivism" were fostered by the development of a new kind of higher educational institution in the United States, the research university. By the early twentieth century, the university had developed into an institution where research and service were added to the traditional mission of developing the liberally educated individual. Universities trained experts in the law, in medicine, in agriculture, in business, and in education.

Further professionalization of education took place within the context of the developing university. Graduate schools of education appeared where future administrators learned the principles of scientific management and curriculum specialists learned scientific curriculum making. Normal schools, generally two-year programs with low admission standards, began to be replaced by four-year teacher's colleges where teachers would receive broader and more sophisticated training. Established colleges began to add departments of education. College professors of education became influential in the placement of graduates and as educational consultants.

The Progressive Era, then, was an era of dramatic development in American education. From the Seven Cardinal Principles to the school as community center, from the kindergarten as a vehicle for social reform to the further professionalization of education, the impact of the Progressive Era is unmatched in significance. It is certainly ironic that during this period of major reform, one group of Americans received none of the benefits society derived from the era. Nevertheless, debate over the education most appropriate for this group reflected some of the questions that progressive education left for the larger society.

Jim Crow and Black Education

One of the most unfortunate results of the failure of late nineteenth-century Populism—the political movement of farmers against the monied interests in banking, transportation, and industry that preceded the Progressive

Era—was the position in which it left Southern blacks.[19] Both Populists, looking for a scapegoat for the failure of their movement, and conservatives, anxious to use any means to keep poor white and black farmers from uniting, turned against blacks and attempted to circumscribe their role in southern society. The result was the development of Jim Crow laws, segregating the South and disfranchising its black minority. Thus, the late nineteenth and early twentieth centuries, the period of "progressive reform," saw the development of the worst forms of segregation in the South. Blacks were disfranchised by the wide use of literacy tests and poll taxes. Segregation in "separate but equal" facilities was approved by the Supreme Court in *Plessy* vs. *Ferguson* (1896). Racism ran rampant. (It should be noted that racism and segregation of minorities were not exclusive to the South. Discrimination against a local minority existed in other regions of the nation. For a complete discussion of the issue in the context of equality, see Chapter 12.)

These developments had a particular impact on black education. While mixed schools had never been popular with whites in the South and few had existed before the appearance of Jim Crow, the new legislation formally instituted segregation. Given the fact of segregation, many blacks, retaining their faith in education as a means to foster equality with whites, hoped that "separate but equal" would mean just that. Their hopes were dashed. Throughout the South, expenditures for black education were only a fraction of that for white. In early twentieth-century Mississippi and Alabama, for example, public expenditures per pupil for white students were five to six times those for blacks.

The black response to these developments was shaped by Booker T. Washington, whose ideas provided the basis for a debate over the kind of education that best served the needs of the black community.

Booker T. Washington

Booker T. Washington, a quiet, conservative ex-slave, was the moving force behind the Tuskegee Institute, a normal school for blacks in Alabama. The heart of the curriculum at Tuskegee was a program of industrial education: agriculture, mechanics, commerce, and domestic service. It was through efforts by blacks in these areas, Washington believed, that advancement in Southern society could take place. Not only would training in manual labor provide an economic base for blacks, it would also foster such virtues as industry, perseverance, and thrift. Virtue and economic independence would eventually lead to acceptance by whites. Washington stated: "If the colored man will only improve his opportunities and persevere, I believe the time is not far distant when a great portion of them will be equal in education, in wealth, equal in civilization, and equal in everything that tends toward human advancement, to any nation or people on earth."[20]

Until whites recognized the value of blacks, however, Washington cautioned blacks to accommodate themselves to the existing social and political climate:

> *I believe it is the duty of the Negro—as the greater part of the race is already doing—to deport himself modestly in regard to political claims, depending upon the slow but sure influences that proceed*

from the possession of property, intelligence, and high character for the full recognition of his political rights.[21]

Equality would eventually come as a result of education, but that education had to be practical:

> *Our greatest danger is that in the great leap from slavery to freedom we may overlook the fact that the masses of us are to live by the productions of our hands, and fail to keep in mind that we shall prosper in proportion as we learn to dignify and glorify common labour and put brains and skill into the common occupations of life; shall prosper in proportion as we learn to draw the line between the superficial and the substantial, the ornamental gewgaws of life and the useful. No race can prosper till it learns that there is as much dignity in tilling a field as in writing a poem.[22]*

Washington's position seemed to be well suited to the political and social realities of his day. White leaders in the North and South lauded his words, and his influence grew tremendously. By the early 1900s, he was the preeminent spokesman for the black community in the nation. Some blacks, however, argued that Washington, in emphasizing industrial education and accepting the social and political inferiority imposed by whites, was giving up too much. The most eloquent spokesman for that group was W. E. B. DuBois.

W. E. B. DuBois

DuBois, some ten years younger than Washington, was born, raised, and educated in New England. The first black man to receive a Ph.D. from Harvard, he was a noted sociologist and historian. As a teacher of history and economics at Atlanta University, DuBois became aware of the plight of Southern blacks. He became convinced that Washington's conciliatory approach to race relations was ineffective.

In 1903, Dubois published *The Souls of Black Folk,* an account of black history, traditions, music, and customs. In that account he devoted a chapter to Booker T. Washington. Recognizing Washington's contributions to the black community, DuBois nevertheless criticized Washington's techniques:

1. He is striving nobly to make Negro artisans business men and property-owners; but it is utterly impossible, under modern competitive methods, for workingmen and property-owners to defend their rights and exist without the right of suffrage.

2. He insists on thrift and self-respect, but at the same time counsels a silent submission to civic inferiority such as is bound to sap the manhood of any race in the long run.

3. He advocates common-school and industrial training, and depreciates institutions of higher learning; but neither the Negro common-schools, nor Tuskegee itself, could remain open a day were it not for teachers trained in Negro colleges, or trained by their graduates.[23]

DuBois called for political power, civil rights, and higher education for talented black youth. DuBois' purpose was to develop an educated black leadership that would be discontented with the status quo, work for black

Photo 4.3
W. E. B. DuBois argued for
the liberal education of
talented black youth.

rights, and struggle against oppression. Simple industrial education would not provide that kind of leadership. DuBois, in short, called for a traditional, academic education through which black students studied the great ideas and ideals of the Western democratic tradition.

In 1905, DuBois and other blacks formed the Niagara Movement as an alternative voice to that of Booker T. Washington. A few years later, the Niagara Movement joined forces with other groups interested in black advancement to create the National Association for the Advancement of Colored People (NAACP). Yet it would be another fifty years before DuBois saw the kind of movement he envisioned in the early twentieth century. Nevertheless, black Americans' faith in education as a device for social improvement remained. As in the larger society, debate raged over the kind of education most suited to their needs.

Progressivism: 1920–1950

As a result of the influence of progressive educators in the universities and teachers' colleges, progressive educational ideas came to dominate the educational agenda from the 1920s through the 1940s. Yet, as we have seen, progressivism was not at all monolithic. Some educators argued that the schools should focus on the immediate needs of children. In general, their ideas included an emphasis upon preparation of the child for "effective living" through a curriculum designed cooperatively between the child and teacher and focusing on student interests.

The recommended teaching strategies were activity oriented. In *The Child-Centered School* (1925), for example, Harold Rugg and Ann Shumaker argued that the new school emphasized "self-expression and maximum child growth" where students "dance; they sing . . .; they model in clay and sand; they draw and paint, read and write, make up stories and dramatize them; they work in the garden; they churn, and weave, and cook. . . ."[24] Diverse student abilities were recognized, and cooperation rather than competition was the order of the day. Special emphasis was given to the relationship of the school program to the wider community. "The newer school," wrote William H. Kilpatrick (1871–1965), major spokesperson for the child-centered, activity-oriented school, "aims explicitly to have its pupils engage actively in life, especially in socially useful work within the community, thus learning to manage life by participation in life. . . ."[25]

Other educators continued the "scientific" approach to schooling, emphasizing the importance of student adjustment to their future roles in society. This could be achieved through "activity analysis", that is, analyzing the actual tasks of a particular role or job. W. W. Charters, for example, who was asked to help develop a curriculum for Stephens College, a private women's college in Columbia, Missouri, surveyed some 95,000 women for descriptions of what they actually did during the week. Charters found 7,300 different activities that were ultimately organized into such categories as food, clothing, and health. The curriculum was to be designed around these actual areas of future activity. Franklin Bobbitt summed up this line of thought: "Education is primarily for adult life, not for child life. Its fundamental responsibility is to prepare for the fifty years of adulthood, not for the twenty years of childhood and youth."[26]

Implicit in the social efficiency educators' call for educational reform was acceptance of the social status quo. That is, these educators never questioned the nature or direction of the society in which they lived, nor did they question the roles society assigned to individuals. Other educators did, however. During the 1920s, George S. Counts (1889–1974) argued that public schooling in the United States was characterized by class distinctions: Secondary schools served primarily those students from higher social and economic levels, and local school boards—the members of which shaped educational policy—were composed of individuals from that same social stratum. Thus, Counts argued, schooling in the United States tended to maintain social distinctions that already existed. Counts believed that schools should do just the opposite—promote a new and better vision of society.

By the 1930s, as the United States fell deeper into the Great Depression, a number of educators were attracted to Counts' arguments. In *Dare the School Build a New Social Order?* (1932), Counts called upon the schools to foster critical-mindedness among students, challenge the rampant individualism that seemed to characterize American society, and promote social reform. Yet, while a number of educators sympathized with Counts' social reconstructionism—the Progressive Education Association, for example, which had been child centered in its orientation, adopted and promoted a number of Counts' positions—there is little evidence that it had much impact on the day-to-day operation of the schools. And as World War II approached, the natural tendency to defend America's institutions in the face of totalitarian threats undercut Counts' arguments.

Thus, during the 1930s, "progressive education" reflected three distinct orientations: child centeredness, social efficiency, and social reconstructionism. Yet in practice, as unlikely as it may seem, two or more of these orientations were often combined. By the 1940s, a new phrase captured the imagination of educational reformers and came to represent progressivism: life adjustment education. Charles A. Prosser, the educator who coined the term and member of the group of social efficiency reformers, felt that subjects should be judged by their utility to everyday life. In a 1939 lecture he argued, ". . . business arithmetic is superior to plane or solid geometry; learning ways of keeping physically fit, to the study of French; learning the technique of selecting an occupation, to the study of algebra; simple science of everyday life, to geology; simple business English, to Elizabethan classics."[27] I. L. Kandel, critic of life adjustment education claimed, "It implies that all the contingencies which human beings are likely to encounter in their lives must be anticipated and education must be adjusted to them. Among these contingencies are dating, marriage, mating, rearing of children, work experience, vocations, and all the social issues which make up the day's headlines in the newspapers."[28]

With the arrival of life adjustment education, progressive education had moved to a position almost diametrically opposed to that of the late nineteenth-century Committee of Ten. However, while the progressive focus on community and individual needs may have made sense to many Americans during the years of depression and World War II, by the late 1940s and early 1950s, the nation faced new challenges. It was not clear that progressive educational ideas as they existed in the life adjustment movement would serve the nation well.

National Priorities and the Schools

By the 1940s, a number of critics had sounded alarms concerning progressive education, pointing specifically to the deemphasis of academic learning. Their criticisms were reinforced when, in October 1957, the Soviet Union launched Sputnik, man's first successful space effort. Concern that the United States was falling behind in the space race brought another wave of reform—this time, however, sponsored by the federal government. From that point through the 1970s, the federal government played a much larger role in the shaping of educational policy than it had at any earlier time. This federal involvement in education—and the use of the public schools to address national priorities—reached a peak during the 1960s with President Lyndon Johnson's efforts to create a Great Society.

Reemphasizing Academics

While Dewey urged educators to begin with student interests and needs as a springboard into more sophisticated and traditional subject matter, many progressives of the 1940s had dropped the sophistication altogether. For example, in 1942, life adjustment advocate Donald C. Doane surveyed 2,069 American youth to determine just what they felt their needs were. Their major concerns, predictably enough, were such questions as how to find a job, make friends, behave on a date, protect one's health, and get the most for one's money. Although it is difficult to tell just how widespread curriculum revision—and revised classroom practice—actually was, some schools did, in fact, shape their curricula around these "needs of youth." In a high school in Altoona, Pennsylvania, science education focused on housing, fuel, and clothing; social studies on interpersonal relations; English on free reading; mathematics on practical applications; and home economics on consumer practices. The twelfth-grade curriculum in the schools of Garrett County, Maryland, consisted of courses in family living, role of education, making a living, health and safety, consumer problems, and technology of living. In name, at any rate, none of the traditional courses were retained.[29]

These developments upset a number of Americans, and criticism of progressive education began to grow. Some of the critics were extremists of the political and religious right, caught up in the anticommunism of the day, who saw in progressive education a plot to undermine American society. Many, however, were serious academicians, and their criticisms of progressive education were reminiscent of the arguments of the Committee of Ten. Philosopher Mortimer Adler wrote in *And Madly They Teach* (1949) that progressive education was anti-intellectual and undemocratic. It was anti-intellectual because it failed to pass on the "traditional knowledge of the race," and it was undemocratic because it failed to attempt to "reach every student, bookish and nonbookish, with the world's wisdom." Worse yet, the progressive's reliance upon experts to determine the direction children's educations should take and these experts' emphasis on adjusting children to society fostered bureaucratic control of society by experts and undermined individual freedom.

History professor Arthur Bestor, in *Educational Wastelands* (1953), continued the attack along similar lines. Bestor argued that the job of the schools was to provide intellectual training. The assumption of progressive educators that many children were not capable of rigorous intellectual challenge was undemocratic. The substitution of "life-needs" education for the traditional disciplines, Bestor argued, undermined teaching the power to think. Furthermore, such curricula were simply wrong-headed. "It is a curiously ostrichlike way of meeting life needs to de-emphasize foreign languages during a period of world war and postwar global tension, and to de-emphasize mathematics at precisely the time when the nation's security has come to depend on Einstein's equation. . . ."[30]

Bestor's comment about mathematics seemed especially prescient when, a few years later, the Soviets were the first to successfully launch a satellite into space. Earlier critics of American educational practices were joined by those who saw a threat to national security in a weak educational system. In *Education and Freedom* (1959), for example, Admiral Hyman Rickover, often called the father of America's nuclear navy, argued that the United States was losing to the Soviets in the technological and military race of the 1950s. In fact, he argued, it was not so much what the Soviets were doing but what Americans were failing to do that was so damaging. Americans were failing to adequately challenge and educate talented youth as future scientists and engineers.[31]

Suddenly, American schools were seen as a vital link in America's system of national security. National security, however, was a federal issue, and it was that issue that brought the federal government into educational decision making. Federal involvement in education, of course, antedated considerably the 1950s. Provisions of the Land Ordinances of 1785 and 1787 fostered public support for schools. The Morrill Act (1862) established land grant, agricultural, and mechanical colleges. The Smith-Lever (1914) and Smith-Hughes (1917) Acts supported agricultural and industrial education, respectively. But federal involvement in the 1950s would have a much more pervasive influence. In 1958, Congress passed the National Defense Education Act (NDEA). The NDEA dramatically increased appropriations to the National Science Foundation to support curriculum development. It supplied funds to improve the teaching of science and mathematics and support the purchase of equipment. Graduate fellowships were provided to prepare students for careers in college teaching. Foreign-language teaching was promoted.

All of these programs were categorical. That is, the federal government would provide funds for a specific project. School systems, of course, did not have to participate in these projects, but when they did, they were—in effect—letting the federal government make curricular and instructional decisions for them. It was in this indirect manner that the federal government shaped educational policy to meet national needs.

During the 1960s, dozens of curricular projects, joint efforts between university scholars and public school people, attempted to reform teaching and learning. In general, these projects developed materials that reflected what psychologist Jerome Bruner called the structures of the academic disciplines: the major concepts, principles, and methods of inquiry that shaped an area of study. In effect, the programs were designed to teach students to think like mathematicians, scientists, or social scientists. Through the use of inquiry, problem-solving, and discovery techniques, students were to learn to process information rather than merely memorize it.

Although these developments have been called the curriculum revolution of the sixties, there was no revolution in curriculum and instruction. Studies done in the 1970s showed that despite the time and effort applied to them, these curricular projects had little impact on day-to-day classroom practice.[32] The fate of the "new mathematics" pointed up a number of the problems associated with these programs. The conceptual approach of the new math was so different from traditional approaches to the subject that teachers balked at its use. Some studies found that the conceptual emphasis was too sophisticated for slower or younger students. Other studies indicated that the students taught in the new math had deficient computational skills. Perhaps the single most significant cause of the demise of the curriculum revolution of the sixties was a change in national priorities. By the mid-1960s, a new movement had garnered the attention of the nation: the movement for racial justice.

Education and the Great Society

In the late fall of 1955, black seamstress Rosa Parks was arrested and fined in Montgomery, Alabama, for failing to give up her bus seat to a white man. The resultant black boycott of the Montgomery bus system focused the nation's attention on the plight of blacks in America. The focus on black rights eventually led to a broader concern with poverty, leading to a series of federal actions that had a tremendous impact on education. The pursuit of excellence gave way to a concern for the disadvantaged in American society.

Civil Rights   Some fifty years after W. E. B. DuBois had called for a black leadership that was discontented with the race's inferior status and willing to work to promote civil rights, such a leadership had emerged. Unable, however, to get U.S. presidents and members of Congress who were wary of controversy to act, blacks turned to the courts to defend their rights. In 1954, NAACP lawyer Thurgood Marshall, using sociological evidence, convinced the Supreme Court of the United States that separate educational facilities for blacks and whites could not be equal. Thus, he argued, separate facilities violated the Fourteenth Amendment's provision for equal protection under the laws. On May 17, 1954, the Court delivered its opinion in *Brown* vs. *Board of Education of Topeka:* "We conclude that in the field of public education, the doctrine of 'separate but equal' has no place." *Plessy* vs. *Ferguson* had been overturned. Later decisions found other forms of segregation unconstitutional and called for integration of schools in the South. White southern resistance to change, however, led blacks to demonstrate for their rights, and incidents like the Montgomery bus boycott captured national attention.

During the 1950s and early 1960s, blacks used nonviolent tactics to demonstrate the inherent injustice of a racially segregated society. The vast majority of Americans were horrified when they saw television news reports of white police brutally responding to nonviolent sit-ins and marches. A growing recognition among Americans of the discrepancy between national ideals and the plight of blacks finally led to federal action. In 1956, the first civil rights legislation since Reconstruction passed the Congress. In 1957, President Eisenhower sent federal troops to Little Rock, Arkansas, when federal court orders for desegregation were flaunted. President John F. Kennedy used federal marshals to protect civil rights demonstrators and federal agencies to foster desegregation. Finally, under President Lyndon B. Johnson, major pieces of legislation ensuring equality before the law—the Civil Rights Act of 1964 and the Voting Rights Act of 1965—were passed.

Some of the civil rights legislation would have a significant impact on education. Title VI of the Civil Rights Act of 1964 stated that no person, because of race, color, or national origin, could be excluded from or denied the benefits of any program receiving federal financial assistance. In the presence of such exclusion, federal support to the participating project or institution would be dropped. The combination of that statement with provisions of the Economic Opportunity Act of 1964 and the Elementary and Secondary Education Act of 1965, providing funds for various educational purposes in the war against poverty, brought the federal government even further into educational policy making.

War on Poverty   By the early 1960s, many civil rights activists recognized that equality before the law alone would not fully address the deeper problems of American blacks. The problems were those related to high unemployment, concentration in low-skill jobs, and poor housing and education. Recognition of these factors, reinforced by the publication of Michael Harrington's *The Other America: Poverty in the United States* (1962), led to a national effort against poverty. Both the Economic Opportunity Act (EOA) and the Elementary and Secondary Education Act (ESEA) were elements of this effort—President Lyndon Johnson's declaration of War on Poverty.

Much of the antipoverty legislation was based on the reasoning found in a 1964 report of the President's Council of Economic Advisers entitled *The Problem of Poverty in America*. In part, the report argued that poverty was cyclical: Poor education led to restricted job opportunities; consequently lower income caused low standards of living characterized by poor medical care, housing, and diet; these factors adversely affected education.

The Problem of Poverty in America was a classic statement of Americans' faith in education as an ameliorating agent. "Equality of opportunity is the American dream, and universal education our noblest pledge to realize it," wrote the Council. "The severely handicapping influence of lack of education is clear. The incidence of poverty drops as educational attainments rise for nonwhites as well as white families at all ages." In phrases that call to mind the reasoning of Horace Mann, the report claimed that "Universal education has been perhaps the greatest single force contributing both to social mobility and to general economic growth." Thus, the report concluded, "The school must play a larger role in the development of poor youngsters if they are to have, in fact, 'equal opportunity.' "[33]

The EOA and ESEA attempted to break the cycle of poverty through education. Title II of the Economic Opportunity Act provided for Urban and Rural Community Action programs, the most popular of which was Head Start. Head Start was designed to provide a wide range of services to impoverished children so that they might get a "head start" in developing those characteristics that seemed to predict successful schooling. The most important part of the Elementary and Secondary Education Act, Title I, provided improved educational programs for educationally deprived children. Other sections of the Act provided funds for books and other instructional materials, educational centers, research, and the strengthening of state departments of education.

Taken together, the Civil Rights Act of 1964, the Economic Opportunity Act of 1964, and the Elementary and Secondary Education Act of 1965 formed the basis for a comprehensive program attacking segregation and poverty. As with the National Defense Education Act, federal funds were made available to those systems that incorporated federal goals. Of course, most school systems sought monies anywhere they could find them, and federal programs spread dramatically.

By the end of Johnson's administration, the nation had seen some sixty pieces of legislation and the appropriation of roughly $1.5 billion related to education. The results of these efforts were unclear, however, and evidence of their success was mixed. However, as historian Vaughan Davis Bornet observed, "One result was certainly clear to any who looked closely: Education at every level fell, during those years, increasingly under the direct or indirect control of the federal government."[34]

Criticism Renewed   During the mid- to late 1960s, a new wave of criticism swept the schools. Dissatisfaction among blacks with the slow pace of change in society—despite legislative triumphs—combined with a growing disenchantment on the part of many Americans with U.S. involvement in the Vietnam War produced a climate of criticism directed at all traditional institutions. The development of the youth counterculture, with its rejection of middle-class values, also contributed to the critical atmosphere. Applied to education, the new criticism rejected the idea of schooling to meet national needs and advocated instead a renewed focus on human needs and the use of child-centered practices.

The new wave of criticism was led by Paul Goodman who, in *Growing Up Absurd* (1960) and *Compulsory Mis-Education* (1964), decried a society that no longer provided the kind of community necessary for the full development of humanity. Rather, he argued, modern society was merely an organized system that impeded human growth. Schools functioned to socialize students to this impersonal system. In schools, students learned "that life is inevitably routine, depersonalized, venally graded; that it is best to toe the mark and shut up; that there is no place for spontaneity, open sexuality, free spirit."[35]

Goodman was followed by a host of other writers, all pointing out the shortcomings of the schools. John Holt, in his 1964 book *How Children Fail*, attacked the notion that there is an important body of knowledge that teachers should pass along to students:

> *Behind much of what we do in school lie some ideas, that could be expressed roughly as follows: (1) of the vast body of human knowledge, there are certain bits and pieces that can be called essential, that everyone should know; (2) the extent to which a person can be considered educated, qualified to live intelligently in today's world and be a useful member of society, depends on the amount of this essential knowledge that he carries about with him; (3) it is the duty of schools, therefore, to get as much of this essential knowledge as possible into the minds of children. Thus we find ourselves trying to poke certain facts, recipes, and ideas down the gullets of every child in school, whether the morsel interests him or not, even if it frightens him or sickens him, and even if there are other things that he is much more interested in learning.*
>
> *These ideas are absurd and harmful nonsense. We will not begin to have true education or real learning in our schools until we sweep this nonsense out of the way. Schools should be a place where children learn what they most want to know, instead of what we think they ought to know. The child who wants to know something remembers it and uses it once he has it; the child who learns something to please or appease someone else forgets it when the need for pleasing or the danger of not appeasing is past.*[36]

The schools of the 1960s, Holt argued, caused children to become dependent on authority and fearful of being wrong, destroyed self-confidence, and inhibited intelligence. Children came to see schools as prisons.

Charles E. Silberman's 1970 best seller *Crisis in the Classroom* continued the attack. "I am indignant at the failures of the public schools," he wrote.

> *It is not possible to spend any prolonged period visiting public school classrooms without being appalled by the mutilation visible everywhere—mutilation of spontaneity, of joy in learning, of pleasure in creating, of sense of self. The public schools . . . are the kind of institution one cannot really dislike until one gets to know them well. Because adults take the schools so much for granted, they fail to appreciate what grim, joyless places most American schools are, how oppressive and petty are the rules by which they are governed, how*

intellectually sterile and esthetically barren the atmosphere, what an appalling lack of civility obtains on the part of teachers and principals, what contempt they unconsciously display for children as children.[37]

In the place of the public school's institutionalized authoritarianism, Silberman called for the development of an alternative that many critics had already endorsed—informal education based on the methods of the British infant schools. These schools were child centered, nondirective environments where teachers and students together chose the activities of the day. The basic idea of the British school was, according to one advocate, "that in a rich environment young children can learn a great deal by themselves and that most often their own choices reflect their needs."[38] The term Americans used for these ideas was *open education,* and open education soon became a crusade. Methods and principles originally directed toward early-childhood education were, in America, transformed into a philosophy applied to elementary and secondary schools as well.

Open education became the byword for educational reform and was widely endorsed by innovative educators. New York State Commissioner of Education Ewald B. Nyquist, for example, argued that open education provided "unique opportunities for humanizing and individualizing learning, making it relevant, meaningful, and personally satisfying." He characterized activities in the open classroom as "person-centered, idea-centered, experience-centered, problem-oriented, and interdisciplinary" rather than "information-gathering, fact-centered, course-centered, subject-centered, grade-getting, and bell-interrupted . . ."[39] The Ford Foundation backed open education by funding teacher training, experiments in open schools, and publications. Open elementary schools, whereby children were provided greater choice in the selection of activities and materials, were built.

On the high-school level, alternative schools appeared. Alternative high schools stressed freedom, student choice, openness, and community involvement. The best known of these was the Parkway Program in Philadelphia, the "classrooms" of which spread out from the Benjamin Franklin Parkway. John Bremer, Parkway's first director, explained the concept: "There is no schoolhouse, there is no separate building; school is not a place but an activity, a process. We are indeed a school without walls. Where do the students learn? In the city. Where in the city? Anywhere and everywhere."[40] Thus, a Parkway student might "study science at a nature center, creative writing at the University of Pennsylvania, law and justice at city hall, library skills at the Philadelphia Public Library, office procedures at a bank, or mechanics at a local auto body shop."[41]

Open education was not welcomed by all, however. Many teachers, uncomfortable with the philosophy and its implications for classroom practice, balked at the concept. In some open schools, bookcases were placed as walls and movable desks were rearranged into traditional, straight lines. Noisy classrooms, students who seemed to crave more structure, and parents who decried the lack of "basics" undermined the movement. By the mid-1970s, the educational pendulum began to swing again. Reflecting a new, conservative mood in the nation, Americans began to call for a return to traditional practices.

An Era of Conservatism

As the 1960s came to a close, the nation faced a host of problems. Inflation soared. The problems of the inner cities remained unsolved. Desegregation was incomplete. The Vietnam War divided national opinion. Underneath all of this, many Americans were beginning to believe that America's bounty could not cure all social ills. The rapid pace of change during the sixties and into the seventies left many Americans alienated and suspicious. Many craved what they perceived as a more simple and stable past. They called for the reestablishment of traditional American values. Many Americans became, in short, more conservative. James Reichley, in a 1969 article in *Fortune* magazine, described this growing attitude among a majority of middle-class Americans:

> *They have at least temporarily become conservatives, in the sense of believing that they are more likely to lose than gain from social change. The economic issues that now concern them most, inflation and high taxes, reinforce their social conservatism. More deeply, they are disturbed by challenges to the system of values that has guided their lives.*
>
> *Hippies and black power militants, drug addicts, Mafiosi, "welfare mothers"—and to some extent expense account executives —are perceived as transgressors against the moral verities that have always been accepted by most Americans, poor as well as rich and middle class, black as well as white.[42]*

This renascent conservatism manifested itself in education on two levels: a reaction to busing and a call for a return to academic essentials.

Reaction to Busing

In the late 1960s, a new instrument had been adopted in the attempt to ensure equal educational opportunity for black students—busing. In the 1966 report of a team of social scientists led by James S. Coleman, *Equality of Educational Opportunity,* evidence seemed to indicate that social class integration might effectively improve the academic achievement of lower-class students. Impoverished black students, it was reasoned, if sent to school with whites, should see improved achievement. The Coleman Report was widely interpreted as an endorsement of busing to achieve integration.

In the late 1960s, federal courts, backed by the reasoning of the Coleman Report, frequently required busing as a means to end racially segregated schooling and foster integration. Busing was not a popular remedy, however. Many Americans had grown tired of "social experimentation," and the conservative mood of the nation was reflected in the regular adoption of antibusing amendments by the U.S. House of Representatives. President Richard Nixon, sensing this mood and responding to political pressure from the right, frequently attacked "wholesale compulsory busing." Nevertheless, the Supreme Court in *Swann* vs. *Charlotte-Mecklenburg Board of Education* (1971) endorsed the use of busing—along with racial quotas, gerrymandering of districts, and the creation of noncontiguous attendance zones—to achieve desegregation. Yet resistance to busing increased. In some cases, violence broke out. In others, however, more affluent whites simply moved out of the cities. As the nation moved into the 1980s, the educational problems of urban minorities remained unsolved. Resistance to busing, however, portended yet another major manifestation of the nation's growing conservatism, a call for the schools to return "back to basics."

Back to Basics

In 1977, *Ladies Home Journal* columnist Mary Susan Miller responded to a reader's inquiry about "back to basics" with this description of "basic" education:

> *"Back to Basics" is a reaction against the recent innovations that are aimed at developing the child in his totality rather than just in intellectual areas. Thus a school that goes Back to Basics may do away with open classrooms, individualization, independent studies, electives, and values clarification in an attempt to raise the level of reading, writing, and arithmetic. Your child will see the difference in a more teacher-centered classroom, in a lessened choice of curriculum, in fewer non-academic enrichment courses, in greater emphasis on performance and test scores.*[43]

Part and parcel of the reaction to disturbing changes in the sixties—drug use, sexual freedom, crime, the counterculture—the back-to-basics movement was endorsed by individuals reflecting a tremendous diversity of perspectives. Two of those perspectives are of particular interest to us, that of the New Right and that of the academic essentialists.

The New Right   In April 1974, Kanawha County, West Virginia, schoolboard member Alice Moore, the wife of a fundamentalist Christian preacher, complained that a number of the textbooks adopted for the following fall were inappropriate. (For a full discussion of the impact of "informal" groups—that is, groups outside the formal political structure—on educational policy, see Chapter 9.) Some, she argued, contained filthy language; others encouraged disrespect for authority and religion. Over the summer, opposition to the books spread, compromise failed, and in the fall, protest leaders organized a boycott. "When the books go out," they promised, "the children go back in!" The boycott, however, buttressed by sympathetic, striking coal miners, soon became violent as protestors attempted to stop school buses and block the entrances to schools. To halt the spread of violence, the local superintendent was forced to close the schools.

The incident in Kanawha County captured national attention. It also revealed a growing dissatisfaction among conservatives and Christian fundamentalists with the content and practices of the public schools. Convinced that the nation was experiencing a period of sharp moral decline, the protestors wanted the schools to serve as a moral anchor, a conservator of traditional values. To their dismay, however, the schools seemed to be fostering the very attitudes that were antithetical to their beliefs.

The initial issue with which Christian fundamentalists were concerned was sex education. In the late 1960s, national concern over the social implications of teenage pregnancy had led to widespread adoption of sex education curricula in the public schools. That disturbed fundamentalists. The topic was one best left to families, they argued, especially since the schools' treatment seemed to be, at best, amoral. Concern over sex

Box 4.2
National Reports of
the 1970s

It is interesting to contrast the aims and assumptions of the national educational reform reports of the 1970s with those of the 1980s. Chapter 1 pointed out that the reports of the 1980s called for the following:

Stress literacy in English	Upgrade textbooks
Increase graduation requirements	Require more homework
Stress proficiency in a second language	Use standardized tests
Stress productive employment	Emphasize quality teaching and teachers
Lengthen school day and year	Provide more money for education
Increase teacher salaries	

In the 1970s, however, concerns were distinctly different. Below are some of the concerns from two of the reports of that era, the Kettering Foundation's *Reform of Secondary Education* (1973) and the *Martin Report* (1974) of the National Panel on High Schools and Adolescent Education:*

Reform of Secondary Education	*National Panel on High Schools*
Involve community participation in determining secondary school expectations.	Extend high school out into the community.
Ensure against bias in textbooks.	Provide schooling during hours other than the regular school day.
Ensure against bias in counseling.	Remove barriers to student opportunities for work and volunteer service.
Stop calculating rank in class and GPA.	Decentralize schools through alternative schools.
Develop and adopt a code of student rights and obligations.	Reduce compulsory attendance at all-day sessions to a two-to-four hour day.
Outlaw corporal punishment.	Encourage citizen and student participation in changes of school structure and programs.
Eliminate sexism in the schools.	Give attention to staffing and scheduling needed for economic reasons.
Plan for affirmative action.	

*Adapted from Sharon O'Bryan, "Reports on the Reform of Secondary Education: An In–Depth Analysis" *Viewpoints in Teaching and Learning* (Spring 1979).

education soon blossomed into concern over a variety of issues, all revolving around the belief that the schools were fostering secular humanism, the concept that people could solve their own problems without recourse to God. Sex education, drug education, "values" education, the teaching of evolution, the "removal" of prayer from the schools, all seemed to undermine religion, authority, the family, and—on a broader scale—the very moral fiber of the nation. By the late 1970s, fundamentalists had developed a number of organizations that attempted to deal with these threats to their perception of the good society. Textbook censors, advocates of prayer in the schools, proponents of creationist theory (as opposed to evolution) abounded in their efforts and grew in influence. Where these groups were especially strong, state legislatures passed laws incorporating their views. Where efforts seemed to have little effect, private "Christian schools" were founded.

Fundamentalist concerns received a significant endorsement from Presidential candidate Ronald Reagan. By 1980, Reagan had promised to support the teaching of creationism, to fight the "anti-family" Equal Rights Amendment, to denounce secular humanism in the schools, to protect the tax-exempt status of fundamentalist Christian pressure groups, to return America to Christian values, to endorse tuition tax credits for parents who sent their children to private schools, to return "back to basics," and to support parental rights in education.[44] After his election, Reagan continued to speak out on these issues. Resistance on the part of most Americans to the fundamentalist right agenda, however, prevented substantive action on many of these points. Yet by the early 1980s, Reagan's support of the back-to-basics concept helped trigger another widespread movement for academic reform in American schools.

The Academic Essentials

Christian fundamentalists were not the only Americans concerned with the direction of the schools in the 1970s. Critics, in fact, abounded, and probably the most important were those who simply called for a reemphasis on the traditional academic subjects. This group of critics ranged from concerned parents who felt that their children were deficient in basic skills and knowledge to businesspeople and college professors who decried the inadequate preparation of employees and college students. Growing dissatisfaction in the 1970s was reinforced by a number of national reports published in the early 1980s that were critical of the schools. These reports sparked an educational reform movement that appears to have set the educational agenda for the rest of the decade.

The 1970s saw a decade-long decline in the average score achieved by high-school seniors on the SAT. Other indicators of academic achievement seemed to confirm that academic standards were down at both the elementary and secondary levels. Critics argued that educational experimentation in the sixties and seventies was at fault. Untested innovations, social promotion, permissiveness, emphasis on nonacademic electives, all deemphasized the academic nature of the school. Robert Ebel reflected the thoughts of many when he wrote:

> *There is, I believe, a . . . fundamental and powerful cause for the decline in achievement. It is the widespread acceptance in our schools*

of a specious, unsound, anti-intellectual philosophy of education. At various times in this century the philosophy has marched under the banner of progressive education, life-adjustment education, and, most recently, humanistic education. It has given us two generations of warm-hearted but soft-headed pedagogy. During this time the cultivation of cognitive competence has not been a high-priority goal of many of our public schools.[45]

To remedy the situation, critics called for an emphasis upon basic skills in reading, writing, and arithmetic in the elementary schools and stressed the importance of academic courses in English, basic sciences, mathematics, and history in the secondary schools. Instruction, many felt, should be textbook oriented, include drill and recitation, require homework, and feature more frequent testing and evaluation.[46] Finally, and most significantly, many critics were determined to hold schools—and students—accountable. As a result of this demand, many states, by the late 1970s, had turned to minimal competency testing—the use of standardized tests of basic skills and knowledge—to determine student promotion and/or graduation.

Yet the schools remained under siege. In April 1983, the National Commission on Excellence in Education, a blue-ribbon panel of citizens and educators, published *A Nation at Risk: The Imperative for Educational Reform*. The opening lines of the report shocked the nation:

Our Nation is at risk. Our once unchallenged preeminence in commerce, industry, science, and technological innovation is being overtaken by competitors throughout the world. This report is concerned with only one of the many causes and dimensions of the problem, but it is the one that undergirds American prosperity, security, and civility. We report to the American people that while we can take justifiable pride in what our schools and colleges have historically accomplished and contributed to the United States and the well-being of its people, the educational foundations of our society are presently being eroded by a rising tide of mediocrity that threatens our very future as a Nation and a people. What was unimaginable a generation ago has begun to occur—others are matching and surpassing our educational attainments.[47]

The report went on to detail a variety of shortcomings in the schools—from the failure to challenge gifted students to the inadequate use of learning time—and make a series of recommendations. The chief recommendation was a call for emphasis on the "new basics" in high schools—science, mathematics, English, social studies, and computer science—and the development in students of a sound basis for those studies in elementary schools. The report also endorsed upgraded textbooks; greater use of homework; extension of the school day and year; continued programs for special students; the use of standardized achievement tests for diagnosis, promotion, and credentialing; and greater attention to discipline problems. The report advocated a wide range of reforms designed to improve the quality of the nation's teachers. Finally, and reflecting the Reagan administration's deemphasis on the federal role in education, the report argued that state and local officials held the primary responsibility for financing and governing the schools and for incorporating the reforms recommended by the Commission.

A Nation at Risk was followed by a series of reports from other organizations, most outlining similar concerns and remedies, and a host of books and articles. Suddenly, educational reform was again in the national limelight. Educational reform in the 1980s would, however, as the Commission had recommended, be spearheaded by the states. By 1985, roughly two thirds of the states had initiated reform in an attempt to follow the recommendations of the Commission.

Summary

What knowledge is of most worth? What kind of schooling is most appropriate in a democracy? These are questions that have been debated throughout the twentieth century and will continue to be debated in the forseeable future. A number of positions in this debate have been identified: Some people advocate the traditional academic subjects, others advocate schooling designed to serve the whole child, and still others feel that schooling should prepare children for their future social roles. Sometimes these positions are mixed. The educational reform of the 1980s, for example, while it emphasizes academic basics, certainly receives much of its impetus from modern advocates of social efficiency and their concern that the nation produce workers suited to a technologically oriented economy. As one position becomes ascendant—invariably as a result of larger national concerns or developments—the schools respond and shift their emphases. Although professional educators are criticized for this characteristic of the schools, it is hard to imagine that critics would advocate any system that did not respond to the concerns of the people.

The late nineteenth-century Report of the Committee of Ten set the tone for what has become a traditional emphasis on subject matter in the schools. During the early twentieth century, educational reformers argued that traditional subject matter failed to consider either the developmental characteristics of the child or the adult social role the child would fill. It was during the Progressive Era that so many of the nonacademic trappings that we now associate with schooling began: playgrounds, lunches, nurses, etc. It was the period that brought us the professionalization of teachers. In fact, the Progressive Era transformed schooling to shape the modern school. Since that time, however, progressive assumptions about the nature of schooling and progressive practices have periodically been challenged by a call for a return to basic subject matter. During the 1950s and the 1980s, in particular, schools were challenged to reemphasize the academic essentials. The debate over the nature of schooling has been further complicated by the appearance of the federal government as a major decision maker. The use of public school policies—often supported by federal funds—to address national priorities has become a major part of the current American educational scene.

In the course of the century, public schools grew to be the most significant institution in the formal education of the population. They also served the nation in other areas of social concern. What generated the considerable debate over the nature of education in a democracy was the fact that as the century progressed, more and more of the population came to be served by the schools. In the 1889–1890 school year, only 11.4 percent of American youth in the 14–17 age group were enrolled in high schools. By 1980, 75 percent of American youth graduated from high school and 45 percent went on to college. Just as significantly the gap in educational attainment between whites and minorities was narrowed dramatically. In 1960, for example, although 67 percent of the white children in the country graduated from high school, only 47 percent of the black youngsters did. By 1980, however, the respective figures were 82.5 percent and 70 percent.

Although the impact of higher educational attainment on the continuing problem of poverty is still unclear, the public schools played a major role in the fight against racial segregation. Thus, by the 1980s, schools were enrolling and graduating more Americans and were providing better teachers and materials, more courses, and better physical environments than ever before. Yet schools would remain under fire. The debate over the nature of education in a democracy—because of the very nature of democracy—would continue.

Key Figures

John Dewey	Arthur Bestor
G. Stanley Hall	Jerome Bruner
Franklin Bobbitt	Lyndon B. Johnson
Booker T. Washington	Paul Goodman
W. E. B. DuBois	John Holt
William H. Kilpatrick	Charles E. Silberman
Charles A. Prosser	James S. Coleman
Mortimer Adler	Ronald Reagan

Discussion Questions

1. Consider your own high-school experience. Can you cite any evidence for the influence of the seven cardinal principles in your education?

2. Who do you feel more adequately addressed the needs of the black community at the turn of the century, Booker T. Washington or W. E. B. DuBois? Who do you think has been more influential in modern times? Why?

3. What is your reaction to the criticisms of figures such as Goodman, Holt, and Silberman?

4. Chapter 2 referred to Joel Spring's criticism of the use of schools to respond to what was seen as a national crisis during the early and mid-1980s. What evidence in this chapter indicates that such a response has become a standard part of the American experience?

5. What issues are uppermost in the minds of Americans as you read this text? Can or should the schools address any of these issues?

For Further Reading

Callahan, Raymond E. *Education and the Cult of Efficiency.* Chicago: University of Chicago Press, 1962.

Dewey, John. *The School and Society.* Chicago: University of Chicago Press, 1899.

———. *Democracy and Education.* New York: Macmillan Publishing Co., 1916.

Karier, Clarence. *Shaping the American Educational State, 1900 to Present.* New York: Free Press, 1975.

Kliebard, Herbert M. *The Struggle for the American Curriculum: 1893–1958.* New York: Routledge & Kegan Paul, 1987.

Krug, Edward. *The Shaping of the American High School: Vol. 1.* New York: Harper & Row, 1964.

———. *The Shaping of the American High School: Vol. 2.* Madison: University of Wisconsin Press, 1972.

Ravitch, Diane. *The Troubled Crusade: American Education, 1945–1980.* New York: Basic Books, 1983.

Notes

1. John and Evelyn Dewey, *Schools of Tomorrow* in Henry J. Perkinson, *Two Hundred Years of American Educational Thought* (New York: David McKay Co., 1976), p. 234.

2. Quoted in Joel Spring, *The American School: 1642–1985* (New York: Longman, 1986), p. 173.

3. Quoted in Perkinson, p. 210.

4. John Dewey, "My Pedagogic Creed" in James W. Noll and Sam P. Kelly, *Foundations of Education in America* (New York: Harper & Row, 1970), p. 238.

5. *Ibid.,* p. 240.

6. Quoted in Perkinson, p. 212.

7. *Ibid.,* p. 228.

8. Quoted in Herbert M. Kliebard, *The Struggle for the American Curriculum: 1893–1958* (New York: Routledge & Kegan Paul, 1987), p. 98.

9. John and Evelyn Dewey, pp. 234–235. See also Clarence Karier, *Shaping the American Educational State, 1900 to Present* (New York: Free Press, 1975); and Edward Krug, *The Shaping of the American High School: Vol. 1* (New York: Harper & Row, 1964) and *Vol. 2* (Madison: University of Wisconsin Press, 1972).

10. Commission on Reorganization of Secondary Education, *Cardinal Principles of Secondary Education* (Washington, D.C.: U.S. Government Printing Office, 1918), p. 7.

11. Quoted in Spring, p. 203.

12. *Cardinal Principles,* p. 9.

13. *Ibid.,* p. 19.

14. Quoted in Spring, 197.

15. Quoted in Spring, p. 161.

16. *Ibid.,* p. 162.

17. Robert Wiebe, *The Search for Order: 1877–1920* (New York: Hill & Wang, 1967), p. 166.

18. See Raymond E. Callahan, *Education and the Cult of Efficiency* (Chicago: University of Chicago Press, 1962).

19. See C. Vann Woodward, *The Strange Career of Jim Crow* (New York: Oxford University Press, 1966).

20. Quoted in Perkinson, p. 179.

21. Booker T. Washington, *Up From Slavery* in *"Three Negro Classics"* (New York: Avon Books, 1965), p. 156.

22. *Ibid.,* p. 147.

23. W. E. B. DuBois, *The Souls of Black Folk* in *Three Negro Classics* (New York: Avon Books, 1965), p. 247.

24. Quoted in Diane Ravitch, *The Troubled Crusade: American Education, 1945–1980* (New York: Basic Books, 1983), p. 50.

25. William H. Kilpatrick, "The Case for Progressivism in Education" in Glen Hass, *Curriculum Planning: A New Approach* (Boston: Allyn & Bacon, 1983), p. 26.

26. Kliebard, pp. 119–121.

27. Quoted in Ravitch, p. 66.

28. Quoted in Kliebard, p. 250.

29. Ravitch, pp. 63–67.

30. *Ibid.,* p. 76.

31. Hyman G. Rickover, *Education and Freedom* (New York: Dutton, 1959).

32. See, for example, Iris Weiss, *Report of the 1977 National Survey of Science, Mathematics, and Social Studies Education* (Research Triangle Park, N.C.: Research Triangle Institute, 1978).

33. "The Problem of Poverty in America," in *The Annual Report of the Council of Economic Advisors* (Washington, D.C.: Government Printing Office, 1964).

34. Vaughn Davis Bornet, *The Presidency of Lyndon B. Johnson* (Lawrence, Kansas: University Press of Kansas, 1983), p. 226.

35. Quoted in Perkinson, p. 286.

36. Quoted in William Van Til, *Secondary Education: School and Community* (Boston: Houghton Mifflin Co., 1978), p. 7.

37. *Ibid.,* p. 8.

38. Quoted in Ravitch, p. 240.

39. *Ibid.,* p. 248.

40. Quoted in Van Til, p. 12.

41. K. C. Cole Janssen, *Matters of Choice: The Ford Foundation Report on Alternative Schools* (Ford Foundation, 1974), p. 7.

42. Quoted in Godfrey Hodgson, *America in Our Time* (New York: Vintage Books, 1976), p. 422.

43. Samuel G. Sava, "The 'Back to Basics' Movement," *Graduate Woman* 71, no. 6 (May 1978), p. 22.

44. Joe L. Kicheloe, *Understanding the New Right and Its Impact on Education* (Bloomington, Indiana: Phi Delta Kappa, 1983), p. 8.

45.   Robert L. Ebel, "The Case for Minimum Competency Testing" *Phi Delta Kappan* 59, no. 8 (April 1978), pp. 546–549.

46.   Gerald L. Gutek, *Basic Education: A Historical Perspective* (Bloomington, Indiana: Phi Delta Kappa, 1981), pp. 9–12.

47.   National Commission on Excellence in Education, *A Nation At Risk* (Washington, D.C.: Government Printing Office, 1983), p. 5.

5 Educational Belief Systems

"Every (human) has a function as a (human). The function of a citizen or a subject may vary from society to society, and the system of training, or adaptation, or instruction, or meeting immediate needs may vary with it. But the function of a (human) as (human) is the same in every age and in every society, since it results from (human) nature. . . . The aim of an educational system is the same in every age and in every society where such a system can exist: it is to improve (human) as (human)."

Robert M. Hutchins, *The Conflict in Education* (1953)

"Our Progressive schools . . . cannot rest content with giving children an opportunity to study contemporary society in all aspects. This of course must be done, but I am convinced that they should go much farther. If the schools are to be really effective, they must become centers for the building, and not merely for the contemplation, of our civilization. . . . We should . . . give to our children a vision of the possibilities which lie ahead and endeavor to enlist their loyalties and enthusiasms in the realization of the vision. Also our social institutions and practices, all of them, should be critically examined in the light of such a vision."

George S. Counts, *Dare the School Build a New Social Order?* (1932)

The last section of Chapter 2 suggested that a thorough understanding of the historical, philosophical, and social foundations of American education is necessary for informed decision making on educational issues. The treatment given the history of education in this text should suggest that a variety of perspectives shape opinion on educational issues. Any number of factors might influence a specific individual's perspective: the individual's educational level, socioeconomic status, age, marital status, age of children, and so on. This chapter treats the major belief systems and their implications for educational debate.

Chapter 4 argued that much of the twentieth-century debate over the nature of education in America revolved around aspects of progressive education. Should the "whole child" be educated, or should schools focus on traditional academic subjects? Should education serve the individual or serve society? An individual's answers to such questions depend upon the beliefs the individual brings to the questions. Thus, when a person is asked, "What is the best education in a democracy?" the answer may well depend on his or her understanding of the nature of knowledge or belief concerning the nature of the good life. These are philosophical questions. One's philosophy, then, influences one's perspective on educational issues. The bulk of this chapter focuses on philosophies, both general and educational, and their significance in shaping opinion on educational issues.

Other factors may also play a role in influencing answers to educational questions. Given the massive development of state-supported schools in the United States, it may seem fruitless to ask, "Who or what institutions should educate?" Yet that is an important question. Not all Americans believe that the public schools are the best agency for the education of their children. Private schooling has remained an important alternative to public schools, and in recent years more parents have opted to teach their children themselves in their own homes. While choices such as these may be based upon philosophical—especially religious—concerns, they may also reflect political beliefs. Beliefs concerning the role of government in society also influence individual's opinions about educational issues.

Philosophy

People's opinions concerning education may (and should) be shaped by their basic beliefs concerning such issues as the nature of life, the nature of knowledge, and the source of moral values. These are traditional philosophical issues and as such have received a great amount of attention through the ages. This section provides an overview of these issues, the treatment given them by both traditional and modern philosophical schools, and the consequent educational implications of these schools of thought.

Philosophical Inquiry

At one time or another most thinking individuals wonder about the meaning of their lives, the nature of their being, the meaningfulness of the cosmos. When they speculate about such issues, they are asking philosophical questions. In fact, traditional philosophy has revolved largely around inquiry into the nature of reality, knowledge (or truth), and value. Philosophers have specific terms that reflect these areas of inquiry. When philosophers inquire into the nature of reality, they are pursuing *metaphysics*. When they inquire into the nature of truth or knowledge, they are pursuing *epistemology*. When they inquire into the nature of values, they are pursuing *axiology*. Each of these realms of inquiry has implications for educational issues.

All of us make assumptions about the nature of reality. We assume, for example, that what we see is real, and we act based on sight and other sense perceptions. But we also act based upon ideas that we hold. Are these ideas real? Of course, you say, but they certainly can't be measured in the same way that a physical object can. Metaphysics, then, asks questions about the ultimate nature of reality. Among metaphysical concerns are questions concerning the origin, development, and purposefulness of the universe; the existence of a primal cause or God; and the nature of being and of humanity. Differences of opinion concerning these issues will produce differences of opinion over educational goals. For example, one who believes that God created the universe and gives the universe purpose might well be concerned over the possibility that secular education subverts these beliefs.

Epistemology is the study of the nature, sources, and validity of knowledge. How do we know what is true? Can the truth even be known? Is truth transcendental or ever-changing? Is truth dependent upon—or independent of —human experience? Is knowledge based upon sensory perception, rational processes, or intuition? Answers to these questions are obviously important in shaping educational opinion. In a broad sense, the development of knowledge is the primary purpose of education. Major curricular and methodological positions, then, will be based upon epistemological assumptions. Emphasis upon the scientific method, for example, is based upon certain assumptions concerning knowledge that is empirically justified.

Axiology is the study of the nature of values. It attempts to define that which is good. Axiology is subdivided into the studies of ethics—moral values—and of aesthetics—beauty. Each is central to the educative process, but individual or group assumptions concerning their nature differ greatly. Americans have traditionally expected their schools to teach moral values, for example, and the schools do. Frequently, however, one person's concept of morality is quite different from another's, and educational debate is joined. In like manner, opinions differ greatly over artistic beauty. That which creatively or beautifully expresses one point of view may alienate another.

Assumptions concerning the nature of reality, knowledge, and value have obvious implications for education. Where traditional philosophy has considered questions of reality, knowledge, and value, traditional schools of thought have developed. Two of these traditional schools—idealism and realism—are particularly important to us because of their significance in the genesis of modern educational thought.

Traditional Philosophy

When we speak of schools of philosophical thought, it is important to remember that we are talking about the ideas of individuals who might not readily accept such classification. Still, there are enough similarities between the thoughts of these individuals, similarities in terms of the metaphysical and epistemological assumptions that they make, for example, to group them. Such grouping aids in understanding but is by no means definitive. Two such traditional philosophical schools are those known as idealism and realism.

Idealism   Idealism is perhaps the oldest systematic philosophical school in the Western European intellectual tradition. Idealists emphasize the importance of ideas over material reality. Thus, in metaphysical terms, the real world is the world of the mind, the world of ideas, not the material world. This line of reasoning can be traced to the thought of Plato (427–347 B.C.), who argued that man's goal in life should be to search for truth. Truth, however, was perfect and eternal, not transitory like conditions in the material world. For Plato, mathematics was one vehicle for the study of truth. Most people, for example, would agree to the truth of the statement, $1 + 1 = 2$. Plato would argue that this truth exists independent of man's realization of it. It has always been true and always will be true. People should attempt to discover other such truths, in mathematics and other fields of knowledge, but that search had to take place in the mind. The physical world was, argued Plato, merely a shadow of the ideational.[1]

Idealism, then, posited a world of the mind, of ideas, that was anterior and superior to the physical world. Such a philosophy was easily adapted by Christians, who saw God, rather than ideas, as the spirit or essence of reality. For Christians, the search for ultimate truth became the search for God. Augustine (354–430), for example, adapted the dualism of Plato to distinguish between the world of man and the world of God. The world of man was the material world, but the Christian should try to transcend this world by focusing, through faith and prayer, on the reality of God.

In more modern times, philosophers such as René Descartes (1596–1650), George Berkeley (1685–1753), Immanuel Kant (1724–1804), and Georg W. F. Hegel (1770–1831) reflect the idealist distinction between the world of the mind or spirit and the physical world. In general, these idealists argued that reality is the world of the mind or spirit; that knowledge and truth are derived from the contemplation of that reality, either through reason or intuition; and that the ideal world is the source of ethical and aesthetic principles.

An idealist education, then, would foster the search for truth through the mental development of the learner. This would require the study of ideas, reflected in mankind's best works in literature, philosophy, and religion. Students should study these great works, attempting to discover for themselves the transcendent truths about the nature of man and existence that might be found within. Such a study would foster not merely knowledge in the learner but also character development and self-realization. The role of the teacher would be that of a source of knowledge and ideas as well as a model of character and scholarship.

Realism   Nearly as old as idealism, realism traces its roots to the philosophy of Aristotle (384–322 B.C.). Although a pupil of Plato, Aristotle disagreed with Plato's conception of reality. According to Aristotle, the physical world was real, not merely a reflection or shadow of the ideal. Aristotle argued that objects were composed of both matter—the physical aspect—and form—the essence or universal aspect. Man should attempt to understand the universal aspects, the form, but that understanding could be based upon the study of the physical world, matter. Thus, the chair in which you are sitting has both matter and form: Matter consists of its physical reality and form consists of its chairness. You are composed of both matter and form: Matter is your physical reality; form is your humanness. The study of separate, physical chairs will give us insight into chairness just as the study of individual humans will give us insight into humanness. The key to understanding the universal essence of any object is the use of reason, particularly deductive logic.

Aristotle posited an organizing force or principle behind the universe of form and matter. That force or principle, that ultimate reality, was both the primal cause and the end toward which all matter was moving. Such a conception of ultimate reality could be and was interpreted by Aristotelian scholars in both religious and secular ways. Thus, Aristotelian realism formed the basis for both religious realism and modern secular or scientific realism.

Religious realism, often called Neo-Scholasticism, can be traced to the thought of Thomas Aquinas (1225–1274), the premier western Aristotelian scholar of the Middle Ages. In Aristotelian philosophy, Aquinas found a compromise position between the demands of religious faith provided through revelation and common sense notions of reality provided through man's observation and reason. In Aristotelian terms, Aquinas saw the Christian God as that being of pure reason that gave the universe meaning and direction. Since God was pure reason and the universe was God's creation, man could use his reason as well as revelation in his search for truth, in his

---

Box 5.1
Deductive Versus
Inductive Logic

Deductive logic is reasoning from general principles to specifics. Its classical representation is the deductive syllogism—composed of a major premise, a minor premise, and a conclusion: All humans are mortal (major premise). Socrates is a human (minor premise). Therefore, Socrates is mortal (conclusion). The reasoning is from the general to the specific, because one begins with a general principle (all humans are mortal) and applies it to a specific situation (Socrates) to derive a conclusion. Medieval Christian scholars such as Thomas Aquinas pursued just this method, but with the principles or major premises derived from the Bible. This method of reasoning, however, is not that of modern science.

The method of modern science is basically inductive in nature. Inductive reasoning is reasoning from the specific to the general. With inductive reasoning, observations are made and common aspects of those observations form the basis for generalizations. These generalizations can then be used to both predict and explain. For example, meteorologists observe atmospheric conditions to predict the weather. Thousands and thousands of observations in the past have led meteorologists to generalize: Given certain atmospheric conditions, rain is likely. In some areas of scientific inquiry, generalizations are more accurate than others. But the process is the same: Observation of natural phenomena leads to generalization about those phenomena, "scientific" knowledge. The process is the basis for modern science—physical, biological, social. It is a central aspect of modern life.

Photo 5.1
Francis Bacon advocated the use of observation and inductive logic to derive general principles.

attempt to understand God. Aquinas' Aristotelianism (Thomism) forms the basis for most modern Christian thought and is the principal philosophy of Roman Catholicism.

The foundation of scientific realism can be found in Aristotle's belief that the physical world can be studied to derive higher truths. Aristotle, however, emphasized deductive logic in reasoning about reality. In the modern era, thinkers such as Francis Bacon (1561–1626) argued for the use of inductive logic, the "scientific method," to derive truth. Bacon criticized religious Aristotelianism for its application of deductive logic, that is, beginning with *a priori* truths and then reasoning toward conclusions. Bacon argued that man should begin with observations and then reason toward general principles.

Bacon's ideas reflected a revolution in Western philosophy. The physical world took on new significance as scientific thinkers, based upon their observations of nature, challenged traditional notions of reality. Galileo's observations with his telescope, for example, demonstrated that the earth revolved around the sun, while religious leaders deduced that the earth was the center of the universe. While the Church won its confrontation with Galileo, the scientific method became modern people's basic approach to reality.

Bacon's conception of the search for truth was reinforced by John Locke's (1632–1704) inquiry into the nature of human knowledge. Locke argued that an individual's mind at birth was a blank slate—a *tabula rasa*—upon which experience, sensation, and reflection wrote. All knowledge, then, was derived empirically, from sensory experience.

Realism in its scientific form, then, came to posit a universe of physical reality that existed independent of man's conception of it. There were principles or laws by which the universe operated—natural laws— but they had to be discovered through the application of inductive reasoning—the

Table 5.1   Traditional Philosophies

	METAPHYSICS	EPISTEMOLOGY	AXIOLOGY
Idealism	An absolute universe of mind or consciousness with purposeful meaning; spirit or principle is ultimately real, physical objects are not.	Test of truth is unity and coherence of ideas.	Values are real and rooted in the cosmos.
Religious realism	Dualism: mind and matter both created by God.	Truths are available through revelation, intuition, and logical reasoning; test for absolute truth is metaphysical roots, for scientific truth is correspondence to natural law.	Universal moral law has been established by God; we can understand much of it through reason.
Secular realism	Reality is a physical universe governed by natural laws; existence constitutes reality, and reality exists independent of any knowledge of it.	Truth consists of a report on an independent and absolute reality consisting of scientifically ascertained facts; correspondence to natural laws; meaningful statements are those that are empirically based.	Natural law supplies ethical natural rights as well as aesthetic standards of natural order and beauty.

Source: Adapted with permission from Morris L. Bigge, *Educational Philosophies for Teachers* (Columbus, Ohio: Charles E. Merrill Publishing Company, 1982).

scientific method. Realists such as Bacon argued that inductive reasoning had to be applied to all areas of knowledge. Thus, throughout the eighteenth and nineteenth centuries, Western European thinkers, scientists, and philosophers attempted to discover the natural laws that regulated all aspects of life—economic (e.g., supply and demand), social (e.g., survival of the fittest), and political (e.g., natural rights) as well as "scientific." Just as the study of nature produced knowledge, it also produced values in both ethics and aesthetics. Nature, through natural law, supplied ethical natural rights while it also supplied aesthetic standards of natural order and beauty.

A realist education is one in which the student is exposed to knowledge that mankind has developed through study of the natural world. In terms of religious realism, the goal would be to gain insight into the nature of God. For the secular realist, the goal would be an understanding of the principles by which the world operates. In the latter case, the teacher would be expected to provide information to students in the most efficient manner possible. The information provided, of course, is that based upon empirical study and research.

Modern Philosophy

While the roots of modern philosophy can be traced to traditional philosophical schools, modern schools have focused their inquiry in somewhat different directions. Traditional philosophical inquiry revolved essentially around metaphysical questions, questions concerning the nature of reality. Idealists defined reality in terms of ideas, while realists emphasized, in one way or another, the significance of the physical world. The tremendous impact of the scientific revolution on Western culture, however, has greatly reduced inquiry into the nature of reality. The modern mind largely accepts the physical, material world as real. In fact, it is even difficult for most of us to conceptualize the physical world as a mere shadow of ultimate reality. "Reality" for most people is that which can be empirically justified. This assumption concerning material reality has brought tremendous advances in our knowledge concerning the nature of the physical world. The technological advances of modern civilization, those that do so much to shape our cultural and social milieu, are based on the development of new knowledge.

But the handmaiden of new knowledge is change. While traditional philosophies saw the world in terms of systems of constants—either in terms of ideas, essences, or natural "laws"—modern science has challenged those constants. New knowledge continuously challenges and replaces old assumptions. For example, the mechanical world of Newton has been replaced by the relative world of Einstein. The reality of change has led many Western thinkers away from questions concerning the ultimate nature of reality and its implications for truth and value (ultimate reality either does not exist or, at least, we cannot comprehend it) to a more relativistic approach toward these issues. Thus, modern philosophical schools tend to be characterized by metaphysical relativism and turn their attention instead to either society or the individual as sources of knowledge and value or to language analysis as a basis for the clarification of ideas. This section considers three modern philosophical schools: pragmatism, existentialism, and analytical philosophy.

Pragmatism   Pragmatism might be described as a truly American philosophy, a natural outgrowth of the American character. Americans, many have argued, are impatient with "fuzzy-headed" idealism (in the popular sense of the word) and oriented toward results. In fact, when we say someone is pragmatic, we mean he or she is practical. A pragmatic approach is a practical approach, that is, one that works. Pragmatism in philosophy reflects this concern with efficacy, although it certainly does not denigrate thought before action.

The term *pragmatism* was coined by the mathematician Charles Sanders Peirce (1839–1914) to suggest the connection between idea and action. The Greek word *pragma* means act or deed, and Peirce argued that the meaning we assign to any idea is a function of some action or effect we attribute to that idea. For example, words like *fast* and *slow* have no meaning unless they are related to some observable consequence or effect. In a race, "fast" runners pass others while "slow" runners are passed by others. Thus, wrote Peirce, "our idea of anything is our idea of its sensible effects."[2]

Meanings, then, are derived by experience or experiment. They are not individual and private, they are social and public. If there is no way to publicly test the meanings of ideas by public consequences—observable to all—the ideas are meaningless. In this context, Peirce argued for the use of scientific method as a public test of ideas. With the scientific method, knowledge is tentative, arrived at critically, and subject to change when new information appears. Peirce argued all beliefs should be scrutinized in such a way.

Peirce's ideas were particularly influential with William James (1842–1910). James, in fact, argued that pragmatism, rather than positing

Photo 5.2
William James argued that pragmatism was a method for testing the validity of ideas.

creeds or dogmas, was essentially a method for testing the validity of ideas. "(T)he whole function of philosophy," he thought, "ought to be to find out what definite difference it will make to you and me, at definite instants of our life, if this world-formula or that world-formula be the true one."[3] Truth, of course, depended upon the consequences of ideas. If ideas failed to help people solve problems, they were worthless. Particular targets of James' pragmatic method were the various late nineteenth-century abstract theories concerning the nature of man and the universe. James was particularly critical of Herbert Spencer, for example, whose concept of evolution, the philosophical basis for Social Darwinism, was very much in vogue in American intellectual circles at the time. Ridiculing Spencer and reflecting the pragmatist's impatience with abstract theories, he parodied: "Evolution is a change from a nohowish untalkaboutable all-alikeness to a somehowish and in general talkaboutable not-all-alikeness by continuous sticktogetherations and somethingelseifications."[4]

For James, then, truth was not inherent in ideas, rather it happened to ideas. Ideas became true only as they helped someone successfully connect his or her experiences. In this respect, James' pragmatism stayed on a personal, individual level. It was left to his colleague, John Dewey (1859–1952), to fully develop the social implications of pragmatism.

While Peirce and James were the intellectual fathers of pragmatism, Dewey was its most famous practitioner. Dewey argued that philosophers should shift their attention away from metaphysics and epistemology and concern themselves rather with politics, education, and morals. Dewey, like the other pragmatists, was critical of philosophical conceptions of knowledge. He rejected the idea that the mind was passive in nature, that its function was merely that of an instrument for the development of images of physical reality. Dewey felt that the mind was much more active. If human-kind's fate were to struggle with an everchanging environment, he argued, then its primary tool in that struggle was human intelligence. Knowledge and intelligence, then, grew from experience, from problem situations in the environment. Dewey's most complete discussion of the relationship between experience and knowledge came in *How We Think* (1910).[5] There he discussed the process of reflective thinking, where an individual faces a problem situation, considers alternative solutions to that situation in terms of their consequences, and tests the most reasonable solution. If the solution provides the expected consequences, it is true. Truth and knowledge derive from experience. There are no *a priori*, transcendent truths.

Dewey derives value in the same way. There are no absolute principles of ethics and aesthetics. In ethics, that which is good is that which works. Here, however, Dewey introduces the social context. Just as knowledge is public (recall Peirce's argument), so is value. Ethical good, then, is that which is good for human society, not merely for the individual. Humans should make moral decisions in terms of that which was most likely to produce good results in social, not individual, terms. Aesthetic evaluation worked in the same way. If, in the presence of a particular work of art, people saw new meaning in life or derived a closer relationship to their fellow men, then they were in the presence of a true work of art.

The most significant implications of Dewey's thinking lay in the realm of politics and government. Dewey and the pragmatists provided a philosophical justification for the rejection of laissez-faire Social Darwinism. But pragmatism also provided a number of implications for education, the most significant of which was the central importance of experience. Experience is the heart of education, that which provides knowledge. Children learn as they interact with the environment. Learning, then, must be active, not passive. Since knowledge is derived from reflective thinking applied to problem situations, the problem situations of children should form the basis for the curriculum. Thus, rather than have students memorize a certain body of content, the major goal of the school should be to teach children how to learn, emphasizing process rather than content.

Existentialism   Existentialist philosophers are those least suited to the term *school*, yet again there are similarities that are suggestive. Existentialism, although its roots can be traced to an earlier era, is largely a product of the twentieth century, an attempt to assert the importance of individual being in the face of an apparently meaningless universe. Global economic collapse sandwiched between two world wars and the dehumanizing impact of industrialization suggest that there is no ultimate meaning to the universe. Existentialists argue that individual humans must supply meaning for themselves.

For an existentialist like Jean Paul Sartre (1905–1980), individual being is the central aspect of reality. One exists; therefore, he or she is real. Sartre, in fact, argued that existence precedes essence. By that he meant that individuals must define for themselves the meaning of their lives, the meaning of being. Here Sartre reversed traditional metaphysical specula-

Photo 5.3

Jean Paul Sartre argued that idividuals must define for themselves the meaning of life.

tion, which had argued that the essence of humanness, or human nature, or the reason for being, was preconceived by some Ultimate Mind; essence was defined prior to existence. According to Sartre, individual humans first exist and then define themselves. They define themselves by the choices they make in their day-to-day living.[6]

Individual humans are free to be what they choose to be. The axiological implications of this position are clear: Humans make choices; thus, they are responsible for their choices. War, maldistribution of wealth, racial tension, all are attributable not to God or natural law but to decisions humans have made. Since there are no moral absolutes, individuals must make their won ethical decisions. If these decisions are harmful to others, the individual carries the burden of responsibility. Yet if one can act to do harm to human existence, one can also act to do good. Again, each individual is responsible for his or her own actions. In like fashion, aesthetic judgments are individual judgments. Each individual is his or her own judge of beauty.

The individual is the focus of existentialist educators' efforts. Education should recognize the uniqueness of each individual learner and foster the learner's understanding of himself or herself. It should also make the learner aware of the human condition—the burden of human freedom and responsibility. In this process, the teacher serves as facilitator rather than dispenser of knowledge. Content might well consist of those works that help students learn of the human condition. "There are works of art," wrote existentialist educator Maxine Greene, "there are certain works in history, philosophy, and psychology, that were deliberately created to move people to critical awareness, to a sense of moral agency, and to a conscious engagement with the world. As I see it, they ought—under the rubric of the 'arts and humanities'—to be central to any curriculum that is constructed today."[7] Existentialist concepts of education tend to be very child-oriented and unstructured, allowing the child freedom to choose, learn, and grow. Although very few schools today are specifically existentialist, A.S. Neill's Summerhill served as a recent example.[8]

Analytical Philosophy   Analytical philosophy is perhaps the best example of the modern philosopher's rejection of the search for absolutes, since the analytical philosopher turns his back on speculative philosophy and, rather, attempts to establish meaning by clarifying, defining, and verifying language. In effect, analytical philosophers have left the field of discovery of new knowledge to scientists and turned to the task of analyzing complex problems originating in the use of imprecise language.

As with the other "schools" of philosophy, a number of individuals have contributed to this approach, and there are differences among them. In general, however, they attempt to critically examine both scientific and everyday language in an effort to clarify and order meanings reflected in language. Ludwig Wittgenstein (1889–1951), for example, one of the most influential analytical philosophers, argued that "the object of philosophy is the logical clarification of thoughts," and that "the result of philosophy is not a number of philosophical propositions, but to make propositions clear."[9] Bertrand Russell (1872–1970) attempted to formulate the logical rules underlying language usage by proposing a set of mathematical symbols that represented words, concepts, and propositions.

A group of European philosophers, known as the Vienna Circle, analyzed the errors of definition and formulation of earlier philosophers, attempting to reveal errors in their solutions to problems. These philosophers of the Vienna Circle, known as logical positivists, argued that statements had meaning only if they could be categorized as either analytical or synthetic. Analytical statements are those that are "true" by definition and as a result of logical consistency, as with mathematical propositions, while synthetic statements, based upon observation and experience, are "true" if they can be verified empirically. If a statement cannot be verified analytically or empirically, it is meaningful only to the individual making it and thus reflects only opinion or personal preference.

Analytical philosophy can play an important role in education today. Today's society is one that relies upon mass communication, and unfortunately, much of the language used in that "communication" lacks clarity. Jargon abounds. Worse, many statements—from automobile commercials (e.g. "computer designed" parts) to campaign slogans ("the time is now") to educational catch phrases (e.g. "quality education," "self–actualization," and "individualized instruction")—simply cannot be verified either logically or empirically. The analytical philosopher points out those statements that can be verified and those that simply reflect opinion. Thus, in one sense, analytical philosophy can foster the educative process itself by helping individuals analyze the validity of statements and information to which they must react. In another sense, analytical philosophy can foster precision and clarity in the language that educators themselves use to convey meaning.

Educational Philosophy

The preceding passages suggested some of the educational implications of traditional and modern philosophical positions, but there are also specific schools of educational philosophy. While these schools trace their roots to general philosophical positions, they have applied themselves specifically to such educational questions as What is the function of the school? What is the role of the teacher? of the learner? What should be taught?

A discussion of modern educational philosophy begins chronologically with early twentieth-century progressivism and its attempt to break away from traditional conceptions of schooling. As noted in Chapter 4, developments in progressive education quickly spawned critics, as individuals concerned with the direction of American schooling in the 1930s and 1940s reacted to the child-centered curriculum and called for more traditional courses of study. Since the traditional perspectives advocated by the opponents of progressive education antedated progressive ideas, composing in fact some of the ideas and practices against which progressives argued, we shall treat them first here. This section looks at four schools of educational philosophy: the traditional schools of perennialism and essentialism, then progressivism, and finally reconstructionism.

Traditional Perspectives: Perennialism and Essentialism

Educational philosopher Theodore Brameld identified two groups that reacted to progressive education and advocated traditional schooling—those he called perennialists and those he called essentialists. His labels have been adopted in common use. These two twentieth-century educational philosophies have close ties to the traditional philosophical positions of idealism and realism. While some contemporary students of educational philosophy see perennialism as an offshoot of idealism and essentialism an offshoot of realism, there seems to be, in fact, elements of both in each. The bottom line for educators, however, is that both of these modern educational philosophies reflect themes from traditional philosophy and emphasize the importance of traditional subject matter.

Perennialism   Perennialists point out that the major distinction between man and lower forms of life lies in man's ability to reason. Thus, education should foster this ability—man's intellectual capacity. Perennialists also believe that there are important constants in terms of man's existence, principles by which man lives, and important questions that humankind asks. These are the "perennial" issues facing humankind. Education should be designed to introduce students to these questions and principles and the ways in which great thinkers have dealt with them. The best vehicle for achieving this goal is the study of the great works of literature, philosophy, and religion.

Great Books of the Western World, Robert Hutchins and Mortimer Adler's program begun in the late 1940s at the University of Chicago, is reflective of this educational philosophy.[10] The Great Books is a set of what Hutchins and Adler felt are the most significant works in the Western intellectual tradition. Hutchins and Adler felt that the study of such works, under the proper leadership, would give students a better understanding of the nature of the human condition. To help with that study, they developed an index, called the syntopicon, which cross-referenced major concepts. Review of the syntopicon would refer students to appropriate passages in the works of the great thinkers concerning whatever major concept the students wished to study. Thus, one could find what writers from Aeschylus to Marx and Freud felt about truth, beauty, goodness, liberty, justice, or whatever.

The case of the perennialists against child-centered or utilitarian educational orientations was summed up in a speech Robert Hutchins made to the National Association of Secondary School Principals in 1938:

> *If you believe that the aim of general education is to teach students to make money; if you believe that the educational system should mirror the chaos of the world; if you think that we have nothing to learn from the past; if you think that the way to prepare students for life is to put them through little fake experiences inside or outside the classroom; if you think that education is information; if you believe that the whims of children should determine what they should study—then I am afraid we can never agree. If, however, you believe that education should train students to think so that they may act intelligently when they face new situations; if you regard it as important for them to understand the tradition in which they live; if you feel that the present educational program leaves something to to be desired because of its "progressivism," utilitarianism, and diffusion; if you want to open up the youth of America the treasures of the thought, imagination, and accomplishment of the past—then we can agree.[11]*

More recently, William J. Bennett, Ronald Reagan's second Secretary of Education, has voiced perennialist themes. In "The Humanities: We Must Reclaim Our Heritage," Bennett gives a classical description of perennialist concerns:

> *I would describe the humanities as the best that has been said, thought, written, and otherwise expressed about the human experience. The humanities tell us how men and women of our own and other civilizations have grappled with life's enduring, fundamental questions: What is justice? What should be loved? What deserves to be defended? What is courage? What is noble? What is base? Why do civilizations flourish? Why do they decline? . . . We should . . . want all students to know a common culture rooted in civilization's lasting vision, its highest shared ideals and aspirations, and its heritage.[12]*

Mortimer Adler's *Paideia Proposal* (1982) has also made the case for student study of the great products of rational activity from the past.[13] Adler argues that true quality of educational opportunity means that society should provide not just the same quantity but also the same quality of schooling for everyone, that students should not be divided into tracks or special programs based on differences of ability, background, or need. Rather, schooling should pursue three basic goals common to all children: (1) intellectual, moral, and spiritual growth; (2) an adequate preparation for discharging the duties and responsibilities of citizenship; and (3) basic skills common to all work—not particular job training.[14] These goals can be achieved for students when they study the organized bodies of learning; are trained in the basic learning and intellectual skills; and study meritorious, individual works of human artistry—visual or musical as well as literary—including productions in dance, film, and television.[15]

Central to the Perennialist perspective on education is a conception of the role of the teacher. The teacher himself or herself must be liberally educated, well versed in knowledge derived from the major disciplines, able to coach students in the basic skills, and—through the use of the Socratic mode—able to lead the students' inquiry into the perennial issues of human existence.

Essentialism   Essentialism was the second of the two traditionalist reactions to progressivism. In fact, essentialism as here described is probably the most widely shared perspective on education in America today. Like perennialism, essentialism is educationally conservative, calling for an emphasis on traditional subject matter and academic skills and questioning educational experimentation and innovation. The essentialist conception of the basic subjects, however, is broader. While perennialists emphasize the intellectual heritage of the West—the great books and other artistic expressions—essentialists advocate study of all the basic academic disciplines. Elementary school, they argue, should focus on the basic academic skills—the three R's: reading, 'riting, and 'rithmetic. Secondary schools should expose students to history and the social sciences, mathematics, English, the sciences, and foreign languages. William C. Bagley, early advocate of essentialism, made the following argument:

> *There can be little question as to the essentials. It is no accident that the arts of recording, computing, and measuring have been among the first concerns of organized education. Every civilized society has been founded upon these arts, and when they have been lost, civilization has invariably collapsed. Nor is it accidental that a knowledge of the world that lies beyond one's immediate experience has been among the recognized essentials of universal education, and that at least a speaking acquaintance with man's past and especially with the story of one's country was early provided for in the program of the universal school. Investigation, invention, and creative art have added to our heritage. Health instruction is a basic phase of the work of the lower schools. The elements of natural science have their place. Neither the fine arts nor the industrial arts should be neglected.[16]*

Essentialists, then, disagree with progressives on a number of points. Essentialists argue that a lot of important learning is simply hard work and that it is naive to expect student interest to be the basis for all learning experiences. Rather, discipline must often be imposed on the student from without. Thus, the teacher as adult—not the learner—has the principal role in the teaching-learning situation. Finally, formally organized subject matter is the most appropriate target for learning.

Essentialism is obvious in the educational reform movement of the 1980s. That perspective animated *A Nation At Risk* in the early 1980s and appeared again in William J. Bennett's 1987 report, *James Madison High School: A Curriculum for American Students.* Through the description of a hypothetical high school—James Madison—reflecting a common ground that "virtually all our schools can reach and inhabit," the report calls for a rigorous academic curriculum including four years of English, three years each of mathematics, social studies, and science, two years each of foreign languages and physical education/health, and one year of art and music. Other courses such as vocational programs could be pursued through electives, but the academic core provides the heart of the program and is required of all students.[17]

Perennialism and essentialism reflect the modern reaction against progressive educational thought and practice. Educational philosopher Christopher Lucas summarized the general position of the two groups:

> *First, traditionalists or conservatives of varied persuasions have tended to agree that considerations of technocratic utility and efficiency should be subordinated to the paramount intellectual, spiritual, and ethical purposes of general education. Secondly, essentialists and perennialists concur that the crux of the educational enterprise is the transmission and assimilation of a prescribed body of subject matter, one incorporating the basic elements of the social cultural heritage. Thirdly, both groups acknowledge the cardinal importance of effort, discipline, and self-control in the learning process, as opposed to self-indulgent gratification of immediate needs and transitory interests. Fourthly, conservatives come together in endorsing the idea of curricular continuity: the foundations for a collegiate-level liberal education are laid in a systematic, planned, and sequential exposure to the rudiments of learning skills, beginning with the three R's in the elementary school and extending through to an orderly introduction to the basic subject matter disciplines at the secondary school level.[18]*

While critics of perennialism and essentialism argue that in practice, traditional approaches tend to be elitist, advocates disavow that intent. Both William J. Bennett and Mortimer Adler argue that all students should be exposed to the basic academic courses that compose the traditional, liberal education. In fact, many traditionalists argue that to assume some students are capable of academic work and others not is in itself inherently undemocratic.

Progressivism

When considering the progressive orientation toward schooling, it is important to remember the historical context in which it evolved. Recall that progressives were convinced that the traditional forms of education—emphasis upon subject matter in preparation for a liberal education—were divisive in terms of socioeconomic class. Progressives attempted to conceptualize education in such a way as to promote democratization of the school. They attempted to provide an education that recognized individual differences at the same time it fostered the potential for each individual's contribution to society.

In terms of philosophical schools, progressive educators reflect the application of pragmatism to education. In fact, America's most famous pragmatic philosopher, John Dewey, was also her most influential progressive educator. Dewey's work, however, is sometimes difficult to dig through, and individuals such as William Heard Kilpatrick, a professor of education at Teachers College, Columbia University, were actually more influential in popularizing progressive educational thought. (The fact that others popularized progressive education, by the way, led to—and still leads to—many unjustified attacks on the ideas of Dewey.)

In "The Case for Progressivism in Education," Kilpatrick made a number of basic points concerning the progressive orientation.[19] First, he argued that progressives "start with the child as a growing and developing person and help him live and grow best; live now as a child, live richly, live well; and thus living, to increase his effective participation in surrounding social life so as to grow steadily into an ever more adequate member of the social whole." Progressives focus on the child both as an individual and as a member of society.

Second, Kilpatrick contrasted the progressive orientation toward learning with the traditional focus on content. Progressives want to foster a situation where "the learner faces a situation of his own, such that he himself feels inwardly called upon to face it; his own interests are inherently at stake. And his response thereto is also his own; it comes out of his own mind and heart, out of his own very self. He may, to be sure, have had help from teacher or book, but the response when it comes is his." Kilpatrick here reflected the pragmatic view of knowledge as a result of experience. He wrote, ". . . learning has taken place when any part or phase of experience, once it has been lived, stays on with one to affect pertinently his further experience."

Third, "each learner should grow up to be a worthy member of the social whole." Individuals should acquire the culture of their group but in such a way as to "engage actively in life, especially in socially useful work within the community."

Fourth, Kilpatrick argued that children had to be taught to think for themselves, so critical a skill in a rapidly changing society. Traditional schooling, "stressing book study and formal information and minimizing presentday problems . . . failed to build the mind or character needed in modern life."

Finally, the progressive curriculum was "actual living—all the living of the child for which the school accepts responsibility." This kind of curriculum would be built jointly by pupils and teacher, and the teacher would serve as a facilitator of child development in what Kilpatrick calls desirable living.

In summary, the words of Dewey in *Experience and Education* (1938), contrasted ("opposed") the principles of traditional education to those of the new, progressive orientation:

> *To imposition from above is opposed expression and cultivation of individuality; to external discipline is opposed free activity; to learning from texts and teachers, learning through experience; to acquisition of isolated skills and techniques by drill, is opposed acquisition of them as means of attaining ends which make direct vital appeal; to preparation for a more or less remote future is opposed making the most of the opportunities of present life; to static aims and materials is opposed acquaintance with a changing world.*[20]

Table 5.2   Synoptic View of Conflicting Educational Philosophies

PHILOSOPHY	CONTROLLING AIM	CURRICULUM	METHOD	IDEAL OF LEARNER
Perennialism	Cultivation of the rational powers; academic excellence.	Liberal arts; Great Books.	Mental discipline; literary analysis.	Rational being guided by first principles; mind elevated above biological universe.
Essentialism	Academic excellence; cultivation of intellect.	Fundamental academic disciplines.	Mental discipline; mastery of academic subject matter.	Rational being in command of essential facts and skills that undergird the intellective disciplines.
Progressivism	Reflective thinking for social problem solving; democratic citizenship; personal growth.	Comprehensive, unified, problem-focused studies in democratic classroom setting.	Social problem solving through reflective thinking (scientific method) and democratic processes.	Autonomously thinking, socially responsible democratic citizen; organism in biological continuity with nature.
Reconstructionism	Building an ideal democratic social order.	Social problems, corrective programs scientifically determined for collective action.	Critical analysis of societal flaws and programmatic needs for corrective action.	Rebel committed to and involved in constructive social redirection and renewal.
Existentialism	Inner search for meaning of one's own existence.	Themes on the human condition; learning activities free of rational constraints, designed to free the individual to find his own being.	Introspection (examining one's own feelings, impulses, thoughts) in a free learning environment.	Flower in search of the meaning of its own existence.

Source: Adapted with permission of Macmillan Publishing Company from *Curriculum Development: Theory into Practice* by Daniel and Laurel N. Tanner. Copyright © 1975 by Macmillan Publishing Company.

Reconstructionism

Like progressivism, reconstructionism finds its roots in pragmatic philosophy. Reconstructionism, however, takes the social orientation of progressivism one step further, advocating the school as an institution for social reform. Where progressives can be seen as advocates of education as a tool for helping individuals *adjust* to society, reconstructionists feel education is a primary means for *change* in society. Schools, argued George S. Counts (1889–1974), should "give our children a vision of the possibilities which lie ahead and endeavor to enlist their loyalties and enthusiasms in the realization of the vision."[21]

That society is in dire need of reform, reconstructionists argue, there is no doubt. Reconstructionists point to such features of modern life as maldistribution of wealth, pollution, overpopulation, racism, and the irresponsible use of technology. These problems, however, are not merely American problems, they are worldwide. Thus, reform must recognize the interdependent nature of nations and peoples.

Reconstructionists have a utopian view of what human society can become: free of hunger, strife, and inhumanity. We have, they would argue, the technological ability to solve these problems. To achieve this goal, however, educators must present realistic pictures of the human condition to students and then help the students consider alternative futures. To fail to do so makes schools supporters of the status quo. If this means, for example, questioning the capitalist system, so be it. In his *Pedagogy of the Oppressed*, Paulo Freire, intellectual brother of the reconstructionists, argued that traditional schooling has allowed people to be exploited. Rather, Freire believes that education should make students aware of their exploitation and show then how to combat it through the use of knowledge.[22]

The purpose of schooling, then, should be to foster social reform. To do this, students would have to spend much time outside the classroom becoming aware not only of conditions in their own communities but also of international problems. Teachers as well as students should petition, protest, and participate in worthwhile social programs. "The circumference of this kind of participation is as wide as the earth," wrote Theodore Brameld (1904–), a leading reconstructionist, "extending all the way from the family and neighborhood outward to the region, nation, and eventually to distant nations. Learning therefore occurs directly through intra- and international travel (let us not be deluded by financial bugaboos; more than adequate funds are available if we insist upon them enough), and vicariously through films, the fine arts, and contact with experts such as anthropologists."[23] Reconstructionism calls for education to lead to a new social order. Elements of this perspective can be seen in the writings of the radical educational critics of the 1960s and 1970s, figures such as Paul Goodman and Ivan Illich.

An Illustration

To aid in discriminating between the classroom implications of the educational philosophies we have discussed, let us take a look at the different ways the four educational philosophies might treat a current topic. We will focus on a hypothetical situation in which high-school students are going to study the environment. We will explore the ways in which teachers reflecting each of the different philosophical perspectives might treat that topic.

The Perennialist   Perennialists are interested in exploring the "perennial" questions that face humankind. In this case, the focus might well be on the relationship of man to nature, the natural man (an important theme in American literature), or man in a "state of nature." To explore these issues, perennialists rely upon the great works of literature, philosophy, and history. A perennialist, then, if interested in the question of man's relationship to nature, might choose to have his or her students read and discuss such works as Daniel Defoe's *Robinson Crusoe* and Henry David Thoreau's *Walden*. The natural, or innocent, man—and his relationship to civilization—might be explored through Herman Melville's *Billy Budd* or James Fenimore Cooper's *Leatherstocking Tales*. An interesting exploration of man in a state of nature might begin with William Golding's *Lord of the Flies*. Classroom activities might revolve around teacher lecture and directed discussion of the works.

The Essentialist   The essentialist hopes to pass along the knowledge of humankind through a study of the major academic subjects. The various sciences play a significant role in this goal, and so it is to the sciences that the essentialist would probably turn to study the environment. The essentialist would expose students to information from biology or ecology. In many classrooms, the essentialist would rely primarily upon the textbook and lecture. Those essentialists who had been influenced by the work of Bruner and other advocates of inquiry learning would attempt to integrate laboratory work into their lessons. In either case, the objective would be to familiarize the student with scientific knowledge concerning ecosystems and man's place within those systems.

The Progressive   The progressive begins with individual needs and concerns and hopes to foster an adequate member of the social whole. On this topic, a progressive might initiate study with the students' own experiences with litter or air and water pollution. A trip to a local polluted stream, a study of local smog, or a survey of litter in the neighborhood might serve as a springboard into a broader treatment of man's relationship to the environment. Perhaps emphasizing the socially responsible use of technology, the teacher and students would draw from a variety of subject areas as they came to bear. The teacher might pose a variety of issues in problem format or, better yet, let the students frame their own problem issues and allow them to pursue reflective inquiry—Dewey's adaptation of scientific method. In this fashion, students would define a problem, develop possible alternative solutions to the problem, and decide which might work best. If possible, students would then act on their decision, eventually evaluating its effectiveness.

The Reconstructionist   The reconstructionist wants to use the school as an instrument to improve the social order. He or she would likely begin a treatment of the environment in much the same way the progressive did. However, the reconstructionist would push the inquiry further, focusing on the economic system—capitalism, which allows technology to damage the environment. If capitalism inherently fosters the irresponsible exploitation of nature in the pursuit of profit, perhaps other socioeconomic alternatives should be considered.

It is hoped that this brief discussion of some possible classroom implications of different educational philosophies helps clarify your thinking about perspectives. It should be noted, however, that in the "real world" of teaching one rarely finds a pure essentialist, progressive, etc. Many teachers are *eclectic*; that is, their teaching reflects different perspectives in different situations. Many teachers, for example, advocate progressive strategies wedded to the essentialist goal of exposure to the different academic disciplines. By the same token, it is a mistake to confuse a "conservative" educational philosophy with political or economic conservatism. Many conservative educators, those who emphasize study of the traditional subjects, are in fact liberal political thinkers. It is to the question of political perspectives that we must now turn our attention.

Political Ideologies

In his book, *American Education*, libertarian Joel Spring discusses the "Ideological Conflict Over the Purposes of Education."[24] In that discussion, Spring describes three ideological perspectives that shape opinion on educational goals, the neo-Marxist, the liberal, and the libertarian. These three perspectives reflect points along a continuum of political ideology. As Spring's title suggests, these political perspectives play a role in shaping individuals' and groups' positions on educational issues. Thus, they require treatment here.

To understand Spring's use of the words *libertarian*, *neo-Marxist*, and *liberal*, it is important to understand the assumptions behind these terms. As previously noted, the terms reflect positions along a continuum of political opinion. More specifically, they reflect perspectives concerning the role of the state in our lives. Libertarians feel that the state should play a minimal role in the lives of the people. As the power of the state increases, they believe, the freedom of the people decreases. Thus, one maxim by which they live is Thomas Jefferson's famous statement, "that government which governs best governs least." Another slogan of the libertarians is "Toward Anarchy," meaning that they work for less and less government.

Marxism, of course, is a form of socialism, where the means of production are owned and controlled by the state. Thus, Marxism reflects a point on the opposite end of the political spectrum from libertarianism. To most Americans, Marxist communism represents a form of totalitarianism. That is, the state controls all facets of the lives of the people.

Liberalism is between the two extremes of anarchism and *statism*. In the modern sense of the word, however, it would be marginally closer to statism. That is, liberals would argue that governmental power can be used as a positive force in society. To enhance the welfare of the many, government power can and sometimes must be used in such a way as to restrict the liberties of some. For example, a modern liberal would reject the old concept of *caveat emptor*, "let the buyer beware," in favor of government regulations over such things as food and drug preparation and truth in advertising. The liberties of those who produce and market such items are moderated by regulations designed to protect the broader group—the consumers.

The Marxist/Neo-Marxist Perspective

It should be remembered that Marx wrote in the middle part of the nineteenth century, when industrialization was just taking off and workers lived and worked under intolerable circumstances. Hours were long, working conditions were hazardous, and wages were low. Wages were so low, in fact, that most working families barely subsisted. Ill-clothed, ill-housed, and ill-fed, many lived miserable lives. Most workers were, indeed, exploited. According to Marx, the cause of all this misery was, of course, capitalism. Marx attacked capitalism as inherently exploitative of the worker and called for a system that recognized the laborer's contribution to production and gave the laborer a better life. Marx's dialectical view of history saw this better system—communist socialism—growing out of the contradictions inherent in capitalism and eventually replacing it. Yet this development would not occur automatically. Workers first had to recognize their plight and work together to force change. If that change required violent revolution, so be it. "Let the ruling classes tremble at the communist revolution," Marx wrote. "The proletarians have nothing to lose but their chains! They have a world to win. Working men of all countries, unite!"[25] Thus, Marx's ideas provided a theoretical base for the criticism of existing conditions in society while they suggested the significance of a feeling of solidarity among workers as an important foundation for revolution. Both of these aspects of Marxist thought carry implications for education.

Photo 5.4
Karl Marx criticized the
social conditions of his day.

Marxism posits the development of a socialist society replacing capitalism. Education can serve to foster this development by making workers
conscious of their plight—of their exploitation by the capitalist class—by
promoting their feeling of solidarity. This promotion of a socialist consciousness is a major part of educational practice in the communist world
today. Lenin, for example, argued that "the school must become a weapon
of the dictatorship of the proletariat."[26] That is, it must foster worker
solidarity through indoctrination in communist ideology. In practice, that
means the exclusion of competing ideologies from the curriculum. Such
indoctrination is repugnant to most Western educators.

Many Western Marxists and American neo-Marxists are more attracted
to Marx's ideas as a base from which to criticize contemporary society and
education. Samuel Bowles and Herbert Gintis, for example, in *Schooling in
Capitalist America* (1976), argue that the American educational system,
rather than promote equality of opportunity, actually serves to maintain
social inequalities.[27] They point out that in spite of mass education,
economic inequalities have not been eradicated. This is because the
American school replicates the workplace: The division of the day into
specific time periods, the authoritarian hierarchy of command, the behavioral expectations within defined limits, and rewards based on productivity,
all socialize students to the existing economic order.

Even child-rearing practices attributable largely to socioeconomic class
are maintained by the school system. That is, upper middle-class suburban
schools tend to emphasize self-direction in their students—an attribute
associated with higher status, higher income jobs—while lower middle-class
urban schools tend to require submissiveness to authority—an attribute
associated with lower status, lower income jobs. Neo-Marxists (and other,
non-Marxist educational critics) might point to such evidence as the
relationship of social class to educational track (children with higher

socioeconomic backgrounds tend to be concentrated in academic classes), the relationship of social class to educational expectations (teachers appear to have higher expectations of children from higher socioeconomic groups), and the relationship of social class to educational achievement (children from higher socioeconomic backgrounds score higher on achievement tests) to criticize the American educational system.[28]

It is at this point where political neo-Marxism and philosophical reconstructionism tend to overlap. Both viewpoints recognize shortcomings of the basic economic system and advocate schooling as a component of change. The influential reconstructionist George Counts, for example, studied the Soviet educational system. As a result of his studies and thought, he grew increasingly dissatisfied with progressive educational reform:

> *If Progressive Education is to be genuinely progressive, it must emancipate itself from the influence of [the liberal-minded upper-middle] class, face squarely and courageously every social issue, come to grips with life in all of its stark reality, establish an organic relation with the community, develop a realistic and comprehensive theory of welfare, fashion a compelling and challenging vision of human destiny, and become less frightened than it is today at bogies of imposition and indoctrination.[29]*

Counts' ideas sound very much like those of contemporary neo-Marxists. Despite the currency of these ideas in international intellectual circles, however, they have had very little impact on American educational practice. Still, they form a perspective that does influence some people's educational ideas.

The Liberal Perspective

The great majority of Americans feel that state-supported public schools are critical to the maintenance of democracy. This view of the school is described as liberal by Spring, because it posits education as a function of the state. Spring argues that the liberal sees the public school as a primary institution for fostering both political community and equality of opportunity. Chapters 3 and 4 of this book pointed out that the majority of Americans do expect the public school to pass along our culture, to socialize, to "Americanize," that is, to foster a common set of political values. It also provides, many feel, a springboard for social mobility.

Liberals, argues Spring, feel that the control of education should be in the hands of professional educators, with local school boards given a broad policymaking function. This view, he writes, sees the "expert professional educator working, without outside political interference, in the interests of the student." Although this aspect of education might be called progressive—in that sense of the word which suggests efficiency in management—it is not inaccurate to call it liberal. This view, too, has become the norm in American elementary and secondary education.

The liberal view, then, is the mainline view in the United States: Education is properly a function of the state. This perspective influences opinion on educational policymaking in a number of ways. One way, of course, is obviously support for the maintenance and health of public-

Table 5.3 Political Ideologies and Their Educational Implications	IDEOLOGICAL PERSPECTIVE	ROLE OF THE STATE	EDUCATIONAL IMPLICATIONS
	Marxist	Active. Means of production owned by state.	Workers should be educated to recognize exploitation. Schools should promote social consciousness, indoctrination in communist ideology.
	Neo-Marxist	Active.	Marxism provides basis for criticism of American society and education where inequalities remain. Schools must shape social vision, theory of welfare.
	Liberal	Active.	State-supported education critical to maintenance of democracy. Schools foster both political community and equality of opportunity.
	Libertarian	Minimal. "Toward Anarchy."	State-supported schools should be abolished and replaced by schools operated by private groups.

education. Thus, liberals might oppose proposals that they see as threatening to the welfare of the public schools, such as federal tax credits for private school tuition. They also may favor the use of public schools to address other social problems—segregation, for example. Beyond points of agreement such as these, however, liberal opinion may well diverge. Two liberals may believe that education is a proper function of the state yet disagree in terms of educational philosophies. One may argue that schools should address the needs of the "whole child" while another believes the school should focus on academics.

The Libertarian Perspective

Libertarians generally believe that government interference in the lives of the people is unfortunate. Where the government is involved, freedom is hampered. This is as true in education as it is in any realm of life. Government intervention, libertarians argue, usually promotes the ideas of those who control the government. State-supported schools, for example, promote the ideology of those who control the schools, regardless of who or what group that is. Promotion of any ideology restricts the free development of ideas and, consequently, hampers social progress. Libertarians reject the liberal contention that government must act to promote the good of the whole. In fact, they argue, government actions are counterproductive to progress.

Thus, state-supported schools should be abolished and replaced with schools that are operated by parents, teachers, students, or other private groups. What would be the common goals of the schools? Just the freedom to develop the ideas they choose:

Libertarians do not have a blueprint of an ideal school system, because they believe all organizations should be the product of voluntary interactions of individuals, rather than the result of one master plan or another. Once freed from government domination, libertarians believe, there is no telling what kind of educational system will evolve.[30]

Given the nature of schooling in America today, the use of tuition tax credits and vouchers is supported by some libertarians. Such devices make it economically feasible for parents to choose schools other than the public schools to which their children would most likely be sent. The basic idea here is to enhance individual choice in the selection of schools. "For instance," writes Spring, "parents could refuse to give their local school their educational tax dollars and could instead participate in organizing a new school or finding another alternative. In either case, libertarians argue, schools would be forced to respond to consumer demands and would be shaped by the choices of individuals."[31]

In recent years, the idea of tuition tax credits and vouchers has been taken up by many political conservatives. The politically conservative Reagan administration, for example, has touted both as means to give parents greater control over their children's education and to generally improve schooling in the United States.

Summary

A major element in our analysis of educational policy development is the role played by participants. The participants' viewpoints on any particular educational issue might be influenced by a number of things, yet both general philosophical positions and political ideology appear to be major factors about which generalizations can be made. Traditional philosophical schools such as idealism and realism posit metaphysical, epistemological, and axiological positions based on the assumption of a meaningful universe shaped by God or natural law. The educational implications of these positions surface in contemporary educational philosophies like perennialism and essentialism, emphasizing traditional academic disciplines. Modern philosophical schools such as pragmatism and existentialism question traditional metaphysical positions and look more to society or the individual for meaning. While existentialism argues that individuals must assign their own meaning to existence, pragmatists emphasize the individual's place in the social context. The contemporary educational philosophies of progressivism and reconstructionism trace their roots to pragmatism. Ideological perspectives also play a role in educational opinion, as debate revolves around the extent to which the government should be involved in the educational enterprise. While Marxists advocate control by the state in order to foster the welfare of the working class, liberals advocate state-controlled education to foster political community and equality of opportunity. Libertarians feel that education should not be a state function at all.

Key Words

Metaphysics	Analytical philosophy
Epistemology	Preennialism
Axiology	Essentialism
Idealism	Progressivism
Realism	Reconstructionism
Neo-Scholasticism	Eclecticism
Deductive reasoning	Liberal
Inductive reasoning	Neo-Marxist
Pragmatism	Libertarian
Existentialism	

Discussion Questions

1. What is your position on epistemological issues? Is knowledge based upon observation and experience, or can reality be intuited?

2. Describe the differences between deductive and inductive reasoning.

3. How would you describe your educational philosophy? Do you find your ideas in agreement with any of the educational philosophies presented here, or are you *eclectic* (that is, borrowing from a variety of perspectives)?

4. How would you describe your ideological perspective?

For Further Reading

Mortimer Adler, *The Paideia Proposal* (New York: Macmillan Publishing Co., 1982).

Howard A. Ozmon and Samuel M. Craver, *Philosophical Foundations of Education*, Third Edition (Columbus: Merrill Publishing Co., 1986).

Joel Spring, *American Education: An Introduction to Social and Political Aspects* (New York: Longman, 1985).

Samuel E. Stumpf, *Philosophy: History and Problems*, Third Edition (New York: McGraw Hill, 1982).

Notes

1. The treatment given traditional philosophies in this section relies upon George R. Knight, *Issues and Alternatives in Educational Philosophy* (Berrien Springs, Michigan: Andrews University Press, 1982); Howard A. Ozmon and Samuel M. Craver, *Philosophical Foundations of Education*, Third Edition (Columbus: Charles E. Merrill Publishing Co., 1986); and Morris Bigge, *Educational Philosophies for Teachers* (Columbus: Charles E. Merrill Publishing Co., 1982).

2. Samuel E. Stumpf, *Philosophy: History and Problems*, Third Edition (New York: McGraw Hill, 1982), pp. 383–384.

3. *Ibid.*, p. 386.

4. Richard Hofstadter, *Social Darwinism in American Thought* (Boston: Beacon Press, 1955), p. 129.

5. John Dewey, *How We Think* (Boston: D.C. Heath, 1910).

6. See, for example, Jean Paul Sartre, "The Humanism of Existentialism" in Wade Baskin (ed) *The Philosophy of Existentialism* (New York: The Philosophical Press, 1965).

7. Maxine Greene, excerpt from *Landscapes of Learning* in Ozmon and Craver, p. 220.

8. See A.S. Neill, *Summerhill* (New York: Hart, 1960).

9. Quoted in Stumpf, p. 417.

10. Robert Hutchins and Mortimer Adler, eds., *The Great Books of the Western World* (Chicago: Encyclopedia Britannica, 1952).

11. Robert M. Hutchins, Address to National Association of Secondary School Principals, Atlantic City, New Jersey, February 26, 1938.

12. "The Humanities: We Must Reclaim Our Heritage" in *Private Colleges and Universities*, 1988 Edition, p. 31.

13. Mortimer Adler, *The Paideia Proposal* (New York: Macmillan Publishing Co., 1982).

14. *Ibid.*, pp. 16–17.

15. *Ibid.*, pp. 28–29.

16. William C. Bagley, "The Case for Essentialism in Education" *Today's Education* 30, No. 7 (October 1941), p. 202.

17. William J. Bennett, *James Madison High School: A Curriculum for American Students* (Washington, D.C.: U.S. Department of Education, 1987).

18. Christopher J. Lucas, ed., *Challenge and Choice in Contemporary Education: Six Major Ideological Perspectives* (New York: Macmillan Publishing Co., 1976), p. 14.

19. William Heard Kilpatrick, "The Case for Progressivism in Education" in Glen Hass, *Curriculum Development: A New Approach* (Boston: Allyn & Bacon, 1983), pp. 24–27.

20. John Dewey, *Experience and Education* (New York: Macmillan Publishing Co., 1938), pp. 5–6.

21. Quoted in Ozmon and Craver, pp. 138–139.

22. Paulo Freire, *Pedagogy of the Oppressed*, trans. by M.B. Ramos (New York: Seabury, 1970).

23. Theodore Brameld, "A Cross-Cutting Approach to the Curriculum: The Moving Wheel" in Hass, p. 30.

24. Joel Spring, *American Education: An Introduction to Social and Political Aspects* (New York: Longman, 1985).

25. Karl Marx, *The Communist Manifesto* trans. by Samuel Moore (London: Penguin Press, 1967).

26. Quoted in Ozmon and Craver, p. 267.

27. Samuel Bowles and Herbert Gintis, *Schooling in Capitalist America* (New York: Basic Books, 1976).

28. These generalizations can be found in works such as A.B. Hollingshead, *Elmtown's Youth* (New York: John Wiley, 1949); James Coleman, *Equality of Educational Opportunity* (Washington: Government Printing Office, 1966); and Christopher Jencks, *Inequality* (New York: Harper & Row, 1972).

29. Quoted in Ozmon and Craver, p. 138.

30. Spring, p. 27.

31. *Ibid.*, p. 28.

6 School/Society Relationships

> ". . . Education, then, beyond all other devices of human origin, is the great equalizer of the conditions of men—the balance wheel of the social machinery."
>
> **Horace Mann, "Fifth Annual Report to the Massachusetts Board of Education" (1842)**

> "None of the evidence we have reviewed suggests that school reform can be expected to bring about significant social changes outside the schools. More specifically, the evidence suggests that equalizing educational opportunity would do very little to make adults more equal."
>
> **Christopher Jencks, *Inequality: A Reassessment of the Effects of Family and Schooling in America* (1972)**

> "By focusing on an economic bottom line, by narrowing their concern to accountability and basics, by ignoring the realities of inequity, the prevailing school critics do warn us of a grave social risk. But the risk they signal in the new standard of merit will become in practice new mechanisms for stratification and, ultimately, another means for pushing unwanted students out of the system. Massive school failure for the other half is not the core crisis that the meritocrats choose to address in their vision for change."
>
> **Ann Bastian et al., *Choosing Equality* (1985)**

Citizens of the United States are involved in a heated debate about the role of schooling in their society. Differing perceptions about the social functions of schooling have made public schools one of the most controversial

133

Figure 6.1   Social Issues Addressed Through Schooling

Issues Addressed		Programs/Activities in School
Promotion of social mobility based on meritocracy		Develop competence skills
		Promote meritocratic ideal
		Deal with social class biases in school programs
Socialization of children and youth		Promote acculturation/enculturation
		Foster understanding of and adaptation to changing social roles
Promotion of equality		Desegregate schools
		Provide compensatory/remedial education
Elimination of injustice		Prevent school dropout
		Promote cultural pluralism
		Accommodate ethnic, racial, sexual, religious differences
Changing demographic structure		Provide sex education
		Provide drug and alcohol abuse education
Changes in institutions such as the family		Prevent juvenile delinquency and crime

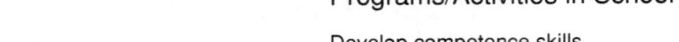

of U.S. social institutions. The debate has generally focused on two major questions. The first concerns the kinds of social outcomes that citizens should expect as a return on their investment in schooling. Is functional literacy the most important goal of public schooling? Is schooling the best vehicle to "equalize the conditions of men," as Horace Mann suggested? Will equalizing schooling opportunity eliminate the problems of poverty in American society? What is the proper role of schools in socializing children and youth in American culture? Are investments in public education society's best hope for producing a generation of workers who have the values and skills that will keep the U.S. economic system competitive in the world economy? Are schools the most appropriate institutions to address pressing problems relating to teen pregnancy, drug and alcohol abuse, and discrimination? Will devoting energy and resources to the preceding activities hinder the schools from doing what many citizens perceive as the school's most important task—helping students to achieve basic literacy and functional skills? Figures 6.1 and 6.2 illustrate the impact these social and economic issues have on the schools and the kind of responses that schools make to deal with those issues.

The second question concerns the impact of social/cultural factors on schooling outcomes. Is it possible for schools to overcome the effects of socioeconomic status on student academic achievement? Can schools overcome the effects of socialization carried out by the electronic media, family, and peer groups?

A considerable body of literature has evolved out of this debate over school/society relationships. There is little doubt that differing perceptions about the role of schools contribute to recent criticism of public schooling.

Photo 6.1
Healthy, safe school environments are a primary expectation of parents for their children.

Citizens judge schools on the basis of how well they carry out the social improvement agenda assigned implicitly or explicitly to them by society. The work of teachers and administrators in public schools is so directly affected by these issues in school/society relationships that the issues deserve treatment in a textbook about the foundations of education. Questions inevitably arise about priorities. How should a teacher's time be divided between helping students learn literacy and cultural skills and helping students appreciate the dangers of alcohol and drug abuse? This chapter examines the school's role in the socialization of children and youth, the promotion of social mobility through the development of merit, and some of the relationships that exist between social class and educational achievement in the United States.

Schooling and the Socialization of Children and Youth

Passing on an appreciation for and an understanding of the characteristics of a culture is a part of the socialization process. All societies have implicit and explicit ways to teach people the mores, values, loyalties, and social roles that are a part of that culture.

Figure 6.2   Economic Issues Addressed Through Schooling

Issues Addressed	Programs/Activities in School
Training of work force	Develop basic competency skills
	Develop specific job skills
	Socialize students in career and work ethic
Consumer education	Promote consumer education curricula
	Require students to study principles of economic system
Appreciation for free enterprise capitalism	Sort students on basis of merit
	Base credentialing process on merit
	Administer special job training/ retraining programs
Inequality in the work force	Provide sex education
	Provide drug and alcohol abuse education
Poverty and unemployment	Prevent juvenile delinquency and crime

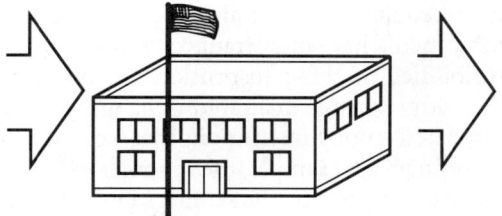

Photo 6.2
Schools in the United States are located in diverse rural, urban, and suburban neighborhoods.

Societies have geographical boundaries and share common political and economic systems. In reality, however, members of any society belong to many different subcultures based on such factors as race, ethnicity, geography, and religion. Families with a combination of cultural identities based on race, ethnicity, geography, and religion rear their children to understand and appreciate the unique set of roles, values, mores, and loyalties that arise from the combination of factors that define culture for those families. The term *enculturation* is used to describe the process by which one learns to achieve competence in one's own culture. Obviously, a child born into a Christian fundamentalist family in the Arkansas Ozarks would have a different enculturation experience from a child born into a Jewish family that lived in an upper-income neighborhood of New York City.

If the more global values, roles, and loyalties associated with sharing a common political, social, and economic system are to survive, members of the diverse subcultures must learn to understand and appreciate aspects of a common cultural heritage. Arrangements must be made for members of the diverse subcultural groups to come into contact with each other to learn a minimum degree of tolerance for differences and common cultural appreciations. This aspect of socialization is described by the term *acculturation*. As you examine the list of socialization agencies in Box 6.1, reflect on the enculturation/acculturation roles of each agency.

Changing Roles Among Socialization Agencies

Societies develop and maintain a number of different kinds of institutions to promote enculturation and acculturation. Unique roles and responsibilities emerge and change for the different socialization agencies in a given society. In the United States, the family, school, church, peer group, work place, and electronic media have important roles in socializing children and youth. The responsibilities of these institutions in the socialization of children and youth undergo change in a rapidly changing society. Socialization activity is so interrelated among institutions that a change in one institution inevitably affects another; for example, the school is expected to carry out socialization tasks once carried out by the family. Many other factors determine how well socialization agencies can carry out their roles in a given culture, some examples of which follow:

> **Degree and rate of social change.**   Rapid change tends to obscure which loyalties, roles, and values should be preserved and transmitted.

Box 6.1
Socialization
Agencies

The following socialization agencies may be utilized by society to perform socialization tasks with children and youth:

> Family
>
> Schools
>
> Youth organizations
>
> Churches
>
> Mass media
>
> Peer groups
>
> Correctional institutions
>
> Leisure and recreational agencies

As you examine this list, reflect on the changes in socialization functions that may be occurring for each agency. How will changes in socialization roles for one agency affect the socialization functions of other agencies? Which agencies would you add to the list?

Degree of cultural diversity within the larger culture based on race, ethnicity, religion, or geography.   Arriving at a definition of a common cultural heritage for the larger society is more difficult where cultural pluralism is a prevailing social value.

Perception of learning.   Since socialization is a learning process, conflicts arise over the most efficient method of carrying out the socialization process.

Evidence regarding the restructuring of the American family raises important policy questions regarding socialization of children and youth. The U.S. Census Bureau projects that by 1990, thirty percent of all children in the United States will be living in single-parent families because of divorce, birth out of wedlock, or desertion. By the same date, one half of all children will have spent some time in a single-parent family before they reach age eighteen. By a large majority, single-parent families are headed by females.

A 1983 U.S. Civil Rights Commission report documents the growth in single-parent households headed by women and the growth in poverty in this type of family. In 1960, 8.4 percent of the nation's families were headed by women, and members of these families constituted twenty-four percent of those in poverty. By 1982, fatherless families made up fifteen percent of the population and forty-six percent of the poor. It appears that a growing number of children in the United States are being reared in family structures that have limited resources to carry on the tasks of socialization. Figure 6.3 documents the incidence of poverty by family type in the United States.

Nearly eighty percent of mothers who head a single-parent family are employed outside the home. Approximately two-thirds of the children age

Figure 6.3   The Hierarchy of Poverty

Percentage of children in 1983 in poverty in each group

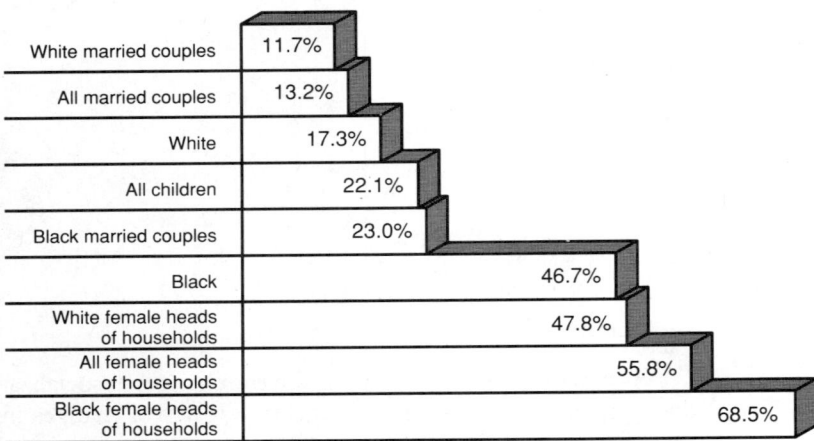

White married couples	11.7%
All married couples	13.2%
White	17.3%
All children	22.1%
Black married couples	23.0%
Black	46.7%
White female heads of households	47.8%
All female heads of households	55.8%
Black female heads of households	68.5%

six to seventeen living with both parents are members of households where both parents work outside the home. Evidence presented to the U.S. House Select Committee on Children, Youth, and Families in 1984 established that more and more children from all types of family structures are spending more time without adult supervision. In some cities, research studies indicate that more than one third of nine- to eleven-year-olds were spending significant portions of their time alone, unsupervised by adults.

Latchkey children prompt many questions about the socialization of children and youth in the United States. Commercial self-help manuals, latchkey survival kits, television spots, and milk carton instructions on how children should take care of themselves when their parents aren't home are some indications that our society is willing to allow "self-socialization" of children and adolescents. Are "helpful hints for self-care" the best socialization practices our affluent society can offer its children? How do we go about reassessing and reassigning roles among different socializing agencies to achieve the most optimum socialization experience for children? What socialization functions do we define for the public schools in response to the changes occurring in other institutions in our society?

Socialization Roles of Peer Groups

If children and adolescents are spending more time without adult supervision, it is logical to assume that they have greater control over their own socialization. Typically, children have had two social worlds affecting their socialization. Adults, consisting of parents, teachers, church and organization leaders, and business owners, make up one world. Peer groups of children and youth their own age constitute the other social world.

Diverse types of peer groups affect socialization—from informal play groups consisting of neighborhood kids to more formal organized youth groups. Some peer groups tend to be in open conflict with adults, whereas other peer groups are formed as a result of adult planning. Except in the latter instance, peer groups are not instituted by society to be a formal agent of socialization. They are not governed by any formal, explicit socialization functions. Yet it appears that peer group influences in socialization are increasingly pervasive.

What has perpetuated the growing influence of peer groups? The labor of youth has been marginally needed in economic productivity. Consequently, youth remain economically dependent on their families for longer and longer periods of time. Youth are more mobile, since a growing number have their own cars. Youth spend more time with peers in schools and recreation programs. Some school administrators have argued that court decisions granting youth constitutional protections of free speech, press, and assembly have enhanced the influence of peer groups.

Peer groups serve various socialization functions among young people:

They teach young people how to get along with others.

They teach sex roles and mores.

They serve as reference groups in the process of establishing self-identity.

They teach the culture, building on, changing, and elaborating on what was first taught in the family.

They teach concepts associated with the social status system which includes having their own system of recognition and rewards.

How should school officials respond to the changing socialization functions of peer groups? Several schools have creatively utilized peer group influence to promote academic achievement and drug and alcohol abuse education. Peer teaching and tutoring programs have been successfully launched in many schools. Many schools are attempting to build new relationships with youth serving agencies to foster more positive peer influence over students enrolled in school.

Socialization for Work

Modern societies are dependent on a reliable source of competently trained adults to fill work roles necessary to sustain social life in a particular culture. What is frequently unclear is the connection between the ways used to socialize individuals for work and the economic conditions within the culture. How should individuals be trained for work roles? Where should socialization for work take place? Is there a connection between the way a society trains its youth for work and the ability of that society to compete in the international marketplace? These and many other questions are being raised about socialization of youth for work in the United States.

The Marginality of Youth and Socialization for Work

In the eighteenth and nineteenth centuries, American youth were engaged in agricultural and industrial enterprises that dominated the economy during those times. In the early twentieth century, growing numbers of youth were displaced from the work place because of the mechanization of agriculture and improved technology that required fewer workers to produce larger amounts of consumer products. School enrollment rose rapidly as society used schooling to delay employment and to socialize larger numbers of adolescents and young people for work through the new vocational education programs being introduced in the schools.

Youth labor talents remained marginal during the depression years. It was not until World War II that the economic efforts of the younger age cohort (specific age group in the population) were needed; consequently, school enrollment tended to decline. After the war, large numbers of young people began to attend college under the opportunities created by the GI Bill and National Defense Student Loan programs. College enrollment continued to rise rapidly during the 1960s and 1970s because of the large youth age cohort of the post-war baby boom and the economic prosperity of the period. The entry of youth into the work force was delayed through the increased opportunity for schooling.

Youth countercultures tend to arise during periods when youth are displaced from the work place. The flapper phenomenon of the 1920s and the hippie counterculture of the 1960s are good examples of what can happen when youth are marginally needed in the economic system.

Current demographic characteristics among the youth age cohort are posing new questions about socialization of youth for work in this society. The population of eighteen- to twenty-four-year-olds that had reached an all-time high of 30.4 million in 1980 had dropped to 28.5 million in 1986. During the next fifteen years, the size of this age cohort is expected to decline by another seven million. Additional concern is created by the reality that a growing percentage of this younger age cohort will come from minority population groups that have not been well served by the public school system (see Table 6.1). These changing demographic realities suggest that school officials need to exhibit greater sensitivity to multicultural and ethnicity issues, discussed in Chapter 12. (See Box 6.2 for evidence suggesting that many of these students will be at risk in regard to academic achievement in school due to family background and socioeconomic factors.)

Furthermore, labor analysts are predicting that most of the new jobs in the next few decades will be in the low-paying categories (see Figure 6.4). The result, as these analysts predict, will be the creation of a bipolar labor force. A few people will hold high status, high-paying jobs, while the vast majority of new entrants to the work force will become locked into low-skill, low-income job roles. According to this analysis of demographic realities and labor trends, the American middle class is threatened.[1]

Table 6.1
Characteristics of the Labor Force in 2000

People under 25 will have a smaller share.
People 55 and over will have a smaller share.
Women will have a larger share.
Blacks will have a larger share.
Asians and others will have a larger share.
Hispanics will have a larger share.

Source: *Occupational Outlook Quarterly*, U.S. Department of Labor, Bureau of Labor Statistics, Fall 1987, p. 6.

Figure 6.4

Occupations That Will Account for More than One Half the Total Job Growth

Numerical growth, 1986–2000

Percentage of growth, 1986–2000

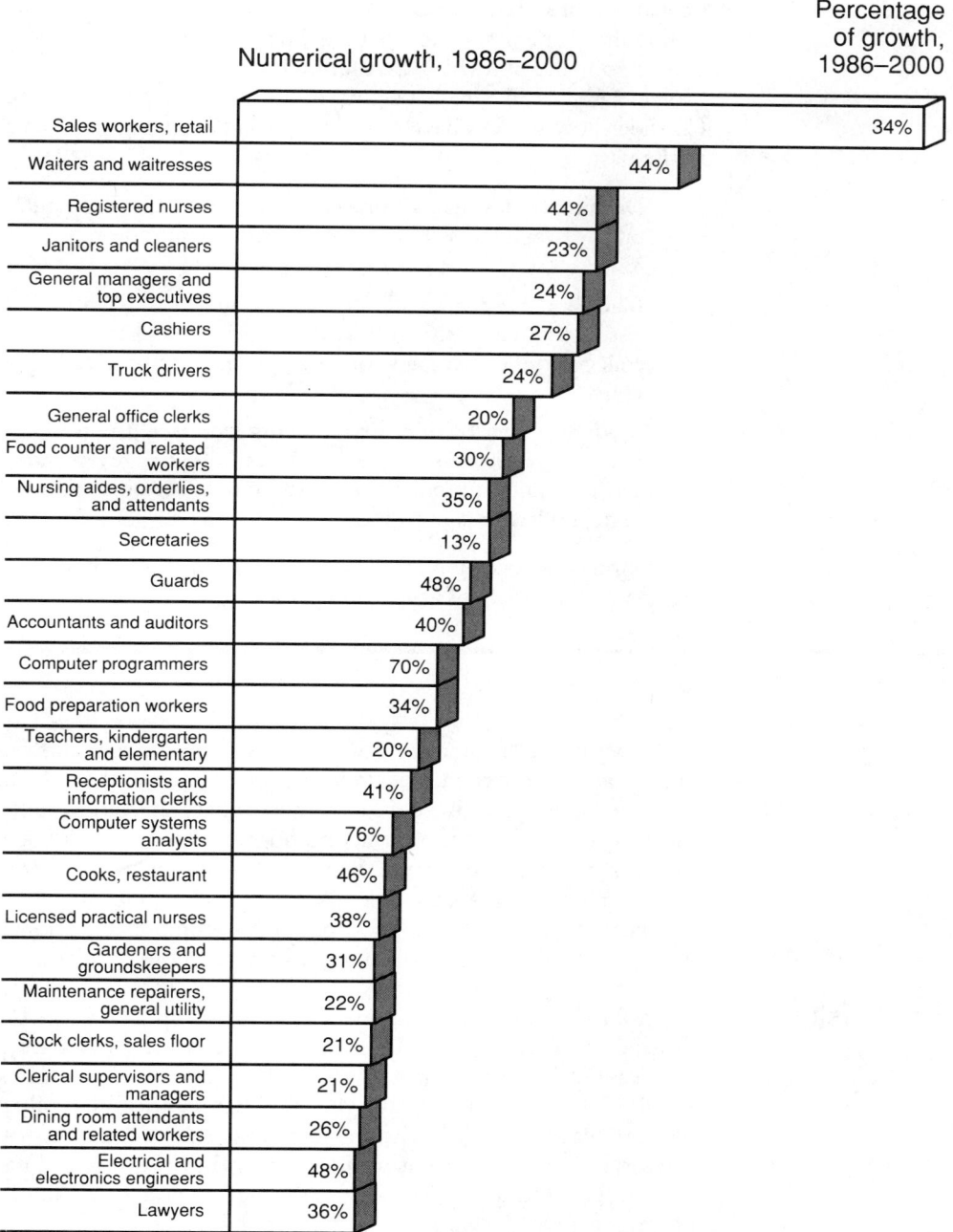

Occupation	Percentage
Sales workers, retail	34%
Waiters and waitresses	44%
Registered nurses	44%
Janitors and cleaners	23%
General managers and top executives	24%
Cashiers	27%
Truck drivers	24%
General office clerks	20%
Food counter and related workers	30%
Nursing aides, orderlies, and attendants	35%
Secretaries	13%
Guards	48%
Accountants and auditors	40%
Computer programmers	70%
Food preparation workers	34%
Teachers, kindergarten and elementary	20%
Receptionists and information clerks	41%
Computer systems analysts	76%
Cooks, restaurant	46%
Licensed practical nurses	38%
Gardeners and groundskeepers	31%
Maintenance repairers, general utility	22%
Stock clerks, sales floor	21%
Clerical supervisors and managers	21%
Dining room attendants and related workers	26%
Electrical and electronics engineers	48%
Lawyers	36%

Most of these occupations are growing faster than the average for all occupations. Those growing less rapidly are very large, so that the numerical increase is still great.

Source: *Occupational Outlook Quarterly,* Fall 1987.

Box 6.2
Schooling Policy and
At Risk Students

In the immediate future, American educators will be working with a cohort of children more ethnically and racially diverse than ever before. A larger percentage of public school students will bring with them an array of risk factors that bode ill for their potential development. A growing proportion will be poor and nonwhite, have limited English proficiency, and come from broken families in which parents have limited educational backgrounds. Consider how schools have served students possessing these characteristics in the past.

> Despite modest gains in recent years, black and Hispanic children on the average continue to score below white peers on standardized tests.

> Black and Hispanic children who do graduate from high school are less likely than white graduates to enroll in college. Furthermore, college attendance rates for these groups has been falling in recent years.

> As the number of minority students increases, the scarcity of minority teachers is increasing. Sweeping changes in state teacher certification requirements are expected to shrink the pool of minority teachers even more.

What kind of schooling policy changes would you recommend to deal with the growing number of at-risk students?

Other analysts interpret the changing job structure differently. They argue that the slower rate of growth in the large number of occupational categories that typically require post-secondary education will offset the faster rate of growth in the smaller number of categories of low-paying jobs. They point out the continuing likelihood of workers with more education earning more and facing less likelihood of being unemployed. This evidence, they suggest, is a good reason to promote educational opportunity as a vehicle to help individuals achieve economic success.[2]

Emerging Questions Relating to Socialization of Youth for Work

The reality of global international economic competition, the prospects of a smaller, less well-prepared age cohort, and other factors are producing significant policy dilemmas regarding how and where youth should be socialized for work. Historically, the family, apprenticeship, military service, the work place, and schools have assumed varying roles in preparing citizens for work. Given the current realities, which institution should assume the major responsibility for this task over the next decade? If schools are given this responsibility, what is the most appropriate method for carrying out the task? Should we emphasize specific job skills in vocational and technical education programs, "learning how to learn" skills in general literacy, work ethic principles, or a combination of these emphases? Should schools require some work experience or community service as a condition for receiving the high-school diploma? These are typical questions being raised in the debate over socialization of youth for work.

The following suggestions are frequently cited in the school reform literature as options that need to be considered in facilitating more adequate socialization of youth for work in the next decade:

> Involve youth in a mixture of work and study.
>
> Give instruction in specific job skills in the work environment.
>
> Encourage youth-serving organizations.
>
> Create new liaisons between educational institutions and the work place.
>
> Change labor laws that keep youth out of the work place.
>
> Provide a separate minimum wage for youth.
>
> Provide educational vouchers for youth beyond age sixteen for work training.
>
> Create more federally funded public service jobs to train youth.

Policymakers will continue to evaluate these and other options as they work to develop policies related to the socialization of youth for work in our society.

Social Class and Schooling

Every society has some form of ranking or stratifying members of that society. Inevitably, all societies exhibit some degree of social inequality based on the distribution of political power, possessions, prestige, or other factors. Joseph Kahl uses the following seven factors to describe the stratification of the population into social classes in the United States:

1. Prestige.
2. Occupation.
3. Possessions, or wealth, or income.
4. Social interactions, pattern of social contacts.
5. Class consciousness.
6. Value orientation.
7. Power or ability to control.[3]

Democratic societies promote the notion that their class systems are open with regard to the preceding dimensions. That is, members of the society can achieve mobility through the acqusition of varying amounts of the preceding factors. Equality of opportunity is promoted to allow any member of society an equal chance to achieve those factors associated with higher rank. Status is achieved through merit. Theoretically, all members of society occupy their positions as a result of merit and not as a result of family wealth, heredity, or other special cultural advantage. Such societies are regarded as meritocracies and offer many opportunities for social mobility in the stratification system.

Many have argued one's social position in the United States is determined by both ascribed (inherited) and acquired (achieved) factors.

Figure 6.5
Unemployment Rates for
Persons 18 Years Old and
Over, By Years of School
Completed: March 1986

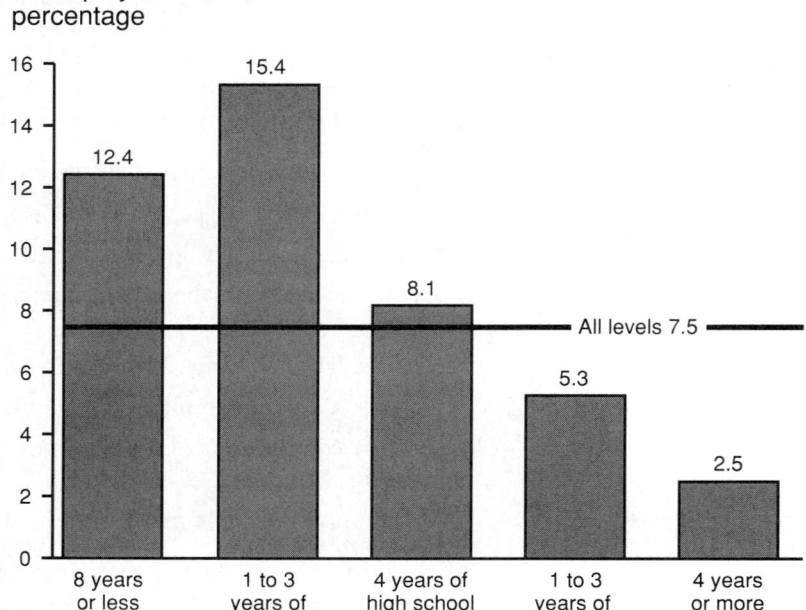

Unemployment rate,
percentage

Source: U.S. Department of Labor, Bureau of Labor Statistics, Office of Employment and Unemployment Statistics, "Educational Attainment of Workers, March 1986."

Females, in spite of educational achievement, frequently face an ascribed position in the economic system because of sex. Ethnicity and race still weigh heavily in the allocation of social position.

Policymakers have recurringly debated the relationship between social class and schooling in the United States. Horace Mann, along with many others, has argued that schools could provide poor people with a means of upward mobility. The evolution of common schools was closely tied to this expectation of social mobility as an outcome of schooling. This expectation explicitly stated that schools will promote openness and flexibility in the social system. Data collected by the Bureau of the Census on unemployment rates and annual income suggests that there is a relationship between level of schooling and social class. This data is summarized in Figures 6.5 and 6.6.

As public schools developed and more students were enrolled from diverse population elements, another dimension of the social class relationship to schooling became apparent. Differences existed in the amount and kind of schooling accessible to members of different social classes. The thesis developed that schooling policy and practice were dictated by social class realities. According to this view, educational programs reflected and transmitted the social class standing the student brought to school. By the 1970s, the possibility of social mobility through schooling was perceived by some as another political myth that needed debunking. Each of these hypotheses concerning the relationship between social class and schooling has generated a considerable amount of debate regarding schooling policy and needs to be explored further.

Figure 6.6
Median Annual Income of Full-time Workers 25 Years Old and Over, By Years of School Completed and Sex: 1985

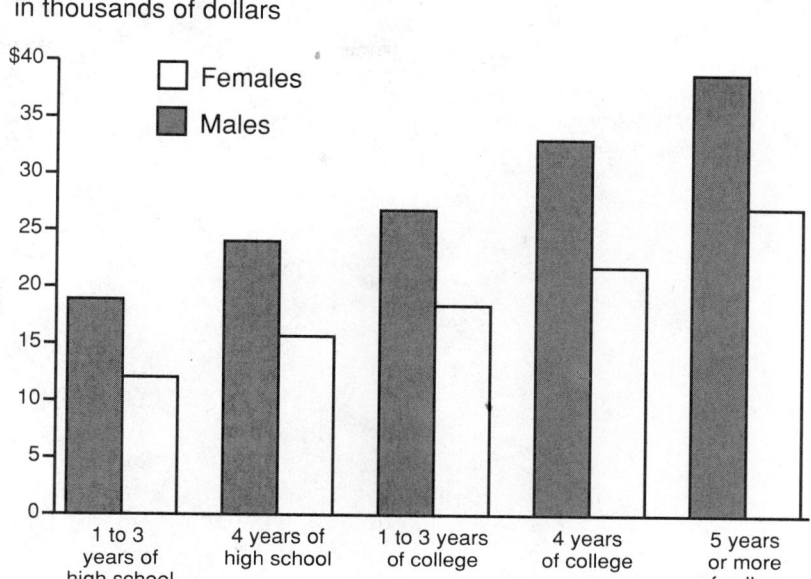

Median annual income, in thousands of dollars

□ Females
■ Males

1 to 3 years of high school | 4 years of high school | 1 to 3 years of college | 4 years of college | 5 years or more of college

Source: U.S. Department of Commerce, Bureau of the Census, *Current Population Reports*, Series P-20, "Money Income of Families and Persons in the United States," and Series P-20, No.154, "Money Income and Poverty Status of Families and Persons in the United States."

Social Class Impacts on Schooling Outcomes

Children in different social classes grow up with different attitudes toward schooling and with different expectations regarding the effect of schooling on their social and economic destiny. Different social classes have different values regarding the work habits and attitudes associated with achievement in school. Upper-class parents tend to view education as a matter of proper rearing and not as an avenue of economic opportunity. Middle-class parents

Photo 6.3
School age populations are changing in the United States, with minority children making up a growing percentage of school enrollments.

Photo 6.4

Parents contribute significantly to student achievement in school through promoting learning activities at home.

tend to see schooling as a means to move into professional careers. Parents of children from different social classes practice different child-rearing procedures and devote differing amounts of material and nonmaterial resources to the development of cognitive and emotive skills of their children. Parents have varying degrees of educational aspirations for their children that are frequently associated with social class status.

Values and practices are communicated to teachers and school personnel in ways that often affect their expectations of students. Teachers begin to expect certain types of behavior and performance of students associated with certain social groupings. This stereotyping results in higher expectations of students from middle-and upper-class families. Children from lower classes are not expected to do as well. Research on the effect of expectations on achievement, such as that done by Rosenthal and Jacobson in *Pygmalion in the Classroom,* suggests that students live up to these expectations. If students are expected to do well, they do well; if they are expected to do poorly, they do poorly. Numerous other research studies indicate that the effects of teacher expectations were overstated in studies done by Rosenthal, Jacobson, and others, since their findings could not be replicated in later research efforts.

In Patricia Sexton's *Education and Income* study, a direct correlation was found between the income level of the parent and the child's performance on achievement tests, placement in ability groups, and curriculum track in high school. Children from lower income backgrounds tended to be placed in lower ability groups and in non-college preparatory tracks. This pedagogical grouping influenced test scores in elementary school and increasingly affected a child's placement and performance as he moved through the later years of schooling. Similar relationships between social class and schooling were detected in Hollingshead's studies completed several decades earlier.[4]

Table 6.2 Relationship Between Achievement Test Results and Students' Socioeconomic Status	PERCENT ABOVE STANDARD		
	MATH	READING	WRITING
GRADE 6			
Not on free lunch	77.9	83.7	87.5
On free lunch	49.2	55.9	63.1
On reduced price lunch	62.7	69.3	76.0
Unknown	55.2	68.6	71.2
GRADE 8			
Not on free lunch	72.1	82.1	84.0
On free lunch	38.4	52.2	40.1
On reduced price lunch	52.3	65.2	73.2
Unknown	57.1	60.9	64.3

Data from the South Carolina statewide Basic Skills Assessment Tests indicate the relationship of economics and social class to achievement test scores. The tests are used to determine whether students are meeting grade-level achievement objectives in math, reading, and writing. The student's socioeconomic status can be estimated by whether the student does or does not participate in a free or a reduced price school lunch program. The data in Table 6.2 summarize the statewide results for sixth- and eighth-grade students for 1986.

Many states, including South Carolina, are beginning to use competency test scores to determine whether students will receive state-approved diplomas for high-school graduation. It appears that a student's socioeconomic status will play an important role in determining who will pass the "exit" test and receive such a diploma.

Periodic evaluations of school achievement collected by the National Assessment of Educational Progress (NAEP) also clearly indicate a close relationship between social class and educational achievement. As shown in Table 6.3, reading scores for selected students in 1979 were directly related to the educational achievement levels of parents and the type of community where the students lived.

Table 6.3 Reading Scores and Socioeconomic Status: 1979	AVERAGE READING SCORE OF STUDENTS (% CORRECT ANSWERS)
PARENTAL EDUCATION	
Not graduated from high school	53
Graduated from high school	60
Attended college	65
TYPE OF COMMUNITY	
Rural disadvantaged	59
Urban disadvantaged	53
Urban advantaged	68

Source: National Assessment of Educational Progress. *Three National Assessments of Reading: Changes in Performance 1970–80* (Denver: Education Commission of the States. 1981).

Figure 6.7
NAEP Reading Proficiency
Scale Scores of Young
Adults Age 21 to 25, By
Race/Ethnicity and
Educational Level: 1985

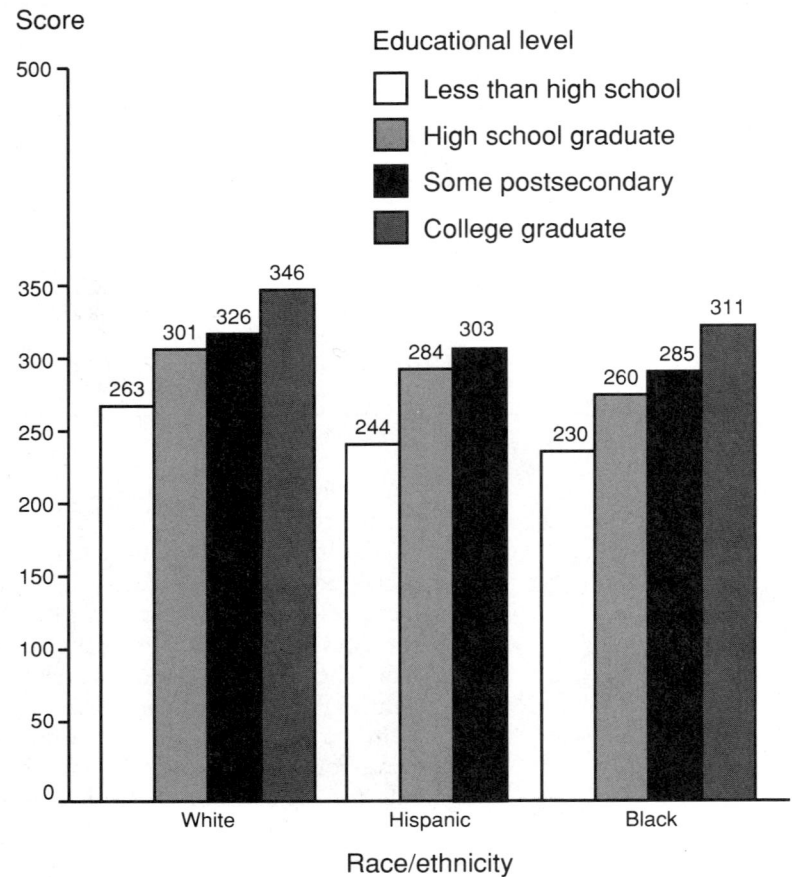

Black young adults, on the average, perform significantly below white young adults on the NAEP reading scale. These differences appear at each level of educational attainment. Hispanic young adults generally perform midway between their black and white peers.

Performance on the NAEP reading scale rises markedly with each additional level of education.
Source: National Assessment of Educational Progress, Young Adult Literacy, 1985.

Numerous studies could be cited that indicate that other educational outcomes are related to ethnic and racial backgrounds of the student. Figure 6.7 shows the relationship between race/ethnicity and educationl level and reading proficiency among adults age twenty-one to twenty-five. Figure 6.8 shows the relationship between race/ethnicity and writing proficiency among fourth-, eighth-, and eleventh-grade students.

Race, ethnicity, social class, and other factors seem to be associated with dropping out of school. Table 6.4 documents how these factors relate to sophomore students who dropped out of school in 1980.

During the 1960s, a school of "revisionist" historians developed a general thesis that historically the public schools in the United States had systematically schooled citizens to serve the interests of the upper middle class. The revisionists claim that since the 1850s, the public schools have attempted to make the children of the lower classes satisfied with low levels of academic performance in school. Public schools were administered in

Figure 6.8
Writing Performance, By
Race/Ethnicity: 1984

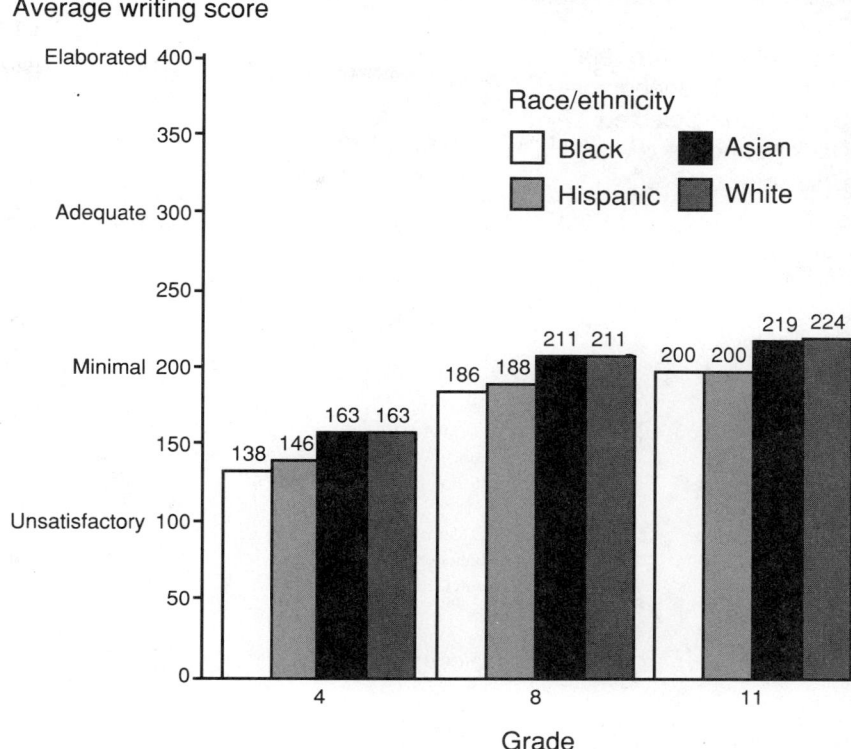

Average writing score

On the average, students at all grade levels were unable to express themselves well enough to ensure that their writing would accomplish its intended purpose. Even in the eleventh grade, average writing performance was only slightly above the *minimal* level.

While the writing performance of eighth graders was considerably better than that of fourth graders, the writing performance of eleventh graders was only slightly better than that of eighth graders.

The writing performance of Asian and white students was higher than that of black and Hispanic students.

Source: National Assessment of Educational Progress, *The Writing Report Card,* 1986.

ways that resulted in the lower-class students entering low-status, low-paying occupations. The revisionist historians claim that sufficient data exists to demonstrate that children of the poor have experienced very little upward social mobility as a result of schooling.[5]

More radical conclusions about the relationship of schooling to social mobility evolved in the 1970s. A number of economists and political scientists argued that education in capitalist societies is bound to work against the interests of the poor. School reforms repeatedly fail to provide opportunity for the lower working-class students. Neo-Marxists see the schools as a part of a larger system designed to produce workers for jobs at the bottom end of the social structure. This occurs through an arrangement that neo-Marxists call the correspondence principle. By emphasizing similar values to those that prevail among families in which poor children grow up, schools merely reproduce the prevailing social class structure.[6]

Table 6.4
Dropout Rates for 1980
High-School Sophomores
By Sex and Selected
Background
Characteristics

	DROPOUT RATE (PERCENTAGE)		
BACKGROUND CHARACTERISTIC	TOTAL	MALE	FEMALE
ALL STUDENTS	13.6	14.7	12.6
RACE/ETHNICITY			
American Indian and Alaskan natives	29.2	27.2	31.8
Hispanic	18.0	18.1	18.0
Black	17.0	20.3	14.1
White	12.2	13.0	11.5
Asian American	3.1	3.5	2.7
SOCIOECONOMIC STATUS			
High	5.2	7.0	3.2
Middle	9.0	9.6	8.3
Low	17.4	17.8	17.1
Unknown	31.6	32.3	30.9
COMMUNITY TYPE			
Urban	18.9	20.8	17.0
Suburban	11.8	12.5	11.0
Rural	12.8	13.6	12.0
GEOGRAPHIC REGION			
Northeast	11.3	13.4	9.0
North Central	12.0	12.2	11.7
South	15.2	16.4	14.0
West	16.6	17.0	16.3
SCHOOL TYPE			
Public	14.5	15.5	13.6
Catholic	2.3	3.2	1.6
Other private	—	—	—
HIGH-SCHOOL PROGRAM			
Academic	4.0	4.5	3.6
General	12.9	12.7	13.0
Vocational/technical	15.1	16.9	13.2

Estimates not presented because of small sample size and high nonresponse in the base-year sample.

Source: U.S. Department of Education, National Center for Education Statistics (1983). *High School Dropouts: Descriptive Information from High School and Beyond*, NCES 83–221b.

The School As a Social Sorter and Selector

School policies and practices that determine "who gets what" educationally give schools a "sorting and selecting" function. If factors other than merit actually determine a student's achievement and the amount of schooling received, questions must be raised concerning schooling's contribution to a meritocracy. Those practices and policies that have come under criticism in recent years include the following:

Use of evaluative instruments to measure aptitude and IQ that tend to favor some groups' cultural experience over that of other groups.

Use of pedagogical grouping programs that tend to isolate some social, racial, or ethnic groups from middle- and upper-income students.

Placement of lower socioeconomic class students into vocational educational programs that result in limited employment opportunities after high school.

Use of high-school curriculum tracking programs that tend to segregate students by race, ethnicity, and social class.

Biases in school guidance and counseling programs that tend to favor college-bound students.

Public school personnel have been responding to the evidence that their institutions have not served some population groups as well as other groups. A large amount of research on effective teaching and effective schools has targeted factors that seek to explain why low-status students do not perform well in school as well as those in-school practices that seem to be associated with achievement among low-status students. The following factors appear to be strongly related to poor academic performance by low-status students:

Inappropriate curriculum materials and instructional strategies.

Lack of parental and peer reinforcement of school-related learning activities.

Lack of previous academic success.

Teacher perceptions of student learning abilities.

Pedagogical grouping patterns resulting in differential treatment of low-status students.

Low standards of performance for low-status students.

Ineffective delivery of services in schools and classrooms with high concentrations of low-status students.

Ronald Edmonds and his colleagues define an effective school as one in which working-class students score as high as middle-class students on tests of basic skills. Their research has identified the following factors that appear to be linked to successful academic achievement in school among working-class students.[7]

Strong instructional leadership on the part of the school principal.

An orderly, humane school environment where students know expectations regarding discipline.

Frequent monitoring of student's academic progress.

High expectations and requirements for all students.

Focus on teaching of basic skills to all students.

Schooling and Social Mobility

Skepticism began to develop about the viability of promoting a meritocracy through schooling in the 1960s. Until that time, most educational historians had generally overlooked the very strong links between social class and schooling outcomes. After the 1960s, Horace Mann's notion that the schools would serve as the "balance wheel of the social machinery" no longer escaped critical analysis. Several factors contributed to the questioning of America's long-standing belief in schooling as the avenue of opportunity.

The 1960s and 1970s were generally a very unsettled period. Many of the country's deepest beliefs and values were under attack. Social scientists challenged traditional assumptions about equality of educational opportunity. Policymakers paid increasing attention to data generated regarding how disadvantaged groups were *actually* served by public schools.

Under the leadership of President Johnson, Congress began to seek remedies to the prevalent inequities in educational opportunity. Congress commissioned a massive national study on inequality of educational opportunity. James Coleman directed the study, which was released in 1966. This study documented the effects of social class on both in-school and out-of-school factors relating to school achievement.[8] Followup studies by the U.S. Commission on Civil Rights[9] and the U.S. Department of Education[10] confirmed Coleman's chief conclusions that the socioeconomic mix of students with which a student attended school and the student's socioeconomic background were the important determinants of academic achievement. These studies cast doubt about the wisdom of attempting to equalize school resources through additional federal funding. Rather, they had the effect of creating additional pressure to racially balance student populations in school to achieve the socioeconomic mix that appeared to be important to school achievement.[11]

In 1972, Christopher Jencks examined evidence of inequalities of educational opportunity; the impact of these inequalities on achievement; and the relationship between schooling, occupational status, and income in the United States. Jencks concluded that educational opportunities in the United States were far from equal but that the inequalities in test scores could not be substantially reduced even if schooling opportunity were equalized. He confirmed Coleman's thesis that family background is the most important determinant of educational achievement. Moreover, Jencks argued that neither family background, cognitive skills, educational attainment, nor occupational status explained the great variations of income in this country. Rather, wealth was largely determined by "luck" and personality. Only large-scale economic measures would reduce income inequality in the United States.[12] However, in a 1979 study, Jencks revised these conclusions and found that family background, test scores, cognitive traits, and amount of schooling were strongly correlated with eventual socioeconomic status and income.[13]

The work by Jencks, Coleman, and others prompted other social scientists to research the connections between educational opportunity and future socioeconomic status in the United States. Many of these studies reached conclusions very different from Coleman and Jencks. Some elements of the preceding debate are continuing in the school reform literature of the 1980s. Different reform reports tie national economic success to improved educational programs and opportunities. It seems most appropriate for policymakers to continue to ask if education is a major factor in determining one's future career and economic success and whether inequitable treatment in school of children from different social classes affects those children's future position in the social structure.

Other discussions confused policymakers as they deliberated public policy relating to schooling and economic opportunity during the 1960s and 1970s. Many psychologists, as a result of research conducted in conjunction with the development and revision of IQ tests, believed that intelligence was determined primarily by heredity. During the 1960s, Arthur Jensen, William Shockley, and Richard Hernstein rekindled this debate by reaching independent conclusions that heredity indeed was the determining factor in accounting for up to eighty percent of the variations in measured intelligence. These authors charged boldly into the policy implications of their conclusions. Hernstein's argument took the following form:(1) "If differences in mental abilities are inherited, and (2) if success requires these abilities, and (3) if earnings and prestige depend on success, then (4) social standing will be based to some extent on the inherited differences among people."[14] Jensen forcefully attacked those scholars, educators, and policymakers who believed children had similar basic potential for mental development. Environmental enrichment and compensatory education programs would never work, according to Jensen, because heredity, not environment, was the primary determinant of intelligence.[15]

State and national policymakers reassessed how many public resources should be devoted to the schooling enterprise during the 1970s in the context of the preceding debate. Skepticism over the efficacy of schools to promote the ideals of meritocracy and openness in the social stratification system must be considered as one of the contributing factors to the financial bind public schools experienced during most of the 1970s.

It appears that the debate is taking a new turn in the school reform literature of the 1980s. Concerns are being expressed about our nation's ability to compete in the evolving world economic market if public schools do not improve their ability to serve all population groups. Probing questions are being raised about how well schools foster the development of the total pool of human resources. Much attention is being directed at sustaining and improving the gains made in school retention and graduation rates for different population groups.

The Debate over Equity Versus Excellence

Critics of the school reform agenda of the 1980s charge that concerns for equity issues are being replaced by an attempt to reconstruct an elitist form of meritocracy that has long prevailed in our educational system. The social value of education is equated with development of human capital sufficient to compete in the global markets. Uniformity and standardization of curriculum and pedagogy are viewed as means to achieve these social ends. Standardized and competitive testing is increasingly promoted as a way to sort and track students. The connection between social class factors and student performance on such tests are subordinated to the greater concern for "excellence." Many of the report writers view the egalitarian emphasis of the social movements of the 1960s and 1970s as responsible for the decline of standards and expectations for the nation's public school students. In essence, according to this view, the promotion of equality has meant a deterioration in commitment to excellence.[16]

It is quite apparent that the ideology concerning the relationships between schooling, social mobility, and social stratification has undergone significant changes over the past thirty years. It is also quite clear that the changing ideology influenced school funding, curricula, pedagogy, and a host of other important educational policy issues. One could predict that the way we define social expectations for schools in the years ahead will have a strong impact on future directions of educational policy.

Summary

Our society is engaged in a heated debate over what it should expect from public schools. This debate affects the way people judge the schools, because different perceptions about the social outcomes of schooling lead to different bases for public evaluation of schooling.

This chapter has reviewed two basic dimensions of school/society relations:(1) the social outcomes that society should expect of schools and (2) the impact that socioeconomic and cultural factors have on a student's schooling experience. The socialization of children and youth is a major assignment given to public schools in our culture, and many forces and factors affect the school's role in socialization. Changes in the family, the pace of change, policies promoting cultural pluralism, and changes in the size and characteristics of the school-age cohort are examples of forces outside the school that affect the school's ability to socialize children and youth.

Since all societies have some type of social stratification system, social institutions are used to promote the preferred stratification arrangements. Americans have generally been very optimistic about using schooling to promote a meritocracy. Until the 1960s, there was little serious questioning of the link between the amount and kind of schooling and one's future economic status and success. Schools could promote social mobility in the social class system and could sort and select on the basis of merit in an objective and democratic manner. Such assumptions came under critical review in the 1960s.

Researchers documented the strong and lasting effects of a student's socioeconomic background on the student's school experience. More pessimistic assessments were announced about the contribution of schooling to one's future socioeconomic status in our culture. Basic policy questions were debated about where society should invest its resources to promote the principles of equity and justice. More recently, research on effective schools seemed to suggest that it is possible for schools to help students overcome the influences of disadvantaged socioeconomic backgrounds.

Debates over school/society relationships affect educational professionals in many ways. The social expectations of schools help to determine the tasks that educators perform in school. Beliefs about the efficacy of schools to promote social outcomes also determine the relative amount of resources devoted to schools to do their tasks.

Key Words

Socialization	Stratification
Enculturation	Meritocracy
Acculturation	Ascribed status
Latchkey children	Achieved status
Demographics	Revisionists
Age cohort	Neo-Marxists

Discussion Questions

1. How do social class factors affect school success or failure in the United States?

2. Are there limits to the socialization functions that can be assigned to the public schools?

3. Do you agree with the neo-Marxist and revisionist arguments? Why?

4. Are investments in schooling society's best hope for producing a personnel source that will keep the U.S. economic system competitive in the world economy?

5. Is the school an appropriate institution to address problems relating to AIDS, teen pregnancy, drug and alcohol abuse, and discrimination? Why?

For Further Reading

Bastain, Ann, et al. *Choosing Equality: The Case for Democratic Schooling.* Philadelphia: Temple University Press,1985.

Bowles, Samuel, and Gintis, Herbert. *Schooling in Capitalist America.* New York: Basic Books, 1976.

The Forgotten Half: Non-College Youth in America. Washington, D.C.: William T. Grant Foundation: Commission on Work, Family, and Citizenship, January 1988.

Fussel, Paul. *Class.* New York: Summit, 1983.

Goodlad, John I. *A Place Called School.* New York: McGraw-Hill, 1984.

Levine, Daniel R. and Havighurst, Robert J. *Society and Education.* Boston: Allyn & Bacon, 1984.

Ravitch, Diane. "The Revisionists Revisited: Studies in the Historiography of American Education," *Proceedings of the National Academy of Education 4.* Palo Alto, California, 1977.

Notes

1. See *The Forgotten Half: Non-College Youth in America* (Washington, D.C.: William T. Grant Foundation, 1988).

2. "Projection 2000, "*Occupational Outlook Quarterly,* U.S. Department of Labor, Fall 1987, p.3.

3. Joseph Kahl, *The American Class Structure* (New York: Holt, Rinehart, & Winston, 1957), pp. 184–220.

4. A. B. Hollingshead, *Elmtown's Youth* (New York: John Wiley, 1959).

5. See Diane Ravitch, "The Revisionist Revisited: Studies in the Historiography of American Education, "*Proceedings of the National Academy of Education, 4* (Palo Alto, California, 1977).

6. See Samuel Bowles and Herbert Gintis, *Schooling in Capitalist America* (New York: Basic Books, 1976).

7. Ronald R. Edmonds, "Programs of School Improvement: An Overview," *Educational Leadership,* December 1982, pp. 4–11.

8. James S. Coleman et al., *Equality of Educational Opportunity* (Washington, D.C.: U.S. Government Printing Office, 1966).

9. U.S. Commission on Civil Rights, *Racial Isolation in the Schools* (Washington, D.C.: U.S. Government Printing Office, 1967).

10. U.S. Office of Education, *A Study of Our Nation's Schools* (Washington, D.C.: U.S. Government Printing Office, 1972).

11. School desegregation data collected during this period of time affirms the impact the Coleman report had on school desegregation.

12. Christopher Jencks et al., *Inequality: A Reassessment of the Effect of Family and Schooling in America* (New York: Basic Books, 1972).

13. ———. *Who Gets Ahead: The Determinants of Economic Success in America* (New York: Basic Books, 1979).

14. Richard J. Hernstein, "IQ," *The Atlantic,* September 1971, p. 58.

15. Arthur R. Jensen, "How Much Can We Boost IQ and Scholastic Achievement?" *Harvard Educational Review,* Winter 1969, pp. 1–123.

16. Ann Bastain et al., *Choosing Equality: The Case for Democratic Schooling.* (Philadelphia: Temple University Press, 1985), p. 22.

7 Curriculum and Instruction

"The curriculum must consist essentially of disciplined study in five great areas: (1) command of mother tongue and the systematic study of grammar, literature, and writing, (2) mathematics, (3) sciences, (4) history, (5) foreign language."

Arthur Bestor, *The Restoration of Learning* (1955)

"(Curriculum is) the planned and guided learning experiences and intended outcomes, formulated through systematic reconstruction of knowledge and experience, under the auspices of the school, for the learners' continuous and willful growth in personal-social competence."

Daniel and Laura Tanner, *Curriculum Development: Theory Into Practice* (1975)

A major product of educational policymaking is curriculum, generally defined as the body of educational experiences sponsored by the school. Although curriculum is best understood as policy, it is included in this part of the text because it offers a bridge between the foundations of education treated thus far and policy issues to be treated in the next part. It supplies this bridge because a number of historical, philosophical, and social issues are directly involved in the discussion of curriculum.

Curriculum—including its subdivision, instruction—is that aspect of educational policy that answers the questions, What do we teach? and How do we teach it? Given the tremendous diversity of opinion toward the variety of issues addressed in this book, it should be no great surprise that answers to these questions differ greatly. Some of that diversity is reflected in the opening quotations. While Bestor describes the curriculum in terms of the teaching of traditional subject matter, Tanner and Tanner choose to emphasize school practices that foster individual growth in what they call personal-social competence. Very real differences exist between these two ideas of curriculum in terms of the assumptions they bring to questions of curriculum development. Given the pluralistic nature of American society, curriculum tends to be shaped through the interplay of this variety of assumptions, interests, values, and demands. This chapter focuses on issues and models of curriculum, those individuals and groups who participate in curriculum development, the varieties of curricular organizational patterns, instructional models, and the effects of the varying curricula on learners. Throughout the chapter, emphasis will be placed upon the relationship of curricular practice to educational goals.

Curricular Issues: A Historical Perspective

While curricular issues are implicit—and often explicit—in much of the material already presented in this book, it is useful to review some of the trends that have influenced curriculum development and practice. This review will be restricted, however, to twentieth-century developments—in part because formal curriculum study is a twentieth-century phenomenon, but also because the dimensions of the early twentieth-century debate over curriculum and instruction (refer to Chapter 4) so clearly anticipate those of today.

In the early years of the twentieth-century, curriculum was largely shaped by the concerns of college educators. High schools attempted to respond to the reports of the Committee of Ten and the Committee on College Entrance Requirements, the latter of which recommended four units of foreign language, two units of English, two units of mathematics, one unit each of science and history, and six units of electives (chosen from the nine areas described by the Committee of Ten) for college entrance. Widespread adoption of the Carnegie Unit also fostered this emphasis. As a result, a typical vertical organization of the schools involved an eight-year elementary education followed by four years of high school. Elementary education emphasized basic reading and writing skills with a general introduction to the various academic disciplines (e.g., history, geography). High schools attempted to provide a more in-depth study of some combination of the academic areas prescribed by the reports. Alternatives to this pattern could be found, of course, in manual training and vocational schools. Another variation was the introduction of the junior high school.

A major concern of Charles W. Eliot, guiding spirit behind the work of the Committee of Ten, was that high-school students were exposed to the academic disciplines too late in their formal education careers. He argued that many subjects could be introduced in the seventh and eighth grades. One result of this argument was the Committee of Ten's recommendation that studies in algebra, geometry, natural science, and foreign languages begin before the ninth grade. This notion was endorsed by a number of other committees, and the "junior" high school—composed of the seventh, eighth, and ninth grades—was born.

Proponents of the new organization argued that the junior high school would provide a number of benefits besides earlier exposure to high-school academic subjects. Studies of enrollment patterns indicated that a large number of students dropped out of school after their eighth year, so the new organization would tend to add another year of education for many. Despite the dropout rate, however, enrollment in high schools expanded rapidly as a result of population growth, child labor restrictions, and the passage of compulsory attendance laws. Overcrowding would be partially alleviated through the creation of the junior high school, removing the ninth grade from the high school. By the early twentieth century, junior high schools were beginning to appear on the educational landscape.[1]

Turn-of-the-century educators also faced other curricular questions. Given that academic subjects were the heart of the curriculum, how should these subjects be organized and taught? Here the ideas of Charles A. McMurry (1856–1929) and Frank W. McMurry (1862–1936) were reflective of the thinking of the period. After teaching for some years in the elementary schools, the McMurrys went abroad to study at the University of Jena, where Johann Friedrich Herbart's (1776–1841) ideas were most influential. Herbart argued that effective teaching depended upon an understanding of psychological principles. A key psychological principle, he felt, was that of apperception, a combination of memory and perception. Learning was most effective when children apperceived, or cognitively assimilated the information to be learned and related it to their own past experiences. To effect this, students of Herbart came up with a five-step teaching process: 1) preparation, 2) presentation, 3) association, 4) generalization, and 5) application.

Upon their return to the states, the McMurrys advocated Herbartian ideas with missionary zeal, Charles at the George Peabody College for Teachers and Frank at Teacher's College, Columbia University. The McMurrys felt that Herbart's ideas provided a systematic method for curriculum development—for selecting, organizing, and delivering subject matter. Charles, for example, wrote some thirty books and developed a course of study for the elementary years demonstrating the selection and arrangement of ideas for instruction according to Herbart's five steps. He also described what he felt were the best teaching strategies for specific subjects.[2]

The influence of Herbart waned rapidly during the Progressive Era, but others reflecting a child-centered orientation remained influential. It was during this period that John Dewy articulated a number of his educational ideas. Dewey, it should be remembered, attempted to develop in the school a microcosm of society, an "embryonic community," where manual training, shopwork, sewing, and cooking—occupations reflective of life in the larger society—were pursued. "We are no longer concerned," he wrote, "with the abstract appraisal of studies by the measuring rod of culture or discipline. Our problem is rather to study the typical necessities of social life, and the actual nature of the individual in his specific needs and capacities."[3] Thus, the curriculum at Dewey's experimental school was organized around four human impulses: the social impulse, the constructive impulse, the impulse to investigate and experiment, and the expressive or artistic impulse. Traditional subject matter was introduced as it informed and broadened children's experiences. Others also emphasized the child's interests as the basis for learning. Junius Merian's experimental school at the University of Missouri organized the school's learning experiences around the normal activities of children—observation, play, stories, and handwork.[4]

Other elements of progressive thought also influenced many educators' concept of the junior high school. Originally perceived as merely a "junior" high school, the junior high school during the Progressive Era came to be seen as a special, transitional school for young adolescents. Dewey's emphasis upon the experiences and interests of the learner, when combined with contemporary study of the psychology of adolescence—most notably that of G. Stanley Hall—provided a new rationale for the junior high school. Most children entered adolescence between the ages of twelve and fourteen, and given the special needs of students during this period of their lives, it seemed logical to place them in the same school. Of course, adolescents varied greatly in their interests and abilities, so another function perceived by advocates was the provision of greater exploration and guidance. Social efficiency educators—those interested in efficiently training individuals for their likely adult roles in society—gave the junior high school the job of providing exposure to vocational courses: business, home economics, shop. In this manner, the junior high school would serve as a steppingstone to the diversification of curricula (academic, vocational, etc.) in the high school. Thus, the exploratory role of the junior high school was established. (In many areas of the country today, the role of junior high school has been taken over by the middle school.)

It was in the context of social efficiency education that the Progressive Era had perhaps its most far-reaching impact on curriculum: the introduction of scientific curriculum making. As noted earlier, schools were seen as institutions for the socialization of children into useful adult roles (beneficial for both individuals and society). To achieve this goal, models of scientific management were applied to schooling. Measurement of student abilities through the new IQ tests (developed during World War I) helped educators predict student areas of strength and weakness and students' contributions to society. Given this information, curriculum developers could design appropriate educational experiences for all children. Thus, the concern for scientific analysis and measurement carried over into the area of curriculum development.

In 1918, Franklin Bobbitt published *The Curriculum*, a book in which he advocated the formulation of a curriculum based upon a scientific analysis of the activities of adult life.[5] These activities, he argued, should be translated into specific objectives. Later, in *How To Make a Curriculum* (1924), Bobbitt prescribed a series of five steps in curriculum making: 1) analysis of human experience, 2) job analysis, 3) deriving objectives, 4) selecting objectives, and 5) planning in detail.[6] Bobbitt's work was supplemented by that of W. W. Charters. In *Curriculum Construction* (1923), Charters argued that curricularists should first identify the ideals and activities of socially efficient persons, analyze these ideals and activities into objectives, and finally arrange the objectives in order of their importance for children.[7] Thus, Bobbitt and Charters provided cookbooklike procedures for developing curriculum.

A further contribution to systematic curriculum development was made by Hollis L. Caswell. Synthesizing a number of the developments just discussed, Caswell argued that curriculum design should be based on three areas of concern: children's interests, social functions, and organized knowledge. Furthermore, Caswell advocated recurring curriculum revision. That is, curricula would need to be revised periodically to ensure that the school continued to meet the personal and social needs of the student. Thus, for Caswell, curriculum development became a process.[8]

The classic approach to curriculum as process appeared in 1949. In *Basic Principles of Curriculum and Instruction*, Ralph W. Tyler organized curriculum development around four basic questions:

1. What educational purposes should the school seek to attain?

2. How can learning experiences be selected that are likely to be useful in attaining these objectives?

3. How can learning experiences be organized for effective instruction?

4. How can the effectiveness of learning experiences be evaluated?

Tyler argued that the purposes of the school should be determined based upon the needs and interests of the learners, the needs of society, and aspects of the traditional academic subject matter. In developing their purposes, or goals, schools were to consider both their philosophies of education and what they knew of the psychology of learning. Tyler's emphasis upon evaluation was an important addition to the process.[9]

Tyler's series of questions became the basis for the vast majority of curriculum development models that followed. For example, they provided the framework for Hilda Taba's well-known approach to curriculum development:

1. Diagnosis of need.

2. Formulation of objectives.

3. Selection of content.

4. Organization of content.

5. Selection of learning experiences.

6. Organization of learning experiences.

7. Determination of what to evaluate and the ways and means of doing it.[10]

In short, Tyler's questions provided a model for the process of curriculum development that others have adopted or adapted.

Generally speaking, today's models of curriculum development recognize four areas of importance in the development of educational goals: (1) student needs and interests (usually based upon an understanding of child growth and development), (2) the needs of society, (3) knowledge from the academic disciplines, and (4) knowledge of the learning process. The models often categorize the various kinds of goals and objectives that might be drawn from these sources: cognitive, dealing with intellectual skills; affective, dealing with values; and psychomotor, dealing with physical skills.[11] (See Box 7.1) The curriculum development process includes the establishment of objectives, decisions concerning content and learning experiences, and the development of evaluation procedures. Yet despite the existence of systematic models, most curricular change occurs in a haphazard fashion, the result of the continuing debate over the nature and purpose

Table 7.1 Contributors to Formal Curriculum Development	CONTRIBUTOR	CONTRIBUTION
	Charles A. & Frank W. McMurry	Adaptation of Herbartian ideas to a systematic method for curriculum development: selecting, organizing, and delivering subject matter.
	John Dewey	Organization of subject matter around four human impulses: social, constructive, investigative and experimental, and expressive or artistic.
	Franklin Bobbitt	Curriculum based upon scientific analysis of activities of adult life translated into specific objectives.
	W. W. Charters	Curriculum based upon identification of ideals and activities of socially efficient persons, translated into objectives, and arranged in order of importance to children.
	Hollis L. Caswell	Curriculum should be based upon three areas of concern: children's interests, social functions, and organized knowledge. Periodic revision important.
	Ralph W. Tyler	Curriculum as process revolving around four basic questions: 1) What educational purposes should the school seek to attain? 2) How can learning experiences be selected that are likely to be useful in attaining these objectives? 3) How can learning experiences be organized for effective instruction? 4) How can the effectiveness of learning experiences be evaluated?

of American schools. James B. MacDonald captures this aspect of American curricular change:

> The development of the curriculum in the American public schools has been primarily an accident. A description of what curriculum exists is essentially a political and/or ethical document rather than a scientific or technical one. It is a statement which indicates the outcomes of a very complex interaction of groups, pressures, and events which are most often sociopolitical in motivation and which result in decisions about what ought to be.[12]

Given this nature of American curriculum development, attention must be turned to the participants and contexts that do, in fact, shape curriculum.

The Shaping of Curriculum: Context and Participants

The preceding historical survey introduced us to a number of the issues related to curriculum development. Most significant, of course, is the continuing controversy over the goals of education. Those who see the school as an institution designed to provide instruction in the basic academic subjects will describe the curriculum in ways quite different from those who argue that schools should foster the development of the "whole child." The staying power of the basic description of curriculum formulated by the Committee of Ten and the Committee on College Entrance Requirements, however, should not be missed. Implicit in the debate over goals is a further debate concerning methodology. While some educators

Box 7.1
Taxonomies of
Educational
Objectives

Educators today frequently rely upon taxonomies in the development of curricular goals and objectives. These taxonomies, which suggest hierarchies of abilities, from simple to sophisticated, that students should develop, are divided into three domains: cognitive (intellectual skills), affective (attitudes and values), and psychomotor (physical coordination).

Cognitive Objective	Performance
Knowledge	Simple recall
Comprehension	Translation, interpretation, extrapolation
Application	Use of information in a new situation
Analysis	Breaking entity into parts for study of relationships to those parts
Synthesis	Creating a new entity from diverse parts
Evaluation	Making a judgment based on criteria

Affective Objective	Performance
Receiving	Attending to certain phenomena
Responding	Complying with given expectations by attending or reaction to stimuli
Valuing	Unforced display of behavior consistent with single belief or attitude
Organizing	Displaying commitment to set of values
Characterizing	Displaying behavior consistent with internalized values

Psychomotor Objective	Performance
Imitation	Observes skill and attempts to repeat it
Manipulation	Performs skills according to instructions rather than imitation
Precision	Independently reproduces skill with accuracy
Articulation	Harmoniously combines more than one skill in sequence
Naturalization	Completes one or more skills with ease and becomes automatic with limited physical or mental exertion

would develop strategies that require students to process information in much the same way academic specialists do, others would emphasize entirely different approaches based upon children's experiences.

A second major point of the previous section was that a systematic process for curriculum development has evolved over the years. As a matter of fact, curriculum development has become an area of specialization within the professional education field.

Finally, the point was made that much curricular change results from the interaction of a variety of viewpoints and is often the result of wider sociopolitical concerns. It is this final point that leads us to a consideration of the various contexts and participants that influence curricular change. The following analysis begins at the level of the school itself, then moves to the community, state, and national levels.

The School

The school is the institution with the primary responsibility for delivering the curriculum. Many factors within the school, ranging from the students and teachers to the actual physical aspects of the school, influence that delivery. Even within the school, the "curriculum" is a compromise between these many factors.

Students   In curricula developed by progressive educators, the students play a key role. Student interests and concerns are frequently cited as a starting point in planning for instruction, and student participation in planning is advocated. In many middle, junior high, and high schools, students have direct responsibilities for a number of experiences provided by the school—student government, club activities, and publications. In some schools, students serve on a variety of advisory committees. In general, however, active student participation in formal curriculum planning is limited.

Students do, however, have a tremendous influence informally. While they may not participate in decisions concerning what is taught, they obviously have a good deal of control over what is learned. And they do influence what is taught—by avoiding courses and teachers they don't like. Perhaps the greatest way in which students affect the curriculum, however, is through the characteristics they bring to the classroom. Students of different ages, abilities, and socioeconomic or cultural backgrounds have different needs, different learning styles, different capabilities. Any curriculum that ignores the developmental characteristics of children is not likely to be successful in achieving its goals.

Teachers   Many curricularists argue that there is much to the old saying, "Teachers are the curriculum." Regardless of goals and objectives that provide the framework for teachers' work, teachers' differences will influence both teaching and learning. Teachers who are more sensitive to individual student needs are likely to present the same material to different students in different ways. Teachers who feel that their strength lies in a particular instructional style may tend to emphasize it and thus influence the delivery of the curriculum. Teachers who feel especially secure in their training in a particular discipline may have their own perceptions about what is and is not important for students to learn. In this regard, Virgil

Herrick once proposed three levels or degrees of teacher responsibility in making curricular decisions. Teachers on the first level merely follow the textbook and school policies. Teachers on the second, more active, level make decisions concerning learning activities and the amount of time that should be spent on particular subjects. Teachers on the third level go beyond the textbook, develop other sources and resources, select concepts and learning activities for emphasis, and provide smooth transitions from learning experience to learning experience.[13]

Teachers also influence curriculum through the various teacher organizations to which they belong. Professional organizations like the National Council for Teachers of English (NCTE) and the National Council for the Social Studies (NCSS) conceptualize issues, develop materials, and thus influence the direction curricular developments take. Teacher unions influence legislation and policy on both the state and national levels. Collective bargaining agreements may include elements that reflect curricular concerns.

Principals   Although the professional literature frequently emphasizes the role of the principal as instructional leader and key factor in curriculum development, most principals actually spend little time on curriculum matters. Rather, their time is devoted to a myriad of other managerial duties. It appears, however, according to some research, that where principals are actively involved in curriculum and instruction, schools are more effective.[14] Also, principals may foster curriculum development by promoting an atmosphere conducive to creativity.

School Building   The physical aspects of the school building itself influence the curriculum. If, for example, desks in classrooms are bolted to the floor, limitations are placed upon the kinds of teaching strategies teachers can use. If, on the other hand, a school building is designed with open spaces and few walls, as were many elementary and middle schools in the late 1960s and early 1970s, there are other implications for the delivery of the curriculum. The absence of facilities also has implications for the curriculum: too few labs, no art or music rooms, no computers, all are obviously significant.

The Hidden Curriculum   Much of the teaching and learning that go on in the school are not a part of the formal curriculum. For example, certain values are taught when students are expected to be on time and to deport themselves within prescribed guidelines. Many educators believe that if ninth-grade junior high school students have to line up under the supervision of a teacher and march quietly to the cafeteria for lunch, a definite message is conveyed to the students concerning their capacity for responsible behavior. Expectations of students from diverse socioeconomic backgrounds frequently differ. This may have a significant impact upon what these students are offered academically and upon what they learn.

Superintendent and Staff   Despite the fact that their time is divided among many managerial duties, superintendents are key figures in curriculum development. As principal administrative officer in the district, the

Photo 7.1
Local and state groups attempt to influence curriculum.

superintendent is responsible for carrying out decisions of the school board as well as state and federal mandates. The superintendent must balance demands for change with the need for stability within the system and is ultimately responsible for the professional development of his or her teachers. In many larger school districts, an assistant superintendent for curriculum is responsible for the curricular duties of the superintendent.

The Community

Local autonomy is a tradition in American schooling. In recent years, however, the influence of the local community in curricular affairs has diminished. Still, community concerns can and do play a significant role in the development of curriculum.

Local School Board   The local school board is the body that represents the community in school affairs. Technically, it is the educational policy-making agency for the school system. In recent years, however, state and national judicial and legislative branches have played a much larger role in educational decision making, thus diminishing that of the local board. Board members increasingly depend upon the advice of professionals in formulating policy.

Local Government   City and county lawmakers play an indirect role in shaping curriculum. If taxes do not produce the revenue a school system needs, programs are cut back or out. This is particularly true where school systems have little or no fiscal independence. Local councils and courts may also serve as arenas in which conflicting demands on the schools are resolved.

The Public   Formal public involvement in curriculum development is minimal. In recent years, however, attempts to more greatly involve the wider community in school affairs have been implemented. A number of school systems have established citizen advisory committees for their schools—sometimes as a result of state legislation. To avoid problems over educational materials, many systems include community representatives on textbook adoption committees.

The ways in which the community informally influences curriculum are myriad. The socioeconomic character of a community influences curriculum in both obvious and subtle ways, through funding levels as well as educational expectations and aspirations. The variety, or lack thereof, of other institutions serving children—YW and YMCA's, Scouts, 4-H Clubs, recreation leagues—helps shape demands placed upon the schools. Local mores influence what is taught. Teachers will avoid issues that they know are controversial.

In fact, local concern over curricular matters increases most dramatically when controversial issues surface. Groups tend to develop around special interests—those advocating a particular program, such as gifted education, or those opposed to some aspect of school life, such as the opposition of religious fundamentalists to secular humanism in the schools. Among the most active of citizens' groups are those that oppose tax increases.

State Government

In recent years, state governments have become more and more influential in the shaping of curriculum. Based on state constitutional provisions, the power of state legislatures to influence what is taught is unequaled. Furthermore, as more laws are passed, the influence of state departments of education over curriculum delivery increases. State reliance upon accrediting agencies also plays a role in curriculum.

Legislatures   State legislatures are tremendously influential in shaping curriculum. They may and routinely do prescribe the number of course credits required for graduation; specific courses, such as U.S. government, economics, or health and physical education; and the number of hours per week spent on a specific subject, such as reading, in an elementary school. Through statewide adoption procedures, many state legislatures control the textbooks used in the schools. State laws prescribe the qualifications of professional educators. State funds may foster specific curricular projects, and their availability (or absence) may promote (or impede) a variety of elements influencing curriculum, from more equitable per-pupil expenditures to the building of physical plants. In recent years, under the banner of the minimal competency movement and fueled by reports such as *A Nation At Risk*, state legislatures have tended to play a more significant role in curriculum development—proportionately reducing local control.

Boards and Departments of Education   When state legislatures pass education laws, the implementation of those laws is usually left to the state boards and departments of education. Boards may be responsible for developing the specific regulations that put the laws into effect, and departments of education are the administrative agencies responsible for the actual execution of state educational policy. Therefore, as state legislatures play a larger role in curriculum, so generally do state departments of education. While state departments of education have traditionally made curriculum specialists or consultants available to the schools, in recent years the monitoring role of these agents has increased considerably. The net effect, of course, is the reduction of local control of curriculum.

Accrediting Agencies   A number of states rely upon accrediting procedures to help maintain the quality of their schools. Standards may be developed by the state department itself or by professional or regional organizations (e.g., the National Association of School Principals or the Southern Association of Colleges and Schools). The standards that schools must meet to receive accreditation generally focus upon a wide variety of factors—from number and variety of courses to teaching strategies, pupil-teacher ratios, and physical facilities. These requirements obviously influence curriculum, and schools must adjust their programs when new standards are mandated. Thus, accrediting agencies may play a significant role in curriculum development.

The University   College entrance requirements traditionally have had an influence on school curricula. The influence of the Committee of Ten at the turn of the century has already been noted, but the tradition continues. In the 1970s, as colleges dropped foreign languages from their admission requirements, the quantity of such courses in the high schools (and the numbers of students taking them) dropped. In the 1980s, colleges began to reinstate foreign-language requirements, and high-school curricula for the college bound will certainly reflect that change.

National Influences

National influences on curriculum development are by no means limited to the federal government. Testing agencies, publishers, foundations, and pressure groups may all influence the curriculum that is ultimately delivered to the student.

The Federal Government   The role of the federal government in American education has been discussed at length in other sections of this book. The federal government was particularly involved in curricular development activities from the late 1950s to the early 1970s. Under the auspices of the National Science Foundation and the U.S. Office of Education and funded by the National Defense Education Acts, a great number of curricular projects were pursued. These projects ranged from those that produced materials reflecting the "new math," "new sciences," and "new social studies" to those concerned with such topics as career education. Furthermore, federal funds were made available to schools that implemented project materials, the effect of which was to disseminate these curricular materials nationally. Other pieces of federal legislation—usually responding to some national concern or pressing national issue—have had a tremendous impact on curriculum. The Civil Rights Act of 1964, the Elementary and Secondary School Act of 1965, and the Education for All Handicapped Children Act of 1975 (P.L. 94–142) offer examples. Legislation such as the Morrill Act of 1862 and the Smith-Hughes Act of 1917 reflect a traditional concern on the part of the federal government over vocational education.

In the 1980s, as a result of criticism of federal activities in education and the ascension to power of political groups opposed to federal involvement, the federal role in curriculum appears to have diminished. President Ronald Reagan, for example, rather than promote federal funding, chose to use his office as a "bully pulpit" to promote educational reform by the states. Nevertheless, the Reagan administration's emphasis upon the academic essentials shaped the nature of educational debate throughout the decade. (See, for example, the discussions of perennialism and essentialism in Chapter 5).

Curriculum is also influenced by decisions of the federal courts. Chapter 8 discusses how the courts become involved in educational issues as the result of questions concerning constitutional rights. Chapter 12 outlines cases related to the question of equal educational opportunity, while Chapter 13 reviews significant cases related to religion and the schools. Many of the issues that appear before the courts have specific curricular implications. A 1986 district court decision in Tennessee (later overturned in circuit court) required school systems to provide alternative materials to students whose religious beliefs are violated by the standard materials used.[15]

Testing Agencies   One aspect of the minimal competency movement and educational reform by the states has been the widespread use of standardized tests to measure student performance. Whether designed to or not, test scores are frequently used either explicitly or implicitly to hold schools and teachers accountable. Where this is the case, teachers tend to "teach to the tests." That which is tested, then, becomes the curriculum.

Publishers   The most widely used materials in the schools are those developed by commercial publishers. Most teachers rely upon textbooks as their basic sources of information, while many seem to rely upon textbooks almost exclusively (refer to Virgil Herrick's proposed levels of teacher involvement discussed earlier in this section). As a result, research shows that nearly seventy-five percent of students' classroom time and ninety percent of their homework is structured around commercially produced materials.[16] Obviously, publishers play a significant role in curriculum development.

Foundations   Foundations influence curriculum through funding and research. For example, the Ford Foundation was actively involved in supporting the academic curricular innovations of the 1960s and, later, the alternative school movement.[17] In recent years, the Carnegie Foundation has sponsored research on the teaching profession that has had an impact on the educational reform movement in the states.

Pressure Groups   Professional educational organizations have already been mentioned in the context of teacher influences on curriculum. Groups like the National Education Association and American Federation of Teachers also operate on the national level. These groups lobby congress and effectively use the mass media in support of their viewpoints. They are by no means alone. Other groups interested in education, such as the National Congress of Parents and Teachers (PTA) and the Council for Basic Education (advocates of basic skills), make themselves heard. The School Boards Association often plays an adversarial role with regard to demands of the teacher organizations. Groups whose concerns are not solely focused on education may also influence curriculum. In other chapters of this book, the influence of such groups as the National Association for the Advancement of Colored People (NAACP), the National Organization for Women (NOW), and various groups of fundamentalist Christians has been noted. Even labor unions and major corporations are in the curriculum business, frequently offering free instructional materials to teachers.

Who Decides What Is Taught?

It is clear that in reality many factors and individuals play roles in curriculum formation. Which are most influential? Perhaps the best answer to that question is found in the following statement by curriculum policy analysts Michael Kirst and Decker Walker:

> A mapping of the leverage points for curriculum policymaking in local schools would be exceedingly complex. It would involve three levels of government, and numerous private organization foundations, accrediting associations, national testing agencies, textbook-software companies, and interest groups (such as the NAACP or the John Birch Society). Moreover, there would be a configuration of leverage points within a particular local school system including teachers, department heads, the assistant superintendent for instruction, the superintendent, and the school board. Cutting across all of government would be the pervasive influence of various celebrities, commentators, interest groups, and the journalists who use the mass media to disseminate their views on curriculum. It would be very useful if we were able to quantify the amount of influence of each of these groups of individuals and show input-output interactions for just one school system. Unfortunately, this is considerably beyond the state of the art.[18]

It is difficult, then, to tell which groups are most influential. There is no doubt, however, that many factors and individuals play a role in the development of curriculum. The point might be illustrated more graphically by focusing on one element of curriculum and instruction, the textbook. The following section briefly considers the example of an American history textbook, the content of which might be influenced by any number of interests.

Case Study in Curriculum: A History Textbook

Who influences the material that goes into a textbook? Of course, the publishing company—through its editors—has the final say, but publishers are sensitive to the concerns of both professional educators and the public. Therefore, many groups influence the content. The following case study of a history textbook will consider just a few such groups.

Subject Matter Specialists   Textbooks today are generally written by teams of authors, usually including at least one subject matter specialist (in

Photo 7.2
In many cases, the textbook is the curriculum.

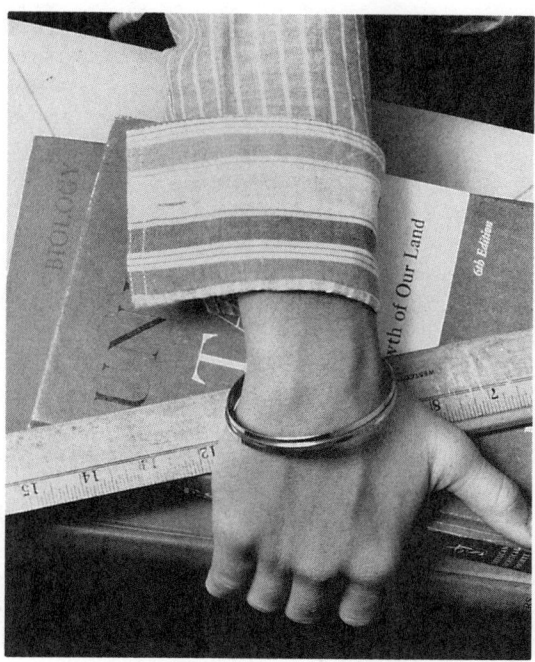

this case, a professional historian) and, frequently, an educator. The historian provides the basic content, attempting to balance the need to provide traditional narrative (and coverage of traditional topics) with a desire to reflect the most recent scholarship in the field. If recent scholarship provides new insights into a historical period, the phenomenon known as revisionism—that is, reinterpretation—may occur. If a historian is a specialist in a particular field (for example, social history or political history), he or she may very well have a tendency to emphasize particular kinds of historical information.

Educators   Educators influence the content of texts in a number of ways. Educators are generally included on writing teams, and these educators supply the pedagogical materials associated with the text—end of section, chapter, and unit exercises as well as student workbooks and tests. Thus, they too may influence the "curriculum" in specific ways. They may, for example, emphasize critical thinking or other higher-order thinking or information-processing skills in their exercises.

Classroom teachers also influence the content of texts. Publishers will frequently survey classroom teachers before the production or revision of a text as a part of their market analyses. Data derived in such a way may indicate strengths and shortcomings in current texts, topics that teachers would like to see emphasized in the narrative, and the kinds of ancillaries teachers would prefer. Such surveys reveal that one of the major concerns of classroom teachers is the reading level of the texts. Publishers know that if the reading level is too high, teachers will not like the text, and it will not sell. Consequently, the phenomenon occurs which in recent years has been called "dumbing down." Various formulae are applied by editors to simplify the language. In the process, of course, some damage may be done to the conceptual sophistication of the information.

Minorities   For some time now, historians have explored much more thoroughly the contributions of ethnic and racial minorities to American life. While the inclusion of these contributions in textbook histories has been a natural outgrowth of historical research, advocacy groups exist that review texts to assure such inclusion. Thus, editors take care to present the culturally diverse nature of American society. Such items as pictures and biographical profiles may be carefully chosen to include blacks, Native Americans, Hispanics, Italian-Americans, and other groups.

Sometimes advocacy groups are able to influence a specific topic. Recently, for example, the Texas Education Agency, acting on a state legislative resolution, suggested that American history texts under consideration for adoption in that state include the contributions of Bernardo de Galvez, Spanish governor of Louisiana, to the American effort during the Revolutionary War. This will almost certainly assure that De Galvez's name will appear in future U.S. history texts.[19]

Women   Just as historians have focused on the contributions of minorities, so too have they begun to more adequately treat those of women. Again, as with minorities, this natural outgrowth of historical research has been fostered in textbooks by advocacy groups. Often the demands of these groups go beyond concern for coverage of women's contributions to include sensitivity to sexual stereotyping and sexist language. In response to this concern, editors have been known to rewrite entire passages of texts to avoid the use of common words incorporating references to male gender (e.g., Englishman, middleman, mankind). To combat stereotyping, women's advocacy groups also want to see women pictured in nontraditional roles. This desire, however, may conflict with demands of other advocacy groups, especially those on the religious right.

Fundamentalists   In recent years, a number of fundamentalist religious groups have become more militant in their efforts to combat the expansion of secular humanism in the schools. One part of that effort has been to review textbooks (and library holdings) in an effort to weed out those that they feel subvert authority or are anti-Christian or antifamily. One such group, for example, has been particularly influential in the Texas adoption procedure. Since Texas represents a huge textbook market, publishers are particularly sensitive to developments there. Unwilling to risk censure by such advocacy groups, editors will avoid historical issues and teaching strategies that might offend. The result is that many religious topics will be left entirely untreated in textbooks, and strategies related to values or valuing will be omitted. In a case familiar to one of the authors of this book, an editor questioned a reference to nineteenth-century Unitarians and their disbelief in the divinity of Christ. The editor feared that such a reference was potentially controversial.

It should be clear, even with this limited example, that many factors can influence the material covered in a U.S. history textbook. You can probably think of more. Remember, however, that in many classes the textbook *is* the curriculum.

Box 7.2
Concerns of
Fundamentalist
Christians

The following is excerpted from a set of educational guidelines derived by a fundamentalist group in the early 1980s. "This list may seem extreme," argued a spokesperson for the Moral Majority, "but we have got to stop teachers today from meddling in the private moral lives of students. . . . lists like this are a reaction to the amoral attitude of the public school system." These guidelines have obvious implications for curriculum and instruction.

Dont's for Students

Don't get into science-fiction values discussions or trust a teacher who dwells on science fiction in his/her "teaching."

Don't discuss the future or future social arrangements or governments in class

Don't discuss values.

Don't write a family history.

Don't answer personal questions or questions about members of your family.

Don't play blindfolded games in class.

Don't exchange "opinions" on political or social issues.

Don't write an autobiography.

Don't keep a journal of your opinions, activities and feelings.

Don't confide in teachers, particularly sociology or social studies and English teachers.

Don't role-play or participate in socio-dramas.

Don't get involved in school-sponsored or government-sponsored exchange or camping programs which place you in the homes of strangers.

Don't get into classroom discussions which begin: What would you do if . . . ? What if . . . ? Should we . . . ? Do you suppose . . . ? Do you think . . . ? What is your opinion of . . . ?

Don't fall for books like "Future Shock," which are intended to put readers in a state of panic about "change" so they will be willing to accept slavery. Advances in science and technology don't drive people into shock. It is government and vain-brain intrusions in private lives which cause much of the unbalance in nature and in people.

What appears to be the major concern reflected in this list of "don'ts"? Given a literal application of this list, what subjects and instructional practices with which you are familiar would be hampered?

Source: Ina Hughs, "Do You Accept Education Goals 'Concerned' Parents Set Down?" *Charlotte Observer*, February 27, 1982.

Organizing the Curriculum

The variety of goals in education is matched by a variety of strategies to achieve those goals. One major area of strategic concern for curricularists is the organization of curriculum. When curricularists speak of organization, they are addressing some of the basic elements of the school setting: the conceptualization of content (e.g., courses based upon separate academic subjects, interdisciplinary topics, or the psychological needs or interests of children), vertical patterns (e.g., first grade, second grade) and horizontal patterns (e.g., groupings of students and teachers). If the goals of schooling are academically oriented, with emphasis on basic skills and knowledge, certain organization patterns may suggest themselves. If, however, goals focus upon the whole child, quite different patterns logically emerge. This section reviews the variety of patterns that have been and are being used to organize the curriculum.

Organization of Content

As just noted, content can be organized in any number of ways, including academic subjects, interdisciplinary topics, and social-psychological needs of students. Content organization by traditional subject matter is usually found where schools emphasize student command of academic material. Alternatives to this pattern are generally associated with a more progressive orientation to schooling, emphasizing the development of the whole child.

The most traditional pattern for the organization of content is that based upon the academic discipline or subject matter. Thus, schools offer courses such as U.S. history, English, mathematics, and biology. Critics of this arrangement, however, point out that it creates artificial barriers between aspects of knowledge. There are few teachers, for example, who have not heard complaints such as "This is science class, not English. You shouldn't grade writing!" To address this problem, curricularists have advocated a number of arrangements that correlate or combine traditional subjects. In one such pattern, subjects are correlated in such a way that relationships between them are made an aspect of study. Thus, the study of the early national period in American history might be correlated with that same period in American literature. A second pattern combines separate subjects into broad fields: history, geography, and government become social studies, and reading, writing, and spelling become language arts. This organizational pattern is frequently found in elementary schools where, most educators agree, exposure to knowledge and skills should be on a general level. A third pattern attempts to integrate the subjects through interdisciplinary or multidisciplinary studies.

Many progressive educators argued—and contemporary proponents of this perspective still argue—that if schools are to promote the healthy psychological and social development of children, they need to organize content around student needs and concerns. As noted earlier, Dewey's experimental school at the University of Chicago organized learning experiences around "human impulses": the social impulse, the constructive impulse, the impulse to experiment and investigate, and the expressive impulse. Other progressives have organized topics around life skills, such as production, consumption, and communication, or social roles, such as home, community, and occupational group membership.[20] In some cases, these topics formed the focus of "core" curricula. In each of these patterns, varieties of sources of information are used to focus on life concerns.

Vertical Patterns

Along with decisions concerning the conceptualization of content, curricularists must make decisions concerning when and to what extent students are exposed to the content. Two basic patterns emerge: graded and nongraded.

In the graded school pattern, content is divided into one-year increments covering knowledge and skills that educators think are appropriate for a particular age group. That is, it is assumed that all seven-year-olds, for example (called second-graders), should learn a certain amount of math in a school year. Continuation is dependent upon completion of each increment (at some acceptable level of mastery) in the prescribed period of time. In the nongraded pattern, a sequence of skills or knowledge within a particular content area is developed, and students are allowed to progress through that sequence without reference to age. When students demonstrate mastery of knowledge or skill at one level, they proceed to the next. No assumptions are made that all students of a certain age should be exposed to the same information at the same rate. Students can progress at their own rates of learning.

In practice, some schools combine the two patterns. That is, students are labeled as second-graders or third-graders but in specific content areas may, as individuals or groups, be at various points along a continuum of skills. Thus, a rapid learning eight-year-old (third-grader) may be studying the same information or skills as a slower learning ten-year-old (fifth-grader). This variety of learning speeds and ability levels leads curricularists to consider another set of organizational questions, those dealing with the assignment of teachers and students.

Horizontal Patterns

Variety also characterizes the assignment of teachers and students to learning groups. The two most common patterns found for the horizontal organization of teachers are the self-contained and departmentalized patterns. In the self-contained classroom, usually found in elementary schools, a single teacher has a single group of students for the whole day and is responsible for instruction in all content areas. In a departmentalized arrangement—usually found in middle and secondary schools but seen also in elementary schools—a teacher will have several groups of students, each of which he or she instructs for only a part of the day in a single content area. Again, in practice, schools will often adopt some combination of these patterns.

One arrangement that reflects elements of both the self-contained and the departmentalized patterns is the organization of teachers into teams. Teams may be interdisciplinary or hierarchical in nature. The interdisciplinary scheme assigns a number of teachers specializing in different academic areas to a larger group of students for a block of time during the day. Thus, for example, a group of four teachers composed of specialists in math, science, English, and social studies may be assigned a group of 100 students. In a hierarchical scheme (often called differential staffing), a master teacher may be teamed with other teachers and paraprofessional personnel and assigned to a large group of students.

Curricularists must also make decisions concerning the composition of the groups of students. In this regard, some recommend homogeneous grouping while others advocate heterogeneous groups. The homogeneous scheme assigns students to groups according to common attributes such as ability level or interest. The heterogeneous scheme assigns students without reference to attributes. Advocates of the former claim that such grouping makes the teacher's task easier (the range of ability levels is reduced, thus simplifying instructional preparation), enhances achievement at all levels, allows slower pupils to be leaders in their own groups, and receives better support from parents (particularly those whose children are in the upper ability groups). Advocates of the latter argue that research evidence is unclear concerning the benefits of homogeneous grouping; that such grouping fosters labeling, is a form of segregation, and is generally undemocratic; and that it is difficult to find teachers who want to work with lower ability students. These advocates further argue that heterogeneous grouping provides advantages: groups are more analogous to real life, foster a greater range of developmental characteristics, and provide a forum for a greater number of instructional and participation strategies.[21] In fact, debate over the various organizational patterns discussed here is very often informed by the philosophical stances of those involved in the debate. Ultimately, then, the curricularist is again forced to recognize the importance of differences of opinion concerning the goals of schooling.

Organizational Patterns and Goals

Some organizational patterns are more amenable to some goals than to others. That is, certain organizational patterns tend to be found in association with academically oriented goals, where content is defined as subject matter, while other patterns tend to be associated with more "progressive" goals, where content is defined in terms of students' personal and social needs. This characteristic is best illustrated by contrasting patterns of organization found in subject-centered curricula to those found in child-centered curricula.

Subject-Centered Curricula

Subject-centered curricula have a long tradition, one that can be traced from Aristotle and his first description of the liberal studies to the current emphasis on traditional academic content. Of course, there are many variations in between, but the subject orientation has remained a constant. The curriculum of Benjamin Franklin's academy included writing (including penmanship), drawing, arithmetic, geometry, astronomy, English, speech, history, geography, and natural history.[22] Horace Mann also thought in terms of subjects: bookkeeping, surveying, navigation, geometry, chemistry, and physiology, for example.[23] William T. Harris argued that elementary students should be exposed to the "five windows of the soul," grammar, literature and art, mathematics, geography, and history.[24] An academic emphasis characterized the Report of the Committee of Ten. More recently, the curricular innovations of the late 1950s and 1960s were based on an analysis of the "structures" (concepts, principles, and methods of inquiry) of the academic disciplines.[25]

When content is conceptualized in terms of subject matter, certain patterns of curriculum organization tend to follow. The graded vertical pattern of sequencing skills (i.e., first grade, second grade, etc.), for example, is as commonplace as the subject orientation. In terms of horizontal patterns, blocks of time during the school day are assigned to the subjects. Thus, in the elementary school, an hour in the morning devoted to mathematics might be followed by an hour of reading, and so on through the day. The subjects might be taught in a self-contained classroom by the same teacher or divided between teachers who specialize in the particular subjects. In the secondary school, the typical day is divided in such a way as to produce six class periods, each devoted to a particular subject taught by a specialist in that subject and each taught in the same time slot every day. Students may be grouped either homogeneously or heterogeneously in subject-centered curricula, but there seems to be a tendency to group students according to ability when academics are emphasized.

Child-Centered Curricula   In 1762, Jean Jacques Rousseau published *Emile,* a novel in which he described the ideal education of a young man. In the novel, Rousseau rejects traditional schooling in favor of what he feels is a more natural process. During the first twelve years of his life, for example, Emile is allowed freedom (albeit within a prepared environment) to pursue his own interests without formal schooling in reading, writing, or mathematics. At age twelve, a more formal phase of schooling begins, but it still exploits the child's natural curiosity:

> *Put the problems before him and let him solve them himself. Let him know nothing because you have told him, but because he has learnt it for himself. Let him not be taught science, let him discover it.*[26]

Many educators trace the modern child-centered curriculum to Rousseau. Rather than emphasize cognitive development, Rousseau argued that the development of a mature, well-balanced, and emotionally stable character was the most important goal of education.

There have been many proponents of the child-centered orientation since Rousseau. Nineteenth-century American educator Bronson Alcott, for example, argued that the true goal of education was self-knowledge. With that knowledge, Alcott felt, individuals could recognize their God-given potential and grow in spirit as well as knowledge. To achieve such a goal, Alcott substituted "encouragement for competition, explanation for memorization, persuasion for coercion." Furthermore, Alcott closely studied children in an attempt to understand their nature so that teaching could proceed "in due accordance and harmony with the laws of (the child's) constitution."[27]

During the twentieth century, progressive educators have been the spokespersons for the child-centered orientation. The arguments of Dewey and more recent educators/educational critics in the progressive tradition have already been treated fully in this text. In the 1980s, the child-centered tradition is still very much alive, despite the national attention on academic basics.

A curriculum based upon a child-oriented philosophy would likely emphasize different patterns of organization from those of the subject orientation. For example, the child-centered philosophy of the British primary school movement, introduced in the United States during the 1960s through the efforts of Joseph Featherstone, was a nongraded, self-contained team pattern with "family" grouping—children of different ages in the same class. There was little emphasis on basics. Rather, subject

Photo 7.3
Physical characteristics of the school can influence curriculum.

matter was used to facilitate classroom interaction. In fact, content was largely unplanned, growing out of student interest in a question, observation, or experience. A topic of study thus derived would be approached from an interdisciplinary perspective. The self-contained classroom allowed a team of professionals and paraprofessionals to more intimately learn the needs and interests of their charges while freeing student learning from the constraints implicit in a schedule that moves students from teacher to teacher or subject to subject.[28]

During the late 1960s and early 1970s, a number of secondary schools also attempted to shape their curricula in a more child-centered fashion. The John Dewey High School in Brooklyn, New York, was one such school. The curriculum at Dewey attempted to foster the following elements:

1. Individualization of student learning rates.

2. An array of course offerings designed to meet the needs and interests of students of all ability levels.

3. Individualization of instruction and a serious attempt to avoid the impersonalization of large, overcrowded schools.

4. The development of a sense of self-reliance and independence among students and an ability to learn on their own outside the formal classroom.

5. Teacher and student involvement in the development of the educational program.

It was hoped that the preceding could be achieved through innovative curricular practices, including the following:

1. An eight-hour day.

2. Independent study (approximately twenty five percent of the student's day) based upon self-contained independent study kits.

3. Flexible modular scheduling, where the eight-hour day is divided into twenty-minute modules; courses meet for one, two, three, or more modules; and the number of modules devoted to a particular course can vary from day to day.

4. Cyclical programming, where the year is divided into five seven-week cycles and courses last for one or more cycles, thus allowing the students to "avoid the 'long corridor of failure' associated with annual or semiannual organization."

5.   A broad array of courses, including academic (e.g., in English: "The Bible as Literature," "The Generation Gap," "Literature of Science Fiction and Fantasy"), practical, and interdisciplinary offerings.

6.   Mastery learning (no numerical grades, rather, indication of mastery—or lack thereof—on objectives of course).

7.   Heterogeneous grouping.[29]

In many ways the John Dewey experience was a compromise between the traditional, subject-matter orientation and the child-centered, more progressive curriculum. In reality this is often the case. It should be remembered, however, that curricular patterns can and should be designed to complement the goals of the school.

Instruction

The major subdivision of curriculum is instruction, which refers to the actual classroom strategies that teachers use to foster student learning. Over the years, a debate has developed concerning instructional strategies: On one side are those who argue that teaching is an art; on the other are those who feel it is a science. Regardless of the position one ultimately takes on the issue, a great variety of models for instruction are available to teachers in the 1980s.

Teaching As an Art

In his book, *The Art of Teaching*, Gilbert Highet argues that teaching cannot be a science:

> *Teaching involves emotions, which cannot be systematically appraised and employed, and human values, which are quite outside the grasp of science . . . . "Scientific" teaching, even of scientific subjects, will be inadequate as long as both teachers and pupils are human beings. Teaching is not like inducing a chemical reaction: it is much more like painting a picture or making a piece of music, . . . like planting a garden or writing a friendly letter. You must throw your heart into it, you must realize that it cannot all be done by formulas, or you will spoil your work, and your pupils, and yourself.[30]*

Much in teaching, then, depends upon such things as a teacher's sensitivity to the mood of a class, the value the teacher places on human achievement, or the choice of disciplinary techniques to match the teacher's personality. Such things are hard to teach to prospective teachers. Nevertheless, most educators feel that there are many elements in successful teaching that can be described and taught.

Teaching As a Science

As scientists have learned more about the nature of knowledge and learning, educators have attempted to apply that knowledge to the production of more effective teaching strategies. As Paul Woodring wrote, "The fact that teaching is held to be an art rather than a science does not mean . . . that methodology cannot be taught. Every artist learns his methods from another artist who acts as teacher. The genius will develop his own methods, but it cannot be expected that all of the more than a million American teachers will be geniuses."[31] In fact, the body of scientific research in teaching has grown to the point that some educators are willing to say that "scholarship and empirical research in education have matured, providing a solid base for an intellectually vital program of professional studies."[32] Various groups have advocated specific methodological practices derived from this "knowledge base." Thus, much time is spent by teacher educators in preparing their charges in methodology. If, as noted earlier, teachers play a significant role in curriculum, it is important that they be aware of the wide range of instructional techniques available to them and the educational purposes to which each of these different techniques is suited.

Instructional Models

In *Models of Teaching,* Bruce Joyce and Marsha Weil describe four families of teaching strategies: information-processing strategies, designed to teach facts, concepts, and generalizations; personal strategies, focusing on the individual and the development of his or her unique personality; social strategies, focusing on the human group, interpersonal skills, and social commitment; and behavioral strategies, applying models of operant conditioning to the classroom.[33] Just as with curriculum organizational patterns, some teaching strategies seem to be more amenable to certain educational goals than to others.

Information-Processing Models The information-processing models attempt to teach both content and process, the techniques by which individuals acquire and manipulate information. These models are drawn from theories of learning, studies of the scholarly disciplines and their structures, and developmental studies of the human intellect. If one feels that the major purpose of schooling is to teach information, then these are the models most likely used.

Personal Models As the name of the family suggests, the personal models are designed to focus on individual needs. A number of these strategies are based on models of counseling or psychological therapy. They tend to place more control of the selection of experiences in the hands of the children. They also tend to downplay the significance of academics. Carl Rogers, for example, argues that instruction should be based upon concepts of human relations rather than concepts from the academic disciplines. In his model, the teacher serves as a guide to the student's growth and development. He or she serves to foster student self-exploration and problem solving. "Philosophically," write Joyce and Weil, "it is the emphasis on the maximization of unique personal development that characterizes [these] models. . . ."

> *Each focuses on the individual's construction of his or her own reality—on the task of finding personal identity and living a life in which one's own dignified search for meaning is recognized on its own terms. The individual's life validates itself—his or her unique existence and experiencing of life are what counts. The long-term dispositional changes in the student are thus more important to this group of model makers than the short-term instructional effects, for they hope to nurture development of the whole personality.*[34]

Social Models   The social family of models includes instructional strategies that emphasize social relations. One subgroup of this family attempts to develop ideal citizens for democracy, teaching students how to reflect on social and political issues. Another subgroup is concerned with improving interpersonal relations. Many of these models can be traced to John Dewey and his concept of reflective thinking. They stress the relationship between the development of the individual and the individual's functioning in society. Thus, both the social and personal families of models tend to find advocates among modern-day progressive, child-centered educators.

Behavioral Models   The final group of models discussed by Joyce and Weil are adaptations from behavior theory. Principles of operant conditioning suggest that for many students, learning tasks should be broken down into small steps and immediate reward be applied for the successful completion of those steps. Joyce and Weil believe, for example, that developments in the application of behavioral techniques are largely responsible for recent progress in the field of special education. With its emphasis upon visible learner behaviors and manipulable environmental conditions, behavior theory seems to be one of the most scientific studies of teaching. The behaviorist's emphasis on specific, observable behaviors has been incorporated into the current concern for accountability in schooling. Thus, teachers are required to state behaviorally the learning objectives for their children. Those objectives can then be easily measured. A number of educators, however, argue that many of the outcomes of the teaching-learning process defy precise measurement. Many also decry the manipulative aspect of behaviorism.

Evaluation

Normally, when a student reads the term *evaluation,* a number of images arise. One is reminded of tests, reports, and recitations. Student evaluation is, indeed, one part of what curricularists consider when they refer to evaluation, but another, and for the curricularist, more significant aspect is the determination of whether or not the curriculum achieves its stated purposes or goals. This section considers both aspects of curricular evaluation.

Evaluating Students

The traditional conception of evaluation suggests assessment of the quality of student work. This is usually done by the classroom teacher through the use of a variety of devices: teacher-made tests, research papers, book reports, special projects, and so on. During the twentieth century, however, the development of the testing movement has had a profound effect on the measurement of student performance. Early experiments by Frenchmen Alfred Binet and Theodore Simon, fueled by the work of people like E. L. Thorndike in the United States, led to the development of standardized intelligence and achievement tests. As the century progressed, and despite the continuing controversy over the nature of the tests—from fundamental questions of definition and conceptualization to questions of cultural bias—more and more school systems and states adopted the use of these tests to indicate how their students did in relationship to others across the country. Today standardized tests are widely used to measure student aptitude or achievement at all levels of education.

The educational reform movement of the 1980s has further fostered the use of these tests. In many states, students face one or another form of standardized test yearly. In some cases, appropriate scores are—or soon will be—required for promotion from grade to grade, high-school graduation, and even course credit. Since these tests measure students in a standardized and objective way, they are also a source of data for use in accountability studies. That is, student scores are reviewed to make sure teachers are "doing their jobs."

Tests may also be used to measure general educational trends. One example of such a test is the National Assessment of Educational Progress (NAEP). Instituted in 1964, the NAEP is designed to measure educational achievement among four age groups (ages nine, thirteen, and seventeen and young adults) in ten subject areas. The tests are administered cyclically, and results are reported in terms of geographic region, size and type of community, sex, race or ethic group, and parental educational background. With this data, general trends can be observed and comparisons made. Areas in need of curricular revision may be revealed. Another such measure of student achievement is the IEA study. Sponsored by the International Association for the Evaluation of Educational Achievement, the IEA is a cross-cultural study of achievement in several academic areas. Study data has revealed a number of significant factors influencing educational achievement and has indicated some major differences in mean scores in academic areas among high-school students of various countries.

When national comparisons are made, American mean scores tend to be lower than the means of students in other industrialized nations. Consequently, this data is often used in support of arguments indicating the inferiority of American schools. As Torsten Husén of the Institute of International Education has pointed out, however, such comparisons must be made with care. Husén notes, for example, that many of the European systems tend to be elitist in nature, while the American system is comprehensive. That is, admission into secondary schools in Europe has traditionally been very selective, while that has not been the case in the United States. When only the scores of the top U.S. students are compared, the United States fares better:

> *The international surveys of both mathematics and science demonstrated that the top 5% to 10% at the end of secondary education (i.e., the elite) tended to perform at nearly the same level in both comprehensive and selective systems of secondary education. Thus the elite among U.S. high school seniors did not differ considerably in their performance from their age-mates in France, England, or Germany.*[35]

Nevertheless, many Americans remain concerned when U.S. students' scores do not compare favorably with those of other countries. Reports issued in early 1987 indicating that Americans were a nation of underachievers in mathematics skills, for example, prompted calls for major revisions in math curricula in the country.[36]

Program Evaluation

Statements in the preceding section suggesting that data from national and international student evaluations often foment curricular change imply a close relationship between the evaluation of students and the evaluation of programs. Generally speaking, however, the evaluation of programs is designed to determine whether or not the planned activities in the curriculum actually do produce the desired results and, if not, to suggest ways they can be improved. In that respect, curricularists speak of both summative and formative evaluation. Summative evaluation is the final assessment of a program. Formative evaluation is designed to produce feedback on a program while it is still in development.

While many evaluators insist on the scientific nature of their work, evaluation is also a political phenomenon. It, too, falls within the realm of educational policy analysis. As curricularist John D. McNeil argues, ". . . curriculum evaluation can be seen as part of the struggle by different interest groups —educationalists, teachers, administrators, industrialists—to gain control over the forces that shape the practice of schooling."[37] Some of the most interesting uses of evaluation, then, derive from major educational movements.

Perhaps the most famous program evaluation in the history of American schooling was the Eight Year Study, conducted during the 1930s and designed to compare students from progressive high schools with those from traditional schools. Students were matched in 1,475 pairs—each pair comprising a student from a progressive, experimental school and one from a traditional school—according to similar background characteristics. The study followed the students through eight years of schooling, from their first year in high school through college. Comparisons were made between the students on a wide range of measures, including academic honors, intellectual curiosity, systematic thinking, drive, resourcefulness, planning, adjustment, participation in religious and service activities, attitudes about schooling, vocational decision making, and interest in world affairs. Students from the progressive schools equaled or bettered their counterparts from traditional schools in all areas except foreign language. Many curricularists have assumed, then, that the progressive schools must indeed have been fostering more important educational goals than simple academic performance, a basic progressive argument. For that reason, the Eight Year Study is frequently cited by those who advocate progressive educational practices.

In recent years, however, research in "effective schools" has received much attention. Based on early studies by Ronald Edmonds and others on exemplary schools for the urban poor, effective schools research has emphasized the importance of school characteristics such as strong principal leadership, especially the principal's involvement in the instructional program and his or her expectations of faculty and students; emphasis on academic skills; orderly atmosphere; higher teacher expectations of students; better teacher morale; more satisfactory teacher-parent relationships; and longer instructional days.[38] These findings, with their emphasis on academics skills, have formed the basis for many of the state-mandated reforms of the 1980s. It is interesting to note, however, that one of the characteristics often mentioned in the research on effective schools is that of greater autonomy for individual schools. As noted earlier in the chapter, one result of the state reform movement has been just the opposite.

Summary

This chapter reveals that curriculum is often the result of the interaction of diverse educational viewpoints and participants. The politics of education, then, permeates curriculum formation. Even among professional educators, differences appear in perspective. This book has noted the orientation of those interested in education for adult social roles, those calling for a focus on individual development, and those emphasizing command of traditional subject matter.[39] These views influence a number of aspects of curriculum, including curricular issues, curricular organization, instructional methodology, and curricular evaluation. It should not be assumed, however, that these views are the only perspectives on education today, nor are they necessarily mutually exclusive. The reality of everyday schooling fosters a good deal of eclecticism among educators. During the early twentieth century, advocates of the junior high school seemed to combine arguments from both child-centered and social efficiency educators. The educational reform movement of the 1980s appears to be animated by a combination of social efficiency and traditional subject matter. It is important for the student of education, however, to recognize the origins of various curricular positions.

Before leaving curriculum, a final point must be made concerning technology and its impact on education in general and curriculum in particular. The widespread use of the microcomputer, for example, has had and will have a tremendous impact on curriculum, from its usefulness in administrative and organizational tasks to its growing role in classroom instruction. Often, however, technological development is also the harbinger of great change in society. Changes in social concern play a significant role in the development of educational issues. Educational futures are considered in the last chapter of this book.

Key Words

Curriculum	Accrediting agency
Instruction	Content organization
Herbartians	Horizontal patterns
Scientific curriculum making	Vertical patterns
Tyler model	Subject-centered curriculum
Cognitive domain	Child-centered curriculum
Affective domain	Instructional models
Psychomotor domain	Formative evaluation
Hidden curriculum	Summative evaluation.

Discussion Questions

1. Consider your own elementary and secondary education. What elements would you describe as subject-centered? Child-centered?

2. What evidence, if any, is there in your home community of non-school influences on curriculum?

3. What do you feel is the ideal content organization?

4. Describe the vertical and horizontal organizations of your home school system.

For Further Reading

Joyce, Bruce, and Weil, Marsha. *Models of Teaching*. Englewood Cliffs, N.J.: Prentice-Hall, 1980.

McNeil, John D. *Curriculum: A Comprehensive Introduction*. Boston: Little, Brown & Co., 1985.

Ragan, William B., and Shepherd, Gene D. *Modern Elementary Curriculum*. New York: Holt, Rinehart, & Winston, 1977.

Schubert, William H. *Curriculum: Perspective, Paradigm, and Possibility*. New York: Macmillan, 1986.

Tyler, Ralph W. *Basic Principles of Curriculum and Instruction*. Chicago: University of Chicago Press, 1949.

Notes

1. John H. Lounsbury & Gordon E. Vars, *A Curriculum for the Middle School Years* (New York: Harper & Row, 1978), pp. 15–17.

2. John D. McNeil, *Curriculum: A Comprehensive Introduction* (Boston: Little, Brown & Co., 1985), pp. 327–332.

3. Quoted in Merle Curti, *Social Ideas of American Educators* (Totowa, N.J.: Littlefield, Adams & Co., 1974), pp. 525–526ff.

4. William B. Ragan and Gene D. Shepherd, *Modern Elementary Curriculum* (New York: Holt, Rinehart, & Winston, 1977), p. 202.

5. Franklin Bobbitt, *The Curriculum* (Boston: Houghton Mifflin, 1918).

6. Bobbitt, *How To Make a Curriculum* (Boston: Houghton Mifflin, 1924).

7. W. W. Charters, *Curriculum Construction* (New York: Macmillan, 1923).

8. McNeil, pp. 342–343.

9. Ralph W. Tyler, *Basic Principles of Curriculum and Instruction* (Chicago: University of Chicago Press, 1949).

10. Hilda Taba, *Curriculum Development: Theory and Practice* (New York: Harcourt, Brace & World, 1962), p.12.

11. See Benjamin S. Bloom, ed., *Taxonomy of Educational Objectives, the Classification of Educational Goals—Handbook I: Cognitive Domain* (New York: David McKay Co., 1956); David Krathwohl, Benjamin Bloom, and Bertram Masia, *Taxonomy of Educational Objectives, The Classification of Educational Goals—Handbook II: Affective Domain* (New York: David McKay Co., 1956); and Anita J. Harrow, *A Taxonomy of the Psychomotor Domain—A Guide for Developing Behavioral Objectives* (New York: David McKay Co., 1972).

12. Jon Wiles and Joseph Bondi, Curriculum Development: *A Guide to Practice* (Columbus, Ohio: Charles E. Merrill, 1979), p.15.

13. McNeil, p. 236.

14. Gilbert R. Austin, "Exemplary Schools and the Search for Excellence," *Educational Leadership,* Vol. 37, No. 1, October 1979, p. 12.

15. Kirsten Goldberg, "Of Religion in Schools, Rights of Parents," *Education Week,* Vol. VI, No. 9, November 5, 1986.

16. Sherry Keith, *Politics of Textbook Selection* (Palo Alto: Stanford University Press, 1981).

17. See Ford Foundation, *A Foundation Goes to School* (New York: Ford Foundation, 1972), and K.C. Cole Janssen, *Matters of Choice: The Ford Foundation Report on Alternative Schools* (New York: Ford Foundation, 1974).

18. Michael Kirst and Decker Walker, "An Analysis of Curriculum Policy Making," *Review of Educational Research,* Vol. 41, No. 5 (1971), p. 488.

19. S.C.R. No. 56, 69th. Legislature of Texas (1985).

20. Ragan and Shepherd, p. 202.

21. *Ibid.,* pp. 125–127.

22. Henry J. Perkinson, *Two Hundred Years of American Educational Thought* (New York: David McKay Co., 1976), pp. 23–30.

23. *Ibid.,* p. 75.

24. Curti, p. 315.

25. See Jerome S. Bruner, *The Process of Education* (Cambridge: Harvard University Press, 1961).

26. Quoted in E. H. Gwynne-Thomas, *A Concise History of Education to 1900 A.D.* (New York: University Press of America, 1981), p.177.

27. Lawrence A. Cremin, *American Education: The National Experience* (New York: Harper & Row, 1980), pp. 84–86.

28. Joseph Featherstone, "The British and Us," *The New Republic,* September 11, 1971, pp. 20–25.

29. Sol Levine and Michael J. Costelloe, "The John Dewey High School Adventure" in Glen Hass, *Curriculum Planning: A New Approach* (Boston: Allyn & Bacon, 1983), pp. 405–407.

30. Gilbert Highet, *The Art of Teaching* (New York: Vintage Books, 1957), pp. vii–viii.

31. Paul Woodring, *A Fourth of a Nation* (New York: McGraw Hill, 1957),p. 52.

32. The Holmes Group, J.E. Lanier, Chair, *Tomorrow's Teachers* (East Lansing, Mich: The Holmes Group, 1986), p. 50.

33. Bruce Joyce and Marsha Weil, *Models of Teaching* (Englewood Cliffs, N.J.: Prentice-Hall, 1980).

34. *Ibid.,* p. 146.

35. Torsten Husén, "Are Standards In U.S. Schools Really Lagging Behind Those in Other Countries?" *Phi Delta Kappan,* Vol. 64, No. 7, March 1983, p. 456.

36. Robert Rothman, "Mathematics Scores Show U.S. Is a Nation of Underachievers," *Education Week,* Vol. VI, No. 17, January 21, 1987.

37. McNeil, p. 205

38. Ronald Edmonds, "Effective Schools for the Urban Poor," *Educational Leadership,* Vol. 37, No. 1, October 1979, pp. 15–24.

39. Curricularist William H. Schubert, for example, in his comprehensive *Curriculum: Perspective, Paradigm, and Possibility* (New York: Macmillan, 1986), makes excellent use of three orientations toward curriculum: the intellectual traditionalist; the social behaviorist, emphasizing the effective development of human capital through scientific measurement and educational treatment; and the experientialist, or progressive.

P A R T

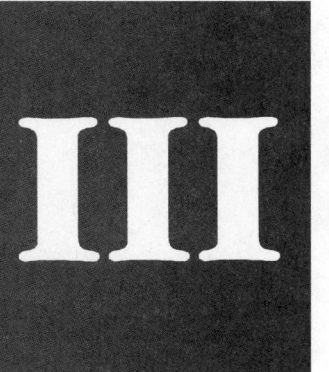

III EDUCATIONAL POLICY

Public policy evolves out of perceptions of problems that citizens and policymakers believe should be addressed by some agency or institution. As indicated in Parts I and II on Education Today and Foundations of Education, notions about educational problems are shaped by views about the educational profession and professionals, historical precedents in schooling, educational belief systems, school-society relations, and ever-changing notions about how and what schools should teach.

Part III focuses on policies relating to elementary and secondary educational institutions in the United States. Chapters 8 and 9 review the formal and informal policy systems and processes that are involved in the shaping of educational policy. Chapters 10–14 review some major areas of schooling policy where significant bodies of law, court rulings, and administrative rulings have developed to resolve the policy problems that have evolved over time. These areas include policies relating to the teacher, the student, equality in schooling, church-state relations, and school funding. Chapter 15 reviews the pressing policy problems that can be predicted to shape educational policy development in the near future.

8 Legal Structures for the Development and Administration of Educational Policy

" . . . Education is the principal responsibility of local school systems, teachers, parents, citizen boards, and state governments. By eliminating the (Federal) Department of Education less than two years after it was created, we can not only reduce the budget but ensure that local needs and preferences—rather than the whims of Washington—determine the education of our children."

Ronald Reagan, Broadcast Address to the Nation (1981)

" . . . . Governors want to help establish clear goals and better report cards, ways to measure what students know and can do. Then, we're ready to give up a lot of state regulatory control . . . if schools and school districts will be accountable for the results. We invite educators to show us where less regulation makes the most sense.

 . . . . We're not ready to bargain away minimum standards that some states are just setting. But we have learned that real excellence can't be imposed from a distance. Governors don't create excellent schools; communities— local school leaders, teachers, parents, and citizens—do."

Lamar Alexander, *Time for Results: The Governors' 1991 Report in Education* (1986)

Since different levels and branches of government are involved in developing and administering educational policy, assigning appropriate roles and responsibilities to the local, state, or federal government is a very difficult

191

task. Who really decides educational policy in the United States? What kind of legal structure exists to allocate and delegate authority for developing and administering policy in this country? What steps or processes usually occur in the development of educational policy? How do lay citizens in the United States influence the direction of policy for their schools? How do teachers and other professionals influence the development and administration of educational policy? Chapters 8 and 9 explore answers to these questions regarding the organization and governance of schools.

Some of the basic problems of educational policy development are the determination of who gets what kind of schooling, where this schooling will be delivered, how and when it will be delivered, and the reasons for its delivery. Determining solutions to the wide range of problems associated with answering these basic educational policy questions is a very complex process involving not only governmental bodies but also citizens. Finding solutions to these policy questions is one of the primary tasks of state and local governments in the United States.

The operation of public schools is usually one of the larger government activities in the United States. Typically, at the state and local level, more money is spent to operate the schools, more people are employed in the schools, and more citizens are directly or indirectly served by the public schools than by other governmental agencies. Nationwide, some type of involvement in formal schooling is the primary activity of approximately sixty-one million Americans. Around fifty-seven million students are enrolled in schools and colleges scattered among the fifty states and are taught by approximately 3.3 million teachers and professors. Public school administration is the primary employment of approximately 300,000 persons in this country. When one adds the other staff members such as custodians, bus drivers, and school building maintenance personnel, schooling becomes a huge enterprise in the United States.

Even through each of the states has assumed legal responsibility for the operation of public schools, the federal government has also been involved in the schooling enterprise. The activities of Congress, the federal courts, and the executive branch of the federal government have influenced the operation and administration of public schools in numerous ways.

The complexities of educational policy development and administration in the United States have led political scientists to use various approaches to explain this political phenomenon. This chapter focuses attention on the use of systems and process approaches to describe the involvement of governmental entities that develop and administer educational policy. Systems models can be used to simulate reality in numerous academic endeavors. Systems and process models are introduced in this chapter and used throughout the policy section of this book to help the reader comprehend the formal and other groups involved in educational policy development and administration, the interaction between these political groups, the process they go through to develop policy, and the kinds of educational policy that result from these processes and interactions. The influence over policy development and administration by interest groups and other entities that have no formal legal authority (the informal stucture) over policy matters is discussed in more detail in Chapter 9.

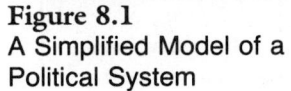

Figure 8.1
A Simplified Model of a
Political System

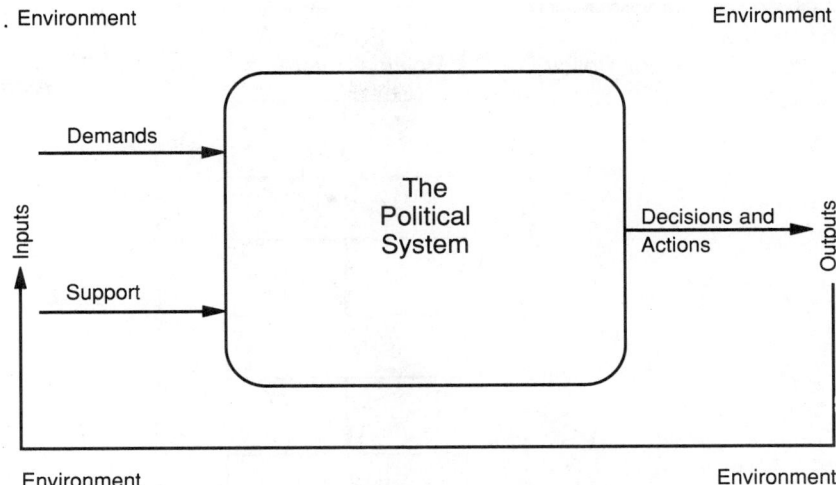

Source: David Easton. *A Framework for Political Analysis*. Englewood Cliffs, NJ: Prentice-Hall, 1965. Reprinted by permission, University of Chicago Press.© 1965 by the University of Chicago. All rights reserved.

Systems and Process Approaches to Describing Policy Development

David Easton's systems model has been helpful in describing the relationships between political agents and public constituents. Easton views political life as a system of behaviors and interactions through which public policy is formed. These behaviors and interactions occur among the holders of formal political authority (legislative bodies, the judicial system, executives in the administrative entities of government) and citizens who have diverse ideas about how the basic public policy questions (who gets what, when, where, how) should be answered. Different answers to these policy questions are demanded in the context of political, social, and economic environments that prevail at a given point in time. Consequently, the formal political systems shape solutions to policy questions in light of the demands and support they get from citizens. Political systems may vary in structure and in ultimate contribution to the development of policy. Any formal policy system must constantly be sensitive to the interests and concerns of the constituents in a particular political environment and must be able to convert these interests and concerns into actual policy.[1] (See Figure 8.1).

The concept of a systems approach to policy development can be applied to educational policy for different levels of government. Local school systems relate to unique political environments as do state educational policy systems. Formal policymakers at the national level must constantly respond to shifts in political interests on the national scene.

The adaptation of Easton's system model in Figure 8.2 more specifically identifies the formal and informal entities that affect policy development and administration in education. It should be remembered that the groups who create demands and build support for the formal political system vary with the political climate of the individual state. Interest groups also come and go in an ad hoc fashion depending on the emergence of diverse social, political, and economic problems.

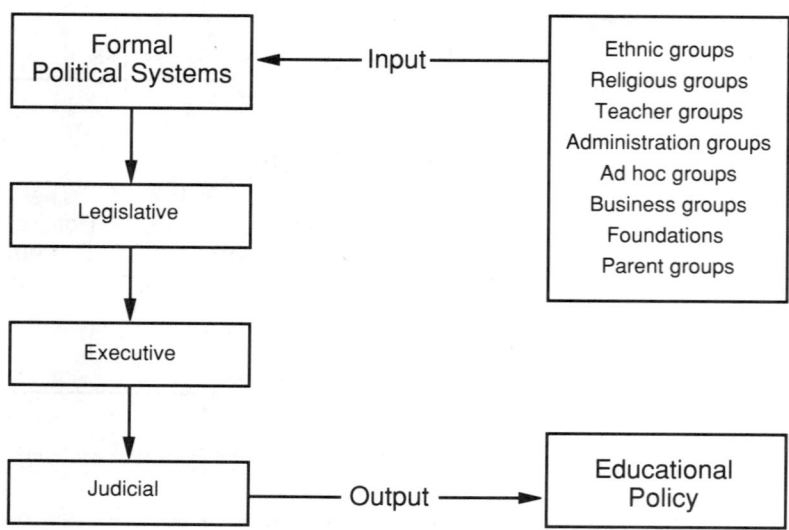

Figure 8.2
Systems Model for Policy
Development

Political environments in the United States are dynamic rather than static. Changing environments produce a variety of informal groups interested in shaping policy development and administration. Because political environments change, such changes affect the identification of diverse needs and interests that must be addressed in educational policy. The varied political environments of the states result in assignment of different roles to different elements of the formal political system. In all states, the legislative branch is protective of the plenary (ultimate) power it possesses over educational policy development. In some states, state court systems are very open to "inputs" from the informal groups and thus serve as a channel for policy development or change. Among the states, the roles and functions assigned to the executive branch of government in educational policy development and administration vary greatly. Political scientists frequently refer to open and closed political systems to describe the relative access that citizens have to the different formal political systems.

Some of the preceding observations about the diverse roles of formal political systems also apply at the federal level. The assertiveness and openness of the federal court system to develop and effect change in

Photo 8.1
State legislative bodies act on many educational policy issues during each legislative session.

educational policy have fluctuated over time in response to changes in the national political environment. For example, the Reagan administration persistently believed that the powers of the executive branch of the federal government (the Department of Education) should be reduced from their previous levels of influence.

The foregoing discussion suggests that systems models can be very useful in explaining educational policy development and administration. Which formal system has the greatest political influence over educational policy in your state? How have changing political environments affected the role of the governor, the legislature, and the courts in the educational reform movement in your state?

Even though systems models are helpful in explaining who is involved in the development of educational policy, they do not adequately explain the steps or processes that typically characterize the evolution of educational policy. Most policy development is "processual" in nature. That is, definite steps and stages in policy development can be identified. In analyzing the process of policy development, the roles of different political systems in the different stages of policy development can be described. Different political environments will also affect the roles that each political system will play in the different stages of policy development.

Charles Jones makes the following distinction between system and process that will be helpful in utilizing the policy models that follow:

> *System refers to two or more persons engaged in patterned or structured interests guided by shared values and working toward the achievement of some goal. . . . Process refers to acts of the system; it is the dynamics of the system and refers to any number of patterned activities in the system.*[2]

Policy models that describe the different phases of policy development and the possible roles of a given political system at a given stage in policy development provide a more complete and helpful basis for explaining educational policy development. Three general phases usually occur in policy development processes. In the predecisional or problem identification stage, problems that need some policy solution are identified and formulated. One group of policy participants (formal or informal) will convince another group that the problem they are focusing on is indeed a problem in need of a solution. For example, diverse formal and informal groups who have been a part of the recent educational reform movement have been able to convince other policy participants that test scores of students in the United States compared with those of students in other countries are a real problem that must be addressed.

The second general phase of policy development involves determining the solution to the problem. In the example just cited, more rigorous curriculum standards, increased high-school graduation requirements, and high-school exit tests are "solutions" that have been "decided" and "legitimized" (made policy) by the formal political system.

During the third general phase of policy development, the "solutions to the problem" or "policy" will be applied and administered. This phase is important because the policy will be interpreted by the parties who have

---

Policy Model 8.1   Framework for Identifying Political Systems and Political Processes

---

PARTICIPANTS IN POLICY DEVELOPMENT	PROCESS	OUTPUT OF STEPS IN POLICY PROCESS
Formal Political System *Federal* Executive Legislative Judicial *State* Executive Legislative Judicial Intermediate units Local units **Informal Political System** PTA NEA AFT	1. Problem identification. 2. Problem formulation. 3. Legitimization of solution (policy) into statute, court precedent, administrative regulation, etc. 4. Application of solution (policy). 5. Evaluation of policy—judging its effects. 6. Augmentation change of the policy as a result of its application.	1. Defining the problem in terms that it can be acted on in executive, judicial, administrative, or legislative system. 2. Shaping the course of regulative or allocative action in terms of social or political feasibility. 3. Bringing the policy to conform to statutory, constitutional, or other recognized principles or standards. 4. Applying allocative or regulative actions that implement policy. 5. Judging the effects of allocative or regulative actions. 6. Reshaping or extending policy to fit new circumstances or demands.

power to enforce or administer it. Policies frequently are modified in the process of application. In the example previously cited, applying higher curriculum standards for all students might affect the dropout rate or the number of students eligible for athletic teams. In some political environments, the effects of applying such a policy would result in new demands for solutions to the new problem of rising dropout rates and fewer students eligible for athletic teams. As a result, the policy would be modified or "augmented" in response to the new problem.

Policy Model 8.1 attempts to bring together elements of the systems and process approaches to help explain policy development for schooling in the United States. This model utilizes the steps in policy development identified by Jones[3] and recognizes the several formal and informal groups that can influence the development of policy through the different phases of policy evolution.

It should be noted that different elements of the formal and informal political systems can have varying inputs into policy evolution during each phase of policy development. Informal political systems frequently are the first to identify problems that need solutions. For example, many of the policy issues being addressed in the school reform movement of the 1980s were first identified as educational problems by concerned citizen groups. By drawing attention to these problems, these groups frequently determine the issues that will be processed by the formal political systems. In simple language, whoever identifies the problem helps to shape the direction of policy solutions.

At the other end of the policy process, administrative groups are called on to administer policy solutions to problems that they did not help to define. For example, a local board may be called on to administer a policy developed by a state legislative group requiring sex education for middle-school students. Implementation of a solution to a problem that was not perceived by a local board or by parent groups could lead to other problems. The basis for augmentation and change of the policy on sex education would thus be established. The effects that a particular policy has on solving a problem is also frequently shaped by those who apply the policy. Unless very rigid accountability measures are taken, local boards may apply the policy on sex education for middle-school students in many different ways. Implementation of a policy thus could have different intended as well as unintended effects.

One other facet of systems and process models needs to be examined. Since policies are solutions to public problems, policymakers usually have in mind specific kinds of effects they want the policies they adopt to have. These effects can be classified into categories based on the kinds of outcomes desired. The following are some possible categories of policy outcomes or effects:

Allocative policies   Determine who gets what, when, where, how.

Regulative policies   Determine who can do what, when, where, how.

Structural policies   Create authority structures for policy implementation and administration.

Redistributive policies   Change resource allocation or regulative/structural authority.

Policy Model 8.2 pulls together the different aspects of the systems and process approaches to policy examined thus far. Elements of the model will be used to analyze policy problems throughout the policy section of this book.

Decentralization of Educational Policy Development

The preceding discussion of the use of systems and process models implies that the United States has a very decentralized system of governance for public education. In fact, it is more correct to say that it does not have a national school system; rather, it has fifty state school systems.

In European countries, the national government owns the schools, finances them through a national tax system, and administers them through a federal or national school bureaucracy. Such centralized school systems are characterized by greater uniformity and standardization. Decision making about the schools is more centralized and in a sense more "efficient," since the national bureaucracies can administer the schools more independently of local whims and interests.

Some critics of the current school governance system argue that U.S. citizens are facing a dilemma regarding their school governance structures.

Policy Model 8.2   Framework for Identifying Political Systems, Policy Processes, Outputs, and Effects

---

PARTICIPANTS IN POLICY DEVELOPMENT	PROCESS	PROCESS OUTPUT	POLICY EFFECT
FORMAL Administrative Executive Judicial Legislative **INFORMAL** Civil rights groups Taxpayer groups Other interest groups Ad hoc groups Professional groups	Problem identification Problem formulation Legitimization Application Evaluation Augmentation	Defining problem for policy action. Shaping course of policy action. Adopting policy in form that complies with legal standards. Implementation of policy according to legal standards. Judging effects of application of policy. Reshaping or extending policy to fit new circumstances or demands.	**Allocative** Who gets what? when? where? how? **Regulative** Who can do what? when? where? how? **Structural** Additions, deletions to structure involved in policy implementation. **Redistributive** Additions, deletions, changes in resource allocation and authority allocation.

By retaining their preference for decentralization and local governance and administration, Americans may fail to address through their schools some of the important issues accompanying national economic and social change.

Historically, it has been somewhat surprising to see the diverse, decentralized elements of school governance respond to changing national needs and interests. However, great similarities exist in schools throughout the country. These similarities have emerged around certain fundamental goals and objectives. Even though most American schools are governed locally by elected boards, public school children study similar subjects and have school experiences with striking degrees of similarity. Certain national interests have helped to formulate common goals of public education shared among the states.

States and local communities have also had a tendency to watch what other localities are doing in their schools and to adopt policies and programs that seem to be successful. This "constructive imitation" has had a significant effect on producing greater standardization of school programs among the states. An analysis of the current school reform movement would indicate that many states are adopting similar solutions to identified educational problems.

Sources of Law that Determine Educational Policy Development and Administration

A variety of legal traditions in the United States determines the limits and powers of the formal and informal political systems in the development and administration of public schooling policy. These sources of legal guidelines can be classified into four main categories: (1) constitutional law, (2) statutory law, (3) judicial precedent, and (4) administrative rules and regulations. These four categories of policy determine the powers, duties, roles, and responsibilities of the different levels of government in education.

Federal Constitution

The framers of the U.S. Constitution make no mention in the Constitution of education. In the eighteenth century, schooling was not judged to be a government function in the sense that it is today. Schooling was provided by the church or home. The Tenth Amendment describes what is frequently referred to as the reserved powers clause. This amendment states, "The powers not delegated to the United States by the Constitution, nor prohibited to it by the states are reserved to the states respectively, or to the people." Thus, by the reserved powers clause, public education in this country became a state responsibility.

Despite the silence of the Constitution on the responsibility of the federal government for public schooling, the federal government has always shown a considerable interest in education. As discussed in Chapters 3 and 4, the federal government, acting under its constitutional obligation to promote general welfare and provide for national security and defense, encouraged various educational programs. The provisions of the First, Fifth, and Fourteenth Amendments have also provided a legal basis for considerable federal involvement in schools in the United States. The impact of these amendments on educational policy is developed more fully in Chapters 10 and 13.

State Constitutional Provisions Relating to Education

Practically all states have some type of constitutional provision relating to the state's responsibility to provide for public schools. Such provisions are not of recent origin. Six of the original thirteen states had constitutional statements relating to education at the time of the formation of the Union. By 1820, thirteen of the existing twenty-three states had constitutional mandates regarding public schooling. The thrust of state constitutional mandates regarding the state's role in schooling is illustrated by Article XI, Section 3, of the South Carolina constitution.

> *The General Assembly shall provide for the maintenance and support of a system of free public schools open to all children in the State and shall establish, organize and support such other public institutions of learning, as may be desirable.*

Several state constitutions simply mandate that the state legislature provide for the establishment and maintenance of a system of free public schools. In other states, the constitutional provisions may be more specific and prescribe methods of selecting chief state school officers, state board members, and local superintendents; give general prescriptions for taxation policy to operate the schools; or establish the nature of administrative units that will be used to manage the school operation in the state. From a policy perspective, it should be noted that most state constitutional provisions grant to the legislature plenary power over school policy.

Federal Statutory Law

Congress first expressed interest in public education by setting aside public land for its support in the Land Ordinance of 1785. Although there was some federal legislation in the nineteenth and early twentieth century, the largest amount of federal legislation relating to public education began to evolve during the 1950s. In light of the states' responsibility to operate schools, how has Congress justified its increased involvement in educational policy development and administration in the past three decades?

The federal government does have constitutional mandates to promote national security and defense and the general welfare as well as the authority to tax for broad social purposes. The U.S. Congress has generally perceived that encouragement of free public education will help "solve" some of the problems it is constitutionally mandated to address. For example, post-Sputnik legislation helped to address national security and national defense issues.

Promoting desegregation and other forms of equal opportunity through such legislation as the 1964 Civil Rights Act, Title IX Amendments, and other statutes would help to address broader social issues of social justice. Beginning in the mid-1960s and continuing through the 1980s, schools were given important roles in helping the nation address the problems of youth unemployment and the need for job training through such legislation as the Comprehensive Employment and Training Act (CETA) and the Job Training Partnership Act (JTPA).

Indeed, there is considerable evidence to suggest that policies relating to education have been a popular way for Congress to deal with the nation's problems. Frequently, Congress has chosen to address problems that states have neglected. Promoting school desegregation, providing for the handicapped, and offering vocational education are examples.

State Statutory Law

Provisions in state constitutions give broad powers to state legislatures to enact laws relating to schooling. These powers are generally limited only by federal and state constitutional provisions and court decisions.

Given the state's responsibility to operate schools and the state legislature's broad powers to enact educational statutes, it should not be surprising that the bulk of educational law in the United States is state law. The volume of educational law is sufficiently great in most states to warrant the organization of educational law into specialized codes including such broad area as:

1. Governmental/administrative arrangements for schooling.

2. School financing.

3. School programs.

4. Personnel policy.

5. Vocational/higher education.

6. Policies relating to students.

7. Policies relating to private schools.

A plethora of educational bills is introduced at the beginning of any given session of a state legislature. It is not unusual for a state legislative body to have hundreds of statutory proposals relating to educational policy introduced in one regular legislative session.

Photo 8.2

Representatives from various citizen groups seek to influence decisions of local boards of education.

Federal and State Court Decisions

Court decisions greatly influence schooling policy in the United States. Each state has its own court system, as does the federal government. Each state court system operates in a unique political environment that determines its roles and relationships to other branches of government. In some states, the state court system may be a very open political system. That is, it will encourage a variety of groups to use the judicial branch as the vehicle to address problems those groups perceive. In other states, legislative bodies overwhelm the influence of the courts through their powers of appointment to the judiciary.

The role of the federal judiciary in educational policy development also changes with shifting political environments. The decision-making philosophy of the federal appellate court system as well as of the Supreme Court can change with new appointments to these respective courts. Cycles of court influence over educational policy development are obvious in the volume of cases reviewed by the courts and the nature of the decisions made by the courts.

John Hogan identified five discernible historical stages of court influence over educational policy development.[4] The first period, a stage of "strict judicial laissez faire" occurred before 1850, when education was viewed as a local matter and even state courts were reluctant to intervene. From 1850 to 1950, there was a "stage of state control," when few cases went to the U.S. Supreme Court. During this period, a number of precedent-setting cases were decided by state courts permitting policies and practices in education that failed to meet federal constitutional standards and requirements. For example, many states adopted statutes requiring Bible reading in the schools. The "reformation stage" started in the 1950s and continued through the 1970s and was characterized by federal appellate court decisions that brought state educational policy and practice into compliance with contemporary interpretations of federal constitutional guidelines.

Table 8.1 Stages of Federal Court Influence over Educational Policy	STAGE 1 BEFORE 1850	STAGE 2 1850–1950	STAGE 3 & 4 1950–1970	STAGE 5 1980s
	Strict judicial laissez faire	Stage of state control; few federal court cases	Reformation stage—state educational law brought into compliance with federal constitution through supervision of the courts	Period of strict constitutional construction

Hogan also notes a fourth period, "education under the supervision of the courts," which occurred concurrently with the third stage and resulted in federal courts taking on enforcement responsibilities to ensure that minimal constitutional requirements were met. Finally, Hogan suggests that the current period is characterized by "strict construction" of the constitution by the courts. Table 8.1 summarizes these stages of federal court influence.

The federal and state courts influence policy development in education in many ways. Courts interpret the meanings of statutes and federal constitutional provisions and apply these meanings to problems. Courts determine the constitutionality of federal and state statutory provisions as well as administrative rules and regulations. Courts are frequently called on to determine the application of statutes to varied educational settings. Court roles in the resolution of conflicts over educational policy have given the court systems additional opportunity to influence policy in recent years. Finally, courts frequently encourage legislative activity in a policy area by decisions made in the court system. For example, in the 1973 decision *San Antonio Independent School District* vs. *Rodriquez*, the Supreme Court held that since education was not a fundamental constitutional right under the equal protection clause, school finance reform should flow from state legislative processes. This decision prompted a large amount of activity by state legislative bodies and state courts to change state policies on school funding.

Administrative Regulations

Appropriate administrative agencies at different levels of government are given authority to implement and monitor policies developed by formal political systems. Discretionary powers granted to these agencies frequently give the agencies great latitude in developing and administering the rules and regulations necessary to implementation and oversight of policy. Volumes of administrative rules and regulations produced by federal, state, and local administrative agencies exist. These rules and regulations generally cover such categories as the following:

1. Delegated responsibilities assigned by constitutional or statutory provisions.
2. Development of necessary standards for monitoring policy.
3. Responsibilities entailed in gathering, reporting, and disseminating data and records necessary for evaluation of policy.

Policy Model 8.3   Analyzing the Federal Executive Branch's Involvement in Educational Policy Development

RATIONALE FOR INVOLVEMENT	PROBLEM ADDRESSED	ILLUSTRATIVE POLICY SOLUTION	POLICY EFFECTS
Jurisdiction given Office of Civil Rights in Department of Health, Education, and Welfare to enforce Title IX, 1972.	Enforcement of prohibitions against sex discrimination in educational institutions in Title IX.	Twenty-seven three-column pages in *Federal Register* of rules and regulations concerning what schools and colleges must do to prevent sex discrimination.	**Regulative** Who will do what in schools and colleges to prohibit sex discrimination
Jurisdiction given Office of Education in the Department of Health, Education, and Welfare to enforce PL 94–142.	Enforcement of PL 94–142 requirements that schools provide schooling opportunities for handicapped.	Forty-four three-column pages in *Federal Register* of rules and regulations concerning implementation of PL 94–142.	**Regulative** Who will do what to provide schooling opportunities for handicapped children
			Allocative Who will get what resources to implement PL 94–142

4. Interpretation of each agency's own rules and regulations.

5. Provisions for hearings and for dealing with disputes arising out of each agency's exercise of discretionary powers.

6. Provision of supervisory and consultative services related to the implementation of policy.

Obviously, granting discretionary powers to administrative agencies to write and interpret such rules and regulations gives the agencies considerable influence. The power to interpret and monitor standards established for the implementation of an educational policy gives an administrative agency considerable clout in controlling the effects of a given policy.

The Federal Government and Educational Policy and Administration

It should be obvious that the federal government has a strong interest in educational policy. This is particularly true for educational policies that relate to national security, general welfare, domestic problems, and constitutional rights. As discussed earlier, each branch of the federal government constitutes a formal political system that is responsive to changing perceptions of problems that could be addressed through educational policy. Policy Models 8.3, 8.4, and 8.5 illustrate the involvement and output of the different branches of the federal government in educational policy development and administration.

Policy Model 8.4   Analyzing the Federal Legislative Branch's Involvement in Educational Policy Development

RATIONALE FOR INVOLVEMENT	PROBLEM ADDRESSED	ILLUSTRATIVE POLICY SOLUTION ADOPTED	POLICY EFFECTS
Promote general welfare	Encourage states to assume responsibility for education.	1785 Land ordinance	**Allocative** Land grants set aside to support schooling
Promote national defense	Enhance quality of math and science in the schools.	1958—National Defense Education Act	**Allocative** Money grants set aside to support schooling
	Identify talented youth—provide aid to attend college.	1958—National Defense Student Loans	**Allocative** Encourage talented youth to attend college
Promote equal rights	Attack discriminatory practices in public institutions.	1964 Civil Rights Act	**Regulative** Who will do what in public institutions to eliminate discriminatory practices?
Promote general welfare	Drug abuse among youth	1986—Drug abuse legislation	**Allocative** Resources allocated for drug education programs in schools **Regulative** Increase mandatory penalties for distribution of drugs in close proximity to schools
Address domestic social problem	Improve educational opportunities for disadvantaged youth	1965—Elementary and Secondary Education Act	**Allocative** Resources allocated for compensatory educational programs for disadvantaged youth

Federal participation and influence in educational policy fluctuates over time. The level of activity by the different branches of the federal government shifts depending on changes in the political environment. Cycles of influence for the judiciary were described earlier in the chapter. During the twenty-year period 1950–1970, the U.S. Congress expanded its influence by enacting a considerable body of educational law. During the late 1960s, questions began to evolve about the results of the policies enacted by Congress during this era of legislative activism. Formal inquiries into the effectiveness of these initiatives were formally commissioned by Congress.

Policy Model 8.5	Analyzing the Federal Judiciary's Involvement in Educational Policy Development		
RATIONALE FOR INVOLVEMENT	**PROBLEM ADDRESSED**	**ILLUSTRATIVE POLICY SOLUTION**	**POLICY EFFECTS**
Court's role in interpreting the meaning of the U.S. Constitution.	Do segregated schools violate equal protection clause of the Fourteenth Amendment?	1954—*Brown* vs. *Board of Education*	**Allocative** Who goes to what school? **Regulative** Segregated schools inherently unequal; states must end de jure segregation
Court's role in interpreting the meaning of the Constitution.	Do minors have certain constitutionally protected rights while in school?	1969—*Tinker* vs. *Des Moines Independent Community School District*	**Allocative** Student granted certain First Amendment rights **Regulative** Schools must be operated in ways to protect student rights
Court's role in defining the meaning of federal statutes.	Defining the meaning of Title VI or the 1964 Civil Rights Act.	1974—*Lau* vs. *Nichols*	**Allocative** School districts must provide special educational services to students who have limited proficiency in English.

The 1966 Coleman Report was one attempt by Congress to judge the effects of efforts to promote greater equality of educational opportunity through compensatory education.[5] This report cast doubt on the wisdom of allocating federal dollars to compensatory educational programs for disadvantaged students, since a student's family background and who the student went to school with were important determinants of achievement in school. The work of Christopher Jencks raised further questions about the capacity of schools to create equal economic opportunity through equalizing educational opportunity.[6]

The pace of legislative activity slacked off for Congress during the 1970s. However, Congress did enact legislation in 1972 establishing the National Institute of Education, an agency devoted to educational research, and in 1979, Congress established the Department of Education. It was argued that the Department of Education would consolidate educational functions found in other departments of the federal government and would give education a cabinet-level status along with other areas of policy concerns, such as labor, agriculture, and transportation.

Even though Congress went through a period of vacillation in the amount of legislation enacted in the 1970s, some scholars argue that legislation such as Title IX, which promoted sex equity, and Public Law 94–142 requiring educational opportunity for the handicapped, illustrates greater intervention and control over schooling. The rules and regulations accompanying each of these statutes were very extensive and stated explicit directions on how public schools were to meet the conditions of these statutes.

With his election in 1980, President Reagan began a program to restructure the federal government. He proposed the elimination of the Department of Education and "federal deregulation" of schools and mechanisms to encourage the private education sector. Clarck and Amiot characterized President Reagan's efforts to redefine the federal role in education in the following way:

Diminution—an effort to reduce the size and scope of federal expenditures in education.

Deregulation—an effort to reduce federal control in the field of education.

Disestablishment—an effort to eliminate the bureaucratic structure for education at the federal level, that is the Department of Education.

De-emphasis—to remove educational policy from a position of priority on the federal agenda.[7]

Given the cyclical nature of federal influence over educational policy, what projections could be made about the federal government's role in public education in the future? Since federal participation and influence have been around for a long time, they are likely to continue. The language of most federal statutes remained intact during the Reagan years. Given federal budgetary problems, federal money for public schooling will be more difficult to obtain. Each of the branches of the federal government will continue to play its respective role to influence educational policy development and administration. Cycles of influence will continue as society responds to changes in perceptions about which of the social and political institutions offer the greatest hope in addressing domestic, defense, economic, and social problems.

State Government and Educational Policy Development and Administration

States have responded to the reserved powers clause of the Tenth Amendment to make the operation of public schools one of the largest of all state government endeavors. Even though there are forces at work that bring about similarities among state school systems, there are unique forces at work in each state that produce unique approaches to school policy and administration.

Even though some claim that schools should be operated in isolation from partisan politics, in reality each state has its own political ecology that greatly affects the kinds of policies that will be developed and administered in the schools. Consider the following. Each state has its own history and tradition in terms of political party competition. Each state has developed through constitutional and statutory provisions the distribution of political power to the different branches of government. Economic and demographic differences among the states create different "problems" to be addressed by the school system. Differences in religious and ethnic constituencies among the states create different demands for policies regarding private schools and for programs responsive to diverse population groups.

States began to recognize the need for special governance structures for education quite early. By 1812, New York became the first state to have a chief state school officer. Thirty-six states had chief school officers by 1870. State boards of education evolved at roughly the same time as state superintendents of education.

Even though each state has evolved its own governance structure to deal with education, state legislatures, governors, and state court systems have not relinquished control of school policy and governance. In fact, several forces have converged in recent years to enhance the interest in education by the different branches of state government. For example, during the 1970s and 1980s, many governors came to view education as a very viable political issue. Governors have since been adding specialists in education to their staffs to help direct educational reform and to help carry out their policy agenda in education.

Proposals for educational reform have become key issues in the partisian political platforms in the campaigns for seats in legislative bodies. Debates over the allocation of additional tax resources to schools have forced legislative bodies to become more interested in accountability of programs funded. School expenditures for the nation as a whole went up 600 percent between 1960 and 1980, while the gross national product increased only 419 percent.[8] A greater percentage of these additional funds allocated to education came from the states. Thus, state legislative bodies have become more concerned with policy and governance measures to ensure accountability and evaluation of the education programs that consumed additional state tax resources.

State formal political systems have also taken more initiative because of the breakdown in cooperation among teacher/administrator groups historically making up state education coalitions. These coalitions suffered from the labor-management split that occurred while collective negotiations were being established as a way to work out personnel matters for school employees. As Rosenthal and Fuhrman note in their review of change in school governance in the 1970s:

> . . . . *By the end of the decade legislatures were in the thick of policy making in education. Many had wrestled the initiative from state departments and interest groups; and most had started to exercise control over the design, funding, implementation, and assessment of education in their state.*[9]

Plenary Powers of State Legislative Bodies in Education

The constitutional provisions of many states use language that grants plenary power over educational policy to legislative bodies. This power does not mean that legislative bodies have no restrictions on their authority in educational matters. State legislative bodies cannot take actions that are contrary to other state constitutional provisions or federal constitutional guidelines. They cannot exercise their authority in an unreasonable or arbitrary manner. Even though they can delegate certain powers to other governmental entities, they cannot grant their plenary power to another governmental agency.

Given these plenary powers, state legislatures decide most basic policy questions regarding the schools. The statutes they write can be divided into two groups: (1) permissive statutes that define the functions and duties of government agencies and (2) mandatory statutes that establish required activities, minimum standards, or guidelines. The following list includes examples of the broad range of educational policy issues decided by state legislative bodies:

1. Kinds of educational programs offered—early childhood, K–12, vocational, technical, special schools, higher education.
2. Minimum standards for instructional programs.
3. Guidelines for training and certification of school personnel.
4. Standards for school facilities.
5. Responsibilities and methods of selection for state boards of education and state superintendents.
6. Functions of state departments of education.
7. Number, types, and functions of school districts.
8. The methods and level of financial support for schools, including guidelines for tax policy for local school districts.
9. Compulsory attendance laws.
10. Length of school terms.
11. Special programs, such as competency testing and driver education.
12. Guidelines for auxilary services, such as transportation and school lunch.
13. Laws regarding private school operations in the state.

State legislative bodies have recently exerted greater independence in developing their own perceptions of solutions to educational policy problems. They have retained their own consultants and formed their own task forces to help them address specific policy questions. There is some evidence that this independence has made them less affected by special interest lobbying by professional groups in their deliberation over policy solutions.

Governors and Educational Policy

Governors have varying degrees of formal influence over educational policy granted by constitutional or statutory law. Some states have defined very limited powers in such matters as appointments to state boards and school financing. Other states have strengthened the governor's hand in such matters. Even in states where governors have limited powers, there are many avenues by which the holder of this office can influence educational policy. The governor is usually head of his or her political party in his or her state. This position as head of the political party is crucial, especially in a school reform era. The governor has many opportunities to create awareness of educational conditions and aspirations in his or her state.

Box 8.1
Examples of Policy
Priorities Adopted By
the National
Governor's
Association

Time for Results: The Governor's 1991 Report on Education, released by the National Governor's Association in September 1986, raised some tough questions about schooling in the United States. The report also makes some recommendations that could have significant implications for governance and administration of schools. Consider the following recommendations made by the governors:

> States should work out a fair, affordable, career ladder salary system that recognizes real differences in functions, competence, and performance of teachers.

> States should create leadership programs for school leaders.

> Parents should have more choice in the public schools their children attend.

> The nation, the states, and school districts all need better report cards about results—about what students know and can do.

> School districts and schools that don't make the grade should be declared operationally bankrupt and taken over by the states.

> States should work with four- and five-year olds from poor families to help get them ready for school and to decrease the chances that they will drop out later.

How do you think school governance would change if the governors are successful in getting legislation passed to carry out these recommendations?

Governors are directly involved in the budgetary process. They can kill or threaten to kill educational measures through veto. They can call special sessions of legislative bodies to consider pressing budgetary or educational issues. Some governors have significant influence over educational policy matters by their appointment of members to state boards or to the state superintendency. Finally, in recent years, governors have been adding their own special staff members to develop and guide educational policy proposals through the legislative process.

State Boards of Education

The first state board of education was created in Massachusetts in 1837. Early on, state boards tended to be relatively weak, because state legislatures scattered limited powers over a broad range of state entities and officials. Modern state boards are often charged with exercising general control over elementary and secondary education and in a few states have limited jurisdiction over higher education. Most states have separate boards or commissions to oversee higher education and in some cases technical and vocational education.

State boards have policymaking functions in those areas delegated by the state legislature. Also, state board members have the opportunity to support positions taken by the governor and legislature on educational policy questions. Rarely, state boards take significant policy initiatives on their own. Rather, they act mainly to legitimize policy recommendations of the chief school officer, who typically serves as the chief executive officer of the state board.

The size of state boards varies among the states and ranges from three to twenty-seven members.[10] The membership of state boards has changed significantly since the 1960s with more women and minorities now serving on state boards. A vast majority of state board members have at least some post-secondary education. Three-fourths of state board members list their occupations as either managerial or professional.[11]

The specific duties and functions of state boards vary among the states. Generally state boards have the following functions:

1. Determine the areas of service, establish qualifications, and appoint the necessary personnel for the state department of education.

2. Develop a budget for the operation of the state department of education.

3. Authorize needed studies and develop and submit proposals for improving schools in the state.

4. Adopt policies and standards for the administration and supervision of the state educational enterprise.

5. Set standards for training and certification of school personnel.

6. Manage funds earmarked for education.

7. Represent the state on matters pertaining to education that involve relationships with the federal government.

8. Act as a hearing body for disputes arising from administrative rules and regulations.

9. When authorized to do so, adopt policies for the operation of special institutions maintained by the state.

Chief State School Officers

The chief state school officer carries the title of state superintendent of education in most states but is known as superintendent of public instruction or state commissioner of education in other states. Most chief state school officers are constitutional officers, since this position is sanctioned by state constitutions.

States typically established chief state officers during the common school movement between 1820 and 1860. Controversy has prevailed regarding the best method of filling the office. By 1920, two thirds of the states selected chief school officers through popular election. The number of states electing chief school officers has been significantly reduced in the past three decades. More states are allowing appointment of state superintendents either by state boards of education or by the governor. As of 1982, eighteen states elected state superintendents, twenty-seven states allowed appointment by state boards of education, and five states allowed governors to appoint chief state school officers.[12] The method used to fill the office affects the chief school officer's role in development and administration of state school policy.

The functions of chief school officers have changed over time. Superintendents in the nineteenth century had responsibilities that were primarily clerical in nature. As school programs expanded, more regulatory duties were added. Even though the duties of state school officers vary among the states, the responsibilities of a contemporary chief state school officer include the following:

1. Serve as secretary and executive officer of the state board of education.

2. Serve as the administrative head and professional leader of the state department of education.

3. Arrange for studies of schooling and organize committees and task forces to identify problems and to recommend plans for effecting improvements in education.

4. Recommend to the state board of education policies, standards, and regulations relating to public education in the state.

5. Recommend educational legislation to the state legislature.

6. Work with the state board and state legislature to improve funding of schools in the state.

7. Explain and interpret the school laws and regulations.

8. Impartially decide controversies and disputes involving the administration of the public school system.

9. Issue annual reports on the condition of education in the state.

Some chief state school officers have taken very assertive roles in the school reform movement in the past few years. They have frequently worked in cooperation with special task forces to formulate significant reform legislation that may even include new roles and responsibilities of the chief school officer and state department of education.

State Departments of Education

The functions and duties of state departments of education have evolved and changed as educational programs among the states have developed. Beach and Gibbs outlined in general terms the evolution of major functions of state departments of education.[13] Up until roughly 1900, state education departments were concerned with gathering, compiling, and disseminating statistical information on public schools. After 1900, states began to adopt standards for public schools. State departments gradually became the agency to monitor whether or not legislative requirements were being met.

In the third phase of their development, state education departments began to take on leadership roles. Educational specialists and consultants were employed to help intermediate and local administrative units improve the quality of educational programs. This phase of state department development was not evident in many states until the 1950s. The increased tempo of federal activity in education in the 1960s contributed to the support and expansion of state department of education professional staffs and activities.

It appears that in the 1970s and 1980s, state education departments may be entering into a "partnership phase" of development. State departments are being called upon to work more closely with state legislative bodies and task forces—federal educational agencies as well as intermediate and local districts.[14] The contemporary function of state departments of education could be broadly classified into five major categories:

1.   Operational. Some state departments operate special schools for handicapped, gifted, vocational rehabilitation, etc.

2.   Regulatory. These agencies monitor whether or not established regulations and standards are met in state educational institutions.

3.   Service. State departments provide advice, consultants, and publications regarding school operations.

4.   Developmental. State departments engage in planning, research, and other developmental activities.

5.   Public support and cooperation. State departments of education engage in general public relations activity with the general public and the state's formal political entities and in interagency relations with federal and state agencies.

Local School Districts and Intermediate Units

The local school district is the basic administrative entity that has delegated power to operate schools. Public schools in the United States, except in Hawaii, are part of a local school district. The local district system of administration evolved at a time when local control was preferred as a way to operate and administer schools.

Local school districts are a political subdivision of the state. They are subject to the limitations imposed by constitutional and statutory provisions. School district boundaries, powers, and jurisdiction can be changed by state legislative bodies. In legal terms, a school district is a quasi-municipal corporation created to serve the governmental purpose of operating public schools. The geographical boundaries of a school district may be coterminous with a city, county, or township, or they may cover any diverse combination of geographic boundaries.

School districts may vary according to the type of educational services and programs provided. Some school districts operate only elementary schools, some operate only secondary schools, and still others operate both elementary and secondary schools. Many states have statutory provisions for the formation and operation of junior college districts. School districts vary greatly in the number of pupils served, the number of institutions operated, and the financial resources available to operate the schools. Table 8.2 gives descriptive information about the size and number of school districts in the United States.[15]

It should be noted that states have gradually reduced the number of local school districts. In 1930, there were in excess of 130,000 school districts; by 1950, there were still over 83,000 school districts. This number was reduced to 15,625 by 1980–81. Reduction in the number of school districts has been brought about through district consolidation. The goals of consolidation have included greater efficiency in the operation of schools and the creation of administrative units that would have sufficient financial resources necessary to offer the range of educational programs and services needed.

Since states can create governmental entities such as school districts to manage schools, governmental agents can be given delegated powers and duties to operate schools. Local boards are usually considered the state's

Table 8.2 Distribution of Public School Systems By Size of District: 1980–1981	SIZE OF DISTRICT (NUMBER OF PUPILS)	PUBLIC SCHOOL DISTRICTS		PUBLIC SCHOOL STUDENTS	
		NUMBER	PERCENTAGE	NUMBER	PERCENTAGE
	Total operating districts	15,625	100.0	42,851,396	100.0
	25,000 or more	183	1.2	11,907,985	27.8
	10,000–24,999	511	3.3	7,434,630	17.3
	5,000–9,999	1,106	7.1	7,705,372	18.0
	2,500–4,999	2,065	13.2	7,181,460	16.8
	1,000–2,499	3,457	22.1	5,665,386	13.2
	600–999	1,820	11.7	1,437,725	3.4
	300–599	2,316	14.8	1,014,640	2.4
	Fewer than 300	4,161	26.6	504,198	1.2

Source: *Digest of Education Statistics 1983–84* (Washington, D.C., National Center for Education Statistics, 1984). table 50, p 62.

agents and have specifically delegated powers and limited discretionary authority to run the schools. Local boards have policy and decision-making responsibility in such matters as local tax support for schools, provision of physical facilities for schools, and employment of school personnel and limited authority in such areas as school curriculum and student policies. Since their powers are delegated, local boards must comply with mandated state and federal guidelines.

Each state has the prerogative of adopting the methods used to select board members. Most local board members are elected. Some states have permissive statutes allowing for either election or appointment. Board members generally come from middle- and upper middle-class backgrounds and have professional and proprietary occupations. Increasing numbers of females and minorities have been appointed or elected to serve on local boards in recent years. Teachers cannot hold a seat on a board in the district where they are employed but can usually serve on a local board in the district where they reside.

Local school districts and state departments of education were organized long before intermediate administrative units were developed. As state education agencies took on more regulative and service functions, intermediate administrative units evolved. County superintendents were a popular expression of this intermediate level of administration. As state departments began to assume more leadership and partnership roles with local school districts, Regional Educational Service Agencies (RESA, or ESA) became a more popular expression of intermediate administrative units. Some states have county superintendents whose administrative unit shares the same geographical boundary as the local school district. Serious questions could be raised about the overlapping and redundancy of this type of intermediate unit.

Intermediate units usually provide complementary and supplementary services and serve as a link between state departments and local school districts. They are a legal or political extension of the state. With the sweeping educational reforms being approved by legislative bodies in some states, intermediate units are being given more enforcement and regulatory duties. As a result, the number of staff members for these units is increasing as the units add a wide range of consulting and service activities to their functions.

Summary

It is difficult to make a generalized accounting of how policy for public schooling is developed and administered in the United States. Different branches of federal and state governments have varying responsibilities depending on the political ecology of the particular state and the changing perceptions of the role of the federal government in education.

Most educational policy is developed at the state level, since states have assumed legal responsibility for education under the reserved powers clause of the Tenth Amendment. Each state has its own constitutional and statutory provisions that assign policy responsibilities to executive, judicial, legislative, and administrative bodies. State legislative bodies usually have plenary power to delegate responsibilities to various types of administrative units.

Systems and process models are helpful in explaining policy development and administration in education. These models can be used to help describe how both formal and informal political groups participate in the different steps or processes that characterize policy development and administration for American schools.

Key Words

Systems model	Federal deregulation
Process model	Education coalition
Informal political systems	Plenary power
Formal political systems	Permissive statute
Judicial laissez faire	District consolidation
Open political system	Constructive imitation
Discretionary power	

Discussion Questions

1. Which level of government do you think should have primary responsibility for governing schools in the United States?

2. Do you agree that the lack of centralization in school governance in the United States has contributed to the level of standards and performance being criticized in recent school reform reports?

3. Would you favor an amendment to the U.S. Constitution making education a responsibility of the federal government?

4. Describe some of the unique features of the political ecology of your state that influences educational policy development and administration.

5. Should teachers and other educational professionals be able to serve on local boards of education in the school district where they are employed?

For Further Reading

Campbell, Roald F., et al. *The Organization and Control of American Schools,* 5th ed. Columbus, Ohio: Charles E. Merrill, 1985.

Digest of Educational Statistics. Washington, D.C., National Center for Educational Statistics. See latest edition.

Educational Governance in the States: A Report of the Council of Chief State School Officers. Washington, D.C.: U.S. Department of Education, 1983.

Jones, Charles O. *An Introduction to the Study of Public Policy*. Belmont, Calif.:Wadsworth Press, 1970.

Kenezevich, Steven J. *Administration of Public Education*, 4th ed. New York: Harper & Row, 1984.

Kimbrough, Ralph B., and Nunnery, Michael Y. *Educational Administration*, 2nd ed. New York: Macmillan, 1983.

Stoops, Emery, et al. *Handbook of Educational Administration*. 2nd ed. Boston: Allyn & Bacon, 1981.

Notes

1. David Easton, *A Framework for Political Analysis* (Englewood Cliffs, N.J.: Prentice-Hall, 1965), p. 112.

2. Charles O. Jones, *An Introduction to the Study of Public Policy* (Belmont, Calif.: Wadsworth Press, 1970), p. 12.

3. *Ibid.*, p.14.

4. John C. Hogan, *The Schools, The Courts, and the Public Interest* (Lexington, Mass.: D.C. Heath, 1974), pp. 5–14.

5. See James S. Coleman et al., *Equality of Educational Opportunity* (Washington, D.C.: U.S. Government Printing Office, 1966).

6. See Christopher Jencks et al., *Inequality: A Reassessment of the Effects of Family and Schooling in America* (New York: Basic Books, 1972).

7. David C. Clarck and Mary Ann Amiot, "The Disassembly of the Federal Role," *Education and Urban Society* 15 (May 1983), pp. 368–69.

8. *Statistical Abstract of the United States* (Washington, D.C.: U.S. Government Printing Office, 1982) pp. 154, 149.

9. Alan Rosenthal and Susan Fuhrman, *Legislative Education Leadership in the States* (Washington, D.C.: Institute for Educational Leadership, 1981), p. 1.

10. *Educational Governance in the States: A Report of the Council of Chief School Officers* (Washington, D.C.: U.S. Department of Education, 1983), pp. 4–6.

11. David Wiley, *State Boards of Education* (Arlington, Va.: National Association of State Boards of Education, 1983), pp. 15–16.

12. *Ibid.*

13. See F.F. Beach and A.H. Gibbs, *Personnel of State Departments of Education* (Washington, D.C.: U.S. Office of Education, 1952).

14. Stephen J. Kenezevich, *Administration of Public Education*, 4th ed. (New York: Harper & Row, 1984), p. 17.

15. *Digest of Educational Statistics*, 1983–84 (Washington, D.C.: National Center for Educational Statistics, 1984), p. 62.

9

The Informal Structure and Educational Policymaking

"NEA objectives can best be achieved by a federal collective bargaining statute that is based on the power of Congress to regulate interstate commerce, and the February 1985 decision of the United States Supreme Court in *Garcia* v. *San Antonio Metropolitan Transit Authority* indicates that this type of statute would be constitutional."

NEA Legislative Program (1985–86)

". . . The curriculum used in the (Mobile County) school system unconstitutionally advanced the religion of humanism, unconstitutionally inhibited Christianity, systematically excluded history of the contributions of Christianity to the American way of life, denied to teachers and students free speech and free exercise of their religion (as guaranteed under the First Amendment), and violated the Code of Alabama. . . ."

Complainants, *Smith* v. *Board of Commissioners of Mobile County* (1987)

"For schools, the establishment clause (of the First Amendment) always meant that you cannot teach a religious belief. But Judge Hand said the failure to include religion (in the curricula) is itself creating a new religion called secular humanism, which is therefore forbidden. So if you include religion you are establishing religion, and if you exclude religion, you are establishing religion. It's an untenable position for schools."

Attorney August W. Steinhilber, in response to *Smith* v. *Board of Commissioners of Mobile County* (1987)

217

The opening quotations point out that strong views concerning educational policy can be promoted by groups that are not a part of the formal educational policymaking structure. The preceding chapter introduced the formal legal structure of our public educational system. Educational policies made by various parts of this formal structure are developed on the basis of the pressures exerted by individuals and groups interested in particular outcomes. The components of the legal structure must deal with the pressures exerted upon them and make decisions on the basis of the actual or perceived power of the multitude of interested parties. The interested parties include organized groups that are part of the educational endeavor such as teacher organizations, interested parents, and accrediting agencies. Groups organized to promote various interests not directly associated with education also make known their views. They include many organizations representing the business community, civil rights groups, religious organizations, and tax-exempt foundations. In addition, some individuals by virtue of their positions in society, their prestige, or their wealth may have considerable influence on educational policymaking.

The term *informal structure* is used to describe the individuals and groups that exert pressure and attempt to influence educational policy yet are not part of the formal legal structure. Some scholars refer to these groups and individuals as making up the extra legal structure of education. Note that the extra legal, or informal, structure is a part of our democratic heritage and is a means by which citizens can attempt to influence governmental activity.

Any discussion of the informal or extra legal structure of education must include a number of items that are important in understanding the complicated process by which educational policy is formulated. Individuals generally hold memberships in many groups. The same citizen could conceivably belong to a religious group, a service club, the chamber of commerce, a taxpayers' group, and a parent-teacher organization—all centered in a local community. The same person could also be a member of a number of groups that have primary interests in state or national issues rather than local issues. Each of these groups may be interested in educational issues, but the positions they advocate could be markedly different, with variations among individual group members. A member of a parent organization that advocates increased taxes for public schools could also be a member of a taxpayers' group advocating lower taxes for the community. A teacher could be a member of the National Education Association, which might endorse a candidate supportive of education and be in favor of pro choice on abortion legislation. The teacher could also belong to a religious group advocating a pro life position. This type of dilemma is not uncommon, and it complicates assessment of what communities, citizens, and groups really want as educational policy. An understanding of this process is important in trying to determine the real desires of citizens concerning educational policy.

Recently the growth of groups advocating a position on a single issue has become a common part of our political process. Groups supporting a particular position, especially if it is on a controversial issue, have been formed and have in certain instances obtained large monetary donations to advance their position. This has led to support for or opposition to political candidates, school officials, or legislation based on the single issue rather than on an evaluation of total activity or performance. Single-issue groups, such as Mothers Against Drunk Drivers (MADD), could command such intense commitment that support for or opposition to a candidate could rest exclusively on the candidate's position related to that issue.

During the course of American history, a number of influential reports on education have been sponsored and disseminated by tax-exempt foundations. Recent history again illustrates the influence of this type of activity on educational policy development. The Carnegie Foundation, for example, has on numerous occasions provided funds and support to individuals or groups to study and report on educational issues. These reports are then issued and disseminated in a manner that the foundation believes will influence educational policymakers. A discussion of these and other issues together with information concerning some of the major components of the informal structure of education will facilitate a greater understanding of educational policy formulation.

Sources of Informal Pressures

The formal legal structure of American education has national, state, and local components. Each component is subject to pressures exerted by the various groups and individuals interested in educational policy. Groups interested in particular policy solutions must bring pressure to bear on the component of the legal structure that has authority to act on the problem in question. Table 9.1 illustrates the variety of informal groups that exert pressure on the formal legal structure.

Although not all of the fifty state systems of education are similar in all respects, some generalizations can be made. In recent years, the state authorities have tended to centralize more of the decision making at the state level. Local schools have tended to lose some autonomy in the process. Financing of schools has tended to move in the direction of an increased percentage of funds supplied by the state. Though local districts still supply significant portions of the school budget, pressures concerning the financing of schools have been centered on the state's decision-making bodies. At the federal level, the particular political party in power will set the tone concerning the size of the federal role in making educational policy. These relationships are explained in detail in Chapter 14.

A first step in the study of informal pressures is to discuss each of these components and attempt to analyze the informal structure that shapes decisions at each level. In addition, some interest groups and organizations that have played major roles in the shaping of educational policy will be highlighted and reviewed in this chapter.

The Local Community

Pressures can be exerted on any part of the formal system in order to attempt to shape, formulate, or influence educational policy. Some individuals and groups have a distinctly local character and are primarily interested in changing or influencing local school district policy. Questions concerning school bus routes, a specific school discipline regulation, or boundary lines of attendance zones are examples of items that can be local in nature and yet can generate intense pressures on individual school administrators and local boards of education. Occasionally, a local policy can become very contro-

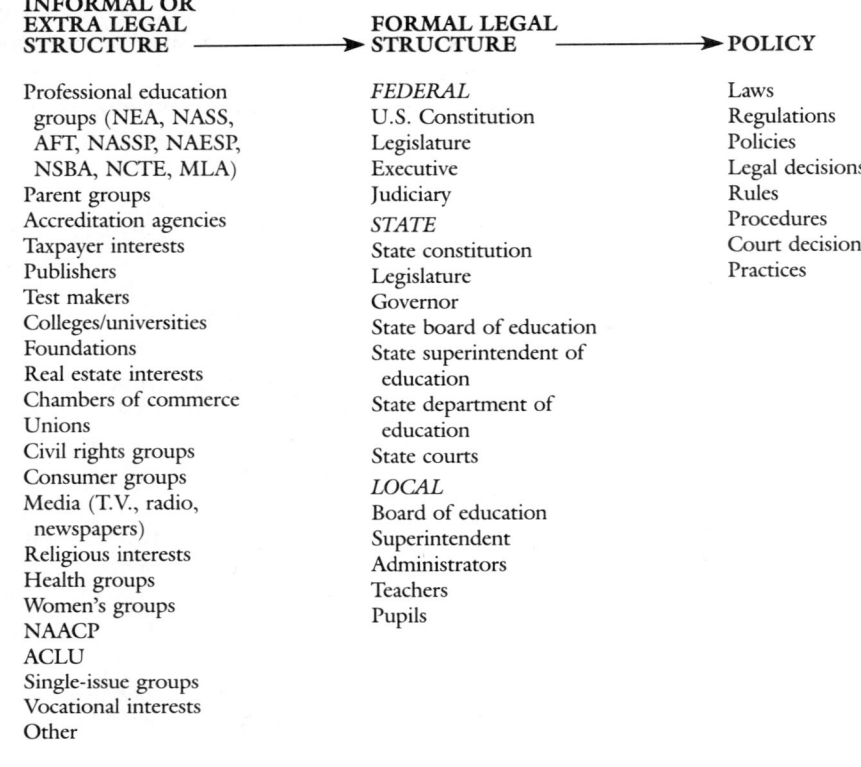

Table 9.1
Influence of Informal Legal Structure on Formal Legal Structure in Educational Policymaking

INFORMAL OR EXTRA LEGAL STRUCTURE →	FORMAL LEGAL STRUCTURE →	POLICY →
Professional education groups (NEA, NASS, AFT, NASSP, NAESP, NSBA, NCTE, MLA)	*FEDERAL* U.S. Constitution Legislature Executive Judiciary	Laws Regulations Policies Legal decisions
Parent groups Accreditation agencies Taxpayer interests Publishers Test makers Colleges/universities Foundations Real estate interests Chambers of commerce Unions Civil rights groups Consumer groups Media (T.V., radio, newspapers) Religious interests Health groups Women's groups NAACP ACLU Single-issue groups Vocational interests Other	*STATE* State constitution Legislature Governor State board of education State superintendent of education State department of education State courts *LOCAL* Board of education Superintendent Administrators Teachers Pupils	Rules Procedures Court decisions Practices

versial, and an entire community can be so divided that confrontation among the various points of view cannot be avoided. Serious conflicts can arise over such issues as sex education, the attempted removal of objectionable reading material from the school library, or complaints concerning instructional material and textbooks used in teaching.

Local pressures are not always obvious, but those involved in the school's day-to-day operation must be cognizant of the many informal pressure sources. Occasionally when there are some obvious disagreements concerning educational policy, the concerns become public, and if the issue is controversial, various community sources may participate in an attempt to resolve the dilemma. Depending on the particular community and the issue in question, a number of alternatives could result. The following are some examples of possible scenarios:

Support for the policy at issue could be strong enough to sustain it.

Support opposing the policy at issue could be strong enough to have the policy modified or eliminated.

Call for changes in school board membership could result.

Increased interest in school board elections could occur.

School administrators could be removed or transferred.

Teacher dismissals could be demanded.

Dissatisfied parties could resort to the judicial system.

In some circumstances, violence could erupt in the community.

An example of the intense pressures and effects on local districts that can be generated by the informal structure occurred in Kanawha County, West Virginia, in 1975. A number of citizens in this school district were upset over the selection of instructional materials used in the district's English program. They claimed the materials were anti-God, anti-American, and communistic. The materials in their view were profane and inappropriate and supported a religion of secular humanism. The board of education was requested to remove the objectionable material from the curriculum but refused. The protesters initiated legal action, seeking a court ruling that would support the removal of the material on the grounds that their religious liberty was violated by the school board's ruling. The Federal district court ruled in favor of the defendant school district. The decision of the court stated in part:

> . . . *The court finds nothing in the defendant's conduct or acts which constitutes an inhibition on or prohibition of the free exercise of religion. These rights are guaranteed by the First Amendment, but the Amendment does not guarantee . . . that nothing offensive to any religion will be taught in the schools.*
> *. . . Plaintiffs and parties . . . with reference to books and materials found offensive and objectionable by them, may find administrative remedies through board of education proceedings or ultimately at the polls on election day.[1]*

The decision did not satisfy the protesting parents, who organized a boycott of the school and public demonstrations opposing the policies of the board. Community feelings were so strained that numerous acts of violence occurred. Two men were shot during the demonstrations, school buses were shot at during their runs to pick up pupils, and a school was bombed. The school board estimated that the cost to taxpayers was over two million dollars. Finally the protesting parents succeeded in gathering enough support to reconstitute the board membership at the next election. Subsequently, the board changed the English curriculum to satisfy the protesters (see Table 9.2). Even though the court agreed that the board of education had the authority to determine curriculum materials, it can be seen that informal groups influence educational policy.

The State Level

In recent years, the formal legal structure concerned with statewide educational policymaking has been very active. The policymakers have centralized much of the decision-making authority in the various state-centered components of the legal structure. The chapters on equality in education and public school finance (Chapters 12 and 14) give detail examples of this process of centralization. It is important, however, to note here that much recent policymaking has been mandated at the state level. The informal structure has had to turn its attention to the state level in order to influence educational policy. The components of the informal structure

Table 9.2
Educational Policymaking Through Informal Pressures Kanawha County, West Virginia

Local board of education approves the use of text material.

Individuals and community groups are critical of the material.

The school board is requested to change the decision.

The board of education stands by the original decision.

The critics resort to the courts.

The court decision supports the board of education.

Community groups boycott the school, violence erupts, school property is damaged, citizens are injured.

Community groups seek change in school board membership.

Election results in the incumbents' losing their seats to those favorable to the groups seeking a policy change.

New board of education reverses previous decision and bans use of controversial material.

have concentrated on influencing state legislators, state education agencies, state boards of education, and state governors. Therefore, more of the action concerning educational policy has been centered in the various state capitals.

Although there are similarities in the way in which the states allocate the authority and control over education, there are also marked differences. Some states have strong executive branches, while others do not. Some state legislative bodies exert strict, detailed control over education, while others give broad discretionary powers to the state education agency. Some state boards of education are elected by the voters, while other states have politically appointed boards. Some state superintendents are elected by the voters of the state, while others are appointed by the state board of education. These variations make it important to look closely at developments in each state. Educational policymaking can take different directions and require different approaches, depending on the allocation of authority and control in a particular state.

Any of a number of reform movements of the past twenty-five years could be used as examples of the power and operation of the informal structure in influencing educational policy at the state level. The school finance reform movement in the 1970s is an example of a rather complicated movement that utilized segments of the informal structure to implement change. The types of finance reform advocated are covered in Chapter 14. Chapter 9 is concerned with the approach used to achieve change. Various groups in the nation became interested in reforming the financial structure of public education. The groups communicated their views and concerns and eventually formed what political scientists call an interstate policy network. The operation and work of the network is outlined in detail in *Schools in Conflict* by Wirt and Kirst.[2] The components of a network include an element that funds the operation, lawyers, private nonprofit advocacy organizations, technical expertise from organizations or individual scholars, and funded graduate students preparing to become activists for the cause.

The network advocating finance reform was funded by the Ford Foundation, which "provided publicity, grants, travel, and recognition as resources to motivate and bond together the network participants. Indeed, it funds, directly or indirectly, all the network's major elements, . . ."[3]

The following is a shortened version of what Wirt and Kirst describe as the method used by the network to achieve reform:

1. The Ford Foundation provides grants to groups interested in school finance reform. These groups provide lawyers to sue the state and to coordinate interstate legal activities. The Western Center on Law and Poverty is an example of this type of group.

2. Private agencies such as the League of Women Voters and the National Urban Coalition publicize general principles the network supported.

3. Scholars testify as expert court witnesses in favor of reform.

4. State politicians and political institutions employ network scholars as chief advisers.

5. Research and action centers oriented to minority groups are funded by the Ford Foundation. These groups continue to publicize minority concerns.

6. Graduate students at universities receive full scholarships to prepare to become reform advocates.[4]

The reform movement in educational finance utilized a well-financed, complex interstate policy network to pursue its goals. Additional illustrations are given to document the increased activity in educational policymaking at the state level.

Recent critical reports concerning public education in America have stimulated a great deal of discussion about the performance of the educational system. Groups and individuals have used some of the findings of these reports as a basis for seeking changes in educational policy. The efforts to change educational policies have been varied and have taken different pathways in the various states. In some states, informal groups seeking change have been influential enough that the formal authorities have responded to the demands for change. Governors and other political office holders in some states noted that it was politically profitable to seek major changes in the state educational system. Programs were presented by the individuals seeking change, and informal groups were sought to support the programs. The changes included the broadening of the accountability movement to include student performance. The use of basic skills examinations, exit tests, and "no pass no play" regulations are examples of the movement. In addition, many of the serious social problems facing our society have focused attention on the use of our institutions of education to help solve the problems. The types of school programs advocated to help solve social problems are usually controversial and create deep differences of opinions. Drug education, sex education, and AIDS education are examples of such controversial issues.

Regardless of whether the policy change originated with a part of the informal structure or the formal legal structure, support from the informal portion of the policy process is vital to successful implementation. The process can be further complicated by showing that one movement that seeks policy change in education can be opposed by another view that also seeks change.

The increase in activity of interest groups working to influence educational policy at the state level can bring conflict between competing interstate policy networks. The finance reform network, which was described earlier, promoted increased state funding as the means to overcome inequality and discrimination in the financing of public schools. Together with other interest groups, it has succeeded in substantially increasing the amount of state money allocated to public education. This increased dependence on state funds has resulted in the coordination of efforts among groups opposing tax increases. California's Proposition 13 (which limited tax rates), balanced budget legislation, and numerous tax expenditure limitation proposals in other states attest to the seriousness of the movement. The coordination of efforts in various states has resulted in a rather loose interstate policy network to promote tax expenditure limitation.

The active area in determining educational policy today is at the state level. As noted earlier, states differ in how the educational enterprise is organized and controlled. Each state must be studied individually to understand particular educational policy decisions. Since the many controversial policy issues described are being debated today, it is imperative that citizens understand the educational policy process and its operation in their state.

The National Level

The formal structure on the national level is composed of Congress, the executive branch, and the federal judiciary. Informal groups exert pressure upon that branch that they perceive to be powerful at a particular time. During the presidency of Lyndon Johnson, for example, the Great Society programs and their goal of eliminating poverty focused pressure on Washington. Congress and the executive branch were perceived as having the money and power to act, and any part of the informal structure that wished to help shape the direction of movement centered its activities there. More recently, the administration of President Reagan attempted to reduce the financial involvement of the federal government in educational programs. The administration viewed its role as the exerciser of leadership and the promoter of state educational programs. Former Secretary of Education William Bennett spoke on behalf of programs such as the use of educational vouchers and tax credits that in his view would provide greater choice for parents. The administration also supported the use of a National Commission to study the public schools. Early on, a report entitled *A Nation at Risk*[5] was issued and disseminated in an effort to influence the programs and the operation of our nation's schools. The implementation of the described programs was expected to be on the state level, and the interested groups had to concentrate their efforts on the state level.

In recent years, individuals and groups have turned increasingly to the courts when the other parts of the formal legal structure were felt to have been unresponsive. A federal court decision could guide the informal groups to that part of the formal structure that has power to respond. For example, during the decade of the 1960s, the National Education Association and the American Federation of Teachers lobbied on a national level to obtain a collective bargaining law for teachers. Members of Congress were intensively lobbied and pressured to support this effort. In 1976, the Supreme Court of the United States issued its decision in *National League of Cities* v. *Usery.*[6] The court in this decision followed a narrow interpretation of the commerce clause in the Constitution by ruling that federal authorities had no right to apply federal minimum wage laws to local government workers. This signified that the court would not support a federal law giving negotiation rights to teachers in state systems of education. The result was that the teachers' organizations moved the area of pressure to the various state capitals. Interestingly, in 1985 in *Garcia* v. *San Antonio Metropolitan Transit Authority,*[7] the Supreme Court overturned the Usery decision. Once again, the teachers' organization will have to decide whether or not to focus their efforts for national collective bargaining legislation on Congress.

Interest Groups

Table 9.1 illustrates the wide variety of groups interested in policymaking in education. Depending upon the nature and location of the issue, many additional groups could be included in this list. The informal structure is made up of many types of interest groups, not all of which are active at any one time. Some of the groups are major in terms of their concern, interest, and power. A number of these important groups are professional education groups or those related to the education endeavor. Other interest groups have major concerns outside of education and attempt to use the schools as a means to accomplish their ends. In addition, some groups are formed in response to a specific crisis. Such groups generally disappear when the crisis ends. This section highlights a representative number of interest groups and their role in policymaking in education.

Professional Education and Related Interest Groups

Among the most important of the professional interest groups are the National Education Association, the American Federation of Teachers, the American Association of School Superintendents, the National Association of Secondary Principals, the National Association of Elementary Principals, the National School Boards Association, and the National Congress of Parents and Teachers. Although these groups are identified as professional interest groups and they do have common interests, they also have deep-seated conflicts on many of the most pressing and controversial issues. The profession does not have a common voice on many questions, and although there are expressions of the need for harmony, the groups remain disunited on many major issues.

The National Education Association (NEA) is the largest and best financed of these groups. Members belong to the local and state associations in addition to the national organization. The NEA has been very active in supporting or opposing educational issues and has screened and endorsed candidates for political office. Each year a representative assembly of members meets and adopts a legislative program that the NEA will support. The first tier of priorities of the 1985–86 legislative program included increased federal funding and support for national collective bargaining legislation. The platform statement on federal funding stated in part:

Figure 9.1
Yearly NEA-PAC Receipts:
1980–1987

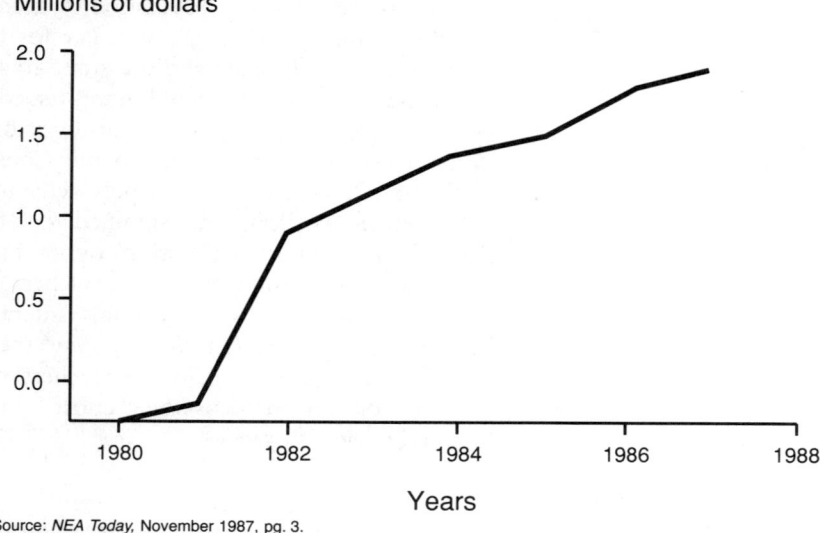

Source: *NEA Today,* November 1987, pg. 3.

> *NEA supports assisting local schools by providing a level of federal funding which equals one-third of the total expenditures for public elementary and secondary education . . . NEA opposes federal control of local schools.*[8]

At this same assembly, a budget of over 97 million dollars was approved for the 1985–86 year. The NEA is well funded and has the ability to apply pressure for its programs very effectively. The state and local associations have their own programs and priorities in addition to the national agenda. With approximately 1.6 million members, the NEA is an important voice in educational policymaking.

The National Education Association Political Action Committee has been very successful in raising money for political purposes. Figure 9.1 shows the growth in PAC funds in recent years. The activity of the NEA-PAC fund is compared to the top contributors to federal candidates in Table 9.3.

The American Federation of Teachers (AFT) is a smaller union with over 500,000 members. The membership is centered in the major urban

Table 9.3
Top Contributors to
Federal Candidates 1986
Two-Year Election Cycle

1. National Association of Realtors PAC	$2,782,338
2. American Medical Association PAC	$2,107,492
3. National Education Association PAC	$2,055,133
4. United Auto Workers V-CAP	$1,621,055
5. National Association of Retired Employees PAC	$1,491,895

Source: Federal Elections Commission report, May 1987.

areas of the nation. The union is affiliated with the American Federation of Labor. Despite speculation concerning a merger with the NEA, considerable differences separate the groups. The major stumbling block is perhaps the AFT's affiliation with organized labor. In recent years, the leader of the AFT, Albert Shanker, has had a high national profile on educational issues. He has participated on numerous national commissions and panels and has been an influential force in attempting to direct educational policy.

The two teacher organizations as well as other professional interest groups such as the National School Boards Association and the American Association of School Administrators have many interests in common but have failed to reach consensus on many issues. Proposed increases in funding and program expansion are usually supported in concert. The teacher organizations, however, support national collective bargaining legislation and the right to strike, while other professional interest groups oppose these issues. Each of the groups has a certain self-interest that prevents a common agenda for educational policy objectives.

Groups related to education, such as professional test-making companies, can also raise complicated educational policy questions. Many states have decided to use standardized test scores as measures of educational achievement. Basic skills testing in the elementary schools, the use of standardized tests in reading and mathematics achievement tests such as the California Battery, exit tests in high school, and college entrance tests such as the SAT are examples of the growing dependence on test scores to measure progress in school. The companies that produce these and other standardized tests have become recognized interests in educational policy decisions. The question of how much influence the test maker should have on curriculum decisions is debated. Does the reliance on test results to measure achievement force the curriculum to be test oriented? Does the test actually measure what should be taught in school? The use of a simple policy process model (Policy Model 9.1) can help in understanding how the educational policymakers are responding to these questions.

Other organizations that have some relationship to the professional groups can be influential on particular policy issues. Accreditation agencies, publishers of instructional materials, and colleges and universities are examples of these groups. Professional education groups and numbers of professionally related groups have special interests in educational policymaking. Any understanding of the policymaking process in education must include an analysis of the involvement of these interest groups as a part of the informal or extra legal structure of education.

Tax-Exempt Foundations and Think Tanks

The tax laws of this nation have provided a means for wealthy individuals and corporations to organize and fund foundations by offering tax shelters for money donated for such purposes. The foundation has been looked upon as an organization that could contribute to the public good by spending its money in a way that would enhance the nation's well-being. Numbers of such foundations have provided money, expertise, advice, and pressure for the promotion of educational change. Foundations, through the years, have been an influential component of the informal structure of education.

Familiar mainline foundation names such as Rockefeller, Ford, and Carnegie have for years been involved in issues that have a bearing on

---

Policy Model 9.1   School Accountability Policy

POLICY ISSUE	PARTICIPANTS IN POLICY DEVELOPMENT	ILLUSTRATIONS OF POLICY SOLUTIONS	EFFECTS OF POLICY SOLUTIONS
How can schools be made accountable for results?	**Formal** Legislative bodies Governors State superintendent State departments of education Boards of education **Informal** Professional groups (NEA, AFT, others) Publishers Test makers Citizen groups Civil rights groups Others	**Statutory Provisions** a. Use test results b. Use exit tests c. Base teacher merit pay on test results **Court decisions** Approve use of tests *Debra P.* v. *Turlington* *Anderson* v. *Banks* **Administrative Rulings**	**Regulative** Who can do what? **Allocative** Who gets what? **Structural** Additions or deletions to present system **Redistributive** Changes in resource or authority allocation

educational policy. Many years ago, the Carnegie Foundation provided for a study that developed the Carnegie unit, which is still the unit used to measure high-school credit. Today under the direction of Ernest Boyer, recommendations have been made and publicized concerning teacher preparation and the national licensing of teachers. The Rockefeller, Ford, and Carnegie foundations have provided research funds, grants to schools and teachers, and funds for university study and publication and dissemination of materials on a national basis.

Recently, the number of tax-exempt think tanks has increased dramatically. These think tanks are privately funded, nonprofit, tax-exempt foundations that engage in public policy research. These newer foundations have become advocacy organizations that represent particular views. Organizations such as the American Enterprise Institute, the Heritage Foundation, the Hoover Institute, and the National Center for Policy Analysis present a conservative view on public policy issues. The Brookings Institute, the Institute for Policy Studies, and the Center for National Policy, on the other hand, advocate more liberal viewpoints. These organizations attempt to influence the national debate on various public policy questions by sponsoring studies, reports, and seminars. Positions on such educational issues as the use of vouchers or tax credits would depend on which of these think tanks has sponsored the study.

The influence and status of these advocacy groups is debated. Some argue that the groups perform a public function by raising vital questions in such policy debates. Others, however, feel that the use of tax-exempt funds

Photo 9.1
Groups with a special interest often attempt to shape the educational agenda in terms of that particular interest.

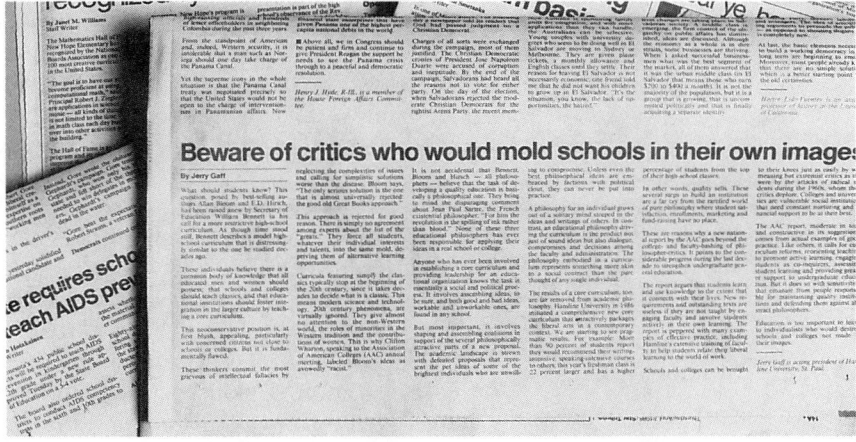

to push certain viewpoints not only gives the individual and corporate contributors too much influence but also removes from the tax rolls money that should be used for other governmental purposes. To fully understand educational policymaking, consideration must be given to foundations and think tanks.

Other Interest Groups

Schools can become involved with groups that have primary interests other than education. Groups can view the schools as the means to accomplish ends that go beyond the schools. If this occurs, pressures can be exerted on the formal structure to obtain the ends desired by the special interest group. These pressures can occur in various ways. Materials such as books, films, film strips, and displays can be provided to the schools for use in the instructional program. These materials could reflect a particular point of view such as pro or anti-free enterprise, pro or anti-United Nations, anti-communism, or promotion of a particular company or industry. Other interest groups might pressure the legal structure to include formal course work designed to achieve a particular end. Promotion of courses addressing social problems such as teen-age pregnancy, drug addiction, alcohol and tobacco use, and the spread of AIDS are recent examples. It should be noted that there has been an increase in the formation of single-issue groups to advocate a particular cause. Although the cause may transcend the school, the educational system can be a target of the single-issue groups as a means to attain its ends. Some examples of these single-issue groups are Mothers Against Drunk Drivers (MADD), pro life or pro choice advocates, and some patriotic organizations.

The groups mentioned all have interests that go beyond school boundaries. The school, however, is viewed as an important means to help accomplish these groups' stated objectives. There are countless groups that can be active in seeking their ends by using the schools. Each state or local school district has its own peculiar history concerning the groups and issues that have been a part of the informal structure affecting the schools and the curriculum.

Summary

The term *informal structure* is used to describe individuals and groups that exert pressure and attempt to influence educational policy and are not part of the formal legal structure. Individuals in our society belong to many groups, and as these groups become interested in questions regarding education, advocacy positions are supported. Frequently, an individual might belong to a variety of groups that disagree on an educational policy question. This can make it difficult for educational policymakers to assess the amount of support that actually exists for a particular point of view.

Informal pressures can exist on national, state, or local levels. The pressures generally focus on the level that is perceived as having the power to decide policy. Recently, state authorities have been considerably more active in promoting policy change in education. Therefore the interest groups have centered their attention on the state level.

Groups representing professional interests are important participants in policymaking. The National Education Association and the American Federation of Teachers are two active teacher interest groups. Other groups represent school superintendents, school board members, and school principals. These professional groups do not always present a united front on issues, and each group's self-interest dictates the group's position.

Many special interest groups have goals that transcend education, and they view the school as a means to accomplish their purposes. Examples include groups interested in health-related problems or social problems such as teen-age pregnancy and drug abuse. Tax-exempt organizations such as foundations and think tanks have influenced educational policymakers.

Key Words

Informal structure

Extra legal structure

Single-issue groups

Tax-exempt foundations

Carnegie Foundation

Secular humanism

Williams v. *Board of Education,* County of Kanawha (1975)

State education agency

Ford Foundation

Interstate policy network

Proposition 13

William Bennett

National League of Cities v. *Usery* (1976)

Garcia v. *San Antonio Metropolitan Transit Authority* (1985)

National Education Association (NEA)

American Federation of Teachers

American Association of School Superintendents

National Congress of Parents and Teachers

Think tanks

Discussion Questions

1. How does the informal structure influence educational policymaking?
2. Why is it difficult to know what the public expects of the school system?
3. Tax-exempt advocacy groups perform a public function and should be encouraged. Do you agree or disagree with the statement?

For Further Reading

Kerr, Donna H. *Educational Policy Analysis, Structure, and Justification.* New York: David McKay Co., 1976.

Mosher, E. K., and Wagoner, J. L., Jr. *The Changing Politics of Education.* Berkeley, Calif.: McCutchan Publishing Co., 1978.

Spring, Joel. *American Education: An Introduction to Social and Political Aspects.* New York: Longman, 1985.

———. *Conflict of Interests: The Politics of American Education.* Longman, 1988.

Wirt, F. W., and Kirst, M. W. *Schools in Conflict.* Berkeley, Calif.: McCutchan Publishing Co., 1982.

Yudof, M. G., and Kirp, D. L. *Educational Policy and the Law Cases and Materials.* Berkeley, Calif.: McCutchan Publishing Co., 1982.

Notes

1. *Williams* v. *Board of Education,* County of Kanawha 388 F Supp. 93 at 96. S.D. W. Va. (1975).
2. F. M. Wirt and M. W. Kirst, *Schools in Conflict* (Berkeley, Calif.: McCutchan Publishing Co. 1982).
3. *Ibid.,* p. 240.
4. *Ibid.,* pp. 240–242.
5. National Commission on Excellence in Education, *A Nation At Risk: The Imperative for Educational Reform* (Washington, D.C.: U.S. Dept. of Education, 1983).
6. *National League of Cities* v. *Usery* 426 U.S. 833 (1976).
7. *Garcia* v. *San Antonio Metropolitan Transit Authority* Su. Ct. (1985).
8. *Today's Education,* "Legislative Programs Adopted by the 1985 Representative Assembly" p. 137 Special Issue 1985–86.

10 Educational Policy and the Teacher

"Demand for teachers is rising fast, and supply shows no sign of following that demand. If we were speaking of medicine, architecture, or accounting, then the economists would tell us professional salaries in the affected field would rise until the supply of applicants willing to work at the higher salaries matched the demand. Unfortunately, in education we do things differently. We lower the qualifications for entrance to the field until there are enough people available who will work at the unchanged salary."

Marc Tucker and David Mandel,
A Call for Redesigning the Schools
(1987)

"States should abolish the undergraduate degree in education and make professional teacher education a graduate level enterprise, building on a base of sound undergraduate education in the arts and sciences."

Carnegie Forum's Task Force on Teaching as a Profession, *A Nation Prepared* (1987)

"The State has the right to adopt academic requirements and to use written achievement tests designed and validated to disclose the minimum amount of knowledge necessary to effective teaching."

The United States Supreme Court in *United States of America v. State of South Carolina* (1978)

Among the many problems facing educational policymakers is the dilemma of providing both the quantity and the quality of teachers needed for our public schools. Recent political proposals have highlighted as a serious

233

Policy Model 10.1   Framework for Educational Policy Analysis

---

POLICY ISSUE	PARTICIPANTS IN POLICY DEVELOPMENT	ILLUSTRATIONS OF POLICY SOLUTIONS	EFFECTS OF POLICY SOLUTIONS
A. Quality of teachers B. Quantity of teachers C. D.	**Formal** a. Courts b. Governors c. Legislators d. e. **Informal** a. Foundations b. Professional groups c. d.	A. B. C. D.	**Allocative** Who gets what? **Regulative** Who can do what? **Structural** Additions or deletions to present system **Redistributive** Changes in resources or authority allocation

problem the quality of teachers and the quality of students in programs preparing teachers. Some of these proposals purport to increase the quality of our nation's teachers. The programs range from making teachers and prospective teachers pass tests of various kinds to eliminating undergraduate education programs completely and making teacher preparation a graduate enterprise. Any of the many alternatives chosen could also affect the quantity of teachers available. Thus, the quantity and quality problems cannot be addressed separately, because most of the materials addressing school problems also predict a coming serious shortage of teachers.

This chapter highlights some selected educational policy issues related to the quantity and quality problem. In addition, the relationship between the rights of teachers as individuals and professionals and the rights given to boards of education to maintain schools is studied. Recent questions relating to tort liability and malpractice in education are also addressed. As you study the chapter, include what you believe to be relevant in addressing the problems in Policy Model 10.1.

Recent reports critical of our nation's schools have been widely circulated and publicized. The result has been a great surge of interest and debate on educational policy. Much of this debate has been focused on the quality of and the role played by the teacher. This concern for quality marks a noticeable change in emphasis.

During the years following World War II through the 1950s, the primary concern was the quantity of teachers available. The demographics of the period and the need for facilities caused educational policymakers to focus on the necessity of producing the number of teachers needed to operate the system. Slowly, the major concern shifted to equality issues in the 1960s and 1970s. Attention moved to the problems of poverty and schooling, equality of educational opportunity, and access to education.

Various studies and reports published during the 1960s and early 1970s were devoted to the relationship of education to poverty, equality, and access. A report entitled *Equality of Educational Opportunity* by James Coleman was widely distributed and became an important work cited as evidence to promote particular educational policy solutions.[1] One of the findings included in the Coleman Report indicated that teachers and teaching have little effect on educational outcomes. Social class standing, according to the study, was the important ingredient. Other studies reinforced these findings. Christopher Jencks' work entitled *Inequality* pointed to family economic and social class as the major determinant of cognitive success in school.[2] These studies, even though some persons disagreed with the findings and methods used, were important and were used as support for recommending particular educational policy solutions.

Recent reports on the schools have been based on information that indicates that our schools do not measure up to standards that are needed to ensure that the United States can continue to compete successfully with other countries. It has been pointed out that the SAT scores of students have been dropping. Various reports have provided information that students in the United States do not compare favorably with students in other nations, particularly in mathematics and science. Other reports have indicated that there are high-school graduates who are functionally illiterate. In addition, unflattering information on the ability of working teachers and the low academic ability of students preparing to teach has been highlighted. This type of information, together with the changing numbers of children attending schools, has led individuals and organizations to begin to question the quality of our teachers. Table 10.1 identifies eight recent studies that have made critical analyses of American elementary and secondary schools. Each of these reports devotes some attention to teachers and teaching, and two reports—*A Nation At Risk* and *Secondary Education in America*—place major emphasis on teachers and teaching.

A number of recent educational policy decisions have been centered on questions related to the quality of the teachers now working in our schools and the quality of the students preparing to teach. Additionally, questions that concern the legal rights and responsibilities of teachers continue to be topics for discussion among the many constituencies that have an interest in public education in America. This chapter describes educational policy development as it relates to the teacher with particular emphasis on some recent areas of controversy.

Teacher Certification and Employment

Certification or the licensing of teachers is a state function. Each of the fifty states has laws, regulations, and procedures outlining its requirements for obtaining a certificate to teach. Thus, the selection of teachers becomes one important way in which the state controls the school program. Though the certificate is not a contract to teach and does not ensure employment, it does legally grant entrance to the profession.

State certification requirements vary but generally include a college degree with a particular pattern of course work composed of general education, some subject matter specialization, and some courses in the field of education. In addition, some states require examinations such as the

Table 10.1
Recent Reports on Public Education

REPORT	SPONSOR	SUBJECT OF TEACHERS	TEACHING INCLUDED
Academic Preparation for College	College Board		Yes
Action for Excellence	Education Commission of the States		Yes
Secondary Education in America	Carnegie Foundation	Yes	
Twentieth Century Fund Report	Twentieth Century Fund		Yes
A Nation at Risk	U.S. Department of Education	Yes	
A Place Called School	Grants from many foundations and the U.S. Office of Education		Yes
Horace's Compromise	National Association of Secondary School Principals and National Association of Independent Schools		Yes
The Condition of Teaching	Carnegie Foundation	Yes	

National Teachers Examination in a teaching area or the commons examination or both, and recently some have instituted a basic skills examination. The right of the state to regulate certification can sometimes clash with the rights of an individual. Does a state have unlimited authority to regulate entry into the profession of teaching, or do the individual rights of a prospective teacher place limits on the power of the state?

The recent reports concerning the status of our educational system have been the catalyst that has made educational policy a popular political subject. A number of state governors have led the way in attempting to renew and change the school systems of their states. The questions raised concerning the quality of teachers and the quality of those preparing to teach have moved a number of states to consider using some form of testing as an assurance of at least minimal competency of teachers. The use of test results has raised some constitutional issues concerning the effect of such tests upon particular identifiable groups, such as minority groups. The perception of educational policymakers that the quality of teachers can be improved through the use of test results has been questioned by groups that feel that tests discriminate against them or others.

The use of test results in making employment decisions has been litigated a number of times. The landmark court case that clarified guidelines for the use of tests was *Griggs* v. *Duke Power*, decided in 1971.[3] Duke Power Company required a high-school diploma or a passing score on a standardized intelligence test as a condition of employment in its labor department or as a requisite to transfer to another department. This practice was said by the plaintiff to result in the rejection of black applicants and the creation of racial imbalance. The court then required Duke Power to demonstrate that the requirement was related to job success. Duke Power was unable to do so, and the court decision held that the employer discriminated against blacks by this requirement and said in part "(a) neither standard is shown to be significantly related to job performance, (b) both requirements operate to disqualify Negroes at a substantially higher rate than white applicants, and (c) the jobs in question formerly had been filled only by white employees as part of a longstanding practice of giving preference to whites."[4] The significance of the decision on the use of tests for employment purposes is that the test must demonstrate a reasonable measure of job performance.

Following the *Griggs* v. *Duke Power* decision a number of states and school systems using tests such as the National Teachers Examination or the Graduate Record Examinations decided not to continue the use of tests for employment purposes. The state of South Carolina, however, continued to use the National Teachers Examination as a certification requirement. In 1977, minority advocates took the state to court, arguing that this requirement discriminated against blacks. In 1978, the U.S. Supreme Court in *United States of America* v. *State of South Carolina* held that the National Teachers Examination score was a reasonable measure of the content mastery of a teacher education program and could determine the minimum amount of knowledge necessary for effective teaching.[5] Thus, the Court in this case indicated that tests that are job related and validated may be used as a measure to ensure minimal quality.

Recent developments indicate that additional states are turning to the use of tests as a means of obtaining some measure of quality in their certification and employment of teachers. A graphic portrayal of the states requiring testing can be seen in Table 10.2. The tests used include basic skills examinations, subject matter examinations, and pedogogical tests. Table 10.2 indicates the type of test used in each of the states requiring a test for certification. Many states are using additional screening devices in their teacher preparation standards. Some of these devices are higher grade point averages, higher SAT scores for acceptance into teacher education programs, additional laboratory experiences, and more subject-matter requirements. Discussion and study of five-year teacher preparation programs is another proposal that is seriously being debated.

Educational policy development relating to the quality of teachers and the use of tests is illustrated in Policy Model 10.2. The model indicates that additional regulation must be developed by the state department of education and that a change in organizational structure might be warranted to administer the testing program. Note that the allocation of funds and the distribution of authority may also be altered. What can you add to or delete from this model to show how educational policy on this issue has developed in your state? The focus on quality has brought the nation full circle on the issue of teacher preparation. The increased requirements may once again point to the educational policy problem of providing the quantity of teachers needed to supply our nation's classrooms in the face of a possible teacher shortage. Will the increase in requirements affect the quantity of teachers available?

Table 10.2 — A Summary of State Teacher Testing Programs: April 1987

STATE	ADMISSIONS TESTS			CERTIFICATION TESTS			RECERTIFI-CATION TESTS	PERFOR-MANCE TESTS	
	TEST	IMPLEMENTATION		TEST	IMPLEMENTATION		In Place	In Place	Under Study
		In Place	When		In Place	When			
Alabama	Custom	X		Custom	X				
Alaska									
Arizona	PPST	X		Custom	X				X
Arkansas				NTE	?		X		
California	CBEST	X		CBEST	X				
Colorado	CAT	X		—		1987			X
Connecticut	Custom	X		NTE		1987			
Delaware				PPST	X				X
Florida	SAT,ACT	X		Custom	X			X	
Georgia				Custom	X		X		
Hawaii				NTE	X				
Idaho				NTE	?				
Illinois				Custom		1988			
Indiana	?		?	NTE	X				
Iowa									
Kansas				PPST,NTE	X				X
Kentucky	CTBS	X		NTE	X			X	
Louisiana	NTE	X		NTE	X				
Maine				NTE		1988			
Maryland				NTE		1987			X
Massachusetts				?		1989			X
Michigan				?		?			
Minnesota				PPST		1988			X
Mississippi	COMP	X		NTE	X				X
Missouri	SAT,ACT	X		?		1987			
Montana				NTE	X				
Nebraska	PPST		1987	PPST		1987			
Nevada	PPST	X		PPST		1990			X
New Hampshire				PPST	X				
New Jersey				NTE	X				
New Mexico	Misc	X		NTE	X				
New York				NTE	X				X
North Carolina	NTE	X		NTE	X		X		
North Dakota	NTE	X		?		?			
Ohio	?		1987	?		1987			
Oklahoma	Misc	X		Custom	X		X		
Oregon	CBEST	X		CBEST	X				
Pennsylvania				NTE		1987			X
Rhode Island				NTE	X				X
South Carolina	Custom	X		NTE,Custom	X		X		
South Dakota				NTE	?				X
Tennessee	PPST	X		NTE	X				
Texas	PPST	X		Custom	X		X		X
Utah	Misc	X							
Vermont									X
Virginia				NTE	X		X		
Washington	Custom,SAT,ACT	X							
West Virginia	PPST,COMP	X		Custom	X				X
Wisconsin	PPST		1989	?		1987			
Wyoming	CAT	X							X
Totals	27	23	4	44	26	18	3	7	17

ACT, CAT, CBEST, COMP, CTBS, PPST, SAT refer to the American College Testing Program, California Achievement Test, California Basic Education Skills Test, College Outcomes Measures Project, California Test of Basic Skills, Pre-Professional Skills Test, and the Scholastic Aptitude Test, respectively.

?-Indicates items that have not yet been decided.

Source: What's Happening in Teacher Testing, An Analysis of State Teacher Testing Practices U.S. Dept. of Education, 1987.

Policy Model 10.2	Providing Quality Teachers		
POLICY ISSUE	**PARTICIPANTS IN POLICY DEVELOPMENT**	**ILLUSTRATIONS OF POLICY SOLUTIONS**	**EFFECTS OF POLICY SOLUTIONS**
Providing quality teachers	**Formal** Courts Legislative bodies Administrative bodies School boards **Informal** Professional teachers' groups (AFT,NEA) Accreditation agencies (NCATE,NASDTEC) Citizen groups Critical reports on the schools Media	**Court Precedents** *Griggs* v. *Duke Power* *U.S.* v. *South Carolina* **Statutory Provision** Require basic skills test Require higher grade point average in college Require National Teachers Exam Additional accreditation requirements for teacher education institutions What about your state? **Administrative Rulings**	**Regulative** State department of education must develop program for test use and make decisions on test **Allocative** Additional resources to the state department of education for program Additional resources to testing companies **Structural** State department of education functions increase to implement testing program **Redistributive** Increase in state department of education authority Less local authority

Termination

If it becomes necessary to terminate the employment of a teacher, the school board has certain powers and responsibilities that vary with the particular circumstance of the dismissal. The three types of teacher terminations that this section focuses on are nonrenewal, dismissal, and reduction in force. Nonrenewal is the termination of a teacher at the end of a contract period, while dismissal is defined as the termination of a teacher within a contract period. Reduction in force is the termination of employees on the basis of reduced enrollment, budget reduction, change in school program, or school consolidation. One important concept that must be understood in any type of termination is the meaning of due process.

Due Process

The laws, policies, and regulations formulated in each of the states for the purpose of protecting individuals from being treated arbitrarily by their employers make up the due process guidelines of the state. The due process or procedural requirements will vary depending on the particular action involved. In general, the greater the impact of the action on the employee, the more detailed the relevant due process procedure.

Box 10.1
Solving the Problem of Providing the Number and the Quality of Teachers Needed in Our Society

If preparation for teaching required six years and a graduate degree, would the quality and quantity problems be resolved?

A group of University deans, called the Holmes group, recently published a report entitled "Tomorrow's Teachers." A task force set up by the Carnegie Foundation's Forum on Education recently published *A Nation Prepared: Teachers for the 21st Century*. Though there are a number of differences between the two reports, the major recommendations of each are similar. Both reports claim that teacher education programs must be reformed if progress is to be made in improving our nation's educational systems. The most controversial recommendation of the reports is the abolition of undergraduate teacher education programs and the establishment of six-year professional graduate programs for the preparation of teachers. A great deal of debate, comment, and controversy has been generated by the proposal. A number of other proposals are included in the reports, and reading and study of the documents could be beneficial to those interested in teacher education. What would the adoption of a six-year teacher preparation program do to the quality and quantity of prospective teachers?

The Fourteenth Amendment to the U.S. Constitution states in part, ". . . nor shall any State deprive any person of life, liberty, or property, without due process of law." If a liberty or property interest of a teacher is involved in a termination, procedural due process must be afforded the employee. A liberty interest is considered to be present if the teacher's future employment or reputation is jeopardized. A property interest is present if the teacher has a legitimate entitlement to continued employment. An example of a property interest would be a teacher working on a tenure or continuing contract.

The procedural due process required might vary considerably from state to state. In general, a written notice of the termination must be given the teacher by a particular date. The notice must provide reasonable time for the teacher to prepare for a hearing. The charges calling for dismissal must be specifically outlined in the notification. A hearing must be provided for the teacher. Usually, it is not as formal as a court hearing. The hearing must provide the names of witnesses, allow for cross examination of the witnesses, provide specific evidence, and give the teacher the option to have counsel and be heard. The teacher must have access to a written record of the proceedings; in addition, an appeal procedure is usually included that leads to the state court system.

Nonrenewal

Nonrenewal of a teacher's contract generally occurs when the school administration decides it does not want to renew a probationary teacher's contract at the end of the contract year. Any state law concerning notification date and type of notice must be observed and followed. The procedure required by the state is all of the due process needed under the conditions described. If the school board or the administration cites particular reasons for the dismissal or has in some manner acted in a way that the teacher has a liberty interest involved, the nonrenewal action may turn into a dismissal for cause and require a much more elaborate due process procedure.

Dismissal

Dismissal for cause is the termination of a teacher within a contract period. The code of laws of each state will generally include a statute outlining the reasons for which teachers may be dismissed. Although the states use varying terminology and do not agree on the same reasons, a general pattern does emerge, and the similarities are easily identified. A statement to the effect that teachers may be dismissed for evident unfitness for teaching generally precedes a set of behaviors that will show this unfitness. The following are some of the most common of these behaviors:

> Persistent neglect of duty.
>
> Willful violation of rules and regulations.
>
> Gross immorality.
>
> Incompetence.
>
> Drunkenness.
>
> Illegal use, sale, or possession of drugs.
>
> Other good and just cause.

If a state does have a teacher dismissal statute that identifies and lists reasons and cause, that list must be utilized and followed in any dismissal action. Statutory provisions in the states and a large body of court precedent have provided safeguards against the arbitrary dismissal of teachers.

It is very difficult to gain agreement on the precise meaning of the previously listed behaviors that supposedly show unfitness for teaching. Reasonable people can disagree on the meaning of such terms as *gross immorality, drunkenness,* and *other good and just cause.* Numerous court cases have revolved around the meanings of these vague terms. The courts have had to deal with this vagueness and make interpretations that resolve specific cases. The state has power through the Tenth Amendment to establish a school system; individual citizens working in the school system or attending schools have individual freedoms established by the Constitution. When the state's powers clash with these individual freedoms, the courts are called upon to interpret and clarify the rights of each party. The courts in this way play a major role in the development of educational policy.

Reduction in Force

Demographic changes brought about by the mobility of the population and birth rate changes have caused some school districts to have more professional staff than needed. Other school districts have experienced shortages of funds so severe that the school board decrees a financial exigency or emergency. In addition, major program changes in a school district or consolidation of schools could also result in an excess number of employees. Recently, school systems faced with such problems have declared emergency status and proceeded to carry out a reduction in force (RIF).

The termination of employees through a RIF may carry a different due process procedure than a dismissal for cause. If a state has passed legislation covering the topic, the requirements of the law must be adhered to. The state law and whatever school board policies have been approved form the basis of the employees' rights. Although the states vary in their treatment of RIF, certain generalizations can be made. The board of education in some manner indicates that an exigency exists, and the severity and the consequences must be outlined. Whatever the district's RIF policy is, it must then be put into operation. Such policies generally include reasons that can implement the policy, procedures to follow such as the use of seniority of teachers or qualification of teachers as priority items, and recall rights. Teachers must be notified of their status regarding the reduction. The due process rights of the employee generally cover only their classification and the board's adherence to the policy.

Due process rights of teachers have been described in different ways depending on the particular circumstance. Due process can simply be written notification by a certain date that a contract will not be renewed. A more complicated procedure involving hearings, presentation of evidence, representation by counsel, or cross-examination of witnesses with the proceedings recorded may be needed in a dismissal for cause. In a RIF proceeding, due process may involve only the placement of the employee on the RIF list and the following of procedure in carrying out the termination.

Freedom of Expression

The First and Fourteenth Amendments to the U.S. Constitution guarantee the citizen a right to freedom of speech. Does the public school have such special characteristics and environment that a teacher must forgo this constitutional right? Can school authorities dismiss a teacher for exercising his or her freedom of speech if the board of education does not like the contents of the speech or the manner in which the right was used? These questions have been troublesome for teachers and boards of education and have resulted in controversy that has been litigated in the courts. Although no one court decision has outlined all of the parameters of teachers' freedom of speech rights, some guidelines for educational policymakers have been formulated by the courts. The most important case that attempts to clarify a teacher's right to freedom of expression is *Pickering* v. *Board of Education* (1968).[6]

Marvin Pickering, a teacher in an Illinois school district, was dismissed from his position for sending a letter that was critical of the school board and the superintendent to a local newspaper. The school board had proposed a tax increase, and Pickering was critical of the school board's handling of previous tax increases and of the board's method of allocating funds to educational and athletic programs. Pickering also accused the superintendent of attempting to prevent teachers from opposing the proposed tax increase. Pickering's letter to the newspaper follows.

Dear Editor:

I enjoyed reading the back issues of your paper which you loaned to me. Perhaps others would enjoy reading them in order to see just how far the new high schools have deviated from the original promises by the Board of Education. First, let me state that I am referring to the February thru November, 1961 issues of your paper, so that it can be checked.

One statement in your paper declared that swimming pools, athletic fields, and auditoriums had been left out of the program. They may have been left out but they got put back in very quickly because Lockport West has both an auditorium and athletic field. In fact, Lockport West has a better athletic field than Lockport Central. It has a track that isn't quite regulation distance even though the board spent a few thousand dollars on it. Whose fault is that? Oh, I forgot, it wasn't supposed to be there in the first place. It must have fallen out of the sky. Such responsibility has been touched on in other letters but it seems one just can't help noticing it. I am not saying the school shouldn't have these facilities, because I think they should, but promises are promises, or are they?

Since there seems to be a problem getting all the facts to the voter on the twice defeated bond issue, many letters have been written to this paper and probably more will follow, I feel I must say something about the letters and their writers. Many of these letters did not give the whole story. Letters by your Board and Administration have stated that teachers' salaries total $1,297,746 for one year. Now that must have been the total payroll, otherwise the teachers would be getting $10,000 a year. I teach at the high school and I know this just isn't the case. However, this shows their "stop at nothing" attitude. To illustrate further, do you know that the superintendent told the teachers and, I quote, "Any teacher that opposes the referendum should be prepared for the consequences." I think this gets at the reason we have problems passing bond issues. Threats take something away; these are insults to voters in a free society. We should try to sell a program on its merits, if it has any.

Remember those letters entitled "District 205 Teachers Speak," I think the voters should know that those letters have been written and agreed to by only five or six teachers, not 98% of the teachers in the high school. In fact many teachers didn't even know who was writing them. Did you know that those letters had to have the approval of the superintendent before they could be put in the paper? That's the kind of totalitarianism teachers live in at the high school, and your children go to school in.

In last week's paper, the letter written by a few uninformed teachers threatened to close the school cafeteria and fire its personnel. This is ridiculous and insults the intelligence of the voter because properly managed school cafeterias do not cost the school district any money. If the cafeteria is losing money, then the board should not be packing free lunches for athletes on days of athletic contests. Whatever the case, the taxpayer's child should only have to pay about 30 cents for his lunch instead of 35 cents to pay for free lunches for the athletes. In a reply to this letter your Board of Administration will probably state that these lunches are paid for from receipts from the games. But $20,000 in receipts doesn't pay for the $200,000 a year they have been spending on varsity sports while neglecting the wants of teachers.

You see we don't need an increase in the transportation tax unless the voters want to keep paying $50,000 or more a year to transport athletes home after practice and to away games, etc. Rest of the $200,000 is made up in coaches' salaries, athletic directors' salaries, baseball pitching machines, sodded football fields, and thousands of dollars for other sports equipment.

These things are all right, provided we have enough money for them. To sod football fields on borrowed money and then not be able to pay teachers' salaries is getting the cart before the horse.

If these things aren't enough for you, look at East High. No doors on many of the classrooms, a plant room without any sunlight, no water in a first aid treatment room, are just a few of many things. The taxpayers were really taken to the cleaners. A part of the sidewalk in front of the building has already collapsed. Maybe Mr. Hess would be interested to know that we need blinds on the windows in that building also.

Once again, the board must have forgotten they were going to spend $3,200,000 on the West building and $2,300,000 on the East building.

As I see it, the bond issue is a fight between the Board of Education that is trying to push tax-supported athletics down our throats with education, and a public that has mixed emotions about both of these items because they feel they are already paying enough taxes, and simply don't know whom to trust with any more tax money.

I must sign this letter as a citizen, taxpayer and voter, not as a teacher, since that freedom has been taken from the teachers by the administration. Do you really know what goes on behind those stone walls at the high school?

Respectfully,

Marvin L. Pickering[7]

The Supreme Court ruled that in general a teacher's freedom of expression is protected but that there must be a balance of interests of teachers as citizens and the employer's promotion of efficient and effective public service. The court did not find that "maintaining either discipline by immediate superiors or harmony among co-workers" was presented as a problem. The court found no evidence that the teacher's classroom performance or the normal operations of the school were affected. Since the court found no harmful effects of the teacher's actions on the school program, the school authorities had no basis for limiting the constitutional right to free expression. The court ruled in favor of Pickering.

Further classification of teacher protected speech rights and limitations was provided in *Mt. Healthy City School District Board of Education* v. *Doyle* (1977).[8] Doyle, a nontenured teacher, telephoned a local radio station and criticized his principal's memo relating to a teachers' dress and appearance code. Sometime later, Doyle was not recommended for contract renewal. He received a statement citing "a notable lack of tact in handling professional matters which leaves much doubt as to your sincerity in establishing good school relationships." Also cited were references to the radio station incident and to an incident where he made an obscene gesture to two female pupils. Doyle claimed his dismissal was in violation of his constitutional rights under the First and Fourteenth Amendments and was based on his call to the radio station which he claimed was protected speech. Although the court ruled that the teacher's call to the radio station was protected speech, there was enough evidence from the other incidents reported to indicate that the board would have reached a decision to dismiss the teacher. The dismissal of the teacher was upheld by the Supreme Court.

In summary, teachers have a constitutional right to express their views on public issues relating to the school district. However, boards of education may restrict freedom of speech rights if such rights interfere with the management of the school. The dismissal of a teacher cannot be based on the protected speech rights of a teacher. At the same time, a teacher cannot use protected speech rights to avoid dismissal if evidence indicates that the board would have come to the same conclusion without the protected speech.

Academic Freedom

The previous section was devoted to the teacher's freedom of speech rights outside the school. This section deals with the teacher's academic freedom rights within the classroom and the school. A close connection and relationship exists between the teacher's academic freedom in the classroom and the school authorities' rights to operate the school and to control instructional decisions. The areas that are most frequently the focus of disputes are the teaching of or use of controversial topics or materials, community objection to classroom materials, the removal of classroom or library material by the board of education, and the selection of text material. These topics lead to the following questions. Who has the authority to determine what material is appropriate for classroom use? What subjects or topics are appropriate for use in a given classroom? Who has the authority to decide on appropriate methods of teaching?

The academic freedom framework in which teachers operate in public elementary and secondary schools has not been outlined by the Supreme Court. A number of rulings in the lower courts have provided some guidelines to be considered in answering the questions raised.

The courts have attempted to maintain a delicate balance between the teachers' interests in academic freedom and education authorities' interests in maintaining control of the public school program to ensure attainment of the objectives of the system. Most of the court involvement in the questions raised has occurred during the past twenty-five years. Teachers, along with others in our society, have been willing to ask the courts to clarify or extend what they view to be their rights. The courts, when considering the relevance of the methods and materials used by teachers, have outlined the following considerations in making the decision:

What age group of pupils is involved?

What is the maturity level of the pupils involved?

Is there a school board policy in existence?

What course is under discussion?

What is the relationship of the activity or material to the objectives of the course?

Does the activity or material have the potential to disrupt the school program?

Has controversial material been objectively treated?

Does the profession agree that the materials and methods used are appropriate?

Although people may not all agree with any particular interpretation of the listed items, the items can be utilized as guidelines for teachers on questions of academic freedom in public elementary and secondary schools. To further clarify the issues, a review of a sample of relevant court decisions on these issues should be studied.

A political science teacher in a high school was interested in having pupils exposed to different political views. The teacher invited four speakers to address his political science class. The four represented the Republican party, the Democratic party, the John Birch Society, and the Communist party. The last of these speakers was the Communist. As was customary, the teacher reported the invitation to the principal. The principal approved. The board of education discussed the invitation and approved. Some citizens were critical of the approval and called a community meeting. A petition was circulated requesting the board to reconsider its decision, and 800 persons signed it. Some letters to the local newspapers opposed the board's decision and threatened to oppose school funding if it were not rescinded. Faced with this community pressure, the board reversed its decision and issued an oral order banning all political speakers from the high school. The teacher and a student instituted litigation and claimed that their freedom of expression rights were violated.[9] The court decision in 1976 concluded that the school board's order was unreasonable and therefore violated the First Amendment. The court reasoned that:

> The order barred political speakers absolutely, yet no disruptions had occurred in Wilson's classes, or at other school gatherings where political subjects were discussed. Further, none were expected in the future.
>
> The defendants have not shown that outside speakers impair high school education. If they did, the board still would lack justification for banning only outside political speakers. Moreover, the evidence demonstrated that the use of outside speakers is widely recommended, widely practiced, and professionally accepted . . .
>
> The board's only apparent reason for issuing the order which suppressed protected speech was to placate angry residents and taxpayers.[10]

This excerpt from the decision illustrates several of the points previously listed. The teacher's method was accepted by the profession and

Photo 10.1

The school library can become the focus of educational policy debate.

appropriate for the age and maturity level of the students. The school board policy in existence was followed by the teacher. The method and procedures utilized were not disruptive to the school's operation, and the material was appropriate for the objective of the course. Controversial material was objectively handled in that various points of view were included and studied. The courts have recognized the rights of a board of education to control the program and objectives of the school system. However, when a constitutionally protected right of a teacher is at issue, the board must show a clear, recognizable, and permissible governmental purpose for the limitation.

Another issue that can become difficult for educational policymakers concerns what text and library material can be used in the school program. When the choice of classroom and library material by the school's faculty is challenged by the board or the community, a heated and serious community debate can develop. In a suburban community near Cleveland, Ohio, in 1976, just such a controversy occurred over what books should be selected as high-school textbooks, purchased for a high-school library, and forbidden to be taught or assigned in a high-school classroom. The school board disregarded the recommendations of the faculty and refused to approve Joseph Heller's *Catch 22* and Kurt Vonnegut's *God Bless You, Mr. Rosewater* as textbooks or library books. The board ordered Vonnegut's *Cat's Cradle* and Heller's *Catch 22* to be removed from the school library and issued resolutions that prohibited teacher and student discussion of the books in class or the books' use as supplemental reading.

The court, in deciding the issue concerning the board of education's approval of textbooks, stated that "we find no federal constitutional violation in this board's exercise of curriculum and textbook control as empowered by Ohio statute."[11] On the question concerning the removal of books from the school library, the court ruled as follows:

Box 10.2
School Board Bans
Books

Board of Education Island Trees Union Free District #26 v. *Pico*,
Supreme Court of the United States (1982)

Can local school boards of education remove books from a school library on the basis that they dislike the ideas contained in the books?

Several school board members attended a conference sponsored by a politically conservative group. Lists of books labeled objectionable were passed out at the conference. Later, it was determined by the board members that the high-school library contained nine of the listed books.*

The board gave an unofficial directive to the administration to remove the books from the library and deliver them to the board's office. A press release was issued by the board characterizing the books as "Anti-American, anti-Christian, anti-Semitic and just plain filthy." The board appointed a book review committee to read the books and make a recommendation to the board. The committee recommended that five of the nine books be retained and that two be removed from the library and made no recommendation on the others. The school board ignored these recommendations and asked that nine books be removed from the school libraries and from use in the curriculum. A number of students objected, claiming that their rights under the First Amendment were violated. The court ruled that local school boards could not remove books from the school library simply because they disliked the ideas contained in the books and by their removal "prescribe what shall be orthodox in politics, nationalism, religion, or other matters of opinion."

*The books in question: *Slaughterhouse Five*, Vonnegut; *The Naked Ape*, Morris, *Down These Mean Streets*, Thomas; *Best Short Stories of Negro Writers*, Hughes; *Go Ask Alice*, anonymous; *Laughing Boy*, LaFargee *Black Boy*, Wright; *A Hero Ain't Nothin' But a Sandwich*, Childress; and *Soul on Ice*, Cleaver.

> *A library is a storehouse of knowledge. When created for a public school, it is an important privilege created by the state for the benefit of the students of the school. That privilege is not subject to being withdrawn by succeeding school boards whose members might desire to "winnow" the library for books the content of which occasioned their discipline or disapproval. . . .*
>
> *In the absence of any explanation of the Board's action which is neutral in First Amendment terms, we must conclude that the school board removed the books because it found them objectionable in content and because it felt it had the power, unfettered by the First Amendment, to censor the school library for subject matter which the Board members found distasteful.[12]*

The court ordered the school board to replace the books in the library.

The school board's decision not to purchase the books recommended by the faculty was upheld, but the removal of the books from the library was held to be unconstitutional censorship. Policy Model 10.3 can be used to analyze the policy issue of providing quality instructional materials such as textbooks and library materials. What would you add to or subtract from this model for analyzing this issue in your school district?

Policy Model 10.3	Providing Quality Educational Materials		
POLICY ISSUE	**PARTICIPANTS IN POLICY DEVELOPMENT**	**ILLUSTRATIONS OF POLICY SOLUTIONS**	**EFFECTS OF POLICY SOLUTIONS**
Providing quality instructional materials, textbooks, and library books	**Formal** Courts Boards of education Administrative bodies **Informal** Professional teachers groups Media Parents Students Citizens' groups	**Court Precedents** *Wilson* v. *Chancellor* *Minarcini* v. *Strongsville City School District* *Island Trees South District* v. *Pico* **School Board Reaction** Board of education policy on book and material selection Use of citizens on committees for selection of material	**Regulative** Board of education develops policy for purchasing instructional materials **Structural** Committees formed to aid in selection using citizens, teachers, and administrators **Redistributive** Teachers may lose some authority Citizen may gain input

Teacher As a Role Model

Through the years, communities have expected school teachers to be role models for their children. The expected rules of behavior were often included in a teacher's contract. These rules were often quite rigid, and it was not unusual for boards of education to expect the teachers to conduct themselves with higher standards than the average citizen of the community. An illustration of such expectations can be seen in the following rules of conduct published by a West Virginia Board of Education in 1915:

1. You will not marry during the term of your contract.

2. You are not to keep company with men.

3. You must be home between the hours of 8:00 P.M. and 6:00 A.M. unless attending a school function.

4. You may not loiter downtown in ice cream stores.

5. You may not travel beyond the city limits unless you have the permission of the chairman of the Board.

6. You may not ride in a carriage or automobile with a man unless he is your father or brother.

7. You may not smoke cigarettes.

8. You may not dress in bright colors.

9. You may under no circumstances dye your hair.

10. You must wear at least two petticoats.

11. Your dresses may not be shorter than two inches above the ankle.

12. To keep the schoolroom neat and clean, you must sweep the floor daily, scrub the floor at least once a week, with hot soapy water, clean the blackboard at least once a day, and start the fire at 7:00 A.M. so the room will be warm by 8:00 A.M.[13]

Historically, teachers have had to conform to the lifestyle that boards of education and the community citizens thought would be an appropriate model for their children. It has long been accepted that one important way in which children learn is by imitation. The role model presented to these children by adults with whom they have daily contact has been accepted as an important factor in influencing children's behavior. Consequently, a higher standard of conduct and character has been expected of teachers than has been expected of ordinary citizens. Boards of education, however, have not been given unlimited authority to regulate the behavior and lives of their employees. Teachers have been more inclined in recent years to question the rules and regulations concerning their lifestyles and have been willing to use the courts if the school board's policy infringes on what they perceive to be their rights as citizens.

The courts have generally agreed that a teacher's conduct can be regulated by the board of education. The regulations, however, cannot be developed merely as a result of board disapproval. A number of questions have been formulated by the courts in deciding the appropriateness of the regulation or the act. Does the conduct in question have some connection with the effectiveness of the teacher? Does the act have an effect on students and other teachers? What is the age and maturity level of the pupils involved? Are the constitutional rights of the teacher adversely affected or limited? These questions deal with a concept the courts have used called nexus, or the connection between the act and the effectiveness of the teacher or the operation of the school.

Many of the controversies between boards of education and teachers have centered on particular issues. One area of concern has been dress and grooming regulation for teachers. This topic has produced litigation over the wearing of neckties and growing of beards and long sideburns by male teachers and the wearing of short skirts or dresses and low-cut blouses by female teachers. Another subject is the sexual conduct of teachers. Areas of concern have been sexual misconduct with students, unmarried teachers living with members of the opposite sex, and homosexual lifestyles of teachers. A study of the court decisions concerning the teacher as an exemplar provides a general guideline for educational policy on such issues.

Teachers that have questioned dress and grooming regulations have claimed that their constitutional rights of free speech, expression, privacy, and liberty have been violated by the requirements. In general, courts have not been favorably impressed by these claims and have usually reinforced the rights of school boards to regulate the dress of teachers. An example of a judicial statement to this effect was made in a case where a high-school teacher was reprimanded for failing to wear a tie while teaching his English class.[14] He sued the board of education for violation of his right of free speech and privacy. Some of the reasoning and the findings of the court were as follows:

The First Amendment claim made here is so insubstantial as to border on the frivolous. We are unwilling to expand First Amendment protection to include a teacher's sartorial choice . . . This claim will not withstand analysis. . . .

By bringing trivial activities under the constitutional umbrella we trivialize the constitution provision itself. . . .

As public servants in a special position of trust, teachers may properly be subjected to many restrictions in their professional lives which would be invalid if generally applied.[15]

Educational policy as pronounced by the courts on sexual misconduct of teachers has been more difficult to categorize. If the misconduct is with students, the courts have left no doubt as to the seriousness of the charge and have upheld the board of education unless serious procedural problems were present. If the misconduct is with a nonstudent, the impact on the teacher's effectiveness has been an important consideration. The courts have generally required that a connection be shown between the teacher's behavior and either the teacher's effectiveness or a disruption of the school. The age group maturity and the grade level of the pupils taught by the teacher have also influenced the decision of the courts.

In a court decision involving the homosexual lifestyle of a teacher, the court ruled that the board of education did prove that the teacher's effectiveness was impaired. The court found:

A teacher's efficiency is determined by his relationship with students, their parents, fellow teachers and school administrators. In all of these areas the continued employment of the appellant after he became known as a homosexual would result, had he not been discharged, in confusion, suspicion, fear, expressed parental concern and pressure upon the administration from students, parents and fellow teachers, all of which would impair the appellant's efficiency as a teacher and injure the school.[16]

This discussion of the teacher as a role model illustrates the various sources that contribute to the development of educational policy. Among these sources are the community pressures, the board of education regulations and policies, and the perception by individuals of their constitutional rights; and the final arbiter of these differing views is the court system. It should also be noted that educational policy is dynamic in that it is constantly being formulated and changed.

Teacher Liability

Citizens in recent years have increasingly looked to the courts to address those contractual and constitutional rights that they feel have been limited or denied. The desired result is the protection of the public from having these rights eroded or violated. The material previously covered in this chapter has highlighted this type of litigation. When an injured party, through civil court action, is concerned with obtaining compensation for the injury sustained, a different and distinct body of law applies. Although

Photo 10.2
The importance of education is expressed here through a parent-teacher conference.

actions against medical doctors, lawyers, and professionals other than teachers have had considerably more publicity, a growing use of the courts involving actions with educators needs to be studied. This section deals with the development of current educational policy regarding the tort and malpractice liability of teachers and highlights some court activity that has played a role in defining this policy.

Tort Liability

For our purposes a general definition of a tort is any civil wrongdoing that leads to student injury. An action in tort is an attempt to get compensation by an individual for injury caused by someone's unreasonable behavior. Educators are concerned about injuries (physical or mental) to pupils that result in tort actions. Defamation of character through pupil records, evaluations, or recommendation for employment purposes could also lead to action in tort. Finally malpractice—usually related to student competence or the placement, treatment, or diagnosis of special students—is the third category that could lead to tort liability.

For the teacher, a tort can be classified as one of two types—through either intentional interference or negligence. The former results from some intentional act that injures someone, such as the corporal punishment of a child. The latter results in injury through the conduct of an educator that falls below an accepted, established professional standard. The law requires that a tort include four elements: standard of care, unreasonable risk, proximate cause, and actual injury. Each element is essential and must be present for a successful action in tort.

Every teacher has a duty to provide an appropriate standard of care for the students. This standard of care varies with the age and maturity of the pupils and the subject taught. An industrial arts teacher with dangerous machinery in the room would have a different standard of care than a high-school English teacher. A teacher taking primary grade school-children on a field trip must provide a standard of care appropriate for the age and maturity level of the pupils. In any test of standard of care, the question, Did the teacher act as a reasonably prudent person would act under the same or similar circumstance? must be answered. If the answer is yes, a proper standard of care was exhibited.

There is an element of risk in most of the activities that make up the school day. It is recognized that choosing a chemistry class, playing football on the school team, and riding on the school bus all involve some risk. The second element of a tort is unreasonable risk. The reasonableness of the risk is also determined by the age and maturity of the pupils and the preparation made by the teacher for the activity in question. The use of appropriate chemicals in a chemistry class provides an element of risk. If safety equipment such as safety glasses or an emergency shower is not available, the risk could be unreasonable.

The third element that is essential is proximate cause. It is not enough that the proper standard of care was missing and that the risk was unreasonable. There must be a connection between these elements and the injury. If a teacher leaves a playground unsupervised and an injury occurs, a connection would have to be made between the teacher's lack of supervision and the injury. If an accident occurs that could not have been stopped had the teacher been present, there may not be proximate cause.

The fourth element, actual injury, must have occurred. If there is no injury, there can be no tort liability. The courts have been called upon to make judgments concerning the tort liability of educators at an increasing rate in recent years. The court actions help define the educational policy that teachers must follow. When a conflict arises over the standard of care provided by a teacher, the court's reasoning and decision must consider the four essential elements that are part of tort liability.

A student in a woodworking class threw a nail toward a trash barrel. The nail struck another pupil in the eye resulting in a severe injury. At the time of the incident, the teacher was working with a student on a special project in a nearby workroom. The parents of the injured student sued the school district and the teacher for negligence, claiming failure to provide proper supervision and failure to discipline students to prevent the throwing of objects. The court found that the student throwing the nail had been reprimanded by the teacher several times for throwing objects at the trash barrel. The decision of the court stated that "there is general agreement that a teacher can be liable for injury to students under their supervision if an injury is caused by the teacher's negligence or failure to exercise reasonable care to protect the students."[17] In this case, however, the court continued in the following manner:

> *Counsel argues that the teacher was negligent because he was not in the classroom at the moment the incident occurred. We disagree. It is, of course, impossible for a teacher to personally supervise each student under his care every moment of the school day. This especially is true in a situation such as woodworking class, in which students are involved in numerous projects, either by themselves or in small groups. A teacher must necessarily rely, to some extent, on the responsibility and maturity of his students to conduct themselves in a proper and safe manner.*[18]

The court did not consider that an unreasonable risk was present or that the teacher did not provide the standard of care needed for the grade level and maturity of the student.

A third-grade pupil went to a girls' rest room following her luncheon recess. In an area adjacent to the rest room, a number of children were playing with apples they had wrongfully removed from the lunchroom. One of the pupils asked another to open the rest-room door, and as the door opened, he threw an apple into the room, hitting the third-grade pupil in the eye. A teacher assigned to supervise the area outside this rest room was not at her assigned post. The court ruled that the removal of the apples from the lunchroom and the absence of supervision in the area were a clear indication of improper supervision. The court awarded damages to the parents of the injured girl.[19] The court recognized the difficulty of supervising the lunchroom, the entrance from the yard, and the area next to the rest room but reasoned that this incident developed over time as the apples were removed from the lunchroom and the children were playing and making noise and were not supervised properly during this entire period.

Malpractice

Another type of tort that concerns educators is malpractice. Although malpractice has been associated in recent years with cases concerning medical practice, other professions have had some activity in this area. Although it has not been a common tort action in the field of education, it is important to know what has happened to this point. The courts have thus far denied tort claims for educational malpractice, but two court actions should be reviewed so that the rationale of the court can be understood.

A student, Peter W., graduated from high school in California. The student claimed he could not gain meaningful employment and survive in society, because he lacked reading and writing skills. He brought suit against the San Francisco Public Schools. The suit alleged that the public schools:

1. "Negligently and carelessly" failed to apprehend his reading disabilities.

2. "Negligently and carelessly" assigned him to classes in which he could not read "the books and other materials."

3. "Negligently and carelessly" allowed him to "pass and advance from a course or grade level" with knowledge that he had not achieved either its completion or the skills necessary for him to succeed or benefit from subsequent courses.

4. "Negligently and carelessly" assigned him to classes in which the instructors were unqualified or which were not "geared" to his reading level, and,

5. "Negligently and carelessly" permitted him to graduate from high school although he was unable to read above the eighth-grade reading level, as required by Education Code 8573 . . . thereby depriving him of additional instruction in reading and other academic skills.

The court stated that:

> . . . *Unlike the activity of the highway or marketplace, classroom methodology affords no readily acceptable standards of care, or cause, or injury. The science of pedagogy itself is fraught with different and conflicting theories of how or what a child should be taught, and any layman might—and commonly does—have his own emphatic views*

on the subject. The "injury" claimed here is plaintiff's inability to read and write. Substantial professional authority attests that the achievement of literacy in the schools, or its failure, is influenced by a host of factors which affect the pupil subjectively, from outside the formal teaching process, and beyond the control of its ministers. They may be physical, neurological, emotional, cultural, environmental; they may be present but not perceived, recognized but not identified.[20]

The court could not in this case determine that any student injury was within the legal definition of negligence.

The New York Supreme Court Appellate Division was called upon to decide a malpractice case similar to the case of Peter W.[21] A student claimed that the public schools failed to teach him varied subjects and failed to properly test him to find his learning capacity and ability. The plaintiff did not have the basic skills in reading and writing and yet received a certificate of graduation. The court ruling questioned the idea that because there is teaching there is learning. The court reasoned that "the failure to learn does not bespeak a failure to teach. It is not alleged that the plaintiff's classmates, who were exposed to the identical classroom instruction, also failed to learn."[22] Although the court ruled against the plaintiff, one may wonder what would have been the decision had other students also failed to learn. The area of malpractice is one that will see increased litigation in the future and must be studied with concern by educators.

Summary

For a number of years the quantity of teachers available for our schools has been the overriding concern of educational policymakers. The quantity issue has been overshadowed in recent years by concerns for equality and equity. Now a movement highlighted by critical reports and led by political office-holders has attempted to focus on the quality of schooling and of teachers. The state through the certification process controls the selection of teachers. Increasingly, the states have implemented the use of testing programs as a part of the certification process. The use of tests for employment purposes has generated controversy that has resulted in judicial intervention outlining the parameters for test usage by educational policymakers.

Educators have frequently turned to the court system to ensure that their constitutional rights are protected. Boards of education, on the other hand, have insisted that they can limit the rights of teachers if the limitation is needed to carry out their purpose of maintaining an orderly, efficient school system that will ensure the proper environment for the children. Educational policy must recognize that the courts have placed limits on both parties.

Intentional interference and negligence are two classifications of torts that educators must understand. Torts have four essential ingredients: standard of care, unreasonable risk, proximate cause, and actual injury, all of which must be present for a tort action to be successful. Malpractice, another type of tort, has assumed importance in recent years. Although the courts have been asked to rule in several malpractice actions, they have not been satisfied that educational malpractice has taken place.

Table 10.3 summarizes court cases that relate to the issues discussed in this chapter.

Table 10.3
Selected Court Cases

CASE	FINDING
Griggs v. *Duke Power* (1971)	If tests are used for employment or promotional purposes, they must be job related.
U.S. v. *South Carolina* (1978)	The National Teachers Examination is job related as it is used in South Carolina.
Pickering v. *Board of Education* (1968)	Teachers have freedom of expression rights if classroom performance is not affected.
Mt. Healthy City School District Board of Education v. *Doyle,* (1977)	Constitutional rights issues will not invalidate dismissal if other incidents warrant the action.
Wilson v. *Chancellor* (1976)	Teachers can utilize methods that are professionally acceptable and do not disrupt the school's operation.
Minarcini v. *Strongsville City School District* (1976)	A school board has the right to approve textbooks but cannot remove books from the library unless an overriding governmental function can be documented.
Bd. of Educ. Island Trees Union Free Dist. 26 v. *Pico* (1982)	A school board cannot remove books from the library simply because they dislike the ideas contained in the books.
East Hartford Education Assoc. v. *Board of Education* (1977)	Dress and grooming regulations for teachers held to be constitutional.
Gaylord v. *Tacoma School District No. 10* (1977)	Homosexual lifestyle of a teacher can be cause for dismissal.
Hammond v. *Scott* (1977)	A teacher is not held negligent for injury to pupil when working with another student outside the classroom.
Carson v. *Orleans Parish School Board* (1983)	Teacher's absence from supervisory post held liable for injury to pupil.
Peter W. v. *San Francisco Unified School District* (1976)	Student's failure to learn to read and write not accepted as malpractice negligence by court.
Donohue v. *Copiague Union Free School District* (1978)	Individual student's failure to read and write not accepted as educational malpractice.

Key Words

Certification

Job-related

Nonrenewal

Dismissal

Reduction in force (RIF)

Due process

Liberty interest

Property interest

Vagueness issue

Balance of interest

Teacher as a role model

Nexus

Tort

Intentional interference

Negligence

Standard of care

Unreasonable risk

Proximate cause

Actual injury

Malpractice

Discussion Questions

1. What is the meaning of the term *due process*?
2. What, if any, limits are placed on a teacher's academic freedom?
3. Should a teacher be held to a different standard of behavior than any other citizen? Why or why not?
4. Malpractice, negligence, and intentional interference are types of torts. Explain the differences and the distinctions.

For Further Reading

Alexander, Kern, and Alexander, M. David. *American Public School Law*. St. Paul: West Publishing Co., 1985.

Beckman, J., and Zirkel, P. *Legal Issues in Public School Employment*. Bloomington, Ind.: Phi Delta Kappa, 1983.

Connors, Eugene T. *Educational Tort Liability and Malpractice*. Bloomington, Ind.: Phi Delta Kappa, 1981.

Delon, Floyd. *Legal Issues in the Dismissal of Teachers for Personal Conduct*. National Organization on Legal Problems in Education, 1982.

Holmes Group. *Tomorrow's Teachers*. East Lansing, Michigan, 1986.

Kerr, D. *Educational Policy Analysis, Structure, and Justification*. New York, David McKay Co., 1976.

LaMorte, Michael W. *School Law Cases and Concepts*. Englewood Cliffs, N.J.: Prentice-Hall, 1982.

McCarthy, M. M., and Cambron, Nelda. *Public School Law Teachers' and Students' Rights*. Boston, Mass.: Allyn & Bacon, 1981.

McCarthy, M., and Deignan, P. *What Legally Constitutes an Adequate Public Education*. Bloomington, Ind.: Phi Delta Kappa.

A Nation Prepared: Teachers for the 21st Century. Carnegie Forum on Education, 1986.

Reutter, E. *The Supreme Court's Impact on Public Education*. Bloomington, Ind.: Phi Delta Kappa, and NOLPE, 1982.

Valente, W. *Law in the Schools*. Columbus, Ohio: Charles E. Merrill Publishing Co., 1980.

Wirt F., and Kirst, M. *Schools in Conflict*. Berkeley, Calif.: McCutchan Publishing Co., 1982.

Yudof, M., Kirp, D., Van Geel, Tyll, and Levin, B. *Educational Policy and the Law*, 2d ed. Berkeley, Calif.: McCutchan Publishing Co., 1982.

Notes

1. James S. Coleman. *Equality of Educational Opportunity* (Washington, D.C.: U.S. Government Printing Office, 1966).
2. Christopher Jencks. *Inequality* (New York: Harper & Row, 1972).
3. *Griggs* v. *Duke Power Co.,* Supreme Court of the United States (1971), 401 U.S. 424, 91 S.CT. 849.
4. *Ibid.*
5. *United States of America* v. *State of South Carolina* U.S. District Court of South Carolina, Columbia Div. (1977), 445 F. Supp. 1094 Aff'd. 434 U.S. 1026, 98 S.CT. 756, 1978.

6. *Pickering* v. *Board of Education*, Supreme Court of the United States (1968), U.S. 563, 88 S.CT. 1731, 20L Ed. 2d 811.

7. *Ibid.*

8. *Mt. Healthy City School District Board of Education* v. *Doyle*, Supreme Court of the United States (1977), 429 US 274, 97 US 568.

9. *Wilson* v. *Chancellor*, United States District Court, District of Oregon (1976), 418 F. Supp. 1358.

10. *Ibid.*

11. *Minarcini* v. *Strongsville City School Dist.*, 384 F. Supp. 698 (N.D. Ohio 1974); 541 F 201 577 (6th Cir. 1976).

12. *Ibid.*

13. Michael W. LaMorte. *School Law: Cases and Concepts* (Englewood Cliffs, N.J.: Prentice-Hall, 1982), p. 216.

14. *East Hartford Education Association* v. *Board of Education*, United States Court of Appeals, Second Circuit (1977), 562 F. 2d 838.

15. *Ibid.*

16. *Gaylord* v. *Tacoma School*, District No. 10 Supreme Court of Washington, (1977), 88 Wash. 2d 286, 559 P. 2d 1340.

17. *Hammond* v. *Scott* 232 S.E. 2d 336 (1977).

18. *Ibid.*

19. *Carson* v. *Orleans Parish School Board*, Court of Appeals of Louisiana, Fourth Circuit (1983), 432 So 2d 956.

20. *Peter W.* v. *San Francisco Unified School District*, (60 C.A. 3d 814 131 Cal. Rptr. 854, 1976).

21. *Donohue* v. *Copiague Union Free School District*, 407 N.Y.S. 2d 874 A.D. 2d 29 (1978).

22. *Ibid.*

11 Student Rights and School Relationships

"First Amendment rights, applied in the light of the special characteristics of the school environment are available to teachers and students. It can hardly be argued that either students or teachers shed their constitutional rights to freedom of speech or expression at the schoolhouse gate."

The U.S. Supreme Court in *Tinker* v. *Des Moines Independent Community School District* (1969)

"Judicial interposition in the operation of the public school system of the Nation raises problems requiring care and restraint. . . . By and large, public education in our Nation is committed to the control of state and local authorities."

The U.S. Supreme Court in *Epperson* v. *Arkansas* (1968)

". . . If the time has come when pupils of state-supported schools, kindergartens, grammar schools, or high schools can defy or flout orders of school officials to keep their minds on their own school work, it is the beginning of a new revolutionary era of permissiveness in this country fostered by the judiciary."

Supreme Court Justice Black's dissent in *Tinker* v. *Des Moines Independent Community School District* (1969)

The individual rights and freedoms of students can be in conflict with the legal mandate given to school authorities to provide a safe and disciplined school environment. At what point can school officials curtail or limit the

---

Policy Model 11.1   A Framework for Educational Policy Analysis

---

POLICY ISSUE	PARTICIPANTS IN POLICY DEVELOPMENT	ILLUSTRATIONS OF POLICY SOLUTIONS	EFFECTS OF POLICY SOLUTIONS
A. B. C. D.	**Formal** a. Courts b. State legislatures c. d. **Informal** a. Parent b. Pupil c. ACLU d. Professional groups e. f.	**Court rulings** a. b. c. d. **Legislative enactments** a. b. **School board policies** a. b. **Administrative regulations** a. b. **Other** a.	**Allocative** Who gets what? **Regulative** Who can do what? **Structural** Additions or deletions to the present system **Redistributive** Changes in resource or authority allocation

constitutional freedoms of the students attending public school? What justification, if any, is acceptable in our society for school policies that limit the individual rights and freedoms of students? These questions have been difficult for our policymakers and have led to conflicts involving the schools, parents, students, and other various interested parties.

This chapter explores the relationship between individual student rights and governmental authority in the operation of our public schools. The conflicts have been so controversial that our court system has been increasingly called upon to settle the disputes and balance the interests. As you read the chapter, note the various groups that attempt to influence educational policymakers. A framework for analysis is provided in Policy Model 11.1. As you study the material on student rights and school relationships, try to add what you believe to be important to the outline.

The state constitution provides the framework for the establishment of schools for children. The state, in using its powers to provide for schooling, often collides with the constitutional liberties granted to individuals (in this case, students). This chapter explores the major areas of conflict and the attempts to resolve these controversies. To understand the issues, a review of the relevant parts of the U.S. Constitution is necessary. The tension between constitutional freedoms and compulsory schooling can then be studied.

Major Constitutional Premises

As noted earlier in the book, the Tenth Amendment to the U.S. Constitution reserved to the states those powers not delegated to the United States or prohibited to the states. The state's power to provide for schooling was established in that manner. Other parts of the Constitution provided individual citizens with certain rights and liberties. The following selected Constitutional provisions are generally at issue when individuals and the state clash over student rights and school relationships.

Amendment I

Congress shall make no law respecting an establishment of religion, or prohibiting the free exercise thereof; or abridging the freedom of speech, or of the press; or the right of the people peaceably to assemble, and to petition the Government for a redress of grievances.

Amendment IV

The right of the people to be secure in their persons, houses, papers, and effects, against unreasonable searches and seizures, shall not be violated, and no Warrants shall issue but upon probable cause, supported by Oath or affirmation and particularly describing the place to be searched, and the persons or things to be seized.

Amendment V

. . . nor be deprived of life, liberty or property, without due process of law; nor shall private property be taken for public use, without just compensation.

Amendment VIII

Excessive bail shall not be required, nor excessive fines imposed, nor cruel and unusual punishments inflicted.

Amendment XIV

Section 1. All persons born or naturalized in the United States, and subject to the jurisdiction thereof, are citizens of the United States and of the State wherein they reside. No state shall make or enforce any law which shall abridge the privileges or immunities of citizens of the United States; nor shall any State deprive any person of life, liberty, or property, without due process of law; nor deny to any person within its jurisdiction the equal protection of the laws.

The First, Fourth, Fifth, and Eighth Amendments provide the individual with protection from federal officials. The Fourteenth Amendment extends this protection to cover state authorities. Figure 11.1 illustrates the manner in which the U.S. Supreme Court can influence student rights and educational policies relating to these rights. Note that the courts can either strengthen or limit the authority of state constitutions, state statutes, school boards, or school officials. The following issues have forced educational policymakers to consider the relationship between individual student rights and compulsory schooling.

Freedom of Speech

The First Amendment freedom of speech rights of public school students have on a number of occasions clashed with the rights of school authorities to provide for schooling. The issue revolves around the question, How much, if any, authority does a school board have in limiting the constitutional freedoms of public school students? This question has been tested a number of times over varied topics. Courts have been asked to rule on

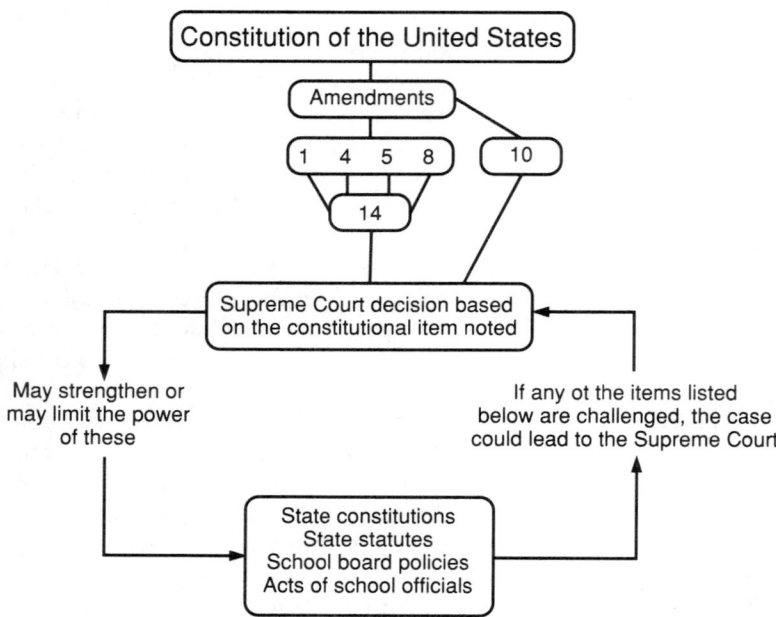

Figure 11.1
Supreme Court Influence on Student Rights and School Relationships

students protesting the Viet Nam conflict, the inclusion of sex-related material in school publications, the distribution of printed material objectionable to the school board, and the utilization of policies that require approval in advance for the use of printed or spoken material.

Due Process

Public school students have due process rights as outlined in the Fourteenth Amendment. Due process was discussed in detail in Chapter 10 and needs only a brief review here. Due process procedures can vary. The greater the impact on the student, the more detailed the required due process. If it can be determined that the student has a liberty or property interest involved, full and complete due process procedures are required. Some major educational policy issues have centered on the balancing of school policy and its administration with the due process rights of the student.

Right to Privacy

In former years, students' privacy rights in a school setting were infrequently a topic of concern. Most of the privacy problems centered on petty theft of some sort and the attempted recovery by school officials of the stolen items. The singling out of an individual to be searched and the search of a student's locker or purse were generally the causes of complaint. In recent years, the privacy rights of students have become a more controversial and complicated issue. Reports of school violence indicating pupil or teacher injury or death have made headlines. The serious problem of drug use in our society has moved into the school. School officials in combatting these trends have utilized search and seizure procedures that some have questioned as an unconstitutional limitation of the privacy rights of public school students. The status of educational policy in the area of student privacy rights and unsettled issues of concern to students, teachers, parents, and educational policymakers are the topics of the next section.

Freedom of Expression As a Policy Issue

Freedom of expression issues can be studied by separating the controversies into two classes. The first of these is student speech. The expression at issue can be typical oral speech, the wearing of buttons carrying a message, or the wearing of something that has symbolic meaning, such as a black arm band. The second topic concerns student publications. This category includes controversies relating to the censorship of written materials in school publications and the distribution of unauthorized written material by students.

Student Speech

A number of emotionally charged, controversial issues have faced our society in recent years. Feelings about View Nam, Black Power, and various civil rights questions have divided the nation. These deep differences have carried over into our public schools, and questions concerning the rights of students to express themselves have arisen. Litigation has resulted from attempts to administer, regulate, and limit expression on controversial issues. A study of representative court cases will provide the guidelines for educational policy as outlined by the courts.

A U.S. Appeals Court announced its decisions in two cases on the same day in 1966. In *Burnside v. Byars,* the court upheld the right of public school students to wear buttons inscribed "One Man One Vote" even though the principal declared that students were not permitted to wear the buttons in school.[1] The court decided that the students were not in any way disrupting the operation of the school and were entitled to wear the buttons as a constitutional freedom of speech right. In *Blackwell* v. *Issaquena Board of Education,* the identical issue was presented to the court.[2] Students wearing buttons similar to those described in *Burnside* were asked to remove the buttons or face suspension. The students in this decision were gathering in an area that disrupted the normal operation of the school and were interfering with those students not wearing buttons by stopping them and asking them to join in their protest. In this decision, the court upheld the right of the school principal to limit the symbolic speech (wearing the buttons) of the students. The major concerns of the court were to uphold the freedom of speech rights of the students and to ensure that the educational process of the school was not disrupted. In the second case, the court found that the students' acts were disrupting the normal operation of the school and thus recognized the right of the school prinicipal to maintain discipline and an orderly school.[3]

A few years later, the Supreme Court agreed to hear a freedom of speech case, *Tinker* v. *Des Moines Independent Community School District.*[4] This is now considered the landmark decision outlining the rights of students and school officials on this issue. The reasoning used in the previously cited decisions was approved and repeated in the Supreme Court's decision. A group of adults and students objected to the Viet Nam conflict. The group decided to publicize their objections by fasting on two days and wearing black arm bands through the December holiday season. The principals of the Des Moines schools became aware of the plan and adopted regulations prohibiting the wearing of the arm bands. Students came to school wearing the arm bands and were sent home and suspended until they would return without the arm bands. The students, citing their

First Amendment rights, brought suit in the U.S. district court. Through appeal, the case reached the Supreme Court. The Court argued in part:

> . . . *The wearing of armbands in the circumstances of this case was entirely divorced from actually or potentially disruptive conduct by those participating in it. It was closely akin to "pure speech" which, we have repeatedly held, is entitled to comprehensive protection under the First Amendment. . . .*
>
> *First Amendment rights, applied in light of the special characteristics of the school environment, are available to teachers and students. It can hardly be argued that either students or teachers shed their constitutional rights to freedom of speech or expression at the schoolhouse gate. . . .*
>
> *The school officials banned and sought to punish petitioners for a silent, passive expression of opinion, unaccompanied by any disorder or disturbance on the part of petitioners. There is here no evidence whatever of petitioners' interference, actual or nascent, with the schools' work or of collision with the rights of other students to be secure and to be let alone. Accordingly, this case does not concern speech or action that intrudes upon the work of the schools or the rights of other students.*[5]

The *Tinker* decision is still the most important statement of the Court in outlining a student's right to free speech. The arm bands were an expression of free speech. The school authorities did not treat all items and topics the same in regulating the wearing of arm bands. No buttons, tee shirts with messages, or other symbols of political ideas were included. The regulation was specifically addressed to the arm bands and protest of the Viet Nam conflict. The Court recognized the rights of school authorities to maintain discipline and order but found no threat of school disruption or disturbance that would justify the limitation of the students' right to free expression. Thus, the Court in this decision has outlined the balance required in protecting the freedom of speech of students and the right of a state to maintain an orderly school environment.

Student Publications

Schools are involved in the publication of student newspapers and literary magazines. Are the constitutional guarantees of freedom of speech and freedom of the press extended without limit to these endeavors? Can students distribute unauthorized underground newspapers on school premises? Can school authorities place limits on the distribution of printed material by students? Can school officials demand the right to see and approve materials before their publication or distribution? Educational policy that attempts to deal with these questions can become controversial and the center of attention in a school district.

The problems can become quite complicated and difficult for school authorities. The standards outlined in the *Tinker* decision are the relevant guidelines for school authorities to follow. Under these standards, material that might be considered obscene by some citizens could be included in school publications. Even though the school may be on sound constitutional grounds in allowing the publication of certain material objectionable

Photo 11.1
Freedom of expression through the school newspaper can be a concern of educational policy makers.

to some citizens, the problem of explaining this action to the community might be difficult. Some groups claim that school authorities who allow the publication of questionable material are responsible for lower morality and a lack of discipline in today's schools. Others, however, claim that free speech and free press are vital to our democracy and that these principles cannot be taught effectively in a civics class if they cannot be practiced in the school setting. The issue has been addressed in a number of court decisions.

The Fairfax County (Virginia) School Board issued a notice prohibiting the schools from offering sex education until a decision was reached by the board on a proposed program. Student reporters submitted an article entitled "Sexually Active Students Fail to Use Contraceptives" for publication in *The Farm News,* the high-school student newspaper. The high-school principal ordered the students not to publish the article as written. The students brought suit to enjoin the authorities from prohibiting the publication of the article.[6] The decision of the court included in part the following findings:

1. *The Farm News* was conceived and established as an instrument for student expression.

2. The newspaper is clearly covered by the First Amendment.

3. The court did not question the authority of the board to regulate curriculum and course content.

4. *The Farm News* was not an integral part of the curriculum offered at the school.

5. The court upheld the right of the students to publish the article in question in its entirety.[7]

In another decision, *Trachtman v. Anker (1977),* school authorities were able to prevent the distribution of a questionnaire concerning the sex

Box 11.1
Students' Freedom
to Speak

Bethel School District No. 403 v. *Fraser,* 106 S.Ct. 778 (1986)

Is Lewd And Indecent Speech By A Student During A School Assembly Protected By The First Amendment?

A high-school assembly was held as a part of the school's program in self-government. The assembly was attended by approximately 600 students. A number of these students were fourteen years of age. A high-school student delivered a speech nominating a student for an elective office. Throughout the speech, the student referred to the candidate by using graphic and sexually explicit figures of speech and gestures. Many of the students at the assembly yelled, screamed, and hooted during the speech. Other students exhibited behavior that indicated embarrassment and bewilderment.

At least two teachers with whom the student had discussed the speech before the assembly had advised the student not to give the speech, as it was inappropriate. The morning following the assembly, a school administrator notified the student that his speech was in violation of the school's disruptive-conduct rule and that it had interrupted the educational process and included obscene and profane language and gestures. The student was suspended for three days and removed from the list of students being considered as commencement speakers.

The student filed suit in federal district court, alleging that his First Amendment right to freedom of speech was violated. The federal district court ruled in favor of the student, saying the First and Fourteenth Amendment rights of the student were violated. The school district appealed, but the appellate court affirmed the district court decision.

The Supreme Court reversed the decision, holding that the First Amendment did not prohibit the school from disciplining a pupil using offensively lewd and indecent speech. The Court also pointed out that although adults may not be prohibited from using an offensive type of expression, the same latitude did not apply to children. In addition, the Court said that an appropriate function of the public schools is to prohibit the use of vulgar and lewd terms in public speech.

habits of students.[8] The student editor of a school newspaper wanted to distribute a twenty-five question survey that included items on contraception, masturbation, and homosexuality. School authorities opposed the use of the survey on the basis that the health and welfare of the students would be jeopardized by the psychological pressures exerted and that significant emotional harm to students might result. The school board offered affidavits from a number of expert witnesses from the fields of psychology and psychiatry to support their contention. The court decided that the school authorities did not act unreasonably and that their action was a measure to protect students. Under the circumstances described in this decision, the school board could, in carrying out its mandate to protect the well-being of students, limit First Amendment freedom of speech rights.

The third decision, *Williams* v. *Spencer (1980),* concerns the distribution of student-written materials on school grounds. An underground newspaper was distributed on school grounds with the permission of the school principal. A short time after distribution started, a school official stopped the procedure and confiscated the papers. The issue contained the promotion of drug paraphernalia and depicted a staff member in a derogatory manner with racial overtones. The school authorities claimed the issue contained information that endangered the health and safety of students and therefore could not be distributed on school grounds. This led to a court suit brought by the students to seek approval to distribute the newspapers.[9] The court ruled that First Amendment rights of students must yield in this case to the superior interests of the school. The materials in question encouraged actions that could endanger the health and safety of the students, and the school authorities acted legitimately in prohibiting the distribution of the paper on school grounds.

The three decisions illustrate the difficulties faced by educational policymakers in the realm of students' First Amendment rights. The *Tinker* decision has been used as the standard, and the guidelines set forth by the court are still important to educational policymakers. It should be noted that the courts have not favored the use of prior restraint by school authorities. If officials attempt to exercise prior restraint, the regulations and procedures must be clear, understandable, and reasonable, and their use must be related to the health, safety, and welfare of the students. Recently, in the view of some legal experts, these guidelines have been altered by the Supreme Court. On January 13, 1988, in *Hazelwood School District* v. *Kuhlmeier,* the U.S. Supreme Court ruled that a school administrator can utilize prior restraint and censor a school-sponsored student newspaper.[10] Journalism students at Hazelwood East High School in St. Louis County, Missouri, interviewed students about their experiences with pregnancy and about the impact of their parents' divorces on their lives. Based on these interviews, two articles were written and included in the school newspaper. The principal objected to parts of the articles concerning birth control and sexual activity. In addition, he was concerned that the parents had not been allowed to respond or consent to publication of the material in the newspaper. The pages containing these articles were deleted from the newspaper, and the students sued in federal district court contending that their First Amendment rights had been violated. On appeal, the Supreme Court majority ruled that schools are not public forums and have different characteristics from those areas used for public assembly. The court concluded that the principal's decision was not unreasonable. The school-sponsored newspaper is therefore not a public forum, and student editors and reporters can be regulated by school authorities.

Policy Model 11.2 analyzes educational policy development in relation to the freedom of expression issue. Additional elements can be added to the model to make it appropriate for your particular area or school district.

Suspension and Expulsion

School authorities have used the removal of students from the school as a means of maintaining order and discipline. If the removal is for ten or fewer days, it is generally labeled as a suspension. If the removal is permanent or

Policy Model 11.2   Student Moral Environment

POLICY ISSUE `	PARTICIPANTS IN POLICY DEVELOPMENT	ILLUSTRATIONS OF POLICY SOLUTIONS	EFFECTS OF POLICY SOLUTIONS
Provide disciplined moral environment for students	**Formal** Courts Legislative bodies Administrative bodies School boards **Informal** Professional teachers' groups ACLU Parents Students Media School boards' associations School administrators' groups	**Board Policy and Administrative Regulations** Limiting student free speech rights by: prior restraint banning of material control of student publications **Court Precedents** *Burnside* v. *Byers* *Blackwell* v. *Issaquena Bd.* *Tinker* v. *Des Moines* *Gambino* v. *Fairfax Bd.* *Trachtman* v. *Anker* *Williams* v. *Spencer* *Hazelwood School District* v. *Kuhlmeier*	**Regulative** School boards must revise policies to conform to court mandates Administrators must implement new policies **Redistributive** Power of school authorities limited regarding prior restraint Students receive some First Amendment protection

for the balance of the semester or year, the removal is generally called expulsion. Expulsions have great impact on the student, and a formal due process procedure must be followed so that the liberty and property rights of the student are not violated. The practice through the years in many school districts was to use immediate suspension for ten or fewer days as a discipline tool without providing any form of due process to the student. This practice was questioned through the courts, and in 1975 the Supreme Court issued a decision, *Goss* v. *Lopez,* that set guidelines for the minimum provisions necessary.[11]

Nine students were suspended from school for ten days. The suspensions were given without hearings in accordance with an Ohio state statute that enabled principals to suspend without hearings. The students brought suit, challenging the constitutionality of the law. The lower court ruled that the law was unconstitutional. The Columbus, Ohio, Public Schools appealed to the U.S. Supreme Court. In upholding the decision of the lower court, the Supreme Court outlined minimal guidelines for due process. These guidelines form the basic foundations for educational policy on the required due process for suspension. The Court indicated that the student must be given oral or written notice of the charges. If the student denies the charges, an explanation of the evidence must be given. Finally, the student must be given an opportunity to present his or her side of the story. The

---

Policy Model 11.3   Student Discipline

POLICY ISSUE	PARTICIPANTS IN POLICY DEVELOPMENT	ILLUSTRATIONS OF POLICY SOLUTIONS	EFFECTS OF POLICY SOLUTIONS
Providing a disciplined school environment	**Formal** Courts Legislative bodies Administrative bodies School boards **Informal** Professional teachers' groups ACLU Parents Students Media School boards' associations School administrators' groups	**Statutory Provisions** School authorities can suspend students for ten days without due process hearing **Court Precedents** *Goss* v. *Lopez*	**Regulative** School boards must revise policy to conform to court mandate **Redistributive** Reduce legislatures' authority to limit due process rights of students

Court pointed out that these requirements would not impose burdensome and unnecessary requirements on school authorities but would provide a measure of safety against erroneous actions. The decision also affirms that the due process requirements vary in relation to the impact of the action on the student.

Policy Model 11.3 deals with the issue of providing a safe, disciplined school environment through the use of a suspension and expulsion policy. What other items can you add to this model to further develop the analysis?

The Student's Right to Privacy

The privacy rights of students reside in the Fourth Amendment, which provides the citizen protection against unreasonable searches. School authorities, in carrying out their responsibilities, have utilized student searches. In recent years, school authorities have had to contend with such serious problems as bomb threats, the use and sale of illegal drugs, and the possession of dangerous weapons by students. These problems have led school officials to search students, student lockers, and student vehicles. Questions have been raised concerning the possible infringement of the privacy rights of students in these actions.

Law enforcement officials must present information to an officer of the court that indicates probable cause for a search. The court official, when satisfied, can then issue a search warrant giving authority for a search. The courts have not required school officials to meet such probable cause standards. Recognizing that school officials have the safety and well-being of students as a priority responsibility, the courts have approved of reasonable cause as justification to search. Reasonable cause is a lower standard than that required of law enforcement officials. A warrant is not needed. The school official need only have reasonable cause to believe that the student possesses something illegal or harmful.

School authorities' searches are not without limits, and a number of court actions have provided guidelines. A number of incidents of petty theft were reported in a class of fifth-graders. On a particular day, a student reported the loss of three dollars. The school authorities searched the cloakroom, including the coats of the children, and the desks and classroom. The school authorities then removed the children to their respective rest rooms and ordered the children to strip to their undergarments. The missing money was not located. The parents of the children sought redress for what they believed to be an unlawful strip search. The court found that the strip search was unreasonable and found no danger present that would require such an undertaking.[12]

School authorities were concerned about the drug use among students at a particular school. A number of incidents indicated to authorities that a drug problem existed. It was decided that a schoolwide search would be conducted using dogs trained to detect drugs. The dogs were used in each room of the school and were allowed to walk past each of the students. If the dog gave an alert, the student was required to empty pockets or purse. An alert was given at a thirteen-year-old female student. No drugs were found in her purse or pockets. The dog continued to return to the girl and seemed highly excited. The student was asked to go to a particular room where she was strip searched. No drugs were found. The parents of the student brought suit against the school officials for what they felt was a violation of the Fourth Amendment rights of their daughter.[13] The decision of the court did not disapprove of the use of a canine search. The emptying of pockets and purses was not considered to be a violation of the Fourth Amendment. The conducting of a nude search of a student on the basis of a dog alert was unreasonable and a violation of the student's rights. This entitled the student to damages. The language of the court was in part:

> It does not require a constitutional scholar to conclude that a nude search of a thirteen-year-old child is an invasion of constitutional rights of some magnitude. More than that: It is a violation of any known principle of human decency. Apart from any constitutional readings and rulings, simple common sense would indicate that the conduct of the school officials in permitting such a nude search was not only unlawful but outrageous under settled indisputable principles of law.[14]

In a very recent decision, the Supreme Court further detailed and emphasized that school searches can be constitutional if there is reasonable cause.[15] A school official discovered two girls smoking in a rest room. Since this was a violation of a school rule, the girls were taken to the vice principal's office. One girl admitted that she was smoking, and one girl denied she was smoking and indicated that she did not smoke at all. The school official asked this student for her purse. Opening the purse, he discovered a package of cigarettes. As the package of cigarettes was being removed from the purse, the vice principal noticed some cigarette rolling paper. This, in the school official's experience, was a possible sign of marijuana use. In a further search of the girl's purse, an amount of marijuana was found, a rather large sum of money, a list of names owing money to the student, and some additional drug-related items. Was this an unreasonable search? Could the drug-related findings be utilized in the disciplining of the student? Should the school authorities' search be limited to the violation related to cigarettes? The Supreme Court upheld the search as being reasonable. The Court indicated that the resulting discovery of evidence of marijuana dealing was reasonable in light of the circumstances and that the evidence could be used in the student's juvenile delinquency proceedings.[16]

School authorities do have the right to search students if necessary for the well-being of the school. The search standard is reasonable cause, which is a lower standard than probable cause. The right to search is not without limits. The courts have been reluctant to approve of nude searches and have been ambivalent concerning the use of sniff dogs. The public views drugs in the schools to be a major problem confronting our society. Thus, the issue of student searches will continue to confront school officials (see Box 11.2).

Corporal Punishment

The use of corporal punishment in public schools has been a much-debated topic. There are some who advocate a "spare the rod and spoil the child" position and others who oppose physical punishment. Through the years, the use of corporal punishment for discipline has been a frequently litigated topic. Most of the questions concerning the use of corporal punishment have been answered through the lower courts. Two cases that seem to best outline the guidelines for educational policy did reach the Supreme Court, and a brief review of these cases follows.

In North Carolina in 1975, a federal court approved of a teacher's use of corporal punishment over the objections of the child's parents.[17] In rendering the decision, the court outlined some safeguards that should be utilized in administering corporal punishment: (1) A policy should be in place informing students of what behaviors will warrant the use of corporal punishment, (2) the use of corporal punishment should be witnessed by another staff member and should not be utilized unless other measures have failed, and (3) a written report of the reasons for punishing the child should be available to the parents. This decision was appealed to the U.S. Supreme Court. The decision was affirmed without a written opinion.

The second case, *Ingraham* v. *Wright,* was decided in 1977.[18] The parents of a child who was severely paddled brought suit alleging that the use of corporal punishment was a violation of the Eighth Amendment. The Court ruled that the cruel and unusual punishment clause of the Eighth Amendment did not apply to corporal punishment in the schools. Some excerpts from the decision follow:

> . . . *All of the circumstances are to be taken into account in determining whether the punishment is reasonable in a particular case. Among the most important considerations are the seriousness of the offense, the attitude and past behavior of the child, the nature*

Box 11.2
What is the Biggest Problem Facing the Public Schools?

Nineteen eighty six marked the first time in the eighteen-year history of the Gallup Poll on public attitudes toward public education that drug use was thought to be the biggest problem confronting public schools. Drug use replaced discipline in the survey as the number one problem facing public schools. Society in general is having a difficult time finding solutions to the drug problem, and considerable pressures are being brought to bear on school policymakers to enter the war on drugs.

Policies that have been advocated in various school districts include the testing of student athletes for drug use, the inclusion of drug education in school programs, and some voluntary and mandatory testing of pupils for drug use as a requirement to participate in extracurricular activities. All of these solutions have some serious implications for educational policymakers. The Fourth Amendment ban on unreasonable search is cited by some people who question the right of school officials to initiate drug-testing programs for students. No court has upheld any form of drug testing in schools, though courts have approved the use of tests for prisoners, bus drivers, and jockeys.

The reliability and validity of the drug tests available have also been questioned. Evidence can be cited to support both sides of the issue. In addition, the testing programs are costly, ranging from $20 to $100, depending on the test's sophistication. Another serious question concerns the consequences of positive test results. The uncertainties described have prompted some insurance companies to exclude liability coverage for school personnel and board members involved in drug-testing lawsuits.

Educational policymakers will have to contend with these complicated problems as they attempt to solve what many consider to be the most serious issue facing American youth. What is the present policy concerning drugs and drug testing in your school district?

and severity of the punishment, the age and strength of the child, and the availability of less severe but equally effective means of discipline.

* * *

Teachers and school authorities are unlikely to inflict corporal punishment unnecessarily or excessively when a possible consequence of doing so is the institution of civil or criminal proceedings against them.

* * *

In view of the low incidence of abuse, the openness of our schools, and the common-law safeguards that already exist, the risk of error that may result in violation of a school child's substantive rights can only be regarded as minimal. Imposing additional administrative safeguards as a constitutional requirement might reduce that risk marginally, but would also entail a significant intrusion into an area of primary educational responsibility. We conclude that the Due Process Clause does not require notice and a hearing prior to the imposition of corporal punishment in the public schools, as that practice is authorized and limited by the common law.[19]

Corporal punishment in schools is a state matter as a part of the state's educational responsibility and is not a constitutional question. Educational policymakers must look to state statutes and local policies in developing their position on the issue. Parents have civil tort actions and criminal assault and battery remedies available if needed. What laws, policies, and regulations apply in your state?

Dress and Grooming

The rights of individual students to dress and groom themselves as they please were controversial issues in the 1960s and 1970s. Recently, there has been considerably less concern on the part of students and school authorities over dress codes and grooming regulations. The courts have addressed a number of these issues in the past and have outlined the appropriate points to be considered in setting school policy. The judicial guidelines and a change in the concerns of the nation have lessened the confrontations between students and school authorities over dress and grooming regulations.

The key item to be considered in regulating dress and grooming is the relationship of the regulation to the educational program or the health and safety of the students. The burden of showing that a legitimate relationship exists is on the school authorities who wish to implement a dress or grooming code. Court decisions have upheld the banning of immodest or suggestive clothing, unsanitary apparel that creates a health hazard, and any type of dress or grooming that creates a disturbance or distraction from normal school operation. The courts have upheld the rights of students to wear blue jeans and boys to wear their hair long if doing so is not a safety hazard. Interestingly, the courts have also stated that grooming issues are frivolous and unworthy of the attention of the federal courts. Do the school districts in your area have dress and grooming codes? If they do, do they bear a relationship to the educational program of the school or the health and safety of the students?

Photo 11.2
Students in public schools exhibit great diversity in their dress.

Photo 11.3

High school marching band is a prominent extracurricular activity.

Extracurricular Participation

A number of issues have surfaced in recent years that have focused on perceived inadequacies of the public schools. The quality of the product has been questioned, and many recent criticisms have pointed to the declining student test scores and the number of high-school graduates unable to read and write on acceptable levels. College athletics has had its scandals and critics also. Major attention has been given to college athletes who do not compare favorably with other students on academic measures. As a result of these criticisms, educational policymakers have focused some attention on the extracurricular programs of the public schools. A number of states have passed what some people call "no pass no play" legislation. This type of legislation usually requires passing grades in all required subjects as a prerequisite for participation in extracurricular activities. Educational policy change in the general area of extracurricular activities has caught the public's interest and continues to develop.

Extracurricular activities are generally described as those activities that take place outside normal school hours. Although they are supervised by school officials, they are noncredit and voluntary on the part of the student. The most common of these activities are athletics, drama, clubs, band, and cheerleading.

Though court jurisdictions have not all agreed on the status of extracurricular activities, some generalizations can be made concerning educational policy. Most of the litigation has involved participation in athletics. Regulations supporting certain training rules, such as no smoking or drinking of alcoholic beverages, have been approved. Rules pertaining to age requirements and transfer requirements have been approved. The major concerns of the courts have centered on the regulations being clearly stated, widely publicized to students and parents, and applied to all without discrimination. The courts have also required that a reasonable due process procedure be utilized in carrying out the regulations. The recent increase in "no pass no play" regulations has led to more litigation in the lower courts. The courts have found that participation requirements, if not arbitrary, can be utilized by school authorities to regulate participation in extracurricular activities. Does your local school have regulations concerning participation? Do these regulations serve an educational purpose?

Student Records

School authorities have tremendous recordkeeping responsibilities. A great amount of information can be included in student records. Personal information; test scores; grades; anecdotal material from teachers, counselors, and administrators; health information; and discipline reports are samples of the type of material that could be a part of a student's record. School policies must consider what information can be included, how confidential the records are, and what the parent and student rights are concerning access to the records. Through much of the history of public education, student records were kept at the discretion of the school authorities with little, if any, access by parents and students. Concern about the privacy rights of students and protection against inclusion of unwarranted or inaccurate information in student records increased in the early 1960s. On a federal level, some legislators became concerned with the information kept on individuals by businesses, credit companies, and schools. Based upon this concern, the Family Rights and Privacy Act, sometimes referred to as the Buckley Amendment, was passed in 1974.

Included in the Family Rights and Privacy Act is a provision that federal funds can be withdrawn from any educational institution that violates the mandates of the legislation. The Act requires that school authorities provide parents access to their children's school records. The parents must also be allowed to challenge the contents of the record and be provided a hearing if requested. In addition, approval must be granted by parents before the school can release anything but directory information to third parties. School authorities must inform parents and students of the rights granted to them by this statute, and they must establish procedures to carry out the provisions of the Act. Since most school districts receive federal funds, their school policies on student records have incorporated the necessary safeguards to protect these funds.

The implementation of the privacy requirements has caused some concerns and difficulties. One criticism is that much material that would be helpful and usable is now routinely excluded from the records. Although negative information is not necessarily inappropriate, some critics contend that records no longer include material that is negative. Some of the specific aspects of school records that school officials must contend with can be difficult. Should student records be released to separated parents? Are only custodial parents allowed access? Are guardians and noncustodial parents included in those having access? How does your local school handle these delicate matters? What are the policies and procedures that are utilized?

Summary

The constitutional provisions safeguarding the individual rights and liberties of students are centered in Amendments I, IV, V, VIII, and XIV. The state's right to provide for schooling is based on the Tenth Amendment. Where there is disagreement concerning the limits of student freedoms and school authority, the issues most frequently involve freedom of speech, due process rights, or the student's right to privacy.

The student's right to freedom of expression does have limits. School authorities must show (1) that the limitation is needed to ensure that the normal operation of the school will not be disrupted or (2) that the exercise of the freedom is harmful to the health and well-being of other students. The limitation cannot be arbitrary and without a legitimate state purpose. The use of prior restraint by school authorities has not been encouraged by the courts. It must be accompanied by procedures that are clear; reasonable; and related to the health, safety, and welfare of the students.

Compulsory schooling laws, once enacted, must provide equal treatment to all eligible for the benefits. The right of a student to attend school cannot be arbitrarily removed; however, authorities can use suspension and expulsion of disruptive students as a means of providing a safe and efficient school system. Students deprived of the right to attend school must be provided proper due process. The actual due process procedures vary in relation to the impact on a student. A short suspension requires less rigorous due process than a permanent expulsion.

The increase in violent crime and drug use in our society has had its impact on the schools. School authorities, in combatting these problems, have utilized search and seizure procedures that have been questioned by some as abridging a student's privacy rights. The courts have recognized that some special and distinct problems face school officials in providing for the health and safety of students. Reasonable cause has been recognized as the basis for search by school officials. The authority of school officials is not without limits. The use of sniff dogs in searches has resulted in both approval and disapproval by different courts. The courts have been reluctant to approve of nude searches.

The use of corporal punishment in schools has not been treated as a violation of the provision against cruel and unusual punishment in the Eighth Amendment. The federal courts have ruled that the use of corporal punishment is a state matter and must be dealt with as part of the state responsibility. Students and parents have recourse to criminal and civil actions if needed.

Dress and grooming regulations must be related to the educational program or the health and safety of the students. Federal courts have ruled that grooming issues are frivolous and unworthy of the attention of federal courts. Recent "no pass no play" regulations regarding participation in extracurricular activities have been upheld by the courts. Regulating participation has been upheld if the rules are widely publicized, clearly stated, and applied to all without discrimination.

The Educational Rights and Privacy Act, passed in 1974, calls for the withdrawal of federal monies from educational institutions that do not provide proper access to student records. The Act also requires that procedures and requirements be publicized and that parents and students be informed.

Table 11.1 summarizes various court cases relative to the issues of student rights discussed in this chapter.

	CASE	FINDING
Table 11.1 Selected Court Cases	*Burnside* v. *Byars* (1966)	Symbolic speech approved.
	Blackwell v. *Issaquena County Board of Education* (1966)	Wearing of buttons (symbolic speech) disapproved for creating school disturbance.
	Tinker v. *Des Moines Independent School District* (1969)	Wearing of black arm bands as protest is protected speech and did not promote disruptive conduct.
	Bethel School Dist. No. 403 v. *Fraser* (1986)	Lewd and indecent speech by a student during a school assembly is not protected speech.
	Gambino v. *Fairfax County School Board* (1977)	Student newspaper included as a part of First Amendment protection.
	Trachtman v. *Anker* (1977)	Court upholds school authorities in preventing sex questionnaire from being distributed to students.
	Williams v. *Spencer* (1980)	Courts uphold school authorities' ban on distribution of underground newspaper on school grounds.
	Goss v. *Lopez* (1975)	Required due process for students suspended from school.
	Bellmir v. *Lund* (1977)	Strip search for missing money unreasonable.
	Doe v. *Renfro* (1981)	Nude search of student on the basis of dog alert is unreasonable and a violation of student's rights.
	New Jersey v. *T.L.O.* (1985)	Reasonable cause search upheld with findings usable as evidence in juvenile delinquency proceedings.
	Baker v. *Owen* (1975)	Court upholds corporal punishment of student and outlines safeguard procedures.
	Ingraham v. *Wright* (1977)	Ban on cruel and unusual punishment does not apply to corporal punishment.
	Hazelwood School District v. *Kuhlmeier* (1988)	Prior restraint and censorship by school authorities affirmed.

Key Words

Freedom of expression	Property interest
Due process	Probable cause
Right to privacy	Reasonable cause
Symbolic speech	Corporal punishment
Underground newspaper	Civil tort action
Prior restraint	Extracurricular activities
Suspension	Educational Rights and Privacy Act
Expulsion	Buckley Amendment
Liberty interest	

Discussion Questions

1. Describe the legal basis for student rights and responsibilities in a public school setting.

2. Why do due process procedures for students vary?

3. Develop a policy model for a student problem that interests you. Identify the participants in the debate, some proposed solutions, and the possible effects of these solutions.

4. Under what conditions, in your view, is prior restraint justified in today's high schools? What procedures would you recommend be included in any school procedures concerning this issue?

5. Review the issue of malpractice in education. What are student and teacher rights and responsibilities regarding malpractice?

For Further Reading

Alexander, Kern, and Alexander, M. David. *American Public School Law.* St. Paul: West Publishing Co., 1985.

———. *The Law of School, Students and Teachers.* St. Paul: West Publishing Co., 1984.

LaMorte, Michael W. *School Law Cases and Concepts.* Englewood Cliffs, N.J.: Prentice-Hall, Inc., 1982.

McCarthy, M. M., and Cambron, Nelda. *Public School Law Teachers' and Students' Rights.* Boston, Mass.: Allyn & Bacon, 1981.

McCarthy, M., and Deignan, P. *What Legally Constitutes an Adequate Public Education.* Bloomington, Ind.: Phi Delta Kappa.

Phay, Robert E. *The Law of Procedure in Student Suspension and Expulsion.* NOLPE, 1977.

Reutter, E. *The Supreme Court's Impact on Public Education.* Phi Delta Kappa and NOLPE, 1982.

Reutter, E. *The Courts and Student Conduct.* NOLPE, 1975.

Valente, W. *Law in the Schools.* Columbus, Ohio: Charles E. Merrill Publishing Co., 1980.

Notes

1. *Burnside* v. *Byars, 363 F.2d 744 (5th Cir. 1966)*

2. *Blackwell* v. *Issaquena County Board of Education 363, F.2d 749 (5th Cir. 1966)*

3. The reading of the two cases in their entirety would prove helpful in understanding the courts' decisions and their effect on educational policy.

4. *Tinker* v. *Des Moines Independent Community School District, Supreme Court of the United States, 1969, 393 U.S. 503, 89 5 Ct. 733.*

5. *Ibid.,* 736-738.

6. *Gambino* v. *Fairfax County School Board, U.S. District Court, Eastern District of Virginia, 1977. 429 F.Supp. 731. United States Court of Appeals, Fourth Circuit, 1977, 564 F.2d 157.*

7. *Ibid.*

8. *Trachtman* v. *Anker, 563 F.2d 512 (2d Cir. 1977).*

9. *Williams* v. *Spencer, United States Court of Appeals, Fourth Circuit, 1980 622 F.2d 1200.*

10. *Hazelwood School District* v. *Kuhlmeier, 56 U.S.L.W.4079 (1988).*

11. *Goss* v. *Lopez Supreme Court of the United States, 1975 419 U.S. 565.*

12.   *Bellmir* v. *Lund United States District Court, Northern District of New York, 1977* *438 F.Supp. 47.*

13.   *Doe* v. *Renfro 631 F.2d 90 (7th Cir. 1980)* cert. denied 451 U.S. 1022, 101 S.Ct. 3015 (1981).

14.   *Ibid.*

15.   *New Jersey* v. *T.L.O.* 105 S.Ct. 733 (1985).

16.   *Ibid.*

17.   *Baker* v. *Owen 395 F.Supp. 294* (D.C. N.C. 1975) 423 U.S. 907, 96 S.Ct. 210 (1975).

18.   *Ingraham* v. *Wright Supreme Court of the United States* 430 U.S. 651, 97 S.Ct. 1401 (1977).

19.   *Ibid.*, pp. 1401-1404.

12 Equality and Education

"If one race be inferior to the other socially, the Constitution of the United States cannot put them on the same plane."

Supreme Court in *Plessy* v. *Ferguson* (1896)

"We conclude that in the field of public education the doctrine of "separate but equal" has no place. Separate educational facilities are inherently unequal."

Supreme Court in *Brown* v. *Board of Education* (1954)

"All that is decided, is that a state may not deny to any person on account of race the right to attend any school it maintains. . . . The Constitution, in other words, does not require integration. It merely forbids segregation."

Supreme Court in *Briggs* v. *Elliott* (1955)

". . . There is no equality of treatment merely by providing students with the same facilities, textbooks, teachers and curriculum: for students who do not understand English are effectively foreclosed from any meaningful education."

Supreme Court in *Lau* v. *Nichols* (1974)

What is equal educational opportunity? Has our society with its vast system of public schools been able to provide equal educational opportunity? Our society has faced many serious controversies and problems in its attempts to provide political equality by providing voting rights. Social and economic

Policy Model 12.1   Differing Views of Equal Educational Opportunity

POLICY ISSUES	PARTICIPANTS IN POLICY DEVELOPMENT	ILLUSTRATIONS OF POLICY SOLUTIONS	EFFECTS OF POLICY SOLUTIONS
Equal Education Opportunity Provide access to all and provide equal amounts of education to all? Provide the same treatment for all children? Provide for individual differences by providing individual programs? Provide for the equality of educational outcomes?	**Formal** U. S. Congress Federal court system State legislature State court systems Administrative bodies **Informal** NAACP Council for Exceptional Children (CEC) National Organization for Women (NOW) ACLU	Federal statutes Federal court rulings State statutes State board policies Local board policies Administration programs	**Allocative** Who is provided what? **Regulative** Who will do what? **Structural** Changes in structures involved in policy implementation **Redistribution** Changes in the allocation of resources or authority

equality have been defined in various ways throughout our history, no definition has really satisfied all the diverse constituencies making up our nation. Our educational history has been one of changing interpretations of what constitutes equal educational opportunity. This chapter focuses upon some of these changing interpretations and the serious and controversial questions our educational policymakers have encountered. Policy Model 12.1 will help you in following the educational policy process. You can use this model, making additions or deletions, as you study equality and education.

Equality of educational opportunity is a concept Americans accept. The struggle to define this concept and to implement the definition as policy in the operation of our public schools has not been an easy task. Various interpretations of the meaning of equal educational opportunity have been advocated, and each view has its supporters and detractors. Individuals base their interpretations on the assumptions they believe to be important, and even though there may be agreement on a conceptual level, there continues to be controversy about specific policy when implemented.

This chapter describes attempts made to define and implement equal educational opportunity. Attention is given to the roles played by the federal government and the various state governments in this process. In addition, the judicial system's role in the development of educational policy relating to equal educational opportunity is highlighted.

Photo 12.1
College preparatory chemistry is provided as a part of equal opportunity.

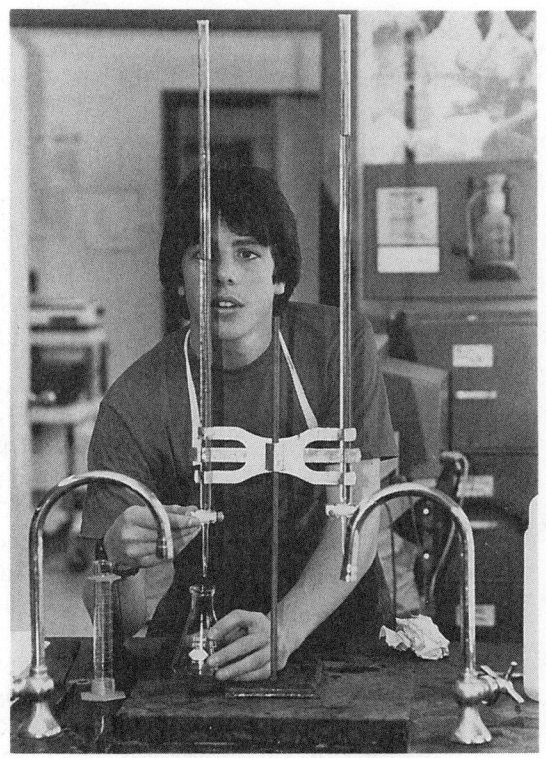

Equality of Educational Opportunity

The meaning of equality as it applies to education has been given various interpretations. One of the more traditional views is that education should be made available and accessible to all children in equal amounts. Thus, equality of access is the key ingredient. If all children have equal access to education, then all children have the opportunity to take advantage of what is available. The student in this view has the responsibility of maximizing the opportunities provided. Those pupils who are serious, are motivated, and apply themselves will benefit. This type of system is known as meritocracy. Advancement would be related to the effort and abilities of the student.

Sameness is another notion of educational equality. That is all programs, all treatments, and all monies should be made available to all students in the same way and in the same amount. This view would insist that all children be treated alike. This sameness would apply to all, and no recognition would be accorded differences in race, sex, ethnic origin, or handicap. This viewpoint also places the responsibility for the success or failure of a student on the student.

Some people began to question the concept of equal treatment or sameness as equality. The wide variation in backgrounds, the apparent individual differences in abilities and motivational levels of the students led to the view that equal treatment would in itself lead to greater inequality. This view concluded that certain children needed to have different treatment to achieve equal opportunity. More dollars per child, longer time periods in school, and programs to compensate for differences were but a few of the conclusions reached by those favoring this view of equal opportunity.

Some social theorists view equality in education as equality of outcomes. This viewpoint would not be as concerned with methods, programs, or curriculum utilized as with the outcomes achieved. Though this view might recognize individual differences among students, it would expect that good teaching, good programs, and different allotments of time would allow learners to achieve equal outcomes. One example of this viewpoint is called mastery learning, advocated by Benjamin Bloom. Bloom's research recognized individual differences. However, by using certain mastery learning techniques, Bloom felt that most individuals could achieve certain basic outcomes.[1] The outcomes of education in this view should be the same for all; thus, equality of outcomes is the operational definition of equal educational opportunity.

Another possible interpretation of equal educational opportunity pays much more attention to individual differences. The emphasis of this view is not only that differences do exist but that education must encourage these differences and provide opportunities that encompass the needs and interests of all children. Statements such as, "The school should provide the opportunity for all children to reach maximum potential," or "Equal opportunity in school is the provision of a program that is fitting and proper for each child," reflect this interpretation. Although this view is attractive to many, it does pose some questions and problems for its proponents. If carried out, it would require classification and eventual segregation of youngsters needing different programs. This in turn could lead to some questions concerning the sorting and classification schemes utilized.[2]

From this brief discussion, it is evident that even though the concept of equality of educational opportunity is acceptable to most Americans, translating the meaning into operational policy is difficult. As various educational policies were implemented under the guise of equality of opportunity, questions were raised concerning impacts on individuals and groups. Frequently, the courts have been called upon to judge these impacts relative to the promises of our Constitution. The courts have introduced the concept of educational equity, meaning fair and unbiased treatment.[3] The concept of educational equality relating to school finance programs is treated in detail in Chapter 14. This chapter presents some policies and procedures that have been a part of our attempts at providing equal educational opportunity.

Discrimination By Classification

Many of the complaints and dissatisfactions concerning unequal treatment in education center on the classification or assignment of a pupil. Sorting and classifying pupils are functions that must be performed by school districts. The decisions made to assign pupils to a school, a classroom, a program, or a teacher are a few examples of these functions. The methods utilized by school districts to select and assign pupils have been questioned by various groups in our society. Generally, the questions relate to assignments that in the view of the critical group are discriminatory and have no legitimate educational purpose. Classifying and sorting pupils on the basis of race, handicap, sex, or cultural difference are examples of the kinds of selection practices questioned. The balance of this chapter reviews some of the crucial educational issues concerning selecting, sorting, and classifying pupils.

Race

The utilization of race as the determining factor in the assignment of pupils in the schools of America has been a controversial and volatile issue. This problem developed early in our nation's history. As society attempted to define equal opportunity as it applied to the education of children of different racial backgrounds, the conflicts became tense and emotional. It should not be surprising that the courts of our nation have been called upon to attempt to clarify, refine, and formulate a definition of equality as it applies to race. A selected number of court decisions instrumental in this process illustrate the historical changes.

Separate but Equal   Sarah Roberts, a black child living in Boston, Massachusetts, was assigned to a public school that was designated for black children. A number of other elementary schools were closer to her home, but they were for white children. The father of the child tried several times to have his daughter assigned to a school closer to home. Failing to achieve an assignment change, Sarah's father hired Charles Sumner, a prominent civil rights advocate, attorney, and U.S. Senator, to bring suit to challenge what he considered to be unequal treatment. This action, taken in 1849, became a precedent-setting decision that formed the basis for the doctrine of "separate but equal." In 1850, the Supreme Court of Massachusetts rendered the decision, reasoning that it was the right of the school board to assign children to schools and that race was one condition that was a legitimate rationale to be used for classification.[4]

The nation continued to struggle with the doctrine of separate but equal for the next one hundred years. Educational policies were implemented, and as individuals or groups dissented, the courts were called upon to define and clarify the meaning of equal treatment. A sample of the issues that reached the courts can be used to trace the slowly changing definition of equal treatment under the law.

It should be noted that the Fourteenth Amendment to the Constitution was enacted in 1868. The Amendment provided in part that "No state shall . . . deny any person within its jurisdiction the equal protection of the laws." The courts in turn were called upon to clarify the meaning and intent of this amendment.

The Supreme Court of the United States used as precedent the reasoning of the Massachusetts court in the *Roberts* decision to decide *Plessy* v. *Ferguson* in 1896.[5] The separate but equal doctrine thus became a national standard. A Louisiana statute passed in 1890 entitled "An Act to Promote the Comfort of Passengers" was the central point of controversy. The act provided in part that "all railway companies carrying passengers in their coaches in this state, shall provide equal but separate accommodations for the white and colored races, by providing two or more passenger coaches for each passenger train, or by dividing the passenger coaches by a partition so as to secure separate accommodations." Ruling that state authorities had wide discretion in promoting peace and order, the Supreme Court upheld the law as constitutional. Although this case concerned transportation, soon the separate but equal doctrine was extended to include education. It is interesting to note that the lone justice dissenting in the *Plessy* decision was Justice Harlan and that his interpretation of equality before the law became that of the Court majority more than fifty years later.

Richmond County in the state of Georgia operated separate schools for blacks and whites. The elementary school for black children did not have physical facilities to accommodate all of the black children. Not having enough money to expand the school, the board decided to close the black high school and utilize the school for elementary children. The sixty black high school students were advised to enroll in church-sponsored schools. The decision did not affect the schools for white children which continued to operate. Challenging the decision, black parents and taxpayers sought to enjoin the school board from operating a high school for white children without at the same time operating a high school for black children. This court case reached the U.S. Supreme Court, and the decision *Cumming* v. *County Board of Education* was rendered in 1899.[6] The Court found for the board of education, reasoning that the matter of education and its conduct was a state concern, and as long as all the taxpayers shared equally in the tax burden, it was not a concern of the federal courts. The separate but equal doctrine was extended to include education.

The question of race and public school assignment did not appear before the U.S. Supreme Court again until 1927. That year, the Court ruled on the assignment of Martha Lum, native-born U.S. citizen of Chinese descent. Was the classification by school authorities of Martha Lum as colored and her assignment to a school for colored children unconstitutional? Did these actions violate the rights of a citizen to equal protection of the law as stated in the Fourteenth Amendment? In coming to a decision in *Gong Lum* v. *Rice,* the Court cited as precedent the *Roberts, Plessy,* and *Cumming* decisions, ruling that the authorities were within their rights in making such an assignment.[7] The separate but equal doctrine was extended to include skin color other than black.

The nation continued to struggle with the doctrine of separate but equal. Educational policies were implemented, and as individuals or groups dissented, the courts were called upon to define and clarify the meaning of equal treatment. A sample of the issues that reached the courts can be used to trace the slowly changing definition of equal treatment under the law. Judicial involvement from the *Roberts* decision in 1850 to the *Gung Lum* decision in 1927 expanded the separate but equal doctrine. By the 1930s, the courts began to shift and constrict the meaning and definition of *separate but equal.*

Lloyd Gaines, a black, was refused admission to the School of Law of the State University of Missouri. His application was sent to Lincoln University, a state school for blacks. Lincoln University did not have a law school. A state law provided that the tuition and fees of a black student could be paid by the state to any university or college in an adjacent state if the course or program was not provided at Lincoln University. Mr. Gaines asserted that by refusing to accept him at the University of Missouri, the state denied equal protection of the law in violation of the Fourteenth Amendment and brought legal action to seek admission on that basis. The Supreme Court in 1938 ordered the university to admit Mr. Gaines and stated in part:

> *The basic consideration is not as to what sort of opportunities other states provide, or whether they are as good as those in Missouri, but*

> *as to what opportunities Missouri itself furnishes to white students and denies to negroes solely upon the ground of color. . . . The question here is not of a duty of the state to supply legal training, or of the quality of the training which it does supply, but of its duty when it provides such training to furnish it to the residents of the state upon the basis of an equality of right. By the operation of the laws of Missouri a privilege has been created for white law students which is denied to negroes by reason of their race. The white resident is afforded legal education within the state; the negro resident having the same qualifications is refused it there and must go outside the state to obtain it. That is a denial of the equality of legal right to the enjoyment of the privilege which the state has set up, and the provision for the payment of tuition fees in another state does not remove the discrimination.*[8]

After this decision, separate but equal legal education had to be provided within a state's own borders.

In 1940, a case arose involving the public schools of the city of Norfolk, Virginia. A black public school teacher contended that he was discriminated against by being paid a lower salary than white teachers with identical qualifications. The plaintiff claimed the practice of paying lower salaries to blacks voilated the due process and equal protection clauses of the Fourteenth Amendment. The U.S. Circuit Court of Appeals ruled that white and colored public school teachers similarly situated and qualified must be provided equal salaries. The court reasoned:

> *The allegation is that the state, in paying for public services of the same kind and character to men and women equally qualified according to standards which the state itself prescribes, arbitrarily pays less to Negroes than to white persons. This is as clear a discrimination on the ground of race as could well be imagined and falls squarely within the inhibition of both the due process and the equal protection clauses of the Fourteenth Amendment.*[9]

The U.S. Supreme Court refused to review the case, and the Circuit Court of Appeals decision was upheld. Although this case was not decided on the question of separate but equal, it centered on the same constitutional grounds of equal protection of the law and due process. Thus, another court had questioned an educational policy treating racial groups unequally.

In 1950, the U.S. Supreme Court rendered a decision after scrutinizing the facts of equality when a state claimed two law schools were separate but equal. Texas maintained two law schools, one for black law students and another at the University of Texas for white students. Herman Sweatt, a black Texan, applied for admission to the University of Texas Law School and was denied admission on the basis of race. He was requested to seek admission to the law school provided for blacks. Mr. Sweatt then brought a legal action to gain admittance to the University of Texas Law School.

The Supreme Court when ruling on *Sweatt* v. *Painter* did not find that the existence of two law schools was in itself separate but equal law education.[10] The Court compared the two schools and found that the separate law school for blacks did not provide black students a legal education equivalent to that available to other races. The Court required the University of Texas Law School to admit Mr. Sweatt. The Court came to this conclusion by stating:

> . . . *We cannot find substantial equality in the educational opportunities offered white and Negro law students by the State. In terms of number of the faculty, variety of courses and opportunity for specialization, size of the student body, scope of the library, availability of law review and similar activities, the University of Texas Law School is superior. What is more important, the University of Texas Law School possesses to a far greater degree those qualities which are incapable of objective measurements but which made for greatness in a law school. Such qualities, to name but a few, include reputation of the faculty, experience of the administration, position and influence of the alumni, standing in the community, traditions and prestige. It is difficult to believe that one who had a free choice between these law schools would consider the questions close. . . .*
>
> *The law school to which Texas is willing to admit petitioner excludes from its student body members of the racial groups which number 85% of the population of the State and include most of the lawyers witnesses, jurors, judges and other officials with whom petitioner will inevitably be dealing when he becomes a member of the Texas Bar. With such a substantial and significant segment of society excluded, we cannot conclude that the education offered petitioner is substantially equal to that which he would receive if admitted to the University of Texas Law School.*[11]

The definition of separate but equal now included a further restriction whereby the existence of separate facilities was not the only criterion for determining equality. The cases outlined were instrumental in setting the stage for the Supreme Court to render its landmark decision in 1954 indicating that separate facilities are inherently unequal.

Separate Is Inherently Unequal   A number of lower court decisions concerning elementary and secondary education were appealed to the Supreme Court. Five of these cases reached the Supreme Court at approximately the same time. The cases originated geographically in Delaware, District of Columbia, Kansas, South Carolina, and Virginia. Each of the cases questioned the practice of classifying and separating children in the public schools on the basis of race. A common legal question seemed to be involved in each of the cases: equal protection of the law versus separate but equal concepts. The Fifth and Fourteenth Amendments provided the constitutional base for the cases, and the Supreme Court decided to hear the cases together as *Brown* v. *Board of Education of Topeka, Kansas*.

The Supreme Court heard arguments concerning the cases in December of 1952 and reached a decision one and one-half years later on May 17, 1954. The consolidated opinion was delivered by Chief Justice Warren and brought to an end the doctrine of separate but equal. The opinion of the Court reasoned in part as follows:

	CASE	YEAR	FINDING
Table 12.1 Selected Cases in Developing the Separate But Equal Doctrine	*Roberts* v. *City of Boston*	1850	Race is a legitimate condition for classification of pupils.
	Plessy v. *Ferguson*	1896	State law requiring separate railroad facilities for the races ruled constitutional.
	Cumming v. *County Board of Education*	1899	Closing of a black high school while continuing a white high school ruled a state concern.
	Gong Lum v. *Rice*	1927	Chinese-American classified as colored for school assignment.
	Gaines v. *Canada*	1938	State having a law school for whites must also provide facilities for all races within its borders.
	Alston v. *Norfolk Board of Education*	1940	Pay in a school system cannot be based on race.
	Sweatt v. *Painter*	1950	Court indicates that equality in fact must be a part of separate but equal.

Today, education is perhaps the most important function of state and local governments. Compulsory school attendance laws and the great expenditures for education both demonstrate our recognition of the importance of education to our democratic society. It is required in the performance of our most basic public responsibilities, even service in the armed forces. It is the very foundation of good citizenship. Today it is a principal instrument in awakening the child to cultural values, in preparing him for later professional training, and in helping him to adjust normally to his environment. In these days, it is doubtful that any child may reasonably be expected to succeed in life if he is denied the opportunity of an education. Such an opportunity, where the state has undertaken to provide it, is a right which must be made available to all on equal terms.

We come then to the question presented: Does segregation of children in public schools solely on the basis of race, even though the physical facilities and other "tangible" factors may be equal, deprive the children of the minority group of equal educational opportunities? We believe that it does. . . .

We conclude that in the field of public education the doctrine of "separate but equal" has no place. Separate educational facilities are inherently unequal.[12]

The court, having decided that segregated schools were unconstitutional, had the task of deciding how the decision was to be implemented. The decision was far-reaching and had potential for great impact on society. All parties to the case were asked to study implementation of the decision and return to the Court and present alternatives. The Court reached its decision on implementation in what is called Brown II in 1955.[13] The lower courts were to oversee the enforcement of the decision. They were asked to balance the interests of the plaintiffs and the public interest and to act with all deliberate speed in the desegregation of the public schools. Did the Court require integration or just the abolition of segregation? What did the impressive language "with all deliberate speed" actually mean? The answers to these questions remained with the states and the courts.

The most visible example during this period of the problems of integrating the schools took place in Little Rock, Arkansas, in September of 1957. Television pictures of federal marshals escorting black students into Central High School through defiant state officials were replayed nightly on the various television networks. This was the result of the Court's saying that it would not permit state officials to nullify directly or indirectly the decision in the *Brown* case.[14] Some areas preferred to close their public schools rather than integrate. In addition, public money provided tuition to private schools that were segregated. In some cases, these private schools were using the public school facilities that had been closed. This problem was litigated in Prince Edward County in Virginia. Closing public schools and using public tax monies to aid students in attending segregated private schools was ruled a violation. Unfortunately for the black students involved, this decision was not rendered until 1965 in *Griffin* v. *County School Board of Prince Edward County.*[15]

A number of school districts used what came to be called freedom of choice plans to integrate their schools. Under this arrangement children could attend any school within the district. After operating for many years under freedom of choice plans, some school districts were still basically segregated. Fourteen years after the *Brown* decision, the Court ruled that freedom of choice plans could be used only if meaningful desegregation resulted. The Court in *Green* v. *County School Board of New Kent County* (1968) would allow freedom of choice only if it resulted in a unitary (nonsegregated) school system.[16] The courts continued to be confronted with questions related to the speed of desegregation. The all deliberate speed criterion was not working, as the meaning of the phase was still unclear fifteen years after the pronouncement that separate was inherently unequal. In 1969, the courts decided that all deliberate speed was unworkable and issued "desegregation now" mandates in a number of cases. In *Alexander* v. *Holmes* (1969), the U.S. Supreme Court ordered that dual school systems be terminated at once and to operate "now and hereafter only unitary schools."[17] The definition of *equality now* included desegregated schools. The Court did not, however, provide the means to attain this end. Two years later, the Court, in rendering a decision that became a landmark case, approved of certain means and standards that could be used to desegregate.

The Charlotte-Mecklenburg school district in North Carolina was ordered in 1969 by a U.S. district court to prepare a plan to desegregate the faculty and the students of the school district. The school system was at this time the forty-third largest in the nation. The district served 84,000 pupils in 107 schools and encompassed an area of 550 square miles. The student population was seventy-one percent white and twenty-nine percent black. The federal court was not satisfied with the desegregation plan submitted by the board of education and appointed an expert in educational administra-

Box 12.1
Has the Busing of Children As a Remedy Solved the Desegregation Problem?

In November of 1986, the U.S. Supreme Court declined to hear two cases from different federal appeals courts concerning school district plans to move from court-ordered busing to neighborhood schools. The first case, *Riddick* v. *School Board of the City of Norfolk,* upheld a court decision approving a student assignment policy that allowed ten elementary schools out of thirty-six to have greater than ninety percent black enrollments. The approval of this return to neighborhood schools is a binding decision in the fourth circuit comprising Maryland, Virginia, West Virginia, and North and South Carolina.

The second case, *Board of Education of the Oklahoma City Public Schools* v. *Dowell,* originated in the tenth district covering Colorado, Kansas, New Mexico, Oklahoma, Utah, and Wyoming. The decision disapproved of a neighborhood school plan that allowed thirty-three of the sixty-four schools in the district to have pupil populations greater than ninety percent black.

Thirty-two years after the *Brown* decision, the nation is still unsettled and uncertain as to remedies and requirements in applying the principle that separate is inherently unequal to educational policy.

tion to devise an alternative plan. Finally, the court accepted a plan that was a combination of those submitted. The ordered implementation of the desegregation plan resulted in an appeal to the Supreme Court. In the subsequent decision—*Swann* v. *Charlotte-Mecklenburg County Board of Education* (1971)—three elements became quite important for future desegregation plans.[18] First, the Court approved the use of ratios as beginning guidelines for desegregation. The district ratio of seventy-one percent white to twenty-nine percent black pupils could not be used as a discrete mathematical solution in each school but could be used as a beginning goal. Second, the housing patterns in the district would not allow for meaningful desegregation if a neighborhood school attendance pattern was followed. The Court therefore approved the gerrymandering of school attendance boundaries to achieve desegregation. The use of pairing and clustering and the zoning of noncontiguous areas for this purpose were declared workable, realistic, and effective. Third, the Court approved the busing of pupils to achieve meaningful desegregation.

The movement from "separate but equal" to "separate is inherently unequal" took a long period of time, with many twists and turns in the educational policies of our nation's schools. Moving from the Brown II deliberate speed mandate to the desegregation now standard some sixteen years later created many problems for educational policymakers. These court decisions were designed to rid the nation of *de jure* segregation. The courts were concerned with those states that had laws forcing segregated education. Many areas of our nation had unitary school systems, but because of housing patterns, they had numbers of schools that did not reflect the racial composition of the school district. This was particularly

Photo 12.2
The photograph provides an example of busing and desegregation in Boston, Mass.

true in many northern and western states. Though these states had no laws requiring segregated schools, the schools were in fact segregated. Was this *de facto* segregation unconstitutional? Did the courts rule only on *de jure* segregation? The assignment of pupils to schools in states having unitary school systems became a concern to parents when the schools seemed to be in fact segregated. The courts were again called upon to rule on equal treatment of the races—this time in a unitary school setting.

The state of Colorado had no laws requiring the segregation of the races. The Denver public school system was operated as a system serving all races and ethnic groups. A number of parents of children assigned to a particular school in a black community in Denver brought court action against the board of education. The parents claimed that the board, through actions in setting attendance zones, selecting school sites, and using neighborhood school policies, created segregated schools. This controversy eventually was appealed to the U.S. Supreme Court and resulted in the case, *Keyes* v. *School District No. 1 Denver* (1973).[19] The Court, in rendering the decision, indicated the difference between *de jure* and *de facto* segregation as being a matter of purpose and intent. The Court agreed with the board that there was no law or specific policy requiring the separation of the races. Certain actions taken through the years by the board of education seemed to the Court to contribute to the separation of the races. Decisions on the location of school sites, drawing of attendance lines, assignment of pupils, transfer decisions, and the use of portable classrooms blurred the distinction between *de jure* and *de facto* segregation. Thus, the Court decided that under these conditions the segregation was *de jure* and unconstitutional and required affirmative action as a remedy. The questioning of assignment practices moved to the Northern states as more parents were willing to ask the courts to intercede against the *de facto* segregation prevalent in the school systems.

The courts struggled with the distinction between *de jure* and *de facto* segregation and the intent and purpose for board policies and state laws. The U.S. Supreme Court refused to approve interdistrict busing as a remedy in one case and found school board policies contributed to segregation in several other instances. The first case involved the public schools of Detroit, Michigan, the population of which was primarily black. The suburban communities surrounding Detroit had predominantly white public school enrollment. Parents of black children in the Detroit public schools felt that meaningful integration could not occur without including the children in the suburban schools. To that end the parents sought, through the courts, a plan for interdistrict busing. The Supreme Court, in *Milliken* v. *Bradley* (1974), ruled against forced interdistrict busing.[20] The Court could not determine that racially discriminatory acts by the state or the local school districts were the substantial cause of the district boundaries. A few years later, in cases involving the cities of Columbus and Dayton, Ohio, the Supreme Court did find that discriminatory acts of public officials contributed to the *de facto* segregation in the schools in both cities and that affirmative remedies were necessary.[21]

The courts were utilized by those citizens who felt separation of the races in school prevented equal opportunity and were used to set limits for educational policymakers. The controversial questions have not, however, been settled to everyone's satisfaction. Thirty-two years after the landmark *Brown* decision, the descendants of Brown, together with the American Civil Liberties Union, are again questioning the policies of the Little Rock School District. On October 6, 1986, the district court heard opening arguments in Brown III, as the plaintiffs alleged that the court-ordered remedy in the original decision has not been carried out. The seriousness of this can be shown by the school board's expenditure of some $350,000 in pretrial preparation.[22] It will be interesting to see if the efforts of a school district can be questioned thirty years after the Court's original mandate.

The many educational policies utilized in attempting to classify and assign pupils in a nondiscriminatory manner have continued to create and cause controversy. Our society is still raising questions as to the appropriateness of busing as a remedy. The Reagan administration questioned the use of busing, and in turn, some state legislatures have been considering the limitation of its use. Although the dominant theme in discriminatory classification has been race, other issues have been addressed in recent years. The balance of this chapter looks at classification problems other than race.

Handicapped

The *Brown* decision in 1954 provided for equal educational opportunity on the basis of the equal protection clause in the Fourteenth Amendment. Racial minorities were not the only citizens concerned about equal protection of the law. The parents of a number of handicapped children thought that the laws of the Commonwealth of Pennsylvania were not providing equal protection to their children. The Pennsylvania Association of Retarded Children (PARC) brought legal action alleging that laws in Pennsylvania allowing the exclusion of handicapped children from the public schools were unconstitutional. The federal district court ruled for the plaintiffs, indicating that the exclusion of the handicapped children did not provide equal protection and that a free and appropriate education must be

Photo 12.3
A special education
classroom is provided as a
commitment to equality.

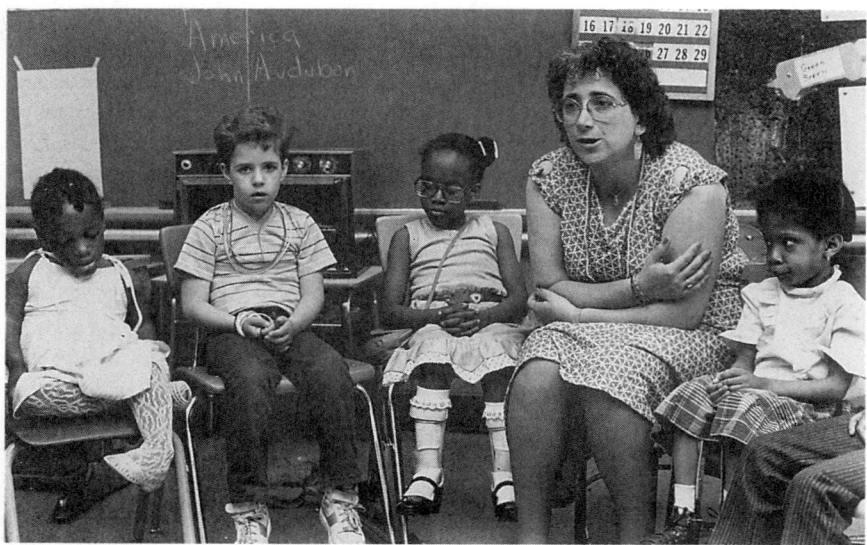

provided for all children. In addition, the court stated that placement in a regular class was preferable to placement of these children in special classes but that special classes in the public school were preferable to other assignments.[23]

Soon after the PARC case, another court decision reinforced and expanded that decision. In *Mills* v. *Board of Education of the District of Columbia* (1972), parents again successfully challenged the exclusion of handicapped children from public school. The court stressed the need for a free and appropriate education for handicapped children.[24] These cases led

Table 12.2
Selected Cases in
Developing the *Separate
Is Inherently Unequal*
Definition

CASE	YEAR	FINDING
Brown v. *Board of Education of Topeka*	1954	Separate is inherently unequal.
Brown v. *Board of Education of Topeka II*	1955	District courts proceed with all deliberate speed.
Griffin v. *County School Board Prince Edward County*	1964	Closing public schools and using public money to support private segregated schools are unconstitutional.
Green v. *County School Board of New Kent County*	1968	Freedom of choice plan must create unitary system.
Alexander v. *Holmes*	1970	From "with all deliberate speed" to immediate compliance.
Swann v. *Charlotte-Mecklenburg Board of Education*	1978	Busing to achieve racial balance is constitutional.
Keyes v. *School District No. 1 Denver*	1973	Board actions may have effect of creating *de jure* segregation.
Milliken v. *Bradley*	1974	Interdistrict remedy is unconstitutional.

Box 12.2
Can School
Authorities Discipline
Special Students?

Does the expulsion of a handicapped child constitute a change in placement that requires an elaborate due process procedure prior to implementation of the punishment? In the first special education discipline case to be reviewed by the Supreme Court—*Honig* v. *Doe,* 108 S. Ct. 592 (1988)—it was ruled that expulsion was considered a change in placement and must be preceded by a completed due process procedure. The Court further contended that Congress in the Education For All Handicapped Act (passed in 1975) stated that there should be no change in placement during the due process review even though the child might be dangerous. The intent of Congress, according to the Court, was to remove the power of school authorities to unilaterally change placements of special children.

to a deepened concern on the part of Congress and eventually to the passage of two major pieces of legislation.

In 1973, Congress passed the Vocational Rehabilitation Act to prevent discrimination against the handicapped in the work environment and in education. Section 504 of the Act, which has been used to question practices in the work place and in educational settings, states in part:

> *No otherwise qualified handicapped individual in the United States . . . shall solely by reason of his handicap, be excluded from the participation in, be denied the benefits of, or be subjected to discrimination under any program or activity receiving Federal financial assistance.*[25]

The second law, P. L. 94–142, was passed in 1975 and was entitled "The Education for All Handicapped Children Act." Several features of this law have had great impact on our public schools and educational policy decisions. First, the law calls for special educational services to be provided to handicapped pupils. Second, the law requires related services to be offered to the handicapped. Third, an elaborate due process procedure is required for assignment and placement of the pupils. Fourth, the education of the handicapped must take place in the "least restricted" environment. These laws have not stopped conflict and disagreement over the definition of equal educational opportunity for the handicapped, and argument still continues over the meaning of the legislation. The complicated nature of defining equality of opportunity for the handicapped can be illustrated by two recent court cases.

Amy Rowley, a deaf youngster, attended a public school. The school prepared for Amy by sending two teachers to sign language classes. In addition, a special teletype was installed in the principal's office and in the child's home to facilitate communication with the girl's deaf parents. The individual educational plan provided the pupil with an FM hearing aid, a special tutor for one hour per day, and a speech therapist's services three hours per week. Amy made progress in school and was promoted to the first grade. The parents thought that Amy would be even more successful in school if she were provided a sign language interpreter in her first-grade classroom. The school pointed to the progress made by the pupil and refused the request for the interpreter. Eventually, this dispute reached the U.S. Supreme Court. Was the education provided Amy "free and appropriate" for a handicapped child, or should an interpreter be included to provide a more optimal experience? The decision of the Supreme Court in the Amy Rowley case was rendered in 1982 and provides some guidelines for educational policymakers.[26] Since Amy was provided free access and a program that enabled her to make reasonable progress, the position of the school authorities was upheld. *Free and appropriate* was defined as providing access and a basic floor of opportunity for the child and did not require the school to maximize the potential of the pupil.

The second example revolves around the meaning of the requirement to provide related services to handicapped pupils. A recent Supreme Court decision provides some help to policymakers but does not completely define the term. Amber Tatro, an eight-year-old, had a physical problem that required frequent clean intermittent catheterization (CIC). This procedure was relatively easy to perform and required about one hour to learn the procedure. Since Amber required CIC every three to four hours, she could not attend school unless the procedure was available for her. Her parents asked that CIC be made a part of the individual educational plan of their daughter. School authorities, feeling that catheterization was a medical procedure, refused the request. The parents sought relief through the courts, and in 1984, the Supreme Court found for the parents and required that CIC be provided.[27] The Court reasoned that the child was required to attend special education classes and could not comply if this service was not available. The definition of equal opportunity in education for the handicapped is still evolving, and policymakers must use court decisions in developing their answers to difficult and controversial problems.

Sometimes, even professional groups of educators have difficulty in defining and agreeing on meanings and procedures. "The least restricted environment" and "mainstreaming" may mean different things to the regular classroom teacher and to the special education teacher. Educational policymakers will continue to have difficulty in providing educational programs that satisfy all the concerned groups, and additional litigation seems a certainty.

Culture, Ethnicity, Language

America has been described as a nation of immigrants. Stories concerning the admonition to "give me your tired your poor" are part of our nation's heritage. The public schools have been called upon at different times to play a role in the Americanization of these immigrants. Recently, the particular role asked of the public schools in coping with the problems of cultural, ethnic, and language diversity of the school population has become controversial. Some feel that the function of the public school is to Americanize the diverse elements of the population. Those who disagree with this position feel that the public schools should recognize diversity and help preserve the cultural, ethnic, and language differences.

The schools are not the only institutions of our society that have been affected by the changing diversity of our population. Large numbers of Spanish-speaking people with their own traditions have settled in various

Box 12.3
Will Federal
Legislation Clarify
and Expand Equal
Educational
Opportunity for
Handicapped
Children?

P.L. 99–457 was signed by President Reagan in October of 1986. The law provides monetary incentives for states to provide services for handicapped youngsters from three to five years of age by the 1990–91 school year. Lobbyists for the Council of Exceptional Children hailed the law as a needed step in providing equal opportunity for handicapped children. Proponents of the legislation claim that 70,000 children not being served at the present time need the services that can be provided by this legislation. Critics of the law, however, point to certain weaknesses and shortcomings. They claim there are not enough trained personnel to make the law operational and that vague terms such as "at-risk children" and "developmentally delayed" will cause serious problems. The law requires each state to designate one lead agency to serve the covered population, and many believe that battles will develop between public health agencies and educational agencies over jurisdiction. Researchers differ on the basic premise of early intervention. Studies to date that support either position are inconclusive. What kind of educational policy will develop in your state as a result of this legislation? Will this policy provide equal opportunity for the handicapped?

parts of our nation. Groups of immigrants from Asian nations with language and cultural backgrounds distinctly different from ours are becoming quite commonplace. This has produced strain and controversy for local and state governmental agencies. In California, for example, the 1986 fall elections included Proposition 63, which was passed by the electorate and declares English the official language of the state, prohibits the use of other languages on election ballots, and requires state and local authorities to use only English in carrying out their duties.

Educational policymakers have been confronted with accusations that certain educational practices are discriminatory on the basis of the language deficiency of groups of pupils. The San Francisco public schools had some 2,800 non-English speaking children of Chinese descent enrolled in school. Approximately 1,000 of these children were provided special help. Parents of the children brought legal action against the school board, seeking special help for all of these students without English background and citing that the cost of the programs did not include all the subject pupils. This case reached the U.S. Supreme Court and was decided as *Lau* v. *Nichols* (1974).[28] The Court decided that providing the same facilities, textbooks, teachers, and curriculum was not equal treatment and that some type of compensatory intervention was needed to give equal opportunity to these "language deficient" pupils. This case is frequently referred to as the case that mandated bilingual programs. It should be noted, however, that the Court did not in fact require any specific remedy—only that some compensatory help be available.

In a case originating in Michigan, a federal judge ruled on the same general question but with an important difference.[29] The parents of a group of black children in Ann Arbor asked that their children be provided special help on the basis that the dialect, Black English, spoken by these children made them language deficient. Ruling in favor of the parents, the court indicated that not only ethnic differences but social differences as well must be taken into account when defining equal educational opportunity. The court did not specify particular methods but insisted that affirmative means be utilized to provide these children equal opportunity. The definition of equality now included not just access to education but also suitable programs recognizing the characteristics of the pupil. Some critics of these decisions claim that the eventual result will be the segregation of children in special programs and will be harmful to the children and the nation. Educational policymakers still face difficult problems in developing policy that provides equal educational opportunity for all children.

Our nation continues to attract immigrants of varied cultural backgrounds. Language and cultural diversity must be considered when addressing the question of equal treatment in our schools. Educators have disagreements over the proper multicultural approach to educating these minorities. Some believe that programs must be transitional in nature, with the goal being to move children as quickly as possible from special programs for minorities to the regular school program for all children. Others believe that special language and cultural programs should be provided and maintained throughout the school experience of the child. Recently, some schools have experimented with "total immersion" programs in various languages. These programs provide a teacher who is bilingual for the first three grades. The teacher, however, speaks only one language to the children. All communication from the teacher is in the one "immersion" language. Studies point to successes and failures in all these programs, and educators continue to seek solutions that will provide equal educational opportunity to the many minority populations who feel our present schools do not provide proper programs for their children.

Table 12.3 Selected Cases in Educational Opportunity for Handicapped	CASE	YEAR	FINDING
	PARC v. Commonwealth of Penn.	1972	Retarded children entitled to a free public education.
	Mills v. Board of Education District of Columbia	1972	Expanded PARC decision.
	Hendrick Hudson Ind. School District v. Rowley	1982	Free and appropriate does not mean maximizing the opportunities for handicapped children.
	Irving Ind. School District v. Tatro	1984	Catheterization is required for handicapped child.
	Lau v. Nichols	1974	Special programs is required for Chinese-speaking children.
	M. L. King Elementary School Children v. Michigan Board of Education	1979	Special programs are required for black children where dialect causes language deficiencies.
	Honig v. Doe	1988	Discipline of handicapped child is ruled as placement change.

Photo 12.4
Athletic activities for girls have increased as a move towards equal opportunity.

Sex

The social, political, and economic norms of the nation are generally reflected in the public schools. Those stereotypes of male and female activities, behaviors, and vocations accepted by society are reinforced in the schools. In the past, this has meant that boys were to be wage earners, prepare for the professions, and participate in athletics, while girls were to be homemakers and cheerleaders and prepare for some type of stenographic or service work. The Women's Rights Movement of the late 1960s questioned these stereotypes. Issues concerning the unequal treatment of women and the classification and assignment of women solely on the basis of sex were raised and litigated.

The expanded interpretation of the equal protection clause of the Fourteenth Amendment included classification by sex. The Civil Rights Act of 1964 and Title IX of the Education Amendments of 1972, together with the Fourteenth Amendment, provided the basis for challenging discriminatory practices in the public schools with regard to placement and classification on the basis of sex. Most of the questions were raised over admission standards to programs, the provision of activities for boys but not for girls, and participation by girls in activities designated for boys only.

The Boston Latin School required the submission of a test score for admission. The girls seeking admission scored higher on the examination as a group than did the boys. In an attempt to balance admissions, school authorities set admission test score standards at 120 for boys and 133 for girls. Some girls who scored higher than boys who were admitted were denied entrance. Parents of these girls brought suit, alleging that the girls were denied equal protection by the admission policy of the school. In *Bray v. Lee* (1972), a federal district court agreed with the claims of the parents and ruled that the policy in question was discriminatory.[30] This decision and other litigation provided educational policymakers with a warning that arbitrary or capricious admission requirements based on sex violate equal protection rights of pupils.

Much of the publicity on the issue of unequal treatment of the sexes has been focused on extracurricular activities, particularly participation on athletic teams. Since Title IX, separate girls' athletic teams have increased in numbers. These separate teams have been provided to ensure comparable athletic opportunities for girls. Serious problems have confronted school officials concerning those sports that are offered on a one-sex basis. Generally, the problems revolve around the competitive skill level, the contact nature of the activity, or the safety of the participants. Many schools have cited the safety of the pupils as the reason for restricting an activity to males. Yet there can be greater differences between the stronger and weaker males than between the stronger males and the stronger, more mature females. Unless the school has established rules protecting the weaker males, such as physical requirements for participation, the courts have been reluctant to exclude females. If the schools have no-cut policies for athletic teams, it is difficult to exclude girls on the basis of weaker competitive skills.

Many of the problems cited have not been completely and satisfactorily solved, and litigation continues at an alarming rate. The one thing that educational policymakers can be certain of is that change will continue. Some examples of the recent past can be used to emphasize the changing athletic environment. A fifteen-year-old girl in Connecticut lost her first two wrestling matches for the school team. A fourteen-year-old girl in New Jersey, after a court order, joined the football team of the high school as a receiver. In Connecticut, a high-school girl not only joined the school's hockey team but also started as a goalie and recorded a shutout in her first competition. A ninety-eight pound girl recently won a junior varsity wrestling match in Maryland, causing considerable publicity for herself and her school. How have educational policymakers in your area handled these matters? Can you use a simple policy process model to trace developments in your school district?

Summary

Equality of educational opportunity is a concept to which most Americans are committed. As attempts are made to translate this concept into meaningful and practical educational programs, disagreement and controversy appear. People view equality in education in different ways. Some look for programs that provide an equality of outcomes, others desire equal treatment for all, yet another view sees individual differences requiring individual treatments.

One function of the school is to classify and assign pupils to schools, classrooms, and programs. The methods used by school officials in making these assignments have been questioned by groups or individuals who allege unequal treatment and discrimination. Classification on the basis of race at one time provided separate facilities for blacks and whites. This type of classification led to the doctrine of "separate but equal" facilities. The nation struggled with this view for many years, and the courts were called upon to clarify and redefine the doctrine's meaning. Finally, in 1954, the U.S. Supreme Court rejected separate but equal and required the elimination of *de jure* segregation. Questions concerning the implementation of the Court's order occupied the nation for many years and remain unsettled today. School programs requiring busing, freedom of choice plans, and the meaning of *de facto* segregation were litigated in attempts to reach agreement concerning equality of opportunity in education.

School policies were also questioned concerning the assignment and classification of pupils on the basis of handicap, cultural background, ethnic origin, and sex. These questions have frequently led to litigation and continue to be controversial. The definition of equal educational opportunity is still being formulated, and educational policymakers must consider the changing definitions in providing education for all children.

Key Words

Equality	**Unitary system**
Benjamin Bloom	**Affirmative action**
Equity	**Vocational Rehabilitation Act**
Equal opportunity	**P.L. 94–142**
Separate but equal	**Least restrictive environment**
With all deliberate speed	**Mainstreaming**
Desegregation	**Free and appropriate**
Integration	**Bilingual program**
Freedom of choice plan	**Transitional programs**
Ratio guideline	**Maintenance programs**
Busing	**Total immersion programs**
De jure	**Civil Rights Act 1964**
De facto	**Title IX**

Discussion Questions

1. What is your definition of equality of educational opportunity?

2. What approaches have been most successful in providing equal opportunity for all children?

3. What recent developments can you outline regarding the education of handicapped pupils? What are the problems or concerns that have not as yet been addressed concerning handicapped pupils?

4. Equality of educational opportunity problems have focused on race, sex, handicap, and on the poor. What in your view are the unresolved issues in providing equal educational opportunity?

5. Should institutions other than the school be involved in educational equality issues? If so, which ones and in what ways?

For Further Reading

Alexander, K., and Alexander, M. *American Public School Law.* St. Paul: West Publishing Co., 1985.

Jarolimek, J. *The Schools in Contemporary Society.* New York: Macmillan Publishing Co., 1981.

Kirp D., and Yudof, M. *Educational Policy and the Law.* Berkeley, Calif.: McCutchan Publishing Co., 1982.

McCarthy, M., and Deignan, P. *What Legally Constitutes an Adequate Public Education?* Phi Delta Kappa Educational Foundation, Bloomington, Ind., 1972.

McCarthy M., and Cambron, N. *Public School Law Teachers' and Students' Rights.* Boston, Mass: Allyn & Bacon, Inc. 1981.

Reutter, E. *The Supreme Court's Impact on Public Education.* Bloomington, Ind.: Phi Delta Kappa, and NOLPE, 1982.

Spring, J. *American Education,* New York: Longman, Inc., 1985.

Spurlock C. *Education and the Supreme Court.* Urbana, Ill.: Univ. of Illinois Press, 1955.

Zirkle, P. A. *A Digest of Supreme Court Decisions Affecting Education,* Bloomington, Ind.: Phi Delta Kappa, 1978.

_____. *A Digest of Supreme Court Decisions Affecting Education: Supplement.* Bloomington, Ind.: Phi Delta Kappa 1982.

Notes

1. Benjamin S. Bloom, *Human Characteristics and School Learning* (Bloom, New York: McGraw-Hill, 1976).

2. John Jarolimek, *The Schools in Contemporary Society* (New York: Macmillan Publishing Co., New York, 1981). A detailed treatment of this topic can be found in Chapter 6.

3. M. M. McCarthy and P. T. Deignan, *What Legally Constitutes an Adequate Public Education?* Phi Delta Kappa Educational Foundation, Indiana, Phi Delta Kappa, 1972.

4. *Roberts* v. *City of Boston,* 59 Mass. (5 Cush.) 198 (1850).

5. *Plessy* v. *Ferguson,* 163 U.S. 537, 16 S. Ct. 1138 (1896).

6. *Cumming* v. *County Board of Education,* 175 U.S. 528, 24 Sup. Ct. 197 (1899).

7. *Gong Lum* v. *Rice,* 275 U.S. 78, 48 S. Ct. 91 (1927).

8. *Missouri Ex Rel Gaines* v. *Canada,* 305 U.S. 337, 59 Sup. Ct. 236–7 (1938).

9. *Alston* v. *School Board of the City of Norfolk,* 112F.2d 992 (CCA 4th 1940) p. 995 311 U.S. 693, 61 Sup. Ct. 75 (1940).

10. *Sweatt* v. *Painter,* 339 U.S. 629, 70 Sup. Ct. 848 (1950).

11. *Ibid.,* pp. 850–851.

12. *Brown* v. *Board of Education of Topeka,* 347 U.S. 483, 74 Sup. Ct. 686 (1954) pp. 690–693.

13. *Brown* v. *Board of Education of Topeka* (Brown II), 349 U.S. 294 (1955).

14. *Cooper* v. *Aaron,* 358 U.S. 178 S. Ct. 1401 (1958).

15. *Griffin* v. *County School Board of Prince Edward County,* 377 U.S. 218, 84 S. Ct. 1226 (1964).

16. *Green* v. *County School Board of New Kent County,* 391 U.S. 430 88 S., Ct. 1689 (1968).

17. *Alexander* v. *Holmes,* 396 U.S. 19, 90 S. Ct. 29 (1969).

18. *Swann* v. *Charlotte-Mecklenburg Board of Education,* 402, U.S. 91 S.Ct. 1267 (1971).

19. *Keyes* v. *School District No. 1, Denver,* 413 U.S. 189, 93 S.Ct. 2686.

20. *Milliken* v. *Bradley,* 418 U.S. 717 94 S.Ct. 3112.

21. *Columbus Board of Education* v. *Penick,* 443 U.S. 449, 99 S.Ct. 2941 (1979). *Dayton Board of Education* v. *Brinkman* 443 U.S. 526 99 S.Ct. 2971 (1979).

22. Lawrence F. Rosson, NOLPE Notes, Vol. 21, No. 11 (1986): p. 1.

23. *Pennsylvania Association for Retarded Children* v. *Commonwealth of Pennsylvania,* 334 F. SUPP. 1257 (E.D. Pa. 1971) 343 F. SUPP. 279 (E.D. Pa. 1972).

24. *Mills* v. *Board of Education of the District of Columbia,* 348 F. SUPP 866 (D.D.C. 1972).

25. Rehabilitation Act of 1973, Section 504, 29 USCA 794.

26. *Hendrick Hudson District Board of Education* v. *Rowley,* 458 U.S. 176, 102 S.Ct. 3034 (1982).

27. *Irving Independent School District* v. *Tatro,* 104 S.Ct. 3371 (1984).

28. *Lau* v. *Nichols,* 414 U.S. 563, 94. S. Ct. 786 (1974).

29. *M. L. King Elementary School Children* v. *Michigan Board of Education,* 413, F. SUPP. 1371 (E. D. Mich. 1979).

30. *Bray* v. *Lee,* 357 F. SUPP. 934 (D. Mass. 1972).

13 Church-State Relations in Education

"The non-public elementary and secondary schools in the United States have long been an integral part of the nation's educational establishment. . . . This government cannot be indifferent to the potential collapse of such schools."

President Richard Nixon (1970)

"(Alabama has) . . . intentionally crossed the line between creating a quiet moment during which those so inclined may pray and affirmatively endorsing the particular religious practice of prayer. . . . This line may be a fine one but our precedents and principles of religious liberty require we draw it."

Justice O'Conner in *Jaffree v. Board of Commissioners* (1983)

"When the U.S. Supreme Court prohibited children from participating in voluntary prayer in public schools, the conclusion is inescapable that the Supreme Court not only violated the right of free exercise of religion of all America; it also established a national religion in the United States—the religion of secular humanism."

Senator Jesse Helms in *Secular Humanism: The Most Dangerous Religion in America* (1979)

Church-State Issues in Education in the United States

Church-state relations in public education involve a broad range of complex constitutional issues. Many aspects of public school programs, curriculum, and administration involve First Amendment questions relating to free exercise of religious beliefs or prohibitions against the establishment of religion. In a political system that espouses the ideal of separation of church

305

Policy Model 13.1   Church-State Issues in Education

POLICY ISSUES	PARTICIPANTS IN POLICY DEVELOPMENT	ILLUSTRATIONS OF POLICY SOLUTIONS	EFFECTS OF POLICY SOLUTIONS
Parental authority over place and content of child's education Use of public funds for private schools State regulation of private schools Proper place of religion in public school curricula and programs Ways that public schools protect free exercise of religion and avoid the establishment of religion	**Formal** U.S. Congress Federal courts State court systems State legislative bodies Federal and state administrative agencies **Informal** Parents Organized parents' groups Religious groups ACLU Other ad hoc groups	Federal statutes Court decisions State statutes Administrative regulations	**Allocative** Who gets to do what? **Regulative** Who will/can/do what? **Structural** Changes, deletions to structures involved in policy administration **Redistributive** Changes, deletions to allocation of resources or authority

and state, questions recurringly arise over the relationship between schools that are operated by religious groups and state education agencies. Other questions arise: How much authority should parents have over both the place and the content of their children's education? Should public funds be used to aid private schools? What type of aid to private schools would constitute excessive entanglement between church and state? Should state education agencies have the authority to regulate private schools? How do public school personnel ensure the ideals of free exercise of religion without violating constitutional principles regarding the establishment of religion?

This chapter examines these and other important questions relating to educational church-state issues in the United States. Policy Model 13.1 lists some of the issues, identifies participants involved in developing the policies regarding these issues, and lists the types and effects of policy solutions developed for dealing with church-state issues in education in the United States.

Church-state issues in education in the United States should be considered in the larger context of church-state relations in the history of Western civilization. Conflicts between church and state have long been a dominant theme in the history of the Western world. Sectarian conflicts have produced wars, political insurrections, and migrations of population that have colored the fabric of Western cultural traditions.

The early Christian church questioned the superior jurisdiction of the state over the Church. Christian martyrs sacrificed life to the cause of eliminating civil authority over religious thought. Later, Church leaders such as Thomas Aquinas argued that the state should be subordinate to the Church. As the Church reached the height of its supremacy over the state in the later Middle Ages, those who questioned Church authority were frequently persecuted or put to death.

The Reformation called into question Church supremacy over matters relating to individual freedom to interpret and adopt personal religious beliefs. However, reformationist leaders did not question the right of secular political leaders to use religion to carry out political activities.

Even though many of the original colonists fled religious persecution to search for freedom of religious expression, state-established religion was a reality in colonial culture. Nine of the thirteen colonies at one time or another levied taxes to support a particular religious tradition. In early colonial history, there were widespread practices of discrimination against minority faiths.

The effort to draft the Constitution generated great debate over church-state issues. Many who were part of this debate believed that separate states should retain the right to enact laws supporting sectarian institutions. After considerable debate, the authors omitted any provisions regarding religious freedom in the proposed constitution. Delegates of two states refused to sign the Constitution until a bill of rights was included as part of the document. Soon after the revolution, Thomas Jefferson and James Madison became the chief architects of the principle of separation of church and state as it found its way into the U.S. Constitution. Jefferson argued that it was tyrannical to tax a person to support religious tenets in which he did not believe. Jefferson's intent in promoting the adoption of the First Amendment was to provide freedom for both church and state so that each could achieve its separate purpose without interference from the other.

Educational policy in early America reflected local control perspectives. Church-state issues were not viewed from the perspective of constitutional rights but in terms of majority rule. The dominant religious group in the local community set the tone for community norms—even the place of religion in the "public" schools. Furthermore, as it was initially interpreted, the First Amendment did not specifically prohibit states from establishing religion or interfering with the free exercise of religious beliefs. For example, in 1845, the U.S. Supreme Court declared:

> *The Constitution makes no provision for protecting the citizens of the respective states in their religious liberties; this is left to state constitutions and laws; nor is there any inhibition imposed by the Constitution of the United States in this respect to the States.*[1]

It was not until the twentieth century that the federal judiciary asserted itself to protect individual First Amendment rights. During the past several decades, the Fourteenth Amendment has been interpreted by the Supreme Court as prohibiting states from violating fundamental liberties protected by the Bill of Rights. For example, the courts have firmly established that

Photo 13.1
Public schools enroll
students from diverse
religious backgrounds.

states must protect First Amendment religious liberties in state governmental enterprises (like schools). Since most of the law and policy in education was originally developed by the states, the federal courts have been very active in bringing state policies regarding church-state issues into compliance with federal constitutional guidelines.

A broad range of factors beyond the historical traditions previously described have emerged to make church-state issues one of the more fertile fields of policy debate in the United States. One such factor is the degree of religious pluralism that exists in this country. Diverse patterns of immigrant settlement into the different geographical regions of the United States also help to account for the extent of religious diversity that characterizes the population of this country. A consolidated high school in the rural South may be attended primarily by students whose families are conservative Southern Baptist or Pentecostal. A middle school in northeastern Indiana may have a cross-section of Mennonite students and students from an Old Order Amish community. In an inner-city school in the East, the student body may be made up of students from Catholic, Jewish, Presbyterian, and Pentecostal backgrounds or from some community cult. The enrollment in any of these schools would no doubt include a number of students who, along with their parents, have no religious affiliation.

Religious affiliation creates one of the strongest of all cultural identities in American life and, along with social class status, appears to have great influence over sex role identity, marriage, divorce, birth rates, child-rearing practices, and many other important lifestyle issues. Public opinion surveys regarding the role of religion in American life indicate that a high percentage of Americans regard their religious beliefs as very important—or at least fairly important—to them.[2] A high percentage of parents in this country believe that their children should have religious training for character building and as a means of keeping the family together.[3] As one author puts it:

> *Religion is much more than a voluntary association of people with a common hobby or pastime. . . . Each faith, even each denomination,*

*is a separate subcommittee as well as a voluntary association. It is a
way of life, with social clubs, athletic leagues, insurance companies,
professional societies, publishing houses, veterans groups, and even
movie-rating committees.[4]*

Different religious traditions do not agree on the impact that religious
identity should have in determining school policies and programs. They also
differ in their interpretations of the principle of separation of church and
state. Some religious groups argue that they want their children exposed to
the perceptions of different ethnic, social, racial, and religious expressions,
while other parents argue that public schools violate their religious liberties
by exposing children to values and mores different from their own.
Developing policies for the operation of public schools that will accommodate these diverse religious commitments while protecting individual liberty
regarding religious belief has been a monumental task—a task that makes
church-state issues in education a prominent policy question.

Frequently, other cultural motifs are closely associated with particular
religious groups. In recent years, public schools have been called on to
respect, in a more global way, diverse cultural identities. Some parents,
arguing that public schools have operated from a monocultural perspective,
suggest that if cultural pluralism means anything in our society, it means the
availability of options. Attempting to operate a monocultural school to
serve a pluralistic society has created a number of extremely difficult
problems in church-state issues in education.

A significant percentage of parents in the United States opt to educate
their children in non-public schools or at home. These parents generally
accuse the public schools of failure on two counts. Public schools do not
provide their children with a challenging educational experience and fail to
provide children with adequate character and moral education—especially
moral and character education based on religious convictions. State and
local school boards throughout the United States are faced with policy
dilemmas in their attempts to accommodate these parents' constitutional
rights while they attempt to safeguard the legitimate interests of children to
receive an adequate education. Also, since the private school sector enrolls
approximately eleven percent of the school-age population in a diverse
cross-section of parochial schools, a sizable number of independent schools
with no religious affiliation, and a growing number of Christian day schools
operated by evangelical groups, policymakers have been forced to deal with
many recurring policy problems related to church-state issues:

1.   How much authority should parents have to control both the content
     and place of their child's education?

2.   Should private schools be funded by public tax funds?

3.   Should states have the prerogative to mandate standards and regula-
     tions for the private school sector?

4.   What constitutes an "adequate" education to meet the intent of state
     compulsory attendance statutes?

5.   In what settings—home, school, etc.—can these minimum standards
     for an adequate education be met?

6.   What are the state's legitimate interests in regulating alternative school options?

7.   How do states implement and maintain these regulations without infringing on First Amendment guarantees of freedom of religious belief?

This chapter reviews the public policy debate over church-state issues in educational policy in several problem areas:

Religious observances and activities in public schools.

Exemptions from state educational mandates based on religious convictions.

Use of public school facilities by religious groups.

State aid to non-public schools.

State regulation of private schools.

Home schooling as an alternative to public and private schooling.

Religious Observances and Practices in Public Schools

Dealing with religious observances and activities in public education has long been a highly charged, emotional activity. Religious concerns constituted the basis for the formation of the first "public" schools in the colonies. Schools would teach people to read so that they could read the Bible. The selection of teachers was based more on religion than scholarship. After the Revolution, instruction in religion and use of the Bible in public schooling were a continuing feature of the school day. One of the great questions of the common school movement from 1830 to 1860 was how to deal with sectarian interests. Massachusetts enacted a statute requiring Bible reading in the public schools in 1826. The McGuffey reader, which sold 120 million copies between 1839 and 1920, was filled with Biblical imagery, stories, passages, and lessons.

Despite the apparent support for religious education in public schools, factors evolved that created controversy over policy. In the mid- and late-nineteenth century, massive waves of immigrants came to the United States. Large numbers of Catholics began to take exception to the widespread use of protestant versions of the Bible in public schools and eventually launched their own parochial school system in the third quarter of the nineteenth century. By the early 1900s, powerful secularizing forces gathered at the schoolhouse door. Progressive, scientific approaches to public education questioned the appropriateness of maintaining religious activities and observances in public schools. By the 1940s and 1950s, the U.S. population had to adjust to the growing reality of cultural diversity, new scientific and technological orientations, and new approaches to Biblical interpretation and criticism. These forces would inevitably raise questions about the role of religion in public schools.

In the first three decades of the twentieth century, several states had responded to the growing secularism in society by enacting statutes requiring Bible reading in the public schools. Pennsylvania, Delaware, Tennessee, New Jersey, Alabama, Georgia, Maine, Kentucky, Florida,

Idaho, and Arkansas had enacted such laws by 1930. Other states followed suit during the 1940s. These statutes spawned numerous state court cases regarding state constitutional issues. State courts reached conflicting conclusions regarding the constitutionality of prayer and Bible reading in the schools. In some states, bans against such practices were upheld by the state courts. In other states, courts upheld the constitutionality of such practices. As a result of this conflict, it should not be surprising that the U.S. Supreme Court had to face the controversy. The First Amendment prohibits the establishment of religion by government entities (the establishment clause) and prohibits government interference with individual rights to hold and freely practice religious beliefs (the free exercise clause). The Supreme Court has established separate tests for assessing government action with regard to these two principles.

The Supreme Court has issued certain guidelines in the *Engel* v. *Vitale* (1962), *Abington Township* v. *Schempp* (1963), and *Murray* v. *Curlett* (1963) decisions that have directed judicial deliberation over religious activities in school since the early 1960s. In the *Engel* case, the New York State Board of Regents had composed the following prayer: "Almighty God, we acknowledge our dependence upon thee, and beg they blessings upon us, our parents, our teachers, and our country." Students in the New Hyde Park district were required to recite this prayer daily. Parents in the district challenged the constitutionality of this requirement for students who were compelled to go to school. The Supreme Court held that this practice violated the establishment clause of the First Amendment.

In the *Murray* and *Schempp* decisions, the Court invalidated Bible reading as a devotional activity in public school classrooms. The Court reiterated its view that state sponsorship of any kind of devotional activity violated the establishment clause of the First Amendment. Furthermore, even if steps were taken to make the activity voluntary on the part of students, it would put the school in the position of violating the posture of neutrality it must take in such matters.

In these two cases, along with *Lemon* v. *Kurtzman* (1971), which questioned whether states could provide direct aid for secular services in private schools, three tests of neutrality were established by the Court to determine the constitutionality of state actions regarding religious observances and activities in public schools. Governments cannot condone actions that (1) advance or inhibit religion, (2) foster excessive entanglement with religion, or (3) promote activities that do not clearly reflect a secular purpose. Any state action that violates any of these tests is considered by the courts to be in violation of the law.

Given the role that religion plays in American life and culture, it is not surprising that there has been intense reaction to the Court's removal of overt religious activities and practices from the public schools. Because a large segment of the public has voiced concern about the growing secular character of the schools, attempts have been made to restore religious symbols and perspectives to public schooling. Recent Supreme Court decisions have been challenged by federal and state legislative bodies through efforts to reinstate voluntary prayer by a U.S. constitutional amendment, requirements to post the Ten Commandments in public school classrooms, establishment of periods of silent meditation in schools, and other means of restoring religious activities as a part of the public school experience.

A large number of parents are concerned that their children are not receiving moral and character education in schools. These parents adamantly argue that moral and character education are tied to religious education and cannot be accomplished in the absence of religious instruction. This attitude no doubt explains the rapid growth in the number of Christian day schools attended by a growing number of students whose parents belong to the evangelical churches that operate such schools.

Inconsistent compliance is another response to the Court's rulings regarding religious practices in public schools. In many communities, church-state issues are still not viewed so much from the perspective of constitutional law as from the perspective of majority rule. In communities where homogeneous religious values are dominant, it is likely that these values will dictate the kind of response that schools make to Court decisions. For example, Bible reading can still be found in public school classrooms of the South.

Justices of the Supreme Court have remarked on different occasions that they have neither "the sword nor the purse" to ensure compliance with their decisions. The three types of power that courts do have to enforce their rulings—coercive, legitimate, and expert—frequently limit compliance. Courts have coercive power to invoke compliance only in the immediate cases under litigation. The courts' legitimate power to bring compliance derives from public acceptance of the courts' right to influence behavior. Obviously, a large segment of the U.S. population questions the courts' legitimate right to determine the behavior of public school systems with regard to religion. The courts' expert power is derived from responsibility to determine the meaning of the Constitution and statutes.[5]

Many people have been disappointed in the degree of compliance to the Court rulings regarding church-state issues. They claim that the decisions were long overdue and that eternal vigilance on the question of religion in education is the price of liberty. Such people view the public schools as places of intense, prolonged human contact and believe that promoting official, government-sanctioned religious activities is divisive and disruptive. Attempts to ally governmental authority with a particular expression of religious practice tends to exacerbate value differences among students and obscure shared values such as freedom, justice, and equality that do not belong to any particular religious expression. Furthermore, defenders of these Court decisions argue that involvement in any genuine religious experience will not grow from a state sanction. Such sanctions will only distort the real meaning of the religious experience and are counterproductive to achieving the ends for which they are so enthusiastically supported.

With the public so divided on the question of religious observances and activities in public schools, it is not surprising that schools have devised many practices that seem to meet the Supreme Court's three-part test. These efforts have centered mainly around teaching about religion, accommodating student-initiated voluntary prayer, and periods of silent meditation.

Teaching About Religion

Careful reading of the Court's opinions in the *Engle* and *Schempp* decisions suggests that the Court did not seek to prohibit schools from teaching about religion or from teaching the Bible or other religious documents from a literary or academic perspective. Justice Clark in the *Schempp* decision noted:

> *. . . It certainly may be said that the Bible is worthy of study for its literary and historic qualities. Nothing we have said here indicates that such study of the Bible, or of religion, when presented objectively as part of a secular program of education may not be effected consistently with the First Amendment.*[6]

Justice Brennan concurred by saying that it "would be impossible to teach meaningfully many subjects in the social sciences or humanities without some mention of religion."[7]

Drawing the line between teaching about religion and teaching religious precepts is sometimes difficult. The motive to ensure that certain values are taught frequently supersedes the interest in conveying information about the past and present religious influences over culture. Efforts to teach about religion and its importance to American culture cannot be used as a guise to advance any particular set of religious beliefs. Courses in history of religion, comparative religion, and the Bible as literature may be offered as a part of the curriculum of a public school without crossing the fine line between teaching religion and teaching about religion.

Silent Meditation and Voluntary Prayer By Students

No governmental authority can prohibit an individual from exercising the private, individual right to prayer. It would be impossible to put restraints on such free exercise or to determine whether or not it was taking place. It appears that the real issue regarding silent prayer is that states have attempted to give official approval or sanction to such prayer. More than half of the states have some type of statute allowing silent prayer or meditation. As long as students are not instructed to carry out a specific religious ritual, such as prayer, during the period of silent meditation, the courts have generally approved the practice. However, during the 1987 Court term, the U.S. Supreme Court refused to let the state of New Jersey provide moments of silence for public school students. The Courts have failed to give a clear hint whether similar laws in other states impermissibly promote school prayer. It is likely that another case testing the validity of the moment-of-silence concept will reach the high court in the near future.

Some states have crossed the boundary regarding establishment of religion by enacting statutes that call for voluntary, overt prayer by students. In 1983, a district court judge struck down an Alabama statute as violating the establishment clause.[8] It seems clear that laws calling for a period of silent meditation guised as a vehicle to encourage prayer are unconstitutional.

Encouraging student-initiated religious activities has been another way to get around the establishment clause. Generally, the courts have concluded that if religious activities are conducted under the auspicies of the school, they violate constitutional principles. A federal appellate court judge declared there is "no meaningful distinction between school authorities actually organizing the religious activity and officials merely 'permitting' students to direct the exercise."[9]

Photo 13.2
The controversy over prayer in school continues in spite of the U.S. Supreme Court's efforts to set guidelines regarding religious activities in school.

Constitutional Amendment to Allow Prayer in School

Perhaps the most aggressive approach used to get around the Supreme Court ban against religious activities in schools has been the effort to pass through the U.S. Congress a constitutional amendment to allow prayer in public schools. In May 1982, President Reagan announced that he would support such a constitutional amendment. Senator Strom Thurmond (R.,S.C.) introduced such an amendment to the U.S. Senate. The intent of this amendment was to remove federal constitutional prohibitions against overt prayer in public schools. The amendment would have allowed states to ban such activities if they desired. The measure has not been successful in Congress even though President Reagan occasionally continued to promote the desirability of this change in the U.S. Constitution.

Released Time for Religious Instruction

Parental pressure has led to released time arrangements for religious instruction. In these arrangements, children whose parents desire are excused from scheduled school activities for a specified period of time each week to engage in religious instruction. Children who do not participate in such activities remain under the supervision of the school. These programs have been challenged on the grounds of advancing religion.

The Supreme Court has issued opinions on two occasions regarding released time programs for religious instruction. In 1948, in the *McCollum v. Board of Education* decision, the Court held as unconstitutional a released time program that allowed religious educators from different groups in the community to provide religious instruction in the public schools. The Court argued that public tax-supported property was being used as a place to aid religious groups in religious instruction. In 1952, the Supreme Court upheld the constitutionality of a released time program in which the religious instruction was provided at places other than in public school buildings. This decision, *Zorach* v. *Clausen,* resulted in several states' adopting statutes permitting students to be released from public schools at specific times for religious instruction each week.

Released time religious instruction has been under litigation since the *Zorach* decision. Generally, the courts have reasoned that voluntary religious instruction conducted off school grounds requires minimum accommodation by public school officials to avoid excessive entanglement between church and state. Also, the courts have concluded that such programs constitute an appropriate accommodation of the free exercise of religious beliefs. Such practices in the future may continue to generate litigation regarding the rights of students whose parents choose not to have their children participate in such activities. Since these children are compelled to be in school, questions have been raised about whether or not they are being deprived of educational benefits during the time that their classmates are involved in religious instruction.

An associated question has arisen over whether or not students should be able to earn credit for Bible study that would apply to high-school graduation requirements. Should the state grant scholastic credit for religious instruction? Would the granting of such credit violate the strict neutrality test established by the courts? Does it constitute advancement of religion by the state?

Other Controversies

Many controversies have arisen over a number of other religious activities and practices in public schools. Several of these controversies have not been resolved.

Religious Proselytization By School Officials

Since students are compelled to attend school, they constitute a captive audience for teachers and school administrators. The courts have ruled that teachers can violate the establishment principle by using their position for religious proselytization. A tenured teacher in New York was dismissed for recruiting students to her religious group, conducting prayer meetings in her office, and using the classroom to espouse her religious faith.[10] In 1982, a state court upheld the dismissal of a public school teacher for refusing to comply with the school superintendent's order to cease religious activities in the classrooms.[11] Other precedents suggest that teachers cannot advance their religious beliefs by disregarding portions of state-prescribed curricula that may conflict with their sectarian views.

Distribution of Religious Literature in the School

Many religious groups rely on the distribution of printed religious material as a way to spread their faith. Millions of children and adolescents enrolled in public school constitute an attractive audience for the distribution of religious literature by sectarian groups. The Gideon organization—the group that has extensively distributed Bibles and other religious materials in hotels and motels—has been involved in several controversies regarding the distribution of Bibles in the public schools. Generally, the courts have reasoned that allowing the Gideons to distribute their materials in schools, even if the distribution was limited to children whose parents had given permission, served to advance religion.[12] Many local school officials have stopped distribution of such materials on the grounds that they might be placed in the situation of having unpopular cults or sects demanding the same rights to distribute their material as were being granted to other groups.

Display of Religious Symbols

Should public schools be allowed to display popular religious symbols and slogans in public schools? This question has generated controversy in several states and has resulted in court decisions setting forth guidelines regulating this practice. In 1978, the state of Kentucky passed a state statute requiring the state superintendent of public instruction to ensure that a copy of the Ten Commandments be posted in each classroom of the state. The U.S. Supreme Court found that a sectarian rather than an educational purpose motivated the enactment of this law and consequently found that it violated the establishment clause.[13] If religious symbols are displayed temporarily for instructional purposes, however, there is no violation of this constitutional principle. Posting plaques with the phrase "In God We Trust" or other religious slogans must be based on secular intentions.

Exemptions from State Educational Mandates Based On Religious Convictions

A considerable number of citizens of the United States have sought various exemptions for their children from public school programs and practices that they claim violate their free exercise of religion. Examples of such exemptions sought by parents include exemption from mandatory immunization, patriotic observances in school, curricular offerings, athletic regulations, and scheduled school activities to participate in religious observances.

The courts have generally concluded that parents have the right to seek alternatives to mandated public school programs but do not have the right to seek relief from the state's authority to require a designated amount of education for all citizens. The courts have stubbornly upheld the constitutionality of compulsory attendance statutes and the state's interest in assuring an educated citizenry. The courts have rather consistently upheld the duty of the state to safeguard the health and safety of children at school. The courts have also taken into account the hardships placed on school officials that may result from granting exemptions to public school programs.

The state's authority to require children who attend public school to be in good health has been respected historically. Students who have not been properly immunized may be denied admission to school. In such matters, the health and safety of a large number of children has to be balanced with the individual parent's freedom to advocate religious practices that are inconsistent with the health and safety of a larger group. Similar principles apply to students who wish to participate in athletic activities but whose parents disagree with regulations that exist as a precondition for participation.

Before 1940, several state courts had upheld the legality of requiring students to salute the U.S. flag. In 1940, the U.S. Supreme Court held that a state statute requiring a salute to the flag and giving a pledge of allegiance did not violate individual free exercise of religion rights. Three years later, the Court reversed this decision. Members of the Jehovah's Witness faith asserted that a West Virginia state board regulation requiring the flag salute impaired their religious convictions against bowing to any "graven image." In this instance, the Court only prohibited school officials from compelling participation in such patriotic observances; it did not ban such practices from the public schools. The courts have also upheld the right of teachers to refuse to take the pledge to the U.S. flag as a matter of personal conviction. Teachers, however, do not have the right to choose to eliminate such observances from the classroom.

Photo 13.3

Title IX guidelines for coeducational physical education courses created controversy in some school districts when they were first implemented.

Other controversies have arisen over state-required curricula offerings that some parents contend violate their religious scruples. For example, in 1972, a Sixth Circuit Court of Appeals concluded that the individual's right to free exercise of religion superseded a school district's right to require R.O.T.C. for graduation.[14] However, in 1974, a federal court upheld the expulsion of a Georgia high-school student for his refusal to enroll in mandatory military instruction.[15]

In several instances, members of different religious groups have contended that required dress for physical education classes in schools offended their religious convictions. Some of these groups have filed grievances based on Title IX requirements for coeducational P.E. classes and have sought exemptions from such regulations for their children. The courts have generally concluded that there are no compelling free exercise of religion claims to compel the schools to exempt students from such arrangements.

Courts have frequently been receptive to parental requests for exemptions to mandated sex education based on religious convictions. States must provide compelling reasons to stifle free exercise rights in order to mandate that students participate in sex education programs. It is highly likely that considerable controversy will prevail on this issue in the next few years as more and more states mandate controversial sex education programs in public schools.

In an isolated instance, the U.S. Supreme Court granted an exemption to compulsory schooling regulations to Amish parents for their children. The *Wisconsin* v. *Yoder* (1972) decision reasoned that requiring Amish children to attend school beyond the eighth grade interfered with the religious practices of the Amish. Requiring additional schooling beyond this level for this group would do little to advance the state's interest. This ruling only applied to the Amish and was not intended to have broad application.

Public school administrators are expected to honor reasonable requests by teachers to be absent from school for religious reasons. These absences must not create universal hardships for the schools or work against the academic interests of students. Conversely, school boards cannot confer special benefits, such as paid leave time, that are tied to religious observances.

Use of Public School Facilities By Religious Groups

In many states, local boards have the authority to permit public school buildings to be used for any lawful assembly by community groups. This policy has created controversies as a result of religious groups seeking to use public school buildings for meeting places. Generally, such use arrangements have been upheld as long as the school district officials function strictly as a landlord. Rental of such facilities at the fair market value does not constitute state aid to religion. These rental arrangements cannot interfere with ongoing school activities and cannot result in religious influences over the public school program. Local boards may not discriminate between groups that may wish to utilize public school facilities.

In the early 1980s, controversy developed over student use of public school buildings for religious purposes. Student clubs, such as the Fellowship of Christian Athletes, YMCA, YWCA, and other groups, have used school buildings for meetings and activities with little controversy, because these groups serve secular as well as religious functions. But, do schools violate the establishment clause if student religious groups are allowed to use school buildings for religious purposes? This question has been the concern of a number of court cases and congressional activity in recent years, because student groups that have religion as their primary focus have sought to use public school buildings for religious activities (see Policy Model 13.2).

In 1981, the U.S. Supreme Court declined to review the *Brandon* v. *Board of Education* case in which the court of appeals upheld the authority of a local board of education to deny the use of local high-school classroom space for a before-school prayer meeting by a group of students that sought such use. Students had challenged the board's decision on the basis of First Amendment free speech and assembly principles. The appellate court reasoned that the right to assemble and to free expression is limited by the establishment clause and indicated that there is a compelling state interest in "removing from the school any indication of sponsoring religious activity."

A week before its decision not to review the *Brandon* case, the Supreme Court in *Widmar* v. *Vincent* upheld the right of college students to use public college buildings for religious meetings. The Court held that college campuses constitute an open forum of ideas and that any infringement of student access to free speech must be justified by a compelling state interest.

Several factors explain the Court's approach to the controversy at the college and university level. The Court has observed on different occasions

Policy Model 13.2	Use of Public School Facilities by Student Religious Group		
POLICY ISSUE	**PARTICIPANTS IN POLICY DEVELOPMENT**	**ILLUSTRATIONS OF POLICY SOLUTIONS**	**EFFECTS OF POLICY SOLUTIONS**
Determining use of public buildings by student religious groups	**Formal** U.S. Supreme Court	*Brandon* v. *Board of Education* (1981) *Widmar* v. *Vincent* (1981)	**Allocative** Students denied use of public school facility for religious meetings. Public college officials must allow use of buildings to student religious groups.
	U.S. Congress	1984 Equal Access Act	**Allocative** If public school officials create open forum and allow one group of students use of building, all groups of students must be given access to use.
	U.S. District Courts	*Clark* v. *Dallas Independent School District* (1987) *Garnett* v. *Benton School District* (1987)	**Redistributive** Equal Access Act may violate establishment clause of First Amendment. School district did not have to accommodate religious clubs.
	Informal ACLU Parent groups Student groups		

that the age and maturity of students is an important factor for consideration. Because college students are less impressionable, less stringent establishment clause restraints could be applied at this level. Also, less faculty involvement would be needed at the college level, creating less likelihood of official use of state resources to advance religion.

In 1984, the U.S. Congress passed a federal statute (Equal Access Act) requiring schools that receive federal funds to provide open access to students who wish to meet before or after school for religious activities. Such programs cannot require involvement of school personnel and must be initiated and conducted by students. When these conditions are met, school

Photo 13.4

There has been recurring debate over the teaching of evolution in school since the Scopes trial in 1927.

officials must allow students to use public school facilities on the same basis as they are made available to other community groups.

During the first four years after the passage of the Equal Access Act, compelling questions were raised by those who opposed and defended the student's right to meet voluntarily in school for prayer and Bible study. The equal access law stipulates that a school creates a limited open forum when it allows one or more noncurriculum-related student groups to meet on school grounds. Thus, according to the law, if a school district grants the use of school property to any student club that is not directly related to the school's curriculum, it must allow all clubs, including religious clubs, to meet in school. To control the use of facilities, some districts are limiting the use of school buildings to only those groups that are curriculum related. Such a closed forum is legal. However, charges are being made that some clubs, such as service and chess clubs, are being allowed to use school facilities. School officials across the country are awaiting further judicial clarification of the intent and meaning of the 1984 equal access law.

Challenges to Public School Curricula Based On Religious Convictions

As noted earlier in the chapter, courts have granted exemptions from public school observances and practices to children whose parents contend that participation in certain activities would conflict with the free exercise of their faith. Another important church-state issue relates to challenges to elements of public school curricula that parents contend interfere with the religious upbringing of their children. These challenges have produced several lawsuits that frequently become the focus of media attention.

One ongoing controversey has centered around the teaching of Darwin's theory of evolution in science courses in public schools. For each generation of students enrolled in school since the 1920s, there have been vocal parents who contend that the theory of evolution conflicts with the Biblical account of creation. They contend that for the schools to teach the theory of evolution and to omit instruction in the Biblical account of creation violated their rights to shape their children's religious views concerning the origin of man and the universe.

In the 1927 Scopes trial, popularized as the "monkey trial," the Tennessee Supreme Court upheld the conviction of John Scopes for teaching evolution under a state law that had been passed to prohibit such instruction in the schools. In *Epperson* v. *Arkansas* (1968), the U.S. Supreme

Court invalidated an anti-evolution statute on the grounds that the state could not limit the knowledge made available to students just to comply with the religious convictions of some parents.

In the 1970s and 1980s, several states passed legislation requiring balanced instruction (evolution and creationism) about human origins. One such balanced treatment statute was signed into law in Arkansas in 1981. This statute was immediately challenged in the courts. A federal district judge ruled the statute unconstitutional on the grounds that the law had no secular purpose and in fact the law was designed to advance religion.[16] During the 1987 Court term, the U.S. Supreme Court heard arguments to review a Louisiana state statute designed to promote such balanced instruction. By a 7 to 2 decision, the Supreme Court concluded that the Louisiana Balanced Treatment Act violated the Constitution's religion clauses "because it seeks to employ the symbolic and financial support of government to achieve a religious purpose" by offsetting the teaching of evolution theory with creation science.

Even though the anti-evolution forces have so far been unsuccessful in getting the courts to approve statutes requiring a balanced treatment of evolution and creationism, they have been successful in getting state officials to require that science textbooks placed on approved textbook lists present evolution as a scientific theory—not a scientific fact. The debate still goes on whether creationism is a scientific or religious belief and whether there is merit in including both views in textbooks.

Teachers frequently require that students read materials that are controversial in nature and that parents contend violate their right to privacy in teaching certain values to their children. More and more parents have claimed that use of such materials constitutes a form of instruction on a secular faith that violates the establishment clause of the First Amendment. In *Mozert* v. *Hawkins County School District* (1986), a federal district judge agreed that several families' rights to free exercise of religion were violated when county school officials gave children the alternative of reading material considered offensive by their parents or leaving the school system. The parents had charged that the offensive reading series encouraged "feminist, humanist, pacifist, and anti-Christian views" and also advocated a "one world government."

An appeals court panel of three judges overturned the district judge's decision and issued the unanimous decision that there was not any proof that students were asked to do anything that required the student to affirm or deny any religious belief. The appeals court reversed the lower court's order that the Hawkins County Board of Education provide the plaintiffs $50,000 for private school tuition and other expenses. In early 1988, the U.S. Supreme Court refused to hear the *Mozert* case, allowing the federal appellate court decision to stand.

The Reverend Tim LaHaye, a California minister and one of the founders of the Moral Majority, attacks public schools for establishing the religion of secular humanism. In his book *The Battle for the Public School,* LaHaye charges that humanism has invaded the public school classrooms, brainwashing children with ideas about evolution, sex, death, socialism, internationalism, and situational ethics. He contends that public schools have become "conduits to the minds of youth training them to be anti-God, anti-moral, anti-family, anti-free enterprise, and anti-American."[17]

Box 13.1
Local Boards Caught
in Catch 22

It appears that local school boards are being caught in Catch 22 situations developing over material being taught in public school curriculum.

In late 1986 in the *Mozert* v. *Hawkins County School District* decision, Judge Thomas G. Hall awarded damages and legal costs to seven fundamentalist Christian families in Greenville, Tennessee, after their children were suspended from school for refusing to read textbooks with materials offensive to their religious beliefs. The controversy began in 1983, when these families began scrutinizing the school district's newly adopted Holt, Rinehart, and Winston reading series. The parents charged that the textbooks systematically advocated feminism, pacifism, witchcraft, vegetarianism, and situational ethics.

In a lawsuit filed in a U.S. district court in Jacksonville, Florida, in December 1986, four parents charged that the local board in Lake City, Florida, had violated their children's rights when it banned a humanistic textbook because of objections raised against the book by a local Baptist minister. The parents, who were assisted in their litigation by the Florida chapter of the ACLU, charged that the board's decision to ban the book had the effect of establishing religious doctrine in the schools.

If you were serving on a local school board, how would you go about protecting the constitutional liberties of parents having an interest in the content of textbooks used by your school system?

In another important case in 1986, a federal district judge heard arguments questioning whether secular humanism is in fact a religion and whether the tenets of secular humanism were being taught in the public schools in Mobile, Alabama. Expert witnesses in this case, *Smith* v. *Board of Commissioners of Mobile County,* gave testimony on these questions as well as on whether or not public school textbooks had essentially eliminated religious elements. Judge Hand issued a decision banning 44 state-approved textbooks from use in Alabama schools. Judge Hand concluded from testimony presented that secular humanism does constitute a religion and this religion was being established through neglect of a fair treatment of religion in the textbooks that were banned. The Alabama State Board of Education appealed the case and Judge Hand's decision was overturned by the circuit court. The U.S. Supreme Court is being asked to decide the question of whether the religion of secular humanism is being established in the public schools in violation of the establishment clause.

Very significant policy questions are being raised in these controversies and observations about the public schools. Since the First Amendment prohibits schools from teaching a specific religion, if the courts determine that, in fact, the schools are favoring secular humanism, these challenges could result in the elimination from school curricula those elements that are discerned to promote it. If the courts refuse to order the schools to stop

> **Box 13.2**
> A Sample of
> Controversies
> Regarding the
> Establishment of
> Secular Humanism

The following are examples of school programs and courses challenged by community groups during the 1985–86 school year for their alleged espousal of secular humanism. This sample was compiled from material developed by People for the American Way, a civil liberties advocacy group.

> California—objections to a drug-abuse prevention program for its use of decision-making techniques and alleged teaching of secular humanism.
>
> Colorado—objections to the implementation of a global education curriculum with a hidden agenda that deemphasizes American patriotism and has no moral absolutes.
>
> Indiana—objection to twelfth grade level health curriculum due to alleged teaching of values clarification and secular humanism.
>
> New York—objections to drug abuse prevention program due to alleged promotion of secular humanism.
>
> Oregon—objections to Holt, Rinehart, and Winston reading series due to discussion of such topics as evolution and sex education and open-ended discussions of these matters.
>
> Texas—objections to use of guidance and counseling programs due to alleged teaching of secular humanism.

Have controversies arisen within school districts in your state over the establishment of secular humanism in school programs and curricula? How have these controversies been resolved?

teaching elements that are defined as contributing to the establishment of secular humanism, then those who contend that secular humanism is a religion could demand equal attention for their religious values to be taught in the schools. The battleground over religious values could be shifted to public school campuses.

It is apparent that many parents will not be happy with the alternatives and exceptions given for their own children with regard to controversial curriculum requirements. They have further claimed that if the schools continue to provide instruction for other students, such instruction advances one religion over another. In 1948, in the *McCollum* v. *Board of Education* decision, Justice Jackson observed:

> *Authorities list 256 separate and substantial religious bodies to exist in the continental United States. Each of them . . . has as good a right as this plaintiff to demand that the courts compel schools to sift out of their teaching everything inconsistent with its doctrines. If we were to eliminate everything that is objectionable to any of these warring sects . . . we will leave the public schools in shreds.*[18]

State Aid to Non-Public Schools

The relationship between private schools and public governments has been in an uneasy state of equilibrium since colonial times. Our society has constantly debated whether private schools should be controlled and funded by government bodies. Historically, First Amendment principles relating to separation of church and state have been used as the source of guidance in developing public policies relating to private schools. But the meaning of separation of church and state has varied with the times.

A major element of the debate regarding the relationship between private schools and government has centered around the use of public resources to fund private schools. This debate has intensified in recent years for several reasons. The increased dissatisfaction with public schooling has stimulated interest in creating ways to make private schools a more available option. For residents in some parts of the country, desegregation has caused many parents to seek refuge in the private schools.

Concern for religious socialization is another factor creating greater interest in private schooling. As a matter of faith, many parents reject values they see public schools perpetuating. Federal educational policy in recent years has had as one of its primary goals to increase the options that parents have in the education of their children. The Reagan administration consistently promoted tuition tax credits and vouchers as good methods to achieve this end. The popularization of research findings by James Coleman that private schools foster greater academic achievement and do more to promote racial equality than public schools has fostered an increased interest in private schooling. In the parochial school sector, rising costs and declining enrollments have raised questions about the future existence of these schools. Some proponents of aid to private schools argue that it would be cheaper to save these schools through some form of aid than to shift the cost of educating children currently enrolled in these schools to the public schools. All of the preceding justifications to fund private schools from public sources meet resistance from opponents to such a policy.

The federal courts have historically protected the right of parents to choose private schooling as an alternative to public schools. In the 1920s, some states began to challenge the right of private schools to operate. Residents in Oregon adopted by referendum a law that would have had the effect of putting private schools out of business. The law required that all children between the ages of eight and sixteen, except those who were "abnormal, subnormal, or physically unable to attend" school, must attend public schools. The Supreme Court's decision in *Pierce v. Society of Sisters* (1925) became a landmark in constitutional law. The Court concluded that states did not have the authority to maintain policies that worked against the existence of private schools. States did, however, have the power to reasonably regulate such schools.

States also have the authority to prohibit public tax funds from being used to support non-public schools. More recent constitutional issues have centered around statutes passed by states to provide financial assistance to non-public schools and their students or to parents of private schoolchildren. Court decisions supporting the use of funds for private schools have generally been based on the child benefit theory. The courts have reasoned that certain types of funding benefits the child more directly than the school or the sponsoring religious body. This theory has been used to provide assistance to private school students under federal funding programs such as the ESEA and subsequent legislation.

Different types of aid have met the child benefit criterion established by the Court. In *Everson* v. *Board of Education* (1947), the Court concluded that states could provide transportation to and from school for private school students. In *Cochran* v. *Louisiana State Board of Education* (1930), and *Board of Education* v. *Allen* (1966), the Court upheld the constitutionality of providing textbooks at public expense to students in private schools. The Supreme Court has declined to review state court decisions holding that it was a violation of state constitutional policy for states to provide such aid. Thus, it seems that states may provide textbooks and transportation, but they cannot be compelled to do so.

In the 1970s, several states attempted to provide direct aid to non-public schools for educational services, teacher salaries, direct lending of instructional materials, etc. In *Lemon* v. *Kurtzman* (1971) and *DiCenso* v. *Robinson* (1971), the Supreme Court ruled that such laws are unconstitutional on the grounds that such aid would result in excessive entanglement between church and state. In 1975, the Court struck down state efforts to provide auxiliary services such as counseling and psychological services to non-public school pupils by public school personnel in *Meek* v. *Pittenger*.

The issue of what is permissible aid was muddled somewhat in *Wolman* v. *Walter* (1977). In this decision, the Court addressed item by item various kinds of services that were provided non-public schools in the Ohio state constitution. The following is a general breakdown of the Court's opinion:

Permissible aid

Purchase or loan of secular textbooks.

Provision for and scoring of standardized tests for secular subjects.

Provision of speech, hearing, and psychological services at the non-public school site.

Provision of the therapeutic and remedial services at a neutral site away from non-public schools.

Nonpermissible aid

Provision of funds to purchase or loan other instructional materials and equipment such as projectors, science kits, globes, maps, and charts.

Provision of travel funds for field trips.

In 1985, the Supreme Court expressed concern over excessive entanglement in the *Aguilar* v. *Felton* and *Grand Rapids* v. *Ball* decisions. The Court invalidated sending public school teachers into private schools for remedial instruction of poor children even if the instruction took place in classrooms in public school buildings that had been leased by a private school system. Even with these decisions, the matter of the type of aid that is permissible is subject to a great deal of interpretation and debate.

Different sets of standards have been applied to determine the constitutionality of aid to private institutions of higher education. Generally, the courts have been less inclined to invalidate state aid to these institutions on the following grounds:

> Because of their age and maturity, college students are less likely to be vulnerable to advancement of religion.
>
> Higher education is voluntary.
>
> Religious and secular functions can be more easily separated in higher education where academic freedom is maintained.

State Regulation of Private Schools

Policy problems over funding the non-public school sector raise questions about accountability for utilization of public resources in nongovernmental entities. Should "he who pays the piper call the tune"? Are attempts by the state to mandate minimum curricula, competency testing, standards for teachers, etc., in private schools an improper infringement of parents' fundamental rights to practice religion? Should states regulate private schools under the guise of looking out for the public interest? How do we balance the private right to practice religion with a larger public good? How much authority resides with parents to control both the content and place of their child's education? It appears that these are pressing policy issues in church-state relations today. Educators and policymakers are being forced to rethink and redefine such concepts as "state interest" and "right to religious belief" as they apply to educational policy.

As educational policy has evolved, it has become firmly established that parents have some control over where, not whether, their children are educated. The state's interest in the universal schooling of its citizens is based on the collective welfare interest of the state and not so much on the individual interest of the child. The judiciary has recognized that states can override parental rights if the welfare of the child is at stake. In a 1944 decision, the Supreme Court elaborated on the relationship between the state's interests and parental rights:

> . . . *Neither right of religion nor right of parenthood are beyond limitation. Acting to guard the general interest in youth's wellbeing the state as* parens patriae *may restrain the parent's control by requiring school attendance, regulating or prohibiting the child's labor and in many other ways. Its authority is not nullified merely because the parent grounds his claim to control the child's course of conduct on religion or conscious.*[19]

In subsequent cases, the courts have defended the compelling interest of the state to protect the welfare of children. Based on this interest, states have the authority to regulate private schools. It must be determined that intervention in the affairs of private schools is motivated by desire to protect the interests of the child. Since it is theorized that education is one of the most important factors relating to one's functioning in society, states must take steps to safeguard children's social and economic interests.

Other arguments have been set forth to justify state regulation of non-public schools:

Preventing the teaching of dangerous social ideas.

Promoting cultural unity.

Protecting children from dangerous business, health, and safety practices.

Providing a suitable criterion for parents to choose non-public schools.[20]

Defining the boundaries of state interest in protecting both the welfare of the child and the state is the troublesome part of policymaking on this question. Few would doubt that the state has an interest in assuring that children meet a minimum level of literacy and competency within a healthy and safe environment. To achieve this, does the state have to license or charter all non-public schools? Since some schools are considered to be an arm of the church, is this tantamount to the state's licensing a ministry of the church?

The limits of state regulation have not been explicitly established in either statutory or case law. There is much inconsistency among the states on policy matters relating to state regulation of non-public schools. The following is but a sample of these differences among the states regarding state regulation of private schools.

In 1983 in Nebraska, Faith Christian School refused to comply with state regulations regarding teacher certification and curriculum standards. A U.S. district court ordered the school closed for failure to comply with these regulations. The U.S. Supreme Court refused to review the case, because it lacked substantive federal questions. The State of Connecticut recently turned down a plan that would have required private schools seeking state approval to submit a statement of philosophy, goals, and description of curriculum to state education officials. In 1982, the Idaho legislature turned down a bill that would have required private schools to inform the state superintendent of the location, enrollment, grade levels, and administration of the schools being operated. Massachusetts has a state law requiring private schools to reveal the names and addresses of students enrolled. Several states require private schools to use state-certified teachers. This cursory sample of state law and recent court rulings illustrates the variety of policy that is evolving regarding state regulation of non-public schooling.

Tax-Exempt Status of Religious Schools

Religious schools have been granted various exemptions under the federal tax code. A volatile dispute arose over the Internal Revenue Service's revoking the tax-exempt status of several institutions that maintained racially discriminatory practices. After 1975, more than a hundred private schools had their tax-exempt status discontinued. One such institution was Bob Jones University in Greenville, South Carolina. Its tax-exempt status was revoked because of its racially restrictive admissions policy and policies prohibiting interracial dating and marriage. In May 1983, the Supreme Court concluded that the federal government's interest in eradication of racial discrimination outweighs any institutional right to claim tax-exempt status under the free exercise clause.[21]

State Regulation of Home Schooling

Dissatisfaction with private and public schools has prompted many parents to choose to educate their children at home. A 1981 survey indicated that thirty-eight states allow home schooling as an alternative to meeting state compulsory attendance regulations. Because of current limitations in getting accurate data on the number of home-schooled children, it is difficult to assess the number of children experiencing this kind of educational alternative. Given current social trends, many school officials estimate that the number of parents choosing to exercise this educational alternative will continue to grow.

The controversy over home instruction turns around the issue of equivalent education. There has been little judicial disruption of the principle that the state has the authority to mandate education of citizens. Questions arise, however, over where this education should take place and whether the optional places allowed are equivalent to those that the state provides or regulates. Related questions include the following:

> Who should have to prove equivalency—the parent or the state?
>
> Who should be the state's agent to determine questions of equivalency—the local board or the state board?

In some states, parents who engage in home schooling do not have to register with either state agencies or local boards of education. Consequently, very few regulations exist for home schooling in these states. In other states, more stringent regulations prevail regarding the qualification of parents to teach and the curriculum taught. Some state courts have observed that children need contact with their peers for their education to be considered adequate under compulsory schooling mandates.

In some states, private schools are virtually unregulated. Thus, some parents who educate their children at home frequently contend that they are operating a private school to bypass the regulations that might apply to home schooling. Consequently, state courts and state boards of education have been moving in many states to establish definitions of private schools. Courts have ruled in several states that religious beliefs cannot be used to disregard statutes that apply to home schooling.

Ongoing controversy and litigation can be expected over the home schooling movement. Addressing the following questions will no doubt stimulate this controversy:

> Should the state assume that the child's educational interests are the same as the parents?
>
> Who should have the burden of proving that home schooling is equivalent to schooling provided in another setting?
>
> How should equivalency be judged—by competency test, review of curriculum, etc.?
>
> Should the state's regulatory authority be reduced in those instances where home instruction is motivated by parents' religious beliefs?
>
> How do you balance the state's interest in the education of its citizens with parental rights to free exercise of faith?

Table 13.1 Significant Court Cases in Church-State Education Issues	CASE	YEAR	FINDING
	Engel v. *Vitale*	1962	Required recitation of prayer prepared by New York regents at beginning of school day was unconstitutional.
	Abington Township v. *Schempp*	1963	Required reading of Bible verses in school was unconstitutional.
	McCollum v. *Board of Education*	1948	Released time religious education courses conducted on school property by community ministers was unconstitutional.
	Zorach v. *Clausen*	1952	Released time religious instruction provided at places other than public school buildings is constitutional.
	Wisconsin v. *Yoder*	1972	Requiring Amish children to attend school beyond the eighth grade interfered with the religious practices of the Amish.
	Brandon v. *Board of Education*	1981	Upheld authority of local board to deny use of public high-school facility for before-school prayer meeting.
	Widmar v. *Vincent*	1981	Upheld right of college students to use public college buildings for religious meetings.
	Smith v. *Board of Commissioners*	1986	Secular humanism constitutes a religion and was being established in public schools through neglect of fair treatment of religion in public school textbooks.
	Pierce v. *Society of Sisters*	1925	State compulsory school attendance law can be satisfied through attendance at a private school.
	Everson v. *Board of Education*	1947	States may provide transportation to and from school for private school students.
	Cochran v. *Louisiana State Board of Education*	1930	Courts upheld the constitutionality of providing textbooks at public expense to students in private schools.
	Lemon v. *Kurtzman*	1971	States cannot directly aid non-public schools by paying the salaries of teachers in these schools.
	Wolman v. *Walter*	1977	Defined permissible and nonpermissible kinds of services that the state could provide non-public schools.

Summary

Many factors make church-state relations in education an important issue for policy debate and formulation. Colonial traditions, characterized by close ties between church and state, established precedents in church-state relations that were difficult to change. The gradual establishment of public school systems that served a religiously diverse population was accompanied with persistent questions about the place of religion in these school systems.

In a society that values education to the degree that the state can make it compulsory, questions inevitably arise about the degree of authority that parents should have to control both the place and content of their children's education. Whether the state should tolerate alternatives to the public schools and whether these alternatives should be regulated and controlled by the state have and will continue to be pressing policy problems in church-state relations in education.

Table 13.1 summarizes the court cases that relate to the church-state issues discussed in this chapter.

Key Words

Establishment clause	Open Access Act
Free exercise clause	Scopes trial
Teaching about religion	Secular humanism
Silent meditation	Child benefit theory
Released time arrangements	Tax-exempt status
Religious proselytization	

Discussion Questions

1. Should private schools be funded by public tax funds? Why?
2. Should states regulate home schooling and private schooling? Why?
3. Would you favor establishing a period of silent meditation at the beginning of the school day in all public schools?
4. Would you favor allowing such organizations as the Fellowship of Christian Athletes to use public school facilities as a meeting place? Why?
5. Do you believe that public schools are promoting secular humanism in ways that violate the establishment clause of the First Amendment? Why?

For Further Reading

Burress, Lee, and Jenkinson, Edward. *The Student's Right to Know.* Champaign, Ill.: National Council of Teachers of English, 1983.

Carper, James C., and Hunt, Thomas C., eds. *Religious Schooling in America.* Birmingham, Ala: Religious Education Press, 1984.

Duncan, Homer. *Secular Humanism: The Most Dangerous Religion in America.* Lubbock, Texas: Missionary Crusader, 1979.

Elam, Stanley, ed. *Public Schools and the First Amendment.* Bloomington, Ind.: Phi Delta Kappa, 1983.

Jenkinson, Edward B. *The Schoolbook Protest Movement.* Bloomington, Ind.: Phi Delta Kappa, 1986.

La Morte, Michael W. *School Law: Cases and Concepts.* Englewood Cliffs, N.J.: Prentice-Hall, 1982.

McCarthy, Martha M. *A Delicate Balance: Church, State, and the Schools.* Bloomington, Ind.: Phi Delta Kappa, 1983.

Pfiffer, Leo. *Religion, State, and the Burger Court.* Buffalo, N.Y.: Prometheus Books, 1984.

Reutter, Edmond, Jr. *The Supreme Court's Impact on Public Education.* Bloomington, Ind.: Phi Delta Kappa and NOLPE, 1982.

Notes

1. See *Permoli* v. *First Municipality of New Orleans,* 44, U.S. 589, 609 (1845).

2. Gallup Poll, *Religion in America* (Princeton, N.J.: Gallup International, 1976).

3. See M. Marty, S. Rosenberg, and A. Greely, *What Do We Believe? The Stance of Religion in America* (New York: Meredith Press, 1968).

4. J. Watson, *Religion in American Society: The Effective Presence* (Englewood Cliffs, N.J.: Prentice-Hall, 1978), p. 278.

5. Richard M. Johnson, *The Dynamics of Compliance* (Evanston, Ill.: Northwestern University Press, 1967), pp. 8–24.

6. *School District of Abington Township* v. *Schempp,* 374 U.S. 203, 225 (1963).

7. *Ibid,* p. 300.

8. *Jaffre* v. *Board of Commissioners of Mobile City,* 554 F Supp. 1104 (S.D. Ala. 1983).

9. *Collins* v. *Chandler Unified School District,* 470 F Supp. 959, 964 (D. Ariz., 1979).

10. *La Rocca* v. *Board of Education,* 406 N.Y. 2d 348 (App. Div., 1978).

11. *Fink* v. *Board of Education,* 442 A 2d 837 (Pa. Commw., 1982).

12. *Tudor* v. *Board of Education,* 100 A 2d 857 (N.J., 1953).

13. *Stone* v. *Graham,* 449 U.S. 39 (1980).

14. *Spence* v. *Bailey,* 465 F 2d 797 (6th Cir, 1972).

15. *Sapp* v. *Renfroe,* 372 F Supp. 1193 (N.D. Ga., 1974).

16. *McLean* v. *Arkansas Board of Education,* 529 F Supp. 1255, 1264 (E.D., Ark., 1982).

17. Tim La Haye, *The Battle for the Public Schools* (Old Tyson, N.J.: Fleming Revel, 1983), p. 13.

18. *McCollum* v. *Board of Education,* 333 U.S. 203 (1948).

19. *Prince* v. *Massachusetts,* 321 U.S. 166 (1944).

20. Donald A. Erickson, *Public Control of Non-Public Schools* (Chicago: University of Chicago Press, 1969), pp. 103–134.

21. *Bob Jones University* v. *United States, Goldsborough Christian Schools* v. *United States,* 51 U. S. L. W. 4593 (May 24, 1983).

14 Policy Issues in Funding Public Schools

"School finance is a complex, complicated subject, entangled in governmental, organizational and legal technicalities that most of our citizens are likely to find baffling. . . . From district to district and state to state, the record shows that the present system of raising and allocating funds for the schools adds up to a rigged lottery that cheats students and taxpayers alike. The need for reform in school financing is crucial and urgent."

Sidney Marland, former U.S. Commissioner of Education (1971)

"It is so easy to vote millions for ABM's and SST's and then to reject money for the ABC's."

Mike Mansfield, former U.S. Senator from Montana (1970)

"Investment in education is an investment in the long term health of our economy and our society. Education has made the American dream a reality for millions. Now is not the time to question that investment. . . . This country will not be served by drastically cutting student financial aid and limiting opportunity for the hard-pressed middle- and lower-income students."

Thomas P. O'Neil, Jr. (1981)

Funding of public school programs involves a broad range of complex issues that must be dealt with by different levels of government in the United States. How much money should be spent on the education of youth? What kind of taxes should be used to raise revenue for the operation of public schools? Which level of government should have primary respon-

---

Policy Model 14.1   School Funding Policy

POLICY ISSUES	PARTICIPANTS IN POLICY DEVELOPMENT	ILLUSTRATIONS OF POLICY SOLUTIONS	EFFECTS OF POLICY SOLUTIONS
How much money should be spent to educate children and youth? What kind of taxes should be used to fund schools? Which level of government should contribute funds to educate children and youth? Should school funds be equalized among/within states?	**Formal** U.S. Congress Federal court system State legislatures State court systems Administrative bodies **Informal** Political systems	Federal statutes Federal court rulings State statutes	**Allocative** Who gets what? **Regulative** Who will do what? **Structural** Additions, deletions to structures involved in policy implementation **Redistributive** Additions, deletions, changes in allocation of resources or authority

sibility for funding education? How should other levels of government share in the responsibility to pay for the education of citizens in the United States? Should efforts be made to equalize the amount of resources devoted to the education of youth in the United States? How should states allocate financial resources to the different administrative units to operate the schools? What kind of changes should be made in school finance policy to bring the schools into line with recent court interpretations of constitutional principles?

This chapter explores the solutions to the preceding problems as they have been addressed by federal, state, and local governments. Policy model 14.1 illustrates the basic school finance questions, policy participants involved in dealing with the finance issues, and the types and effects of the policies adopted to deal with school finance problems.

Funding any public enterprise involves the allocation and utilization of human and material resources to solve public problems. The decisions made about which government program gets what kind of resources are related to perceptions that public decision makers have about the relative contributions that these programs will make to the public good.

Funding public institutions inevitably confronts the reality of scarcity of resources. There are not enough resources to allocate to all government programs the total amount of resources requested by the managers of the governmental agencies. Consequently, budgetary policymaking becomes a value-laden enterprise. Decisions have to be made about which allocations will have the greatest impact on accomplishing public good.

Our society has tended to believe that investments in public educational institutions could address many pressing social problems. Consequently, allocations in education have typically consumed major portions of state and local government budgets. This has occurred in spite of the fact that there has never been a continuing, clear definition of problems to be dealt with by public schooling institutions and the fact that these institutions recurringly compete with other public agencies for resources.

What are some of the fundamental arguments for making relatively large investments in public schooling? Some argue that schools can be an effective, conservative force in society, preserving developments in skills, language, art, music, knowledge, and other cultural expressions. Others justify large allocations of resources to public schools on the basis that the schools are the best agencies to accommodate or foster change that is inevitable in a modern democratic society. The founders of our common school system argued for investments in education so that enlightenment rather than ignorance could guide the political process. Schools could also be used to transmit common political and economic values necessary for the survival of the political system.

Arguments have also been made that schools are a good place to teach the fundamental skills necessary to function in our economic system. In fact, human capital formation has become recognized by some economists as one of the best investments that a society can make for long-term economic growth. Theodore Shultz, Charles Benson, and other economists have documented the relationship between economic growth and educational opportunity.[1] Evidence is gathered to indicate how individual earning increases as a result of schooling. It is noted that society is repaid by the increased tax revenue on these additional earnings of the individual.

Increases in productivity and improvements in technology result from higher skill development. This leads to cheaper products and higher rates of consumption. Increased consumption produces even more jobs and higher rates of employment and eventually a higher standard of living. Higher standards of living make possible greater accessability to more education and additional, recurring social benefits.

Arguments are also made that investments in education reduce other types of welfare costs. People who have adequate opportunities for schooling are more likely to be productively employed and thus less likely to need welfare aid or the rehabilitative services of prisons or similar institutions.

Of course, not all politicians and economists accept the above arguments for investments in education. Segments of the general population doubt the above "faith" in education. The skeptics point to evidence of variations in the benefits of education in our society based on race, ethnicity, or sex. Questions are raised about the real economic returns from the rapidly rising costs of operating public schools. For example, after adjusting for inflation, per-pupil expenditures increased by twenty-five percent between 1970–71 and 1980–81, while public elementary and secondary school enrollment declined from 40.2 million in 1977–78 to 36.7 million in 1982–83. Total school revenue grew by approximately forty-seven percent between 1979 and 1984. The increases in per-pupil expenditures from 1949–50 through 1985–86 are portrayed in Figure 14.1. In spite of budget increases, local school officials have claimed that the schools they manage

Figure 14.1
Trends in Current
Expenditures per Pupil

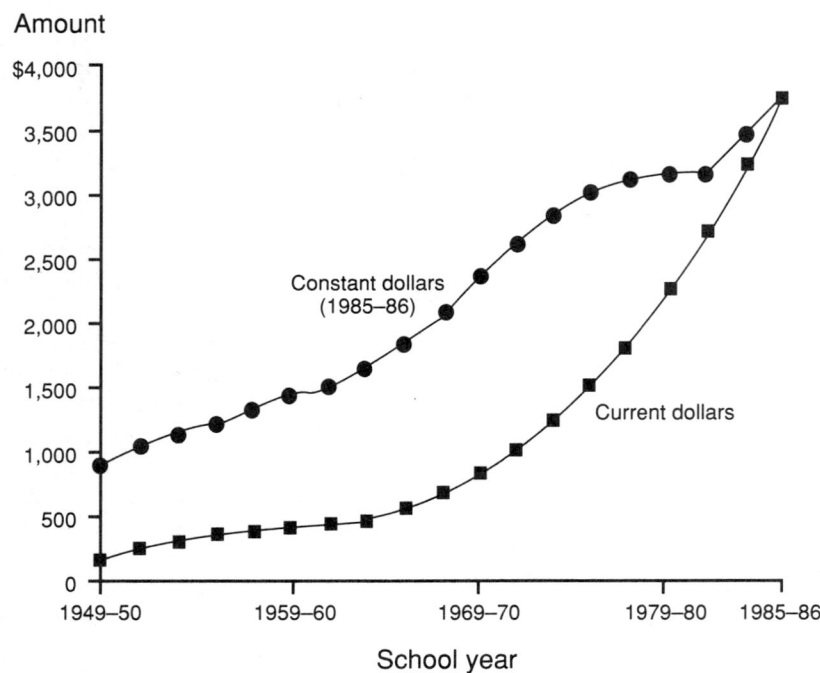

Between the 1949–50 and 1985–86 school years, current expenditures per pupil in constant dollars more than tripled, from $960 to $3,705 per pupil.

Between 1977–78 and 1981–82, current expenditures per pupil in constant dollars remained relatively unchanged but then began rising steadily.

SOURCE: Center for Education Statistics, *Statistics of State School Systems, Revenues and Expenditures for Public Elementary and Secondary Education.* "Common Core of Data" survey, and unpublished tabulations.

have been facing serious budget problems. Increasing staff salaries, rising costs of energy, and the impact of inflation kept officials worried about being able to balance their school budgets.[2]

The debate will continue on how much should be invested in public elementary and secondary education in the United States. Changing demographic factors, economic conditions, and emerging social issues and trends will continue to influence the debate.

Tax Programs to Fund Schools

An important function of different levels of government in the United States is to provide for services that cannot or will not be provided by private enterprise or to provide services that can be better provided by government. Since the argument is generally accepted that many social and economic problems can be addressed through schooling, providing free public education becomes an important government service. Approximately ninety percent of the children attending elementary and secondary schools in the United States are enrolled in public schools, thereby making public education a very large and important government activity. If governments have justified their role in providing schooling, the next fundamental question is related to the methodology of raising revenues to fund public schools.

Governments use taxation policy to achieve different goals. Tax policy can be used to raise revenue, to support government services, to redistribute wealth, or to regulate and promote general welfare. Governments use taxation for schools to achieve some, if not all, of these objectives.

To minimize resistance to taxation, which inevitably involves some type of transfer of resources from the private sector to the state, governments must address certain fundamental questions related to tax policies:

What kind of taxes will be used?

How will different groups in the population be affected by the tax policy?

How will the power to tax be allocated among different levels of government?

Who will collect and allocate the revenue generated through taxation?

Who will be accountable for administering tax revenue to ensure that public interests will be served?

To sustain public support for tax systems, tax policy must maintain certain desirable features. It is difficult for any taxing unit—local, state, or federal—to develop a tax system that engenders universal acceptance by all taxpaying clientele. Yet, certain basic characteristics of tax policy must be maintained.

1. Tax policy should be equitable; that is, it should deal fairly and justly with different groups in the population. For a tax policy to be equitable, it must be related to the ability to pay on the part of the taxpayers. Taxes fall into two categories based on this principle. A regressive tax results in people with lower incomes paying disproportionately more of their income in taxes than do higher income groups. A progressive tax increases the tax obligation as the ability to pay taxes increases.

2. Tax policy should be direct, avoiding hidden taxes. It should be predictable so that the subjects of taxation can know what to expect.

3. Tax policy should possess the quality of economy. Overtaxation may lead to tax evasion or excesses by government. On the other hand, undertaxation may lead to dissatisfaction with the quantity or quality of services delivered or failure to achieve the goals and objectives of government.

4. Tax policy should produce stable and predictable revenues. Stability of revenue is especially important in operating massive public enterprises such as a public school system. Ease and economy in the collecting, allocating, and accounting for tax revenues should also be considered in developing a sound tax policy.

It is important that tax systems among the three levels of government be coordinated and that efforts be made to eliminate excessive duplication in the tax structure. Good tax systems among the different levels of government will have low collection and administrative costs to optimize the amount of dollars available to be spent on public services.

Table 14.1 Percentage of Revenue Receipts for Schools		1975	1978	1980	1982	1984
	Federal	8.1	8.8	9.2	7.4	6.6
	State	43.6	44.3	49.1	48.2	48.7
	Local	48.4	46.9	41.7	44.3	44.7

SOURCE: *Statistical Abstract of the United States* (Washington, D.C.: U.S. Department of Commerce and Bureau of Census, 105 ed., 1985), p. 137.

Which Level of Government Is Responsible for Funding Schools?

Funding public education has involved all three levels of government—local, state, and federal (see Table 14.1). Traditionally, local districts have raised the majority of revenues to support schools. States have gradually—sometimes reluctantly—assumed more important but varying degrees of responsibility for financing education. The participation by the federal government has fluctuated through the years, but for the most part, it has maintained a minor role in providing tax dollars to support schools. National trends in revenue sources over a longer period of time are illustrated in Table 14.2.

In reality the responsibility assumed by different levels of government for funding education was made before the United States had experienced the social, political, and economic benefits of a public school system that served a large percentage of citizens of school age. Policy Model 14.2 focuses on the policy issue of which level of government is responsible for funding schools. The model depicts the parties involved in finding a solution, the kinds of solutions that have evolved, and the outcomes of those solutions.

Table 14.2

Sources of Public School Revenue Receipts and Percentage Spent on Public Elementary and Secondary Schools

	1929–30	1939–40	1949–50	1959–60	1969–70	1979–80	1982–83
Total revenue receipts (in billions)	$ 2.09	$ 2.26	$ 5.44	$ 14.75	$ 40.27	$ 96.9	$116.9
Percent of revenue from:							
Federal government	0.4 %	1.8 %	2.9 %	4.4 %	8.0 %	9.8%	7.1
State governments	16.9	30.3	39.8	39.1	39.9	46.8	48.3
Local sources	82.7	68.0	57.3	56.5	52.1	43.4	44.6
Total %	100.0	100.1 %	100.0 %	100.0 %	100.0 %	100.0%	100.0%
Total expenditures for all public schools (in billions)	$ 2.32	$ 2.34	$ 5.84	$ 15.61	$ 40.68	$ 96.0	$119.1
Percentage of total expenditures for elementary and secondary school current expenditures	79.6 %	82.8 %	80.3 %	70.0 %	84.1 %	90.6%	90.8%

Source: Department of Education, National Center for Education Statistics, *Digest of Education Statistics* (Washington, D.C.: U.S. Government Printing Office, 1980, 1981, 1982, 1983).

Policy Model 14.2	Level of Government Responsible for Funding Schools		
POLICY ISSUE	**PARTICIPANTS INVOLVED IN POLICY DEVELOPMENT**	**ILLUSTRATIONS OF POLICY SOLUTIONS**	**EFFECTS OF POLICY SOLUTIONS**
Which level of government is responsible for funding schools?	**Formal** U.S. Congress	Federal categorical aid legislation Federal blocks grants	**Regulative** Who will do what to get funds? **Allocative** Who will get what?
	Federal courts	*San Antonio* v. *Rodriquez*	**Redistributive** State legislatures and state courts are responsible for bringing school finance plans into compliance with state constitutional requirements.
	U.S. Department of Education	Administrative regulations	**Allocative** Set guidelines for distribution and allocation of funds.
	State legislatures	School finance reform legislation	**Allocative** Who will get what? **Regulative** What local districts must do to get what?
	State courts	*Serrano* v. *Priest* *Robinson* v. *Cahill*	**Regulative** What local districts must do to get what?
	State education administrative agencies	Administrative rules and regulations	**Regulative** Set guidelines for distribution/ administration of funds.
	Informal Local taxpayer groups	Initiatives to limit property taxation	**Allocative** Who will get what? **Regulative** Set guidelines for collection/administration of local property taxes.

Table 14.3 Percentage Distribution of Local Government Tax Collection By Type of Tax During Selected Years	YEAR	PROPERTY TAX	SALES TAX	INCOME TAX	ALL OTHER TAXES
	1940	92.7	1.2	0.4	5.7
	1952	87.5	3.9	0.9	8.7
	1960	87.4	4.8	1.4	6.4
	1972	83.7	5.5	4.5	6.3
	1982	76.0	9.9	5.9	8.2
	1984	75.0	9.7	5.6	9.7

Financing Schools at the Local Level

Even though all states assume responsibility for maintaining schools as a result of state constitutional mandates, the actual operation and funding of schools has been delegated with varying degrees among the states to local districts. Although there has been a trend in recent years to shift more of the financial burden to the state, local districts in most states still contribute a crucial portion of the resources used to fund schools.

As indicated in Table 14.3, the property tax has been the mainstay of revenue for schools at the local level.[3] In most states, both personal and real property may be taxed. Taxes on real property provide the largest percentage of property tax revenue for schools.

The property tax has a tradition dating back to the colonial period. In spite of the fact that it has generated the bulk of revenue for schools, the property tax has frequently been under criticism. Since people are now inclined to invest surplus earnings in investments that escape property taxes, property taxes are not the fair measure of taxpaying ability that they once were. Surveys in the early 1970s revealed that the property tax was considered to be the least fair of all the different taxes used by local, state, and federal governments. Some of the reasons given for the unpopularity of the property tax were as follows:

Property taxes had risen at an uncontrolled pace.

Property taxes had to be paid directly in large sums.

Property taxes gathered a higher fraction of the income of the poor than of the rich, making it a regressive tax.

The property tax base was unevenly distributed among taxing jurisdictions in a state.

The property tax was inelastic—the assessed value of property grew slower than the economy.

The property tax was the only major tax that the electorate voted on directly, making it the scapegoat for negative sentiment regarding other taxes.[4]

Assessment—the practice of assigning a base of value for tax purposes—varies widely among the states. Some states assess property at more than sixty percent of market value, while many states assess it at less than twenty percent. Because of these different assessment practices among and within states, people with equal value property are treated differently in the tax system. Furthermore, since reassessment of property values may occur infrequently, the property tax is not very responsive to rapidly changing economic conditions. Consequently, tax revenues may not keep up with inflation, and actual tax rates may be based on unrealistic market conditions.

Compared with the cost of administering other taxes, the administrative cost of the property tax is high. The process of assessing property for tax collection and policing the collection of property taxes takes a relatively large bite out of revenues generated. The efficiency and clout of tax collection agencies to deal with the various political entities involved in property taxation vary widely across the states.

Another serious defect of the property tax relates to the great disparities of wealth that exist among tax districts. Some districts within a state are much more heavily populated or industrialized than other districts and consequently have a much greater basis of wealth to tax. This results in great differences in ability to support schools among districts within a state.

Cities are faced with demands to provide other services that are also financed by property taxation. This creates competition between government services for limited property tax dollars. School districts in cities have difficulty devoting as large a percentage of property tax revenues to the schools as do districts in rural areas. Cities in some geographic regions are also faced with diminishing tax bases resulting from the migration of industry to the Western and Sunbelt regions of the country.

Cities typically have a disproportionate share of students who come from disadvantaged or low-income groups. These students are more likely to need educational services that are more costly to deliver than programs typically provided to students in other school districts.

Sources of School Revenue Among the States

As noted earlier, states have constitutionally obligated themselves to have primary responsibility for and jurisdiction over public schools. Even though much of this responsibility has been delegated to local districts, states still have very important duties in raising revenues to support public schools. Although citizens have generally tended to favor state financial support for schools, they have maintained the desirability of keeping local control of schools. States have sought ways to achieve certain objectives through state aid to schools that fit into this rationale. These objectives have included the following:

Supporting a program of basic education in every district.

Using state funds to help equalize educational opportunity.

Eliminating place of residence as the primary determinant of dollars available for supporting schools.

Providing incentives for greater local support.

Broadening the tax base for support of schooling.

Stimulating special service programs or providing categorical assistance for transportation, school buildings, etc.

The sources of revenue for school support vary from state to state. Characteristically, states use three categories of taxes for general revenue: (1) income taxes, (2) consumption or sales taxes, and (3) privilege or license taxes (taxes levied on privileges for engaging in some sort of conduct, such as driving a car or operating a business). Table 14.4 summarizes state tax revenues from different types of taxes.[5]

Table 14.4 Percentage of Revenue By Type of Tax Among States	YEAR	PROPERTY TAX	SALES TAX	INCOME TAX	ALL OTHER TAXES
	1957	3.3	58.1	17.5	21.1
	1967	2.7	58.2	22.4	16.8
	1977	2.2	51.8	34.3	11.7
	1981	2.0	48.6	36.8	12.6
	1984 (est)	2.5	48.2	38.1	11.2

Certain trends in revenue collection stand out in the data in Table 14.4. Revenue from individual and corporate income taxes has significantly increased. Sales tax revenues and revenues from other sources have declined. These trends are interesting in light of the fact that the sales tax has historically been used by states as the main source of revenue for schools.

In the late 1970s and the early 1980s, the state's share of general school revenue increased to approximately fifty percent of total tax collections allocated to operate the schools. The state's share of revenue declined slightly in the mid 1980s, so that by 1984, states contributed 45.4 percent of the operating costs of public schools.

The sales tax and personal income tax are the two major sources of revenue states use to fund public schools. As of 1984, forty-two states had some type of sales tax that imposed a levy of 3 to 7.5 percent on the sale value of certain goods and services. Proponents of the sales tax argue that the tax meets many criteria for a good revenue resource. The tax is easy to administer and collect, convenient to pay, and relatively stable and provides an immediate flow of revenue. Its major disadvantage is that it is regressive if it is levied on basic living essentials such as food, clothing, and medicine. Low-income groups spend proportionately more of their income for these items. As of 1984, twenty-nine states exempted food, forty-three states exempted prescription drugs, and five states exempted clothing from sales taxes.[6]

As Table 14.4 indicates, states increased the percentage of their total revenue from income tax between 1957 and 1984 from 17.5 percent to 38.1 percent. The income tax has become the second largest revenue source for states. The income tax is usually considered to be a progressive tax, although loopholes exempting some sources of income from taxation and taxing some types of income at different rates add a degree of inequity to this source of taxation. Also, some states have a flat rate of taxation for the income tax that tends to make the tax regressive. The income tax is easy to collect and can be more easily adjusted to reflect economic conditions.

A number of states have established lotteries in recent years. Some states have earmarked the revenues from these state-run lotteries for support of public education. As of 1983, seventeen states had state-run lotteries that raised from 0.3 percent to 4.9 percent of total collected revenues in the respective state.[7]

Variations in Ability and Efforts Among States to Fund Schools

As with local school districts, not all states have the same potential tax resources to fund public schools. Measuring the relative ability of a state to fund public schools is a difficult task. States have different population characteristics, natural resources, levels of industrialization, and employment opportunities. When compared with local districts, however, states have more types of taxes available to gather revenue for schools.

One of the most common methods currently used to compare the relative financial ability of states to support education compares per pupil expenditures and per capita income indexed to the national average. For example, Table 14.5 shows that Alaska's per capita expenditure for all state and local government functions is about four times that of the national average. Per capita expenditures in Alaska for elementary and secondary education are about three times that of the national average. At the other extreme, Mississippi's per capita expenditure for elementary and secondary education is about eighty percent of the national average.

Per capita income is a good indicator of a state's wealth. Since different states spend different portions of that per capita income on education, there are obviously different priorities among the states when it comes to funding public schools. Even accounting for differences in the purchasing power of a dollar among the fifty states, it is apparent that wide variations exist among the states in the amount of resources devoted to public schooling.

Federal Sources of Revenue for Schools

Historically, the federal government has assumed a rather minor fiscal responsibility for public schools. As noted earlier in the chapter, the total percentage of school operational costs obtained from the federal government fluctuates over time. It should be noted that federal contributions in 1984 were significantly below what they were in 1980.

The Tenth Amendment to the U.S. Constitution has been interpreted as a kind of legal sanction for the states to assume the dominant responsibility for funding public schools. The framers of the Constitution may have had some fears of a nationally controlled, centralized system of schooling. Until the 1950s, the federal government had a policy of deference to the states in matters relating to funding schools. The 1960s and 1970s were characterized by an increased interest in federal financial support for public education. The 1980s can be described as an era of retrenchment on the part of the federal government regarding financial support for public schools. What kinds of arguments have been made to justify federal support for education?

The federal government has a constitutional mandate to provide for national security and promote general welfare. Many politicians believe that national welfare is served by providing minimum levels of support for the schooling of children and adolescents. It is widely held that the social benefits of education are not confined to state borders. Schooling serves national interests and should be supported by the federal government. Our defense interests are served by developing human capital to the greatest extent possible. Human capital development fosters scientific and technological development which in turn facilitates a more secure defense system.

The equity question has also been raised in the debate over federal funding. The role of the federal government, in promoting principles of equal treatment, justifies the government's involvement in reducing interstate and intrastate disparities in educational funding. The argument has been made that the federal government has a more progressive income tax revenue system when compared to the more regressive sales and property tax revenue systems used by the states.

Why has there been a retrenchment in federal funding of schools in the 1980s? The Reagan administration's federal agenda followed a more strict constructionist interpretation of the Constitution's Tenth Amendment,

Table 14.5	Direct General Expenditures Per Capita of State and Local Governments for all Functions and for Education, By Level and State: 1983–84

EDUCATION EXPENDITURES

STATE	TOTAL DIRECT GENERAL EXPENDI-TURES PER CAPITA[1]	TOTAL		ELEMENTARY AND SECONDARY EDUCATION		HIGHER EDUCATION		OTHER EDUCATION[2]	
		Amount	As a percentage of all functions	Amount	As a percentage of all functions	Amount	As a percentage of all functions	Amount	As a percentage of all functions
1	2	3	4	5	6	7	8	9	10
United States	$2,131.13	$ 745.72	35.0	$ 511.93	24.0	$201.61	9.5	$32.18	1.5
Alabama	1,739.38	651.42	37.5	368.11	21.2	222.84	12.8	60.48	3.5
Alaska	8,729.32	2,309.44	26.5	1,673.23	19.2	568.61	6.5	67.60	0.8
Arizona	2,079.95	803.46	38.6	493.20	23.7	282.40	13.6	27.85	1.3
Arkansas	1,477.74	591.60	40.0	399.94	27.1	147.44	10.0	44.22	3.0
California	2,356.96	759.12	32.2	491.92	20.9	245.14	10.4	22.06	0.9
Colorado	2,204.44	841.46	38.2	565.89	25.7	255.31	11.6	20.27	0.9
Connecticut	2,156.39	685.08	31.8	517.06	24.0	130.19	6.0	37.83	1.8
Delaware	2,471.75	951.57	38.5	549.29	22.2	335.28	13.6	67.00	2.7
District of Columbia	3,891.24	743.05	19.1	618.70	15.9	124.35	3.2	—	—
Florida	1,802.98	616.72	34.2	444.42	24.6	140.24	7.8	32.06	1.8
Georgia	1,825.81	612.76	33.6	412.87	22.6	172.00	9.4	27.89	1.5
Hawaii	2,428.89	681.36	28.1	399.89	16.5	270.97	11.2	10.50	0.4
Idaho	1,709.37	636.17	37.2	403.84	23.6	211.45	12.4	20.89	1.2
Illinois	2,030.14	681.92	33.6	472.90	23.3	177.88	8.8	31.14	1.5
Indiana	1,718.59	706.11	41.1	460.56	26.8	210.07	12.2	35.48	2.1
Iowa	2,143.59	843.92	39.4	522.35	24.4	290.25	13.5	31.32	1.5
Kansas	2,079.53	814.71	39.2	534.31	25.7	264.29	12.7	16.11	0.8
Kentucky	1,717.02	608.72	35.5	371.59	21.6	187.32	10.9	49.81	2.9
Louisiana	2,239.22	715.05	31.9	456.31	20.4	214.48	9.6	44.26	2.0
Maine	1,945.91	670.00	34.4	465.54	23.9	168.00	8.6	36.47	1.9
Maryland	2,298.08	811.02	35.3	533.66	23.2	217.14	9.4	60.22	2.6
Massachusetts	2,233.06	645.57	28.9	497.33	22.3	111.34	5.0	36.90	1.7
Michigan	2,387.92	857.03	35.9	591.81	24.8	240.23	10.1	24.99	1.0
Minnesota	2,611.01	893.10	34.2	608.35	23.3	245.44	9.4	39.32	1.5
Mississippi	1,686.57	593.27	35.2	361.91	21.5	198.86	11.8	32.50	1.9
Missouri	1,621.89	602.29	37.1	435.00	26.8	148.32	9.1	18.97	1.2
Montana	2,376.42	915.71	38.5	667.17	28.1	202.84	8.5	45.70	1.9
Nebraska	2,056.30	814.38	39.6	552.19	26.9	237.91	11.6	24.28	1.2
Nevada	2,394.23	609.75	25.5	439.52	18.4	151.93	6.3	18.29	0.8
New Hampshire	1,728.88	596.69	34.5	431.22	24.9	147.84	8.6	17.63	1.0
New Jersey	2,290.13	777.47	33.9	608.15	26.6	145.64	6.4	23.68	1.0
New Mexico	2,465.02	939.08	38.1	626.83	25.4	287.55	11.7	24.69	1.0
New York	3,037.01	884.78	29.1	670.33	22.1	166.04	5.5	48.42	1.6
North Carolina	1,602.38	681.66	42.5	420.84	26.3	229.06	14.3	31.77	2.0
North Dakota	2,464.52	928.75	37.7	559.18	22.7	330.06	13.4	39.51	1.6
Ohio	1,970.94	713.82	36.2	513.26	26.0	184.50	9.4	16.06	0.8
Oklahoma	1,930.63	766.61	39.7	517.33	26.8	219.89	11.4	29.38	1.5
Oregon	2,382.88	901.54	37.8	625.05	26.2	255.97	10.7	20.53	0.9
Pennsylvania	1,835.61	632.12	34.4	474.77	25.9	100.81	5.5	56.54	3.1
Rhode Island	2,355.19	748.57	31.8	487.83	20.7	185.91	7.9	74.83	3.2
South Carolina	1,569.16	641.38	40.9	411.55	26.2	195.60	12.5	34.24	2.2
South Dakota	1,995.05	703.44	35.3	495.03	24.8	184.99	9.3	23.42	1.2
Tennessee	1,590.95	540.44	34.0	342.64	21.5	157.20	9.9	40.60	2.6

Table 14.5   Continued

EDUCATION EXPENDITURES

STATE	TOTAL DIRECT GENERAL EXPENDITURES PER CAPITA[1]	TOTAL		ELEMENTARY AND SECONDARY EDUCATION		HIGHER EDUCATION		OTHER EDUCATION[2]	
		Amount	As a percentage of all functions	Amount	As a percentage of all functions	Amount	As a percentage of all functions	Amount	As a percentage of all functions
1	2	3	4	5	6	7	8	9	10
Texas	1,860.96	796.68	42.8	549.07	29.5	235.10	12.6	12.51	0.7
Utah	2,047.63	865.33	42.3	540.79	26.4	292.37	14.3	32.17	1.6
Vermont	2,220.95	842.58	37.9	508.18	22.9	275.98	12.4	58.42	2.6
Virginia	1,805.81	733.03	40.6	493.13	27.3	208.37	11.5	31.54	1.7
Washington	2,273.96	836.31	36.8	549.95	24.2	252.07	11.1	34.30	1.5
West Virginia	1,815.10	697.96	38.5	494.03	27.2	165.91	9.1	38.02	2.1
Wisconsin	2,363.25	903.29	38.2	573.29	24.3	299.37	12.7	30.63	1.3
Wyoming	3,903.81	1,526.38	39.1	1,104.02	28.3	389.85	10.0	32.51	0.8

[1]Includes state and local government expenditures for education services, social services and income maintenance, transportation, public safety, environment and housing, governmental administration, interest on general debt, and other general expenditures.
[2]Includes state education administration and services, tuition grants, fellowships, aid to private schools, and special programs.
—Data not applicable or not available.

Note: Because of rounding, details may not add to totals.

Source: U.S. Department of Commerce, Bureau of the Census, *Governmental Finances in 1983–84* (table prepared April 1986).

which leaves the function of education to the states. As a function of the state, it is argued, education should be funded at that level. The role of the federal government in education should revert to that of disseminating information and providing assistance to state and local governments.

Brief History of Federal Financial Support for Public Education

Many different departments of the federal government have directly or indirectly appropriated resources to public schooling. Since it is difficult to accurately classify a historical record of all federal funds for public schools, a more general description of types of federal funds for public education is presented in the following sections.

Early Land Grants   Even before the U.S. Constitution was adopted, the Land Ordinance of 1785 included a provision stating that "there shall be reserved the lot number 16 of every township for the maintenance of public schools in each township." The Northwest Ordinance of 1787 also expressed federal interest in education by stating that "religion, morality, and knowledge being necessary to good government and the happiness of mankind, schools and the means of education shall forever be encouraged." Thirty-nine states received land grants for the support of schools from these ordinances. There were varying degrees of accountability for efficient use of these lands to support education among the states that received the grants.

In 1862, Congress, through the first Morrill Act, provided for a grant of 30,000 acres of federally owned land to each state with the provision that income from the sale or rental of these lands be used to establish colleges that would facilitate the study of agriculture, military science, and the mechanical arts. The land grant college, or people's college, as it was called, was the forerunner of many contemporary state universities.

Early Money Grants   Between 1862 and 1917, the federal government confined its primary interest in educational support to institutions of higher education. In 1917, through the Smith-Hughes Act, Congress provided funds to support the study of vocational education, home economics, and agricultural subjects in secondary schools. This legislation marked the first time that the federal government provided annual appropriations for public secondary education. The George-Reed Act of 1929, George-Dean Act of 1937, George-Bearden Act of 1946, and Vocational Education Act of 1963 have supplemented and broadened the original Smith-Hughes Act.

Federal Relief Measures During the Great Depression   Federal interest in education during the Great Depression was incidental to other federal concerns for the high unemployment and general economic displacement suffered during this era. The following are examples of relief measures that gave direct or indirect financial aid to education:

1.   The Civilian Conservation Corps (CCC) was established in 1933 and provided for the vocational training of millions of youth before it was abandoned in 1943. The Job Corps of the 1960s was modeled after the CCC.

2.   The National Youth Administration (NYA) also provided welfare and training programs for unemployed youth as well as financial aid for needy students attending secondary school or college.

3.   The Public Works Administration (PWA) and Works Progress Administration (WPA) provided significant amounts of money for school plant construction and repair. These programs were terminated in 1940.

Educational Aid to Veterans and World War II Education Acts   The Lanham Act of 1941 provided for the construction, maintenance, and operation of educational facilities where defense activities created unusual burdens on local governments. The GI Bill, or Serviceman's Readjustment Act of 1944, provided for the education of veterans and enabled thousands of them to complete college degrees or special training programs. These programs have been amended and extended to aid veterans who have served in the military since World War II.

Aid to School Lunch Programs   In 1935, the newly formed Federal Surplus Commodities Corporation administered the distribution of surplus agricultural commodities to schools for lunch programs. In 1946, the School Lunch Act was passed to "safeguard the health and well being of the nation's children and to encourage domestic consumption of nutritious agricultural commodities." This legislation has been amended to direct more federal funds to provide free lunches for children unable to pay for them.

Educational Funding to Support National Defense   A turning point in the relationship of the federal government to public education occurred

Photo 14.1
Providing food services for millions of students is a major enterprise for school districts in the United States.

in 1958. During the cold war, it was a popular belief that the Russian socialist system could not possibly produce scientific and technological development equivalent to that produced by the United States. The launching of Sputnik brought about shocking evidence that this was not the case. Beginning in 1958, Congress enacted a series of laws designed to encourage scientific and technological development and reduction in unemployment through personnel development and occupational training. Development of human capital came to be viewed as an important security measure. The following laws expressed this concern:

1. The National Defense Education Act of 1958 authorized expenditures of substantial sums for improvement of instruction in science, mathematics, and foreign language.

2. The Manpower Development and Training Act of 1962 was designed to reduce hard-core unemployment by retraining workers whose skills had become obsolete.

3. The Vocational Education Act of 1963 broadened the purpose of the original Smith-Hughes Act to provide occupational training for persons of all ages in any occupational field not requiring a baccalaureate.

Funding Programs to Encourage Equal Educational Opportunity
The 1964 Civil Rights Act provided for the withholding of federal support from school districts practicing racial or religious segregation. The Elementary and Secondary Education Act of 1965 provided federal support for educational programs and materials for children of low-income families. The 1965 Act was divided into different titles and encouraged categorical support of a diversity of activities ranging from compensatory education

Photo 14.2
Handicapped children require individualized learning programs.

and development of school library programs and teacher corps to the initiation of preschool programs for children from low-income families.

The Higher Education Act of 1965 authorized loans and scholarships for students, expanded college construction programs, improved libraries, and provided assistance for improvement of undergraduate instruction. In 1973, Congress enacted a law establishing the National Institute of Education. This agency was charged to strengthen the scientific and technological foundation of education and to help build an effective research basis for educational program development. Public Law 94–142, passed in 1975, encouraged the initiation, expansion, and improvement of programs for the handicapped at the preschool, elementary, and secondary school levels.

Box 14.1
Federal Funding Priorities

A 1986 Louis Harris poll of public attitudes toward the problems of children suggested that three out of four adults in the United States think that the problems facing today's children are more severe than when they were growing up. The survey also indicated that adults were willing to pay higher taxes for better schools, drug treatment, and other services for the nation's children and youth.

Harold Howe, former U.S. Commissioner of Education, argued in a November 1986 *Phi Delta Kappan* article that children in the United States are losing ground. The interests of adults are taking center stage while the interests of children are being pushed into the wings. This has been brought about by demographic changes resulting in a greater proportion of voters who have no direct interest in schools, in child care, or in the health needs of children. Mr. Howe suggests that children have not had persons to champion their cause in Congress the way older citizens have had champions to protect Social Security and other programs.

Do you agree that our society is shortchanging children and youth? Since the federal government has contributed a smaller and smaller percentage of total operational costs for public schools in recent years, is this evidence that children and youth are losing ground in national priorities? Should the federal government increase its expenditures for public education to indicate a greater interest in the welfare of the nation's children and youth?

Photo 14.3
Teachers have been active and vocal in their attempts to improve teacher salaries and to prevent cutbacks in the number of teaching positions.

Allocation Systems: How Does the Money Get to the Schools?

The allocation of revenue collected for schools by different levels of government through diverse tax systems takes place in a variety of ways throughout the United States. Typically, budgets to operate the schools are developed and approved at the local level. Local government bodies such as county councils, county commissions, county boards of education, and city councils have varying relationships with local boards of education in the development and approval of school budgets. Some states and localities permit local school boards to have sole authority for the development and approval of school budgets. Most states prescribe forms and procedures that must be used in developing, approving, and administering the local school district budget.

The local school district budget expresses in dollars and cents who gets what in the school budget on an annual basis. There has been a considerable amount of standardization in classifying school budget items. Educational expenditures are usually grouped into capital outlay, debt service, and current operating expenses. Expenditures for capital outlay include expenses for land and equipment. Expenditures for debt service include payment of interest and principal on borrowed money. Current operating costs include such items as salaries for instructional, administrative, clerical, and maintenance staffs; instructional materials; and transportation. Figure 14.2 illustrates the typical percentage of a school budget that might go to these major categories of expenditures.

Figure 14.2
Typical Priorities in Local School Budgets

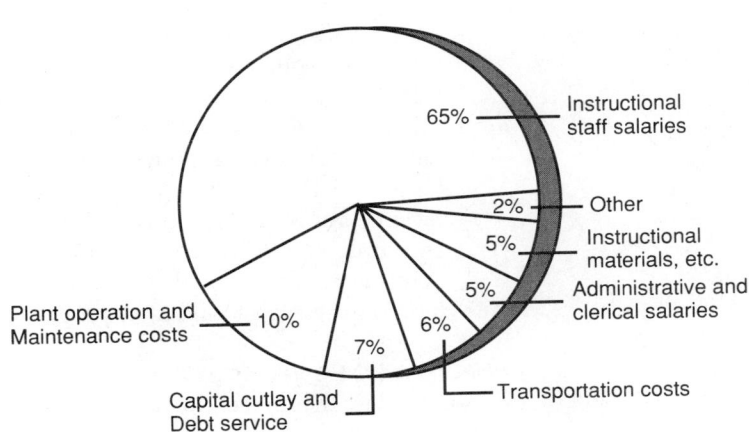

Although there are diverse plans among the states to provide aid for school building construction, local districts have primary responsibility for providing capital outlays involved in the construction and maintenance of school buildings. Local districts must follow state school building construction guidelines in such matters as site selection, architectural planning and specifications, advertising for construction bids, and issuance of bonds to finance construction.

Most school systems do not have the necessary amount of capital on hand to finance construction of school buildings. Consequently, they issue bonds that are repaid from the revenues collected from property taxes. Given the unpopularity of the property tax as a revenue resource in recent years, it has been increasingly difficult for school districts to finance new school building construction. Beginning in the 1960s and continuing into the 1980s, residents in local school districts have voted down an increasing percentage of bond referendums submitted to finance new construction and modernization of existing facilities.

Allocation of State Sources of School Aid

Revenues collected by states through different tax programs are allocated to school operations at the local district level in a variety of ways. Each state is responsible for determining how it allocates money to local districts. Generally, state allocation schemes can be classified into four different models: flat grants, foundation programs, equalization schemes, and categorical funding.

Flat Grants   States used flat grants extensively in their early efforts to aid local school districts. Flat grants usually were based on funds per pupil, funds per teacher, or some type of percentage grant. Flat grants contributed to the inequality of school funding, because rich districts within a state would get the same amount of money per unit as received by poor districts. Rich districts could add the state's flat grant to the revenue collected on their own tax base and have more resources available than poor districts. Also, flat grants did not take into account extra expenses incurred in educating special-needs students or special program costs associated with schooling in poor districts. No state currently depends exclusively on the flat grant model, largely because this approach does not promote equity in school funding.

Foundation Programs   Most states use some form of foundation program to guarantee that a minimum amount of per pupil aid, collected from both state and local sources, will be used to support a minimum school program in every locality within the state. In most states, each local district must put forth a minimum effort to finance its schools under the foundation program. This minimum tax, based on a district's ability to generate revenue, results in greater reliance upon local resources in wealthier districts and consequently on less state revenue. Poor districts would receive a larger percentage of state funds to meet the minimum funding level. Figure 14.3 represents how a foundation program operates.

District Power Equalizing   The goal of district power equalizing is to eliminate the impact that local disparities of wealth have on funding schools

Figure 14.3
Operation of a Foundation
Program

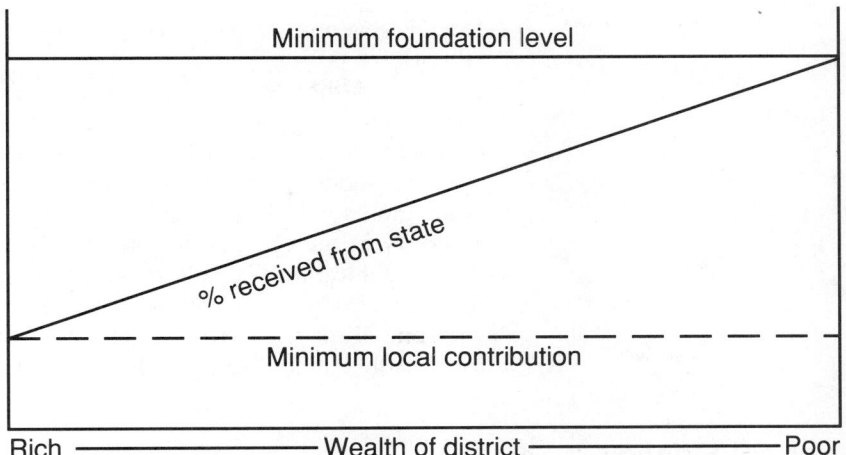

so that the resources allocated to a child's education are not a function of local district wealth. Local districts are allowed to levy their own rate of taxation, but very wealthy districts that raise funds above a certain revenue limit have to pay funds into a state account that is distributed to poorer districts. This plan of financing has been adopted in a small number of states for two basic reasons. First, taxpayers in rich districts do not like to tax themselves for revenue that eventually goes to support school programs in other districts. Second, equalizing all local district resources in a state requires such a commitment of resources by the state that most state legislatures back off from such a commitment.

Categorical Aid   Some states are beginning to incorporate into their funding schemes formulas that take into account the difference in expenditures for special-needs students. Special education and vocational education programs are much more costly to operate than programs offered for typical elementary or secondary pupils. Special-needs pupils are classified and assigned some proportional weighting formula so that the state contribution for these students will be higher than students in basic programs.

Frequently, states have allocation schemes to fund activities such as transportation, driver education, and vocational education. Categorical aid is frequently given to encourage specified education programs, such as programs for gifted students. Such aid may be granted on a matching basis, which requires the local school district to match each dollar received from the state with a similar amount out of local funds.

Allocation of Federal Sources of School Aid

It is apparent from the previous description of federal support for schools that different methods have been used by the federal government to allocate federal money to schools. Allocation of federal funds has fallen into two broad categories: categorical aid and general aid.

Federal categorical aid designates specific needs and programs that are conceived to be in the national interest. Some examples are programs for the handicapped and disadvantaged, vocational education, and school desegregation. It has been argued that through manipulation of categorical aid the federal government has been able to exert undue influence over state educational policy.

During the 1980s, allocation of federal aid to education has moved away from categorical grants to general aid or block grants. It was the position of the Reagan administration that education in the United States is a state function; if there is federal support, it should be in the form of block grants. Block grants allow local and state education officials more authority in the expenditure of federal education funds. Chapter 2 of the Federal Education Consolidation and Improvement Act (ECIA) of 1981 replaced categorical grants for twenty-eight separate funding programs, with one block grant that the state and local education agencies could use for broadly defined educational activities of their choice.

School Finance Reform Movement

In the past decade, a large number of states have modified both their sources of taxation for school support and their methods of allocating state resources to local school districts. Since our culture has been on a quest to achieve more equality in the delivery of all government services, it is not unusual that the concept of equalization of school funding has become a central issue in the larger debate over how to achieve greater equity and justice in the delivery of educational services. More than one half of the states modified their school finance systems in the years between 1970 and 1985. As a result of these reform efforts, school funding became less dependent on property taxation in the 1970s and 1980s.[8]

Equalizing Resource Inputs

Beyond the amelioration of racial and class segregation encouraged by traditional systems of school funding, what has prompted these extensive efforts in school finance reform? In the first place, it is easier for states to focus on the equity of resource inputs, such as expenditures per pupil and equality in physical resources, than on equity of hard-to-measure outputs, such as knowledge, skills, and improved learning potential. It is much easier to address the issue of the comparable number of dollars spent than to attempt to change the factors that affect academic achievement such as the influence of home environments and peer influence. Despite a great deal of skepticism over the efficacy of equalization of expenditures to affect educational outcomes, states have been plodding forward to implement plans to achieve greater equity in resource inputs.

The Tax Equity Question

Achieving greater equity for the taxpayer has been another factor stimulating the school finance reform movement. Holders of different classes of property have been taxed at different rates. Inequities of assessment or reassessment among taxing authorities have resulted in differences in the tax burden to support education. State governments have been called on to deal with these inequities so that funding of a basic service such as education falls more evenly on the property taxpayers across the entire state.

Tax Revolt

In the 1970s and early 1980s, thirty-nine states legislated the use of one or more types of tax limitation devised to control the tax collection or tax allocation authority of local government entities, including school districts.[9] The most dramatic illustration of this revolt occurred in California in 1978 when a voter-initiated referendum called Proposition 13 resulted in the establishment of a maximum annual tax rate of one percent of the fair market value of property. Increases in assessed values were also limited to no more than two percent per year. Idaho and Massachusetts are examples of other states that have put lids on either the amount of taxes to be paid or the rate of increases that can be made in assessed value. These cases of tax revolt illustrate quite well that a majority of voters can reject the entreaties of government officials, professional groups, and labor and business leaders as well as those of the mass media to continue unchecked increases in local property taxation to support government services.

Legal Challenges to State Funding Schemes

Court challenges of state funding schemes have contributed another force spurring efforts by states to reform their methods of school finance. Some state court systems have taken the position of judicial restraint by concluding that education is not a fundamental right guaranteed by the U.S. Constitution. Other courts have viewed education as a fundamental right entitled to judicial protection under a particular state's equal protection provisions. Courts following the latter approach have focused on the disparities of resources expended on education among districts and have promoted the theory that the amount of resources allocated to schools under state funding schemes should not be based primarily on local district wealth.[10]

In the 1971 *Serrano* v. *Priest* decision, the California State Supreme Court expressed this view by concluding:

> *. . . We have determined that . . . (the state of California) funding scheme invidiously discriminates against the poor because it makes the quality of a child's education a function of the wealth of his parents and neighbors.*[11]

In the 1973 *San Antonio Independent School District* v. *Rodriquez* case, the U.S. Supreme Court decided by a five-to-four vote that disparities of school expenditures based on differences in local property wealth did not violate federal constitutional principles. The Court did conclude, however, that such disparities may violate the equal protection clause of a state's constitution. Such a determination had to be made by state courts. Essentially, this decision placed the issue of inequities of school funding as an equal protection issue in the hands of state legislatures and judicial bodies.

Some state courts and legislative bodies have shifted the focus of legal challenges of school funding away from concern for equity of resources to concerns for adequacy of educational programs funded by the state. Such a shift of focus is illustrated in the series of *Robinson* v. *Cahill* decisions issued by the New Jersey Supreme Court between 1973 and 1976.[12] In response to these decisions, the New Jersey legislature enacted an educational reform statute that provided all children within the state "the educational opportunity which will prepare them to function politically, economically, and socially in a democratic state." The legislation specified the major elements of an adequate educational program perceived to be required by the New Jersey Supreme Court's interpretation of that state's constitutional mandate to provide education.

Policy Model 14.3   Equity in School Funding

POLICY ISSUE	PARTICIPANTS IN POLICY DEVELOPMENT	ILLUSTRATIONS OF POLICY SOLUTIONS	EFFECTS OF POLICY SOLUTIONS
How can states promote greater equity in school funding?	**Formal** Federal courts State courts State legislative bodies **Informal** Ad hoc tax reform groups Professional groups	*San Antonio* v. *Rodriquez* *Serrano* v. *Priest* *Robinson* v. *Cahill* Foundation program funding District power equalizing Property tax reform	**Regulative** Who will make what effort to fund schools? **Allocative** Who gets what from state and local sources of funding? **Structural** Changes in state allocation formulas Changes in property tax entities

In the late 1970s and early 1980s, many legal challenges to school funding schemes focused on the rights of special-needs students. Courts and legislative bodies have had to address issues related to the appropriateness of school services being provided to handicapped students, students with language differences, and other students who were perceived to need special instructional assistance. Given the reality of a scarcity of revenue resources, many courts have struggled with the dilemma of dividing these scarce resources between adequate programs for the majority of students and the more expensive appropriate educational opportunities for students with special needs.[13] Policy Model 14.3 summarizes governmental response to equalize school funding resources through the school finance reform movement.

Outcomes of the School Finance Reform Movement

Students of the school finance reform movement have different criteria to judge whether or not a state has actually overhauled its school funding schemes. Even though different criteria are used to make such judgments, there is a great deal of consensus that the school finance reform movement has affected a large number of states. By some criteria, more than thirty states have overhauled their school finance system in the past fifteen years.[14]

School finance reform is still the focus of controversy in many states. Some argue that the reforms have not gone far enough—others that they have gone too far. Certain questions can be used to analyze the effects of school reform in a particular state:

1.   Did the reform provide property tax relief?
2.   Did the reform result in the state's carrying an increased percentage of the burden to fund schools?

3. Did the reform limit local district spending?

4. Did the reform result in equalization of per pupil expenditures among districts?

5. Did the reform facilitate equalization of tax burdens for citizens?

6. Did the reform accommodate differential funding for special-needs students?[15]

School Finance Issues in the Late 1980s

Public schooling policy came under greater scrutiny by state legislatures in all of the states during the 1980s. Demands were made in the school reform literature not only for a continued commitment to equity in educational funding but also to a new commitment to excellence in public education. The suggestions associated with achieving greater excellence in schooling carried price tags that would require substantial amounts of additional financial resources. For example, states have been grappling with the costs associated with implementing the following types of reforms that were frequently suggested in recent reform reports:

Improvement of teacher salaries and implementation of merit pay or career ladders for educational professionals.

Implementation of increased high-school graduation requirements.

Implementation of prekindergarten programs.

Implementation of sequential achievement testing programs.

Revising and upgrading of textbooks used in public schools.

Many states have been mandating that local districts adopt and implement such reform measures. Unfortunately, some states are attempting to pass the burden of funding these reforms on down to the local school districts. Given the retrenchment on the part of the federal government regarding school funding, the elimination of federal revenue-sharing funds to local governments, and the spending and tax limitation activities at the state level, where will the money come from to fund school reform? Is public sentiment toward state and local taxation shifting sufficiently to provide the dollars to fund school reform? These are questions that policymakers in every state will have to address in responding to the educational reform movement.

Another issue associated with funding school reform relates to the decisions that will have to be made about the treatment of individual reform measures. Should they be funded as categorical items, or should they be incorporated as a part of the state's foundation program? School administrators who have been involved in the battle to establish minimum foundation programs are worried that states may use the special categorical approach to fund specific school reform agenda. If this happens, it would make funding of these programs much more vulnerable to shifts in the political pendulum in a state. Cutbacks in funding these programs could easily occur if some of the glamour of focusing on education loses out to some future social or political agenda.

Photo 14.4
Providing students with opportunities to learn computing skills can be an expensive item in school budgets.

Alternative Funding Schemes

The effort to reduce federal involvement in public education has been accompanied by another agenda that would adopt policies and programs designed to increase the options that parents have regarding the education of their children. Instead of providing federal dollars directly to established public education agencies, the Reagan administration attempted to encourage parental choice in the education of their children through tuition tax credits and use of educational vouchers.

Tuition Tax Credits   A tuition tax credit would grant indirect aid to parents through a federal tax credit to offset the tuition paid at a private school of the parents' choice. There are strong arguments on both sides of this alternative approach to funding schools. Some parents who have their children in private schools argue that they bear a double taxation, since they pay the costs of both private and public schooling. Others suggest that it is the function of government in a democracy to encourage options, especially if the quality of services in a private school is perceived to be better than in public schools. Recent research by James Coleman contends that since private schools do a better job of promoting the ideals of both quality and equality, government policy should promote parental choice.[16]

Persons opposed to tuition tax credits have offered many counterarguments. Johns, Morphet, and Alexander refute the argument that public schools operate as an inefficient monopoly. They suggest that it is necessary for the economy to establish certain types of government-approved monopolies such as public schooling.[17] Others argue that private schools primarily serve children from higher income families and that tuition tax credits would be a subtle form of aid to wealthy parents. Senator Ernest Hollings (D., S.C.), one of the more vocal congressional opponents of tuition tax credits, based his opposition on the following points:

A disproportionate amount of federal aid would go to private schools.

Tuition tax credits would result in funding schools that are operated for purposes that run counter to public interest.

Because of federal deficits, the federal government cannot afford the additional burden created by tuition tax credits.

Tuition tax credits would bring about severe infighting between supporters of public and private schools.[18]

Even though the tuition tax credit proposals submitted by President Reagan were designed to overcome some of the preceding criticisms, Congress has not adopted this alternative funding scheme.

Educational Vouchers   Educational vouchers are another alternative funding scheme that promotes parental choice in the education of children. Parents of school-age children would be given a voucher worth X number of dollars that could be applied against the cost of their children's attendance at any school of their choice. Proponents of the voucher system argue that vouchers would promote competition between public and private schools. This competition would result in more efficiency and productivity, especially in the monopolistic public school sector. Based on the economics of the marketplace, good schools would stay in business and improve and bad schools would go under as a result of parental decisions to support or avoid a school.

Opponents of this idea argue that such an alternative system of funding would lead to greater racial and socioeconomic segregation in schooling. The perception of what constitutes a "good" school might not be based on academic issues or the best interests of the child. Skeptics also doubt that principles of competition in the private economic sector apply that well in a public endeavor such as schooling. Critics also contend that vouchers would produce divisiveness and generate dramatic increases in bureaucratic regulation of all schools necessitated by such a scheme.

In 1985 and 1986, then Secretary of Education Harold Bennett strongly defended his proposal to Congress that would distribute compensatory education funds directly to parents in the form of vouchers rather than directly to state and local education agencies. Some state education reform leaders, such as former Governor Lamar Alexander of Tennessee, have also advocated vouchers as an alternative funding program. So, the voucher idea seems to be alive in the school reform movement, and efforts are being made to get it adopted at the state level. Policymakers at both state and federal levels will undoubtedly continue to judge the merits of vouchers as an alternative funding scheme for the rest of this decade and into the 1990s.

Summary

Funding public school activities consumes major portions of state and local budgets. Generating large amounts of dollars to operate schools creates many policy issues over what kind of taxes should be used, which level of government should be responsible, and how money should be allocated to fund school programs.

Questions over equity and adequacy of school funding have prompted many states to examine their traditional methods of school finance. Settling controversies over these issues has generated new policy solutions through the school finance reform movement. Educational policymakers at both the state and local level are now involved in evaluating the outcomes of the school finance reform movement.

Debate over school funding will continue as a result of the school reform agenda outlined in the school reform literature that began to appear in the early 1980s. Retrenchment on the part of the federal government in public school funding will also create additional pressure on state and local education entities to make up for dollars lost through federal cutbacks in educational funding.

Key Words

Human capital formation

Progressive taxes

Regressive taxes

Assessment

Disparities of wealth

Categorical funding

Block grants

Consumption taxes

Tax equity

Flat grants

Foundation programs

District power equalizing

Adequate funding

Tuition tax credits

Vouchers

Discussion Questions

1. Do you think the federal government currently assumes adequate responsibility for funding public education?

2. Should the federal government use block grants or categorical funding to channel federal dollars to public school systems?

3. Given the recent problems associated with property taxation as a way to fund schools, what kind of taxes would you recommend to fund schooling?

4. What would you suggest be done to overcome the inequities in annual per pupil school expenditures between and within states?

5. What would be the advantages and disadvantages of funding schools through a voucher system in your state?

For Further Reading

Burrup, Percy E., and Brimley, Vern. *Financing Education in a Climate of Change,* 3rd ed. Boston: Allyn & Bacon, 1982.

Carroll, Stephen J., and Park, Rolla E. *The Search for Equity in School Finance.* Cambridge, Mass.: Ballinger Publishing Co., 1983.

Changing Public Attitudes on Government and Taxes. Washington, D.C.: Advisory Commission on Intergovernmental Relations. See 1980 through latest edition.

The Condition of Education. Washington, D.C.: U.S. Department of Education. See latest editions.

Digest of Educational Statistics. Washington, D.C.: National Center for Educational Statistics. See latest editions.

Johns, Roe L., Morphet, Edgar L., and Alexander, Kern. *The Economics and Financing of Education,* 4th ed. Englewood Cliffs, N.J.: Prentice-Hall, 1983.

McCarthy, Martha M., and Deignan, Paul T. *What Legally Constitutes an Adequate Public Education?* Bloomington, Ind.: Phi Delta Kappa, 1983.

Significant Features of Fiscal Federalism. Washington, D.C.: Advisory Commission on Intergovernmental Relations. See latest editions.

Statistical Abstract of the United States. Washington, D.C.: U.S. Department of Commerce and Bureau of Census. See latest editions.

Wagner, Ivan, and Sniderman, Sam M. *Budgeting School Dollars: A Guide to Spending and Saving.* Washington, D.C.: National School Boards Association, 1984.

Notes

1. Roe L. Johns, Edgar L. Morphet, and Kern Alexander, *The Economics and Financing of Education* (Englewood Cliffs, N.J.: Prentice-Hall, 1983), pp. 32–37.

2. *See Peggy Odel Gonder. How Schools Can Save Dollars* (Sacramento, Calif.: American Association of School Administrators, 1980).

3. *Significant Features of Fiscal Federalism,* 1984 (Washington, D.C.: Advisory Commission on Intergovernmental Relations, 1985), p. 4.

4. *Changing Public Attitudes on Government and Taxes* (Washington, D.C.: Advisory Commission on Intergovernmental Relations, 1980), p. 4.

5. *Significant Features of Fiscal Federalism,* 1985, p. 51.

6. *Ibid.,* pp. 88–89.

7. *Ibid.,* p. 126.

8. John Augenblick, "The States and School Finance: Looking Back and Looking Ahead," *Phi Delta Kappan* 66 (November 1984), pp. 196–201.

9. *Significant Features of Fiscal Federalism,* 1985, pp. 122–26.

10. Martha M. McCarthy and Paul T. Deignan, *What Legally Constitutes an Adequate Public Education?* (Bloomington, Ind.: Phi Delta Kappa, 1983), pp. 6–22.

11. *Serrano v. Priest,* 487 p 2d, 1241 (California, 1971).

12. McCarthy and Deignan, *op. cit.,* pp. 16–18.

13. *Ibid.* pp. 18–22.

14. Augenblick, *op. cit.,* pp. 196–98.

15. See Stephen J. Carroll and Rolla E. Park, *The Search for Equity in School Finance* (Cambridge, Mass.: Ballinger Publishing Co., 1983).

16. James S. Coleman, "Quality and Equality in American Education: Public and Catholic Schools," *Phi Delta Kappan* 63 (November 1981), pp. 159–64.

17. Johns, et al, p. 27.

18. Ernest F. Hollings, "The Case Against Tuition Tax Credits," *Phi Delta Kappan* 60 (December 1978), pp. 277–79.

15 Educational Policy Development and the Future

"Political confusion and economic uncertainty have shaken the people's faith in education as the key to financial and social success. This retreat ought to be the most pertinent issue in any examination of the country's condition. . . . At stake is nothing less than the survival of American democracy."

Fred M. Hechinger, former education editor of the *New York Times* (1978)

"Our nation has asserted a commitment to the twin goals of excellence and equality: in support of these commitments, quality and justice must go hand in hand. Most of the recent reports on educational excellence and the corresponding reform initiatives, however, have ignored the equity side of educational excellence."

The College Board in *Equality and Excellence* (1985)

"Our ability to compete in world markets is eroding. Growth in U.S. productivity lags far behind that of our foreign competitors. . . . Our world leadership is at stake, and so is our ability to provide for our people the standard of living and opportunities to which they aspire."

Global Competition: the New Reality, The Report of the President's Commission on Industrial Competition (1985)

Policymaking for the decentralized system of education that we have in the United States is complex. It has been the basic rationale of this text that the study of foundations of education can best be addressed from a study of educational policy—both as a process and as a product. Public policy for

361

education—and all other governmental enterprises—evolves out of perceptions of problems. It is the basic function of government to deal with problems—social, economic, political—and attempt to "solve" them. Changing cultural circumstances cause citizens and government to focus their attention on different problems that need to be addressed. In a democratic society, there will always be different perceptions about what problems are most important and what needs to be done to "solve" them. Chapters 3 and 4 focused on a historical review of the various problems that were defined for educational institutions to solve from the colonial period to the twentieth century. Addressing these problems produced diverse policies in different time periods. New institutions, curricula, programs, and standards evolved as schools were expected to deal with the different problems that were defined and assigned to the school to solve.

Chapter 5 reviewed the major belief systems and philosophical perspectives held by different groups. The chapter noted that these perspectives and belief systems affect the way that people perceive problems and their solutions. Chapter 6 explored different dimensions of school/society relations and noted how changing social factors affect the school and how our society evolves expectations for schools in light of these social changes. Two chapters of the text described the formal and informal policy systems that are involved in educational policy development in the United States. Other chapters described possible solutions to selected policy problem areas such as policies affecting students and teachers, policies relating to school finance, church-state issues in education, and school curriculum.

It should be apparent from the review of educational policy in this text that schools have been called on to deal with certain recurring problems since schools were organized. These problems could be classified into the general categories of economic, political, and social problems. Figures 15.1 through 15.3 illustrate how these problems have influenced schools to develop programs and activities designed to help "solve" these recurring problems.

The diagrams in Figures 15.1, 15.2, and 15.3 suggest that policy for schooling is fashioned by political, social, and economic conditions external to the school. Over a period of time, economic, political, and social values change. These changes bring forth demands for different solutions in schooling policy. Some futurists such as Alvin Toffler argue that the pace of change has increased dramatically and has become "a current so powerful today that it overturns institutions, shifts our values, and shrivels our roots."[1] Toffler coined the term *future shock* to characterize the dizzying disorientation brought about by the premature arrival of the future.[2] More recently, this futurist has described the major waves of change that have characterized the development of civilization.

Toffler argues that a new civilization is emerging to challenge our old ways of thinking—old formulas, ideologies, and dogmas. The world of tomorrow cannot be crammed into what Toffler calls "yesterday's conventional cubby holes." One should not despair about the many new relationships—changing energy patterns, world marketing realities, institutional change in families, etc.—springing up, because "many of the very conditions that produce today's greatest perils also open fascinating new potentials."[3] The pace of social, economic, and political change itself causes

Figure 15.1   Economic Issues Addressed Through Schooling

Issues Addressed   Programs/Activities in School

Training of work force   Develop basic competency skills

                                                    Develop specific job skills

                                                    Socialize students in career
                                                    and work ethic

Consumer education   Promote consumer education curricula

                                                    Require students to study principles
                                                    of economic system

Appreciation for   Sort students on basis of merit
free enterprise capitalism

                                                    Base credentialing process on merit

                                                    Administer special job training/
                                                    retraining programs

Inequality in the work force   Provide sex education

                                                    Provide drug and alcohol
                                                    abuse education

Poverty and unemployment   Prevent juvenile delinquency and crime

many problems for policymakers as they attempt to respond to this change. As some wit once suggested, the future is not what it used to be.

Futurism is a field of study concerned with social, economic, and political change and with forecasting future trends and ideas. Futurists hope to assist policymakers in choosing wisely among alternative courses of action as they look to the future and the kinds of policy problems public institutions might be called on to address. In *Future Shock,* Toffler stated:

> *Every society faces not merely a succession of probable futures, but an array of possible futures, and a conflict over preferable futures. The management of change is the effort to convert certain possibilities into probables, in the pursuit of agreed on preferables.*[4]

Figure 15.2   Political Issues Addressed Through Schooling

Issues Addressed   Programs/Activities in School

Citizenship training   Require study of constitutional
                                                    documents/government process
Development of political
leadership   Develop programs that identify talent

Fostering of political
consensus necessary   Require study of cultural
for political stability   and political heritage

Promotion of national security   Foster technical, scientific development
and national defense

Stimulation of patriotism   Engage students in patriotic observances

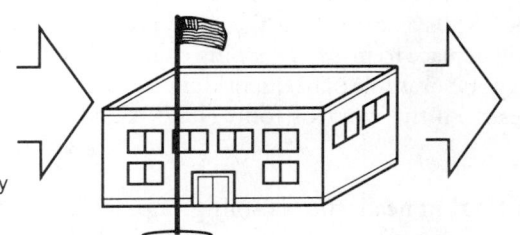

Figure 15.3   Social Issues Addressed Through Schooling

Issues Addressed

Promotion of social mobility
based on meritocracy

Socialization of children
and youth

Promotion of equality

Elimination of injustice

Changing demographic
structure

Changes in institutions
such as the family

Programs/Activities in School

Develop competence skills

Promote meritocratic ideal

Deal with social class biases
in school programs

Promote acculturation/enculturation

Foster understanding of and adaptation
to changing social roles

Desegregate schools

Provide compensatory/
remedial education

Prevent school dropout

Promote cultural pluralism

Accommodate ethnic, racial, sexual,
religious differences

Provide sex education

Provide drug and alcohol abuse
education

Prevent juvenile delinquency and crime

Given the dynamic nature of society in the United States, our ability to predict the future is limited. Likewise, our ability to generate possible alternative futures is restricted. Choosing preferred alternative futures from possible alternative futures is also very difficult in a society that places a high value on maintaining diversity and pluralism. Yet economic, political, and social systems take a future for granted—the assumption is made that there will be a future and that it will be different from the past and the present.

Some knowledge of the future would facilitate planning for educational policy development. If we could accurately predict social, economic, and political problems, we could benefit from past mistakes made in educational policy development and design more effective solutions to these problems in the future.

Historical evidence suggests that schools will always be involved in addressing economic, political, and social problems as they arise. Even though predicting the future in the best of times is hazardous, are there evident problems and current trends that can be identified and documented that will affect future policy development for schools? Much of the school reform literature of the 1980s assumes that there are identifiable trends and directions sufficiently in place to justify sweeping changes in educational policy in this country. A good example of frequently cited evidence of these trends and directions comes from the work of John Naisbitt and the Naisbitt Group.[5]

Megatrends

John Naisbitt heads the Naisbitt group, which provides social and economic trend information to a variety of clients. This group employs a method called content analysis to detect evolving patterns and emerging trends in American society. This analysis of information and media material in bellwether states provides a basis for identifying major trends. The book, *Megatrends,* which appeared at the onset of the 1980s, set the pace for analysis of major trends already under way. It devotes a chapter to each of the following megatrends:

1. **From an industrial to an information society.** This shift is as important as the previous shift from agriculture to industry. This shift is being perpetuated by revolutionary developments in communication technologies. Scientific and technological information will continue to grow at a phenomenal rate.

2. **From forced technology to high tech/high touch.** As new technology becomes employed more widely, society will evolve toward producing a "counterbalancing human response" in the form of increased interpersonal contacts and spiritual awareness. The more intrusive high tech becomes, the more individuals in our society will engage in compensatory "high touch" outlets.

3. **From a national to a world economy.** The United States is changing from a singular, self-sufficient national economy to being a single member of an interdependent global economy comprising a community of countries.

4. **From short-term to long-term.** Over the past several decades, the business and industrial community in this country has been criticized for being shortsighted—showing more interest in immediate short-term rewards than for long-range factors that promote a healthy future.

5. **From centralization to decentralization.** Our culture, economy, and politics are increasingly being affected by a variety of local and regional conditions rather than being primarily influenced by homogeneous national trends.

6. **From institutional help to self-help.** For a period following the Great Depression, citizens began to rely on government and affiliated institutions to provide an array of basic needs. By the 1970s, many citizens had become disillusioned with "collective institutional dependence" as a means of improving the quality of life. A major trend now is to reclaim a sense of self-reliance.

7. **From representative to participatory democracy.** A shift is being made from the traditional form of representative democracy whereby voters elect representatives to a participatory democracy whereby citizens vote on issues directly by referendum.

8. **From hierarchies to networking.** Historically, institutions organized and managed themselves in ways by which power and communication came from the top down. Now the trend is to manage communication and distribute power more evenly among the different layers of authority in an organization.

9. **From north to south.** The migration of the U.S. population from north to south really is characterized by a shift of population to the

West, Southwest, and Florida. It also involves the economic decline of the industrial Northeast and East and an accompanying development of an information-based economy in the West and Southwest.

10. **From an either/or to multiple-option society.**   Until the 1960s, Americans were relatively satisfied with a limited range of personal choices of consumer goods and lifestyles. Since that time, our society has sought greater and greater accommodation of differing tastes and values, including family structure, work arrangements, and ethnic diversity.

The documentation in *Megatrends* of major formative forces already in motion to restructure our society is having an impact on educational policy development. The following questions illustrate some of the policy dilemmas evolving out of the megatrends identified by Naisbitt and his group:

1. What kind of educational programs and emphasis are required to accommodate the shift from an industrial to an information-based society?

2. What role should the schools have in sensitizing children and youth to humane, compensatory responses to new technology?

3. What is the role of the school in socializing children and youth to the new economic realities of international competitiveness? Do schools or other institutions have primary roles in the development of human resources to sustain the competitive position of the United States in a global economy?

4. For educational bureaucracies, what are the implications of the trends to decentralize governmental responsibilities and the formation of new authority and communication structures through networking? Can states provide the economic resources needed to implement necessary reform responses as they assume greater burdens for more and more programs resulting from decentralization? Will state education bureaucracies be willing to develop new authority and communication networks to facilitate educational change?

5. Particular burdens will be placed on states in the South and West to accommodate the migration of populations to these regions. How will states in these regions find the resources necessary to develop the infrastructures of streets, sewers, fire and police protection, health care, *and* educational services? This is a particularly crucial question for those states in the South and Southwest that have historically suffered from educational underdevelopment.

6. If our society is moving from dependence on government help to self-help and self-reliance, what role will educational institutions have in helping us deal with such problems as poverty, unemployment, inequality, delinquency, and teenage pregnancy? This question is particularly crucial, given the fact that the fastest-growing segments of our population are within those population groups more frequently suffering from these problems.

7. What kind of educational policies will be needed to accommodate the preference for diverse tastes and values relating to family structures, work arrangements, ethnic diversity, and cultural pluralism in general?

Policy Model 15.1   Future Economic, Political, and Social Trends

POLICY ISSUE	PARTICIPANTS IN POLICY DEVELOPMENT	ILLUSTRATIONS OF POLICY SOLUTIONS	EFFECTS OF POLICY SOLUTIONS
What knowledge or skills will citizens need in the future? What socialization functions should be assigned to the schools? How will public schools accommodate increasing numbers of students? How will schools accommodate concerns for both equity and excellence? What quantity/quality of teachers will be needed? How many resources will it take for schools to perform tasks assigned to them in the future?	**Formal** U.S. Congress Federal courts State legislative bodies State court systems State administrative agencies **Informal** Futurists Private foundations Parents Ad hoc interest groups	Federal statutes Federal court rulings State statutes State court rulings	**Allocative** Who gets to do what? **Regulative** Who will/can do what? **Structural** Changes and deletions to structures involved in policy administration. **Redistributive** Changes and deletion to allocation of resources or authority.

This cursory review of imminent changes and how they will impact on educational policy indicates that policymakers will be faced with many recurring problems in the future. Policy model 15.1 outlines some problems that educational decision makers will be forced to confront in the immediate future.

The following issues have been selected to illustrate the recurring nature of some of the problems outlined in policy model 15.1 and the ways that policymakers will have to deal with these problems in the future. Each problem will be briefly analyzed for the implications it has for policymakers for the next few years:

1. What knowledge is of most worth? What shall the schools teach in light of economic, political, and social trends already under way?

2. What socialization functions do we assign to the schools in light of changing social roles and social values and changes in our basic institutions such as the family?

3. How will schooling institutions deal with individual differences in light of the demographic changes characterizing the population of the United States? How shall we balance the concern for equity for individuals and larger social concerns for our ability to be economically competitive?

4. How will teachers be selected, educated, and rewarded?

5. How shall we provide the necessary financial and human resources to the schools to help them address the recurring economic, political, and social problems that will inevitably accompany the emergence of the future?

Before analyzing the policy implications that the preceding questions have for the future, we must reassert that dealing with these questions is not an isolated phenomenon. Addressing the questions will occur in the context of major efforts to restructure all of our cultural, economic, and political institutions. If politically powerful groups are successful in drawing our attention away from problems of inequality, political representation, and "people rights" versus "property rights," policy for schooling institutions will support those values. On the other hand, if "people rights" and economic and social justice are the focus of cultural, economic, and political institutions, policies for schools will promote these values.[6]

What Knowledge Is of Most Worth? What Skills Are Basic?

Herbert Spencer raised these questions in a perceptive way when societies in Western Europe and in the United States were attempting to adjust to sweeping changes brought about by the industrial revolution. Spencer premised his answer on "survival of the fittest" principles of Social Darwinism. He argued that societies were growing in complexity and competition as a result of the industrial revolution. To survive in the new order, one needed an education based on scientific and utilitarian objectives rather than on the very general goals associated with education in the liberal arts and humanities.

Recent reform reports have a great deal to say about loss of economic power and position by the United States in the information age and in the international economic community now taking shape in the world. Former President Reagan and the Congress viewed economic competitiveness as a significant political issue to be addressed. Schools are receiving a lot of blame for the perceived loss of this country's ability to compete. The opening words of *A Nation at Risk* illustrate these concerns:

> *Our nation is at risk. Our once unchallenged preeminence in commerce, industry, science, and technological innovation is being overtaken by competitors throughout the world. . . . We report to the American people that while we can take justifiable pride in what our schools and colleges have historically accomplished. . . . The educational foundations of our society are presently being eroded by a rising tide of mediocrity that threatens our very future as a nation and a people.[7]*

America's captains of industry see these educational deficiencies as a clear threat to our economic competitiveness. David Kerns, chairman of

Photo 15.1
What kind of curriculum would best contribute to student understanding of global economy?

Xerox Corporation, claims that U.S. industries spend $25 billion a year training poorly schooled workers. Mr. Kerns suggests that "we cannot compete successfully unless we have a competitive work force—certainly not against Japan. Clearly, we have to rethink our educational system from the ground up."[8]

John Naisbitt argues in *Megatrends* that the revolutionary progress in communication technologies is facilitating a rapidly increasing ability to generate, disseminate, and store information. According to Naisbitt, this information explosion should inspire schooling policy to move us toward educating people to learn how to learn. Naisbitt goes on to describe the "education mismatch" that stems from a lack of intensive emphasis upon science, math, and languages in the United States. Naisbitt also argues that the shift from short-term to "the long-range perspective may signal the need to return to the ideal of a generalist education. If you specialize too much, you may find your specialty obsolete in the long run. As a generalist committed to life-long education you can change with the times."[9]

Decisions concerning what is basic and what knowledge is of most worth have presented real dilemmas for educational policymakers in the past and will continue to do so in the future. In the past, policymakers have lengthened the school year or school day and provided additional resources to teach more skills and more subjects. There is a limit to using this approach now, because both student time and school resources are limited relative to the massive information and technological revolution under way.

If meeting the challenge of economic competitiveness is a primary goal, policymakers have to deal with policy issues that most efficiently relate to enhancing labor force "quality." What kind of curriculum would most effectively enhance labor force quality and promote the goal of making students generalists with life-long learning skills?

Further questions abound regarding vocational and career education. Should schools be responsible for strengthening the "work ethic"? Is productive efficiency down in the United States because of problems with the work ethic? What do schools teach to develop this quality in human capital that would make our country more competitive?

In addition to "basic" or "general" education, specific job skills are a significant component of labor force quality. Should schools be responsible for specific job skills training? Do specific job skills change too quickly and unpredictably for schools to be responsible for these skills?

Paul Woodring argues that in a free society all citizens must be liberally educated to free them from the "limitations of ignorance, prejudice, and provincialism; to enable them to see the world clearly and in perspective; to develop their intellectual capacities, increase their sensitivity, and prepare them to make wise independent judgments."[10] Are the goals associated with the liberal education of citizens just as important as the goals associated with economic competitiveness? How will policymakers balance the demand that schools facilitate greater economic competitiveness with the noble goals of liberal education? What kind of schooling will it take to encourage both objectives? Indeed, deciding what knowledge is of most worth is a pressing policy problem for the future.

What Socialization Functions Do We Assign to the School?

Culture consists of the patterns of values, beliefs, mores, and practices of a group of people who live together in a particular society. It is the total character of life in that group. Societies attempt to transmit their culture from one generation to the next. The process of passing on culture can be called socialization.

In a complex society like the one we have in the United States, cultural pluralism—the maintenance of diverse cultural affiliations—while being encouraged in public policy, is opposed by some sectors of our society and tolerated by others. There are many different cultural patterns based on race, ethnicity, religion, and social class. The encouragement of cultural pluralism complicates the process of socialization. Decisions have to be made about which aspects of the different cultures are important and should be learned. As we learned earlier, *enculturation* is one aspect of socialization that has the objective of helping one to achieve competence in one's own ethnic, racial, religious, or social class group. *Acculturation* occurs when members of different subcultures come into contact and learn from each other. Frequently, these two aspects of socialization are in conflict in the public schools. For example, conservative, fundamentalist parents do not want their children acculturated into acceptance of expressions of popular culture such as rock music. Parents who try to maintain strong ethnic identity in their family do not want their children to lose this identity when they send them to school. It is likely that schools will increasingly be called on to balance the expectations to carry out both enculturation and acculturation functions.

Box 15.1
Curriculum in the
Year 2000

The high-school graduating class of year 2000 entered kindergarten in the fall term of 1987–88. What kinds of curriculum changes are most likely to occur while this age cohort is enrolled in school? Michael Apple, a professor of curriculum and instruction at the University of Wisconsin, reviewed some of the changes most likely to occur in an article in the January 1983 issue of *Phi Delta Kappan*. Some of these changes are summarized as follows:

1. As a result of the activism of conservative groups, educators will have to give more attention to justifying WHY they teach what they do. This will be increasingly difficult, because teacher education programs are putting more stress on HOW to teach.

2. Tension between organized labor and business will manifest itself in curricular content. This friction will be heightened by a growing cooperation between state departments of education and the business community.

3. The basics will be expanded. The teaching of math and science will be strengthened.

4. Just as more time is devoted to math and science, so too will teachers give more time to the topics of ecology and peace.

5. More extensive use of tracking and ability grouping will result in greater differentiation in the curriculum.

6. Fiscal constraints will mean fewer teachers and support services and longer use of textbooks and instructional materials.

7. Closer and more cooperative bonds between teachers and the communities they serve will develop around efforts to save or develop some curriculum programs deemed important.

What is your assessment of Professor Apple's prediction on the curriculum in year 2000? Is he too pessimistic? Too optimistic?

Dynamic societies experience a great deal of tension in promoting socialization because of the necessity of balancing the more conservative functions of cultural transmission and the need to accommodate social change. The institutions involved in socialization processes have difficulty identifying the social learnings that should be taught. Should the institution teach the more traditional values, roles, beliefs, and patterns, or should it attempt to promote social change by encouraging younger members of the culture to adapt new values, roles, beliefs, and patterns? As an example, should the ideals of the National Organization for Women (NOW) be the basis for family courses in school, or should schools base such a curriculum on the ideals of family life promoted by Phyllis Schlafly and the Eagle Forum?

These conflicts over socialization processes make it difficult for policy-makers to make decisions about the roles of different socializing agencies within a given culture. As institutions change, their roles in socialization can change. Changes in mass media technology fostered the evolution of TV viewing as a popular pastime, thus creating new roles for the TV industry in the socialization of children and youth. By the time they graduate from high school, typical youth will have spent more time viewing TV than they will have spent in school. Increasing numbers of single-parent families and families with working mothers employed outside the home have changed the roles of the family in the socialization of children. Should our society be reassessing and reassigning socialization roles among different socialization agencies? In light of changes occurring in the family and other socialization agencies, what socialization functions do we assign to the schools in the future?

How Will We Deal with Emerging Demographic Changes in Educational Policy: Can We Achieve Excellence While We Promote Equity?

Since the 1960s, many Americans have exhibited an interest in facilitating a greater diversity of tastes and values. Naisbitt claims this has produced a "Baskin-Robbins society" where everything comes in at least thirty-one flavors.[11] Residents of the United States attempt to validate a claim to a large number of diverse lifestyles and products. Some examples include the following:

Family   Although the nuclear family dominated the family scene for several decades after World War II, today no family structure exists that could be regarded as typical.

Women   Women have challenged traditional roles. Instead of—or in addition to—raising families, women are now family heads in increasing numbers and are joining the work force, going back to college, entering professional schools, and working in both nontraditional professional and blue-color jobs.

Work   Jobs have become less gender bound. Newly created jobs are increasingly in low-paying service categories. Because of such innovations as part-time jobs, flex time, and job sharing, workers are less frequently required to maintain a rigid work schedule.

Ethnic Groups   Instead of attempting to achieve a homogeneous culture through a melting pot process of assimilation, most Americans are learning to accept, even appreciate, ethnic diversity. This has been perpetuated by the rapid growth of both Spanish-speaking and Asian-American populations.

James Carpenter, formerly of the U.S. Office of Education, made the following observations about the impact of these trends on public schools:

> In 1909 an educator wrote that a major task of education in America was to "break up these immigrant groups or settlements, to assimilate and amalgamate these people as part of our American race, and to implant in their children, so far as can be done, the Anglo-Saxon conception of righteousness, law and order, and popular government. . . .
>
> Sixty years later the Congress of the United States passed the Ethnic Heritage Studies Act giving official "recognition to the

Photo 15.2
Family support is an important factor to academic success in school.

hetergeneous composition of the nation and the fact that in a multiethnic society, a greater understanding of the contributions of one's own heritage and those of one's fellow citizens can contribute to a more harmonious, patriotic, and committed populace.[12]

A demographic profile of the 3.6 million children entering school in September 1986 characterizes the diversity of the age cohort beginning school in that year:

One of four children came from families living below the poverty level.

Fourteen percent of the children were birthed by teenage mothers.

Fifteen percent of the children were mentally or physically handicapped.

Fifteen percent were immigrants who spoke a language other than English.

Fourteen percent were children of unmarried parents.

Over 10 percent of the children had poorly educated, even illiterate parents.[13]

Demographic projections indicate that population diversity, considered as a hallmark of American democracy, will increase. Projections indicate that a growing proportion of American children and youth will be poor and nonwhite, will have limited English proficiency, and will increasingly come from families in which parents themselves lack formal schooling. Figure 15.4 summarizes data from the U.S. Immigration and Naturalization Service that documents the relative growth in immigration to the United States since 1910.

Figure 15.4
The American Melting Pot: Immigration to the United States, 1900–1984

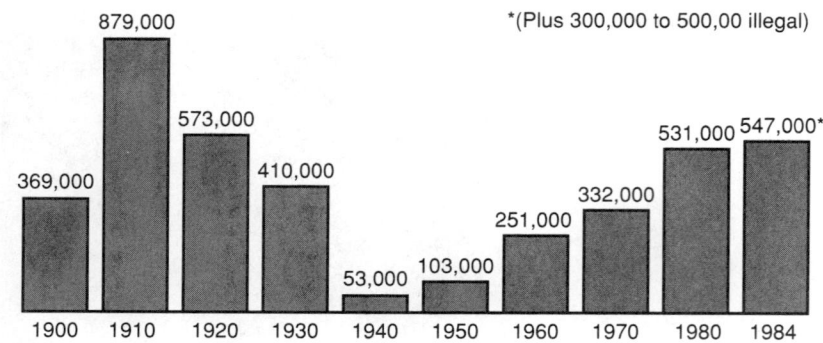

Source: U.S. Immigration and Naturalization Service. Reprinted with permission from *Education Week*, Vol. 5, No. 34, May 14, 1986.

It should be noted that the rate of immigration to the United States in 1984—including the migration of illegal aliens—was greater than at any time since 1900.

How will schools deal with a growing percentage of youth who are "at risk"? Consider some of the comparable outcomes of schooling for selected population groups:

In spite of gains in recent years, blacks and Hispanic children continue to score below their white peers on standardized tests.

In spite of recent improvements, minority students are still far more likely to drop out of high school before graduation. Data from a 1979 Census Bureau study showed that 35 percent of Hispanics and 25.5 percent of blacks ages 18 to 21 had dropped out of school compared with only 15.5 percent of all whites of similar age. Table 15.1

Photo 15.3
Controversy prevails over the kind and extent of educational opportunities that should be provided preschool and kindergarten age children in the United States.

summarizes data from a 1986 U.S. Department of Education report that indicates great diversity of school dropout rates among the different states.

Minority students who do graduate from high school are less likely than white high-school graduates to enroll in college. Moreover, the college enrollment rate for minority high-school graduates has been falling. Almost thirty percent more blacks graduated from high school in 1982 than in 1975. Black student enrollment in college decreased in that time period by eleven percent. Hispanic high-school graduation rate improved thirty-eight percent during that time period, but the enrollment rate in college dropped sixteen percent. Ten percent of all college baccalaureates were awarded to black students in 1976. By 1981, blacks received only 6.5 percent of all bachelor degrees awarded.[14]

Many educators are concerned that policies being adopted in the school reform movement of the 1980s that call for higher standards, longer school days and years, more rigorous graduation requirements, and reforms in teacher certification and school personnel policy may have negative effects on efforts to achieve greater equity in schooling for all groups. Some critics argue that most of the reform reports have paid little attention to equity issues except in the very general sense that equity and excellence ought to be joint goals of school reform.

While it is difficult to oppose higher standards, the effects of such policies must be evaluated carefully. For example, competency tests have caused public school personnel to focus on the "basics." But, questions have to be raised whether the skills targeted in these tests promote rote learning at the expense of higher order cognitive skills that all students need to learn. Likewise, increasing and standardizing requirements for graduation from high school may promote greater uniformity of school experience. But if such policies are administered without sensitivity and flexibility, they may exacerbate dropout rates among disadvantaged student groups. The ultimate effect of such policies could be higher standards for more elite groups of students while other students are allowed to fall through the cracks.

Failure to develop policies that provide appropriate educational services for the growing number of at-risk students will contribute to other social problems. Given the size of the current school-age cohort, business, the military, and academe will be competing for a declining number of young people. For example, some demographers estimate that for the military to maintain its current level of personnel in 1995, it would need to attract fifty-five percent of all eligible eighteen-year-olds with a high-school diploma. To maintain a competitive position in the world economy, the United States will need to pursue school policies resulting in the development of all available human resources.

Undereducated youth cost society in other ways. School dropouts typically earn lower salaries and consequently pay fewer taxes. A large percentage of dropouts end up either in state juvenile institutions or reform schools. Caretaking of these youth in such institutions can cost $25,000 to $30,000 per person per year. It is estimated that the annual cost to American citizens to provide for dropouts and their families is more than

Table 15.1
Making the Grade: High
School Graduation Rate
By State, 1982 and 1984

STATE	1982		1984	
	NUMBER	RANK	NUMBER	RANK
Alabama	62.1	49	63.4	44
Alaska	74.7	25	64.3	41
Arizona	64.6	41	63.4	43
Arkansas	75.2	22	73.4	24
California	63.2	44	60.1	50
Colorado	75.4	21	70.9	31
Connecticut	79.1	11	70.6	33
Delaware	71.1	34	74.7	20
District of Columbia	55.2	51	56.9	51
Florida	62.2	47	60.2	49
Georgia	63.1	45	65.0	39
Hawaii	73.2	30	74.9	18
Idaho	75.8	20	74.4	21
Illinois	74.5	27	76.1	15
Indiana	77.0	17	71.7	29
Iowa	86.0	4	84.1	2
Kansas	81.7	9	80.7	7
Kentucky	68.4	39	65.9	38
Louisiana	56.7	50	61.5	47
Maine	77.2	15	72.1	28
Maryland	77.8	13	74.8	19
Massachusetts	74.3	28	76.4	13
Michigan	72.2	33	71.6	30
Minnesota	89.3	1	88.2	1
Mississippi	62.4	46	61.3	48
Missouri	76.2	18	74.2	22
Montana	82.1	8	78.7	9
Nebraska	86.3	2	81.9	6
Nevada	66.5	40	64.8	40
New Hampshire	75.2	22	77.0	11
New Jersey	77.7	14	76.5	12
New Mexico	71.0	35	69.4	34
New York	62.2	47	63.4	45
North Carolina	69.3	37	67.1	36
North Dakota	86.3	2	83.9	3
Ohio	80.0	10	77.5	10
Oklahoma	73.1	31	70.8	32
Oregon	73.9	29	72.4	26
Pennsylvania	77.2	15	76.0	16
Rhode Island	68.7	38	72.7	25
South Carolina	64.5	43	62.6	46
South Dakota	85.5	5	82.7	5
Tennessee	70.5	36	67.8	35
Texas	64.6	41	63.6	42
Utah	78.7	12	75.0	17
Vermont	83.1	7	79.6	8
Virginia	74.7	25	73.8	23
Washington	75.1	24	76.1	14
West Virginia	73.1	31	66.3	37
Wisconsin	84.5	6	83.1	4
Wyoming	76.0	19	72.4	27
U.S. AVERAGE	**70.9**	—	**69.7**	—

Source: U.S. Education Department; Office of Planning, Budget, and Evaluation; Planning and Evaluation; February 1986.

Photo 15.4
Policy makers in a number of states are concerned about the fact that fewer minorities are choosing teaching as a career.

$75 billion. This figure includes welfare and unemployment costs, lost tax revenues, and crime and crime prevention costs.[15]

It appears to be in the self-interest of taxpaying citizens in the United States to press for educational policies in the future that will ensure a commitment to both equity and excellence.

How Shall We Select, Train, and License Teachers?

The economic, political, and social trends described earlier will have a profound impact on policy relating to school professionals. Decisions made about what knowledge is of most worth and what public school curriculashould emphasize will affect the kinds of teachers and administrators that are needed. If policymakers decide that vocational education and specific job skills training are to be done by other agencies in the private sector, that will affect the kind of teaching cadre recruited, trained, and licensed. If policymakers insist on schools' emphasizing only the "basics," it is likely that the emerging demands that all teachers have a thorough background in the liberal arts and humanities will intensify.

On the other hand, if policymakers choose to address in school settings the problems of inadequate socialization of children and youth being created by changes in the family, it would appear that schools might have different personnel needs. School personnel assigned the task of socialization and "life adjustment" of children and youth would need different training than personnel assigned the tasks of emphasizing only the basics.

Demographic changes producing different clientele for schools will also affect policies relating to school personnel. For example, as the number of minority students enrolled in school increased in the mid-1980s, the supply of minority teachers became more scarce. Trends requiring teachers to pass competency tests for certification are shrinking the pool of minority teachers even more. How will public policymakers balance the concerns for equity and excellence in school staffing in the future? What are the implications for school staffing of applying more rigorous standards to student clientele that includes more at-risk students? Problems relating to balancing concerns for equity and excellence are just as crucial for school staffing as they are for determining the most appropriate curriculum for the growing diversity of students.

It appears that the really crucial problems relating to the selection, training, and licensing of teachers in the future could be summarized by the following questions:

1. How many teachers and other school personnel will be needed to address the problems that schools are asked to attend to?

2. What kind of selection and training procedures would best ensure that schools have the quality and kind of personnel they are called on to address?

3. What kind of licensing procedure will ensure that school personnel are equipped with the appropriate skills needed to deal with the problems that schools are called on to address in the future?

Beginning in 1985, several national policy studies on selection, training, licensing, and retention of teachers were released. These studies included *A Nation Prepared*, from the Carnegie Foundation; *Investing in Our Children*, by the Committee for Economic Development; *Who Will Teach Our Children?*, by the California Commission on the Teaching Profession; *Tomorrow's Teachers*, from the Holmes Group; and *A Call for Change in Teacher Education*, by the American Association of Colleges for Teacher Education. These reports do not agree on all points and do not develop an agenda for a particular state. Rather, they address the three major questions previously listed. The following are common elements enumerated in *Time for Results: The Governor's 1991 Report in Education*. This report contains a synthesis of ideas relating to teachers found in the preceding reports that is likely to influence the development of policy in the future.

1. A body of professional knowledge and effective practices that teachers must learn must be defined.

2. The nation needs to create a national board to define teacher standards.

3. Teacher education programs must be restructured in response to changes 1 and 2.

4. The work environment of schools must be restructured to create productive learning and work environments.

5. Teaching careers must be reshaped and redesigned.

6. Efforts must be made to recruit able teachers that take into account concerns for equity.

POLICY ISSUE	PARTICIPANTS IN POLICY DEVELOPMENT	EFFECTS OF POLICY SOLUTIONS
Five-year preparation programs Career ladders	**Formal** State legislative bodies State boards of education State administrative agencies **Informal** Teacher organizations Colleges and departments of education Private foundations	Fewer lower-class students will choose teaching because of additional costs of teacher preparation. Fewer minorities will choose teaching because of additional preparation costs. Unless teacher salaries are increased significantly, fewer students will choose teaching. Colleges and universities will use five-year program to generate additional revenue based on differences between graduate/undergraduate state funding formulas. School districts would seek to minimize costs by hiring only teachers at the lower end of career ladder. Teacher turnover rates would increase with the use of short-term/nontenured appointments. Professionalization of teaching would be thwarted.

Policy Model 15.2   Possible Unintended Outcomes Resulting from Restructuring Teacher Preparation and Career Patterns

7. Teacher compensation must be improved upon entry into the profession and throughout the career.

8. Teacher incentives and rewards must be aligned with schoolwide student performance.

9. Efforts must be made to facilitate teacher mobility from one state to another.

10. States should establish a "loose/tight" approach to state and local regulation of schools.

Adopting solutions to deal with the preceding issues in the teaching profession could have unintended as well as intended effects, as illustrated in Policy Model 15.2. Career ladders and five-year professional preparation programs are prominent recommendations in the Holmes Group's report, *Tomorrow's Teachers*.

How Should Schools Be Funded in the Future?

Decisions have to be made in every culture about how to cope with problems accompanying economic, political, and social change. Policymakers must decide how to allocate/reallocate responsibilities among different agencies and institutions for "solving" these problems. Trends discussed in this chapter have direct implications for funding education in the United States. The economic shifts taking place—international competition, from centralization to decentralization—are likely to have great influence on policies relating to school funding. This is stated succinctly in the preface to *A Nation Prepared*, a report released by the Carnegie Forum in 1986:

> *Four purposes motivated the Task Force in producing this volume: (1) to remind Americans, yet again, of the economic challenges pressing us on all sides; (2) to assert the primacy of education as the foundation of economic growth, equal opportunity, and a shared national vision; (3) to reaffirm that the teaching profession is the best hope for establishing new standards of excellence . . .; and (4) to point out that a window of opportunity lies before us in the next decade to reform education.[16]*

Many forces will influence policymakers as they attempt to provide resources to the schools to respond to these challenges. In an era of reform, as greater demands are placed on the schools, solutions to funding problems will be affected by the experiences of the past and present as well as by the hopes for the future. The following factors will influence educational policy development on school funding in the future:

The amount of resources needed if schools are assigned more responsibilities.

School finance reform efforts of the recent past.

The amount of resources recently allocated to educational programs.

Fiscal condition of the states.

Public opinion regarding the schools.

School Funding and Role Changes for Schools

Many critics argue that schools must be involved in enhancing labor force quality if the United States is to have a chance to enjoy economic success in the emerging world economy. Varying interpretations of how public schools can enhance labor force quality carry different price tags in terms of resources that would have to be allocated to carry out this task. If schools are given more caretaking roles in the socialization of children and youth, such responsibilities will also require new allocation of resources. Caretaking services, socialization activities, and programs to enhance labor force quality for disadvantaged and different children and youth will no doubt require more resources to aid schools in discharging these tasks.

School Finance Reform Efforts of the Recent Past

Significant progress has been made in addressing the question of equity in the school finance reform movement of recent years. Today it appears that the issues are different and more complex as efforts are made to achieve both equity and excellence. State aid to education has consistently risen. General aid programs to local school districts have been strengthened. Policymakers in many states are examining the possibilities for additional sources of

Table 15.2 Total of Elementary/ Secondary School Expenditures for Selected Years	SCHOOL YEAR	TOTAL REVENUE (BILLIONS)	REVENUE AS PERCENTAGE OF GNP	REVENUE AS PERCENTAGE OF PERSONAL INCOME
	1969	35.5	3.8	4.7
	1979	87.4	3.8	4.6
	1980	95.1	3.7	4.6
	1981	102.8	3.5	4.3
	1982	110.1	3.6	4.3

revenue available to local school systems. A number of states are currently returning a portion of state income taxes to support schools in proportion to amounts collected.

States have dramatically expanded their roles in providing high-cost programs to special and disadvantaged students who need them. The implementation of basic skills testing programs in many states have been accompanied by programs for remedial and compensatory education for students identified as needing such services. States are taking special steps to help poor districts with high tax rates, urban districts that face high prices for educational services, and districts with declining enrollments. Many states are responding to successful efforts to limit property tax collections. All of these changes in school finance reform in the recent past will influence policy directions in school funding in the future.

Amount of Resources Recently Allocated to Education

Educating the masses takes a great deal of money. Implementing reforms to improve the schools and to serve larger school enrollments will take more money. Between 1969 and 1979, expenditures on education as a percent of gross national product (GNP) and of personal income in the United States remained constant—even with the declining school enrollments and increased allocations to government services in noneducation sectors. Data from Table 15.2 indicates that investments in education relative to GNP and personal income began to slip in the early 1980s.

If public schools are called on to fill gaps resulting from perceived failures of other institutions, it would seem logical to expect growth in the percentage of GNP and personal income devoted to education.

Fiscal Condition of the States

The fifty states vary greatly in their ability to raise tax revenues. Many forces are currently at work to affect the relative fiscal conditions of the fifty states. The cost of building the nation's infrastructure of streets, sewers, water systems, etc., is being returned to the states. Servicing the growing national debt is consuming more and more tax revenues that cannot be shared with the states.

The industrial and population migrations from North and East to South and West are redistributing fiscal capacity among the states. The changing economics of natural resources such as oil is negatively affecting the economies of several states. Traditional perceptions of wealthy states and poor states may need to be revised. Certainly the effects of these trends on intrastate and interstate issues of school funding need to be evaluated as policymakers map out ways to fund schools in the future. Table 15.3 projects school funding prospects on a state-by-state basis through year 2000.

Table 15.3
State Education Funding
Prospects Through the
Year 2000

STATES WITH FAVORABLE PROSPECTS	STATES WITH AVERAGE PROSPECTS	STATES WITH UNFAVORABLE PROSPECTS
Alaska	Arizona	Alabama
Connecticut	California	Arkansas
Delaware	Colorado	Georgia
District of Columbia	Florida	Idaho
Illinois	Hawaii	Indiana
Maryland	Iowa	Kentucky
Massachusetts	Kansas	Louisiana
Michigan	Missouri	Maine
Minnesota	Montana	Mississippi
New Jersey	Nebraska	Nevada
New York	New Mexico	New Hampshire
Oregon	Ohio	North Carolina
Rhode Island	Oklahoma	North Dakota
Washington	Pennsylvania	South Carolina
Wisconsin	Virginia	South Dakota
	West Virginia	Tennessee
	Wyoming	Texas
		Utah
		Vermont

Source: "The Prospects for Financing Elementary/Secondary Education in the States," School Finance Project (Washington, D.C.: National Institute of Education, December 1982).

Public Opinion Regarding the Schools

During the 1970s, opinion polls indicated that the American public gave schools poorer and poorer evaluations. Those asked to evaluate the schools in the early 1980s have been more positive in their evaluations. The percentage of the population with a direct stake in public schools by having children in school reached an all-time low as we moved into the 1980s. Recent polls indicate that by a large margin, the public believes that a good education system is more important to the future of the country than a strong industrial system or a strong military force. Parents also firmly believe that schooling offers their children the best hope for economic prosperity and a good job. Recent polls even indicate that the public is willing to increase the resources allocated to the schools if they could be assured that such increases in resources would result in the improvement of schools.[17]

Since one objective of the school reform literature was to awaken the public to such issues, one might conclude that these efforts have been successful. Policymakers should be sensitive to these trends in public opinion as they make decisions about allocation of resources to the schools in the future.

Summary

Public education policy will be influenced by perceptions about the future and the kinds of problems educational institutions will be called on to address. Most societies assume that there will be a future and devote varying degrees of effort to plan for it. Futurists attempt to identify probable trends that aid policymakers in both the private and the public sectors to plan for the future.

The Naisbitt group has produced evidence of future trends that are already in motion in the United States. These trends influence educational policy development as policymakers attempt to facilitate educational reform measures that will help educational institutions provide the kinds of programs and activities that will help children and youth be prepared for the future.

Educational policymakers are having to rethink what knowledge is of most worth in light of the economic, political, and social changes already taking place. Socialization functions of schools are being evaluated in response to changes in roles and responsibilities of other institutions such as the family. Responding to the challenges of international competition will force efforts to balance concerns for equity and excellence in educational programs. Increasingly, policymakers will be concerned about the quantity and quality of teachers needed to staff schools that are taking on more challenging tasks. Since solving public problems costs money, school funding policies will continue to be a major problem for educational policymakers in the future.

Key Words

Future Shock	**At-risk youth**
Futurism	**Equity versus excellence**
Content analysis	**Caretaking roles**
Megatrends	**Nuclear family**
Economic competitiveness	**Baskin-Robbins Society**
Education mismatch	**GNP**

Discussion Questions

1. Do you think John Naisbitt's *Megatrends* accurately portrays the major changes already occurring in our society? What evidence of these trends could you identify in your community?

2. What kind of school curricula do you think would best prepare students for the economic realities they will face as they enter the labor market?

3. Do you think it is possible for schools to promote both equity and excellence in the future? Why?

4. What changes would you recommend be made in schooling policy to accommodate the changing demographic realities occurring in our society?

For Further Reading

"Demographic Portrait," *Education Week,* Vol. 5, No. 34, May 14, 1986.

Naisbitt, John. *Megatrends: Ten New Directions Transforming Our Lives.* New York: Warner Books, 1982.

A Nation Prepared: Teachers in the 21st Century. New York: Carnegie Forum on Education and the Economy, 1986.

The Nation Responds: Recent Efforts to Improve Education. Washington, D.C.: U.S. Department of Education, 1984.

National Commission on Excellence in Education, *A Nation at Risk.* Washington, D.C.: U.S. Department of Education, 1983.

Toffler, Alvin. *Future Shock.* New York: Bantam Books, 1971.

Woodring, Paul. *The Persistent Problems of Education.* Bloomington, Ind.: Phi Delta Kappa, 1983.

Notes

1. Alvin Toffler, *Future Shock* (New York: Bantam Books, 1971), p. 1.

2. Alvin Toffler, "The Future as a Way of Life," *Horizons,* Summer 1965, p. 109.

3. Alvin Toffler, *The Third Wave* (New York: William Morrow & Co., 1980), p. 19.

4. Toffler, *Future Shock,* p. 460.

5. See John Naisbitt, *Megatrends: Ten New Directions Transforming Our Lives* (New York: Warner Books, 1982).

6. See Michael Apple, "Curriculum in the Year 2000: Tensions and Possibilities," *Phi Delta Kappan,* January 1983, p. 321–26.

7. National Commission on Excellence in Education, *A Nation at Risk.* (Washington, D.C.: U.S. Department of Education, 1983), p. 1.

8. "The Brain Battle." *U.S. News and World Report,* Vol. 102, No. 2, January 1987, p. 59.

9. Naisbitt, *op. cit.,* p. 37.

10. Paul Woodring, *The Persistent Problems of Education* (Bloomington, Ind.: Phi Delta Kappa, 1983), p. 6.

11. Naisbitt, *op. cit.,* p. 232.

12. James Carpenter, "Educating for a New Pluralism," in *The Schools and Group Identity,* by Edith Herman (New York: Institute on Pluralism and Group Identity, 1974), p. 3.

13. "Demographic Portrait," *Education Week,* Vol. 5, No. 34, May 14, 1986.

14. *Ibid.*

15. Data taken from materials provided by the National Dropout Prevention Center at Clemson University, Clemson, S.C.

16. *A Nation Prepared: Teachers for the 21st Century* (New York: Carnegie Forum on Education and the Economy, 1986), p. iii.

17. Alec M. Gallup, "The 18th Annual Gallup Poll of Public Attitudes Toward the Public Schools," *Phi Delta Kappan,* Vol. 68, No. 1, September 1986, pp. 43–59.

Index